The Riddle *of* History

THE RIDDLE
OF
HISTORY

*The Great Speculators from
Vico to Freud*

BRUCE MAZLISH

Massachusetts Institute of Technology

Harper & Row, *Publishers*

NEW YORK AND LONDON

Library of Congress Catalog Card Number: 66-12559

CONTENTS

PREFACE

PHILOSOPHY OF HISTORY is interdisciplinary by its very nature. It assumes a willingness to use the epistemological and metaphysical assumptions of philosophy in an attempt to understand and give meaning to the empirical data of history. On occasion, the current is presumed to run the other way, and history to reveal the correct nature of philosophy. In any case, those who enter this boundless land must appeal to the more settled territories of knowledge on each side for intellectual provisioning, if not for steady support. As a result, one is always in debt in philosophy of history to countless and generally unnamed philosophers and historians. I should like to acknowledge this debt in one gesture here.

My especial indebtedness to the great speculators with whom I deal should be obvious in the pages devoted to them. In an effort to leave the pages uncluttered, however, I have made as few footnote citations to the actual works treated as possible: where the references, for example, are to one or two major works of the speculator, such as to Vico's *New Science* and *Autobiography*, I have assumed that the reader will get at the full text for himself and spot the passages again as he reads there; where the references, as in Marx, are to various scattered works, I have felt more obliged to cite them. In the end, I succumbed to the scholar's fondness for footnotes more than I had intended originally; and in many of these footnotes, I have cited other thinkers in philosophy of history who have, by negative or positive means, influenced my views. As for the bibliographies, they are not intended to be complete, but to serve where possible as a critical guide for the reader interested in going further on a particular subject.

In addition to the speculators and scholars cited in the text, I wish to thank friends, colleagues, and other scholars who read various parts of the book: William W. Bartley III, William Dray, Erich Heller, George Lichtheim, and George Nadel. The last named knows only too well how much our association (both personal and on the journal, *History and Theory*) has shaped my thought. I need hardly add that no jury could convict any of these men for the crimes of commission and omission exhibited in this book. Others, too legion to name, have helped in the effort to educate me by their conversations; not least of these have been the students in my successive classes in the Philosophy of History at M.I.T.

I wish also to thank Dean John E. Burchard, Professor Richard Douglas, and Professor Howard R. Bartlett for their generous and general support of my endeavors, and to record my gratitude to the Department of Humanities at M.I.T. for awarding me a Summer Research Grant which enabled me to complete my manuscript.

Lastly, a word of appreciation to the numerous secretaries who have struggled with my handwriting and my version of typewriting. My especial thanks go to Mrs. Ruth Dubois and the other secretaries of the M.I.T. Department of Humanities, as well as to many others, like Miss Ann Allen of the Harvard Business School, who labored outside my department. By their efforts, they often brought clarity to what otherwise looked like a new version of some ancient cryptic language.

BRUCE MAZLISH

The Riddle *of* History

I

Introduction

1

JACOB BURCKHARDT, the great nineteenth-century historian, described philosophy of history as a centaur, because one part of it subordinates and the other part coordinates. This is apt, but I should like to offer another description for this semi-monstrous subject. I would describe philosophy of history as a sphinx-like entity, which poses to man the riddle of his past. Stopping him at the crossroads of time, it inquires enigmatically how he has arisen from an instinctual life of nature to the consciousness of a historical being. Even before Voltaire coined the phrase, philosophy of history, in a work written to satisfy the yearning of his mistress for a meaningful history, men have been involved in a long affair with this riddle.

The metaphor of the sphinx and the riddle is a poetic way of expressing what philosophy of history is about. More prosaically phrased, the subject is concerned with a twofold question: how does man know what has happened; and what is the meaning and mechanism of that happening. The attempt today to answer the first part of the question, "how does man know what has happened," is generally placed under a label called "critical philosophy of history." The attempt to deal with the meaning and the mechanism of history is often segregated under the label "speculative philosophy of history." The great philosophers of history of the last few centuries made no such distinction. They tried to deal with the problem of history as a whole. Consequently, although I refer to them as the great speculators, I do not mean by this to deny them any standing as "critical" thinkers: quite the contrary.

It is true, however, that the central speculative effort has been to explain the origin and development of man as a cultural or historical animal. What Darwin did for the physical evolution of man and the other animals, speculators on history like Vico, Condorcet, Hegel, Comte, Marx, and Freud, attempted to do for *homo culturas*. Imprecise and vague as we may judge their findings and theories, their aim is exemplary and their intention scientific. Surely, the importance of their effort needs no defence. To understand or to have some reasonable conception of the nature and meaning of man's historical origins is an all too pressing problem of the moment, for it is largely by the flickering lights of the past that we perceive and define our present identities and future prospects.

2

The notion of philosophy of history posing a riddle, as well as the title of this book, seemed to emerge from nowhere while I was working on the draft of the final chapters. After some reflection, however, I was able to reconstruct the main elements of its origin, and this reconstruction may be of interest to the reader.

The initial inspiration appears to have come from Hegel's lyric passage, in his *Philosophy of History*, on the meaning of the Sphinx. Interpreting the spiritual significance of the great statue, half-man, half-beast, lying in the desert sands, Hegel perceived in it the symbol of human consciousness emerging from its own bestial and physical qualities. Because I had read Vico's *New Science*, and his account of the emergence of mankind out of bestiality into humanity and consciousness, I was prepared to accept Hegel's insight. Next to serve in the line of my inspiration was Karl Marx. In his youthful *Economic and Philosophical Manuscripts of 1844*, Marx used the precise phrase itself and spoke boastfully of communism as "the riddle of history solved." In his supposed solution, Marx abandoned Hegel's idealistic explanation for the rise of human consciousness and offered a materialistic one instead. It remained for Sigmund Freud, with his concern for the unconscious as well as the conscious, to fuse the images of the Sphinx and the riddle for me. It was Oedipus, of course, who was stopped by the Sphinx on the road to Thebes, and made to answer the riddle. Ultimately, the riddle is the riddle of our existence, and, as Freud tells us, we are all Oedipus. Unlike Oedipus, however, our fate does not require that we blind ourselves to, or be blinded by, the knowledge vouchsafed to us.

That knowledge, it need hardly be said, is only partial knowledge. There may be some presumption that a riddle has an answer; I make no pretence in this book to offer a single, unified solution. Technically, therefore, the riddle of history might more justly be considered a pseudo-riddle. Such a verdict will be reached, however, only by those who demand of science (or knowledge) final answers, rather than probing, tentative attempts to answer key questions concerning complicated phenomena, natural or historical. True, many of the great speculators on the riddle of history, like Hegel and Marx, did aspire to final answers; nevertheless, I shall treat them as offering hypotheses that account for some of the data of history in a useful way, and that then lead on to further empirical inquiries and theoretical formulations. It is, then, in this latter spirit that I approach the riddle of history: the riddle as to man's rise to a more scientific consciousness of his past.

3

In general, I seek in this book to examine the efforts of a number of great thinkers to deal with the riddle of history. Specifically, I attempt to accomplish the following: (1) to write an expository and interpretative history of philosophy of history in its modern period, presenting new and comprehensive portrayals of some of the great speculative thinkers; (2) to bring to bear on the task the insights of the two sorts of modern approaches, that is, the speculative (defined as emphasizing the meaning and mechanism of history) and the critical (defined as emphasizing the epistemology and logic of history); (3) to treat philosophy of history, where possible, as part of the history and philosophy of science; and (4) to perceive in the data and metaphysical assumptions of philosophy of history the origins of a number of the present-day disciplines of the so-called cultural or human sciences.

There are, however, definite restrictions which hedge in my efforts, and these ought to be noted at the outset. First, I have confined myself to thinkers of the modern period: a Thucydides, an Augustine do not figure significantly in this book. Second, as indicated, I have centered my attention upon the great speculators, those of large and sweeping vision, who have sought to discern a *meaning* in history as well as to treat it as a logical and epistemological *problem*. Hence, I am not directly concerned with recent critical philosophers of history such as Dilthey, Collingwood, or Croce, or with any of the logical analysts, except for an interest in the questions they raise. Third, I have not attempted to cover all of the possible candidates for inclusion under the heading of great speculators: on one side, I have left out such modern possibilities as Max Weber and Karl Mannheim; on the other side, such possibly lesser lights as Danilevsky or Brooks Adams. Less justifiably, I have omitted a major figure in speculative philosophy of history, Johann Gottfried Herder. In his case, I seem to have found in Vico the originality and power which have prevented me from becoming enthusiastic again about his German counterpart; however, I might have persevered if I had not come to feel that an adequate treatment of Herder's philosophy of history requried more background knowledge of his theological and literary work than I had, or was willing to acquire. Fourth, and last, I have made little pretense at dealing with historiography per se. Thus for example, my treatment of historicism is in terms of the great speculators, and not in the equally valid terms of the legal humanists of the sixteenth century, or of a Ranke or Burckhardt of the nineteenth. *On fait ce qu'on peut*, and according to one's dominating interests. In essence, then, I have centered my attention on the great speculative thinkers, mainly French, German, and English (though Vico is Italian), who may be considered as the classical philosophers of history.

4

The figures whom I do treat are, generally, major thinkers who have worked not only in philosophy of history but in other areas as well. Thus, a Kant and a Hegel, even if not a Toynbee, ideally must be understood against the background of their total work. This has imposed a heavy burden on me, one which I seek to have my reader share. Therefore, while hoping for an acquaintanceship by my reader with the philosopher's general work, I have also felt it requisite on some occasions to present the overall outlines of a great speculator's thought, to treat him, so to speak, in the round.

Nevertheless, my major concern has been with philosophy of history, and this gives me a definite perspective on the thinkers with whom I deal. It would be hopeless to expect that my treatment will escape the reproach of experts on a philosopher's total work, and I shall be accused of misunderstanding, for example, Kant or Hegel, by specialists in their aesthetics or morality. While this cannot—and should not—be avoided, I hope that every reader will keep in mind that the focus of this book is on the development of speculative thought in the philosophy of history and not on the total work of particular philosophers who happen to have devoted some part of their thought to our subject.

Further, I have frequently ignored the fact that some of the views and theories held by the great speculators treated in this book have been voiced by other thinkers, before or contemporary with them. My concern is less with absolute claims of priority than it is with the effect produced when a certain philosopher of history enunciated his position and thus fixed public attention on the doctrines in question.

Finally, while each of the chapters on major figures such as Vico, Hegel, Comte, Marx, Spengler, Toynbee, and Freud is an independent whole and can be read for itself, I have tried to run certain motifs and lines of development through all of the chapters.[1] Thus, for the fullest comprehension of what I say, for example, about Marx, I assume a reading of the chapter on Hegel.

---

[1] A set of major questions concerns the direction of history. Is man evolving toward greater freedom (however the latter is defined—for instance, as Kant's moral freedom, Hegel's freedom to be rational, or Marx's freedom from alienation)? Toward equality, of a social, economic, or political nature? Toward a new religion, as in Toynbee; or toward the complete displacement of the religious illusion by scientific truth, as in Comte, Marx, and Freud? Is history progressive, in any or all of these ways, or is it merely a never-ending, repetitive cycle? Is culture cumulative, or are there merely different cultures, as Spengler thought, which flourish and die in isolation?

What is the major force at work in history? Is it Providence, as Vico believed, working through man in a naturalistic fashion? Or Reason, as Hegel suggested, realizing its potential as actuality? Or the economic conditions of production, as Marx proclaimed, determining, or conditioning, or influencing (the precise relationship is never made clear) the rest of man's historical world? Are the central characters in history individual heroes (whether self-impelled psychic leaders of their people or mere representatives of Reason), or nations, or God?

How are the stages, or periods, of history to be distinguished? By political, economic, social, technological, scientific or cultural criteria? Are there ages of Gods, heroes, and men, as Vico thought, or ten stages in the progress toward the French Enlightenment, as Condorcet contended? How do these divisions affect or reflect the other views on the meaning and direction of history projected by our speculators? As E. H. Carr puts it, "the division of history into periods is not a fact,

5

In my presentation of the great speculators and their philosophies of history, I have tried to keep three factors in mind, although these factors may appear irrelevant to some students of the subject. The first is that the way in which a man states his views is often as important as the content he presents. Style contains its own meaning, and offers a gloss to the overt message thrust upon us. For this reason, I have allowed each of my figures, when possible, to speak for himself, and I have sought to offer quotations not only as proof for my assertions but as examples of the color and quality of a man's mind.

The second factor is the biography of the thinker. I do not believe that men's doctrines can be divorced from their lives, nor the passion with which they advance "pure thoughts" separated from their personal experiences in the world. While this interrelationship is difficult to establish successfully, it is cowardice not even to attempt it. Thus, in a number of cases I have supplied not only biographical details, but I have also

---

but a necessary hypothesis or tool of thought, valid insofar as it is illuminating, and dependent for its validity on interpretation." (*What is History* [New York, 1962], p. 76.)

Other themes or *motifs* in our work are: the idea of probability (for example, Voltaire's "probable knowledge" is quite different from Condorcet's treatment of the subject); the notion that "man makes his history," and the connection of this notion with pragmatism (a notion that appears in Vico, and enjoys an important career in the theories of Kant, Hegel, and Marx); the related idea that "man has no nature, he has only his history" (to use the phrasing of the Spanish philosopher, Ortega y Gasset); the concept of the unintended consequence ("Man proposes, God disposes"); and the notion of "cultural wholes."

Then, on the critical—as contrasted with the speculative—side, probably the fundamental inquiry is: how can we or how do we know any of the answers to any of the questions above. What, in short, is the epistemology and logic of the discipline known as history? Do we start from Lockean empiricism or Kantian idealism? From "raw data," proceeding thence by induction; or from a priori assumptions, moving onward by deduction? Or from some combination of both, to be identified as the scientific method? What, indeed, is the correct relationship of theory and empirical research?

Do we proceed by intuition, by a method known as *Verstehen*, or by Cartesian analysis into parts? Can historians be "objective"? Do they aim

ventured where possible on the shaky ground of psychological interpretation, without, however, trying to write psychological biographies.

The third factor concerns the social conditions surrounding the thinkers whom I treat. Once again, I do not think the philosophy of history of a Hegel can be torn asunder from the problems facing European society in the post-Napoleonic period, or that of a Spengler from the cataclysm of World War I. In this sense, then, I practice in the sociology of knowledge in some of these studies.

Obviously, I approach philosophy of history from my work as an intellectual historian. Abstract ideas, paraded like self-winding automata across the pages of a book, do not impress me as either true or revealing entities. I believe that ideas—and this includes philosophies of history—are the lively productions of real men operating in actual life situations. Such ideas are efforts to achieve knowledge about the world, in this case historical, which conditions man's condition. My own conviction, that philosophy of history is primarily concerned with man's increasing consciousness, and perhaps therefore control, of his historical nature, emerges without discontinuity from the views just stated.

6

It remains to say a few words more about the general thesis which I hope to sustain in the course of this work: that the basic meaning of history lies in man's developing historical

---

at producing general laws, or only at narrating a unique sequence of events? Even if they themselves do not produce general laws, can historians use general laws derived from other fields in the course of their work? What is a satisfactory "explanation" in history? What do we mean by "causes" in history, and how do we determine what they are? What constitutes adequate evidence for a statement, causal or otherwise? Indeed, what is a "fact," and how does the historian decide what facts to select? These and other such questions will recur constantly, explicitly or implicitly, in all of our chapters.

consciousness. E. H. Carr is surely right when he says, "History begins when men begin to think of the passage of time in terms not of natural processes—the cycle of the seasons, the human life-span—but of a series of specific events in which men are consciously involved and which they can consciously influence." This, as Burckhardt pointed out, is "the break with nature caused by the awakening of consciousness." It is what Hegel intended by his poetic invocation to the Sphinx.[2]

As we know, historical consciousness, only slowly emerging out of myth, was at first largely the property of the Greeks and of the Judaic-Christian peoples (and I am aware of avoiding here the vexed question of Chinese and Indian history), though lapsing for their European heirs after the decline of the Roman Empire. Recovering strength in the modern period for the Occidental world, it is solely in the contemporary period that history—the attempt at *logical, scientific* understanding of the past—has spread to most other cultures than the Western. Only now, with a quest for historical identity, has Africa, for example, sought to discern an African past that is not legendary. So, too, the emergence into historical consciousness of whole groups and classes, previously neglected, has occurred only recently. To quote Carr again, "It is only today that it has become possible for the first time even to imagine a whole world consisting of peoples who have in the fullest sense entered into history and become the concern, no longer of the colonial administrator or of the anthropologist, but of the historian."[3] Such emergence into history and historical consciousness means at least the possibility of *efforts* at logical and rational control of *parts* of our destiny.[4]

It is this thought which lies in back of the idea most closely

[2] For Hegel's invocation, see pp. 164–165. Carr's statement is in *What is History*, p. 178.

[3] Cf. what Hannah Arendt has to say in *The Origins of Totalitarianism* (New York, 1958), Part II, "Imperialism," on the treatment of subject peoples by colonial administrators.

[4] For complicated reasons, I believe that large parts of man's future will always remain outside his control. See, for example, P. B. Medawar, *The Future of Man* (New York, 1959), for the biological side of this

related to the concept of historical consciousness, the idea of progress. Progress in history means not only increased technical mastery of our natural environment, but also an advance in the understanding of ourselves and in the ordering of our societies (an advance, incidentally, without which the technical mastery would falter or not take place at all). It is no accident that the idea of progress arose and gained strength at the same time, in the seventeenth century, as the first sign of the modern historical consciousness significantly manifested itself in the European thought of that period.

Elsewhere I have remarked that

We are coming to realize that the counterpart of the theory of evolution in the biological world is the idea of progress in the historical world. Both relate to processes which have a direction: increased differentiation and complexity. What is missing as yet from the idea of progress is an acceptable explanation of how the process takes place: the equivalent of a theory of natural selection. For example, Hegel's notion of Spirit coming to self-awareness dialectically is too metaphysical; Marx's economic determinism does not cover satisfactorily the empirical data or the manifold activities of man; and so forth. Nevertheless, whatever the mechanism by which it occurs, and however arguable the precise experience the term covers, there is today a widespread conviction that progress—the term for man's *historical evolution*—has been and is taking place.[5]

The aim of the present book is to study at some length this problem of man's historical evolution—his progress; and to do so in terms of how the problem has been dealt with by the great speculators from Vico to Freud. The hope is that by their inspirations we shall gain increased consciousness and additional insights concerning the riddle of history, and thus the riddle of our own being.

---

question. Claude Lévi-Strauss, "Race and History," in *Race and Science* edited by UNESCO (New York, 1961), is suggestive in the matter from the anthropological side.

[5] "The Idea of Progress," *Daedalus* (Summer, 1963), 458–459.

II

Vico

*Riverrun, past Eve and Adam's,
from swerve of shore to bend
of bay, brings us by a com-
modius vicus of recirculation
back to Howth Castle and En-
virons.*

JAMES JOYCE,
Finnegan's Wake

1

IN 1725, having just published his great work, the *New Science*, Vico wrote dolefully to a friend: "In this city [Naples] I
account it as fallen on barren ground. I avoid all public places,
so as not to meet the persons to whom I have sent it; and if I
cannot avoid them, I greet them without stopping; for when I
pause they give me not the faintest sign that they have received it, and thus they confirm my belief that it has gone
forth into a desert."[1] But Vico was wrong. Like the great
English philosopher, David Hume, shortly afterwards (whose
Treatise on Human Nature appeared in 1739, falling "dead-

[1] *The Autobiography of Giambattista Vico*, translated from the Italian by Max Harold Fisch and Thomas Goddard Bergin (Ithaca, N.Y.,
1944). (Also available as a Great Seal Book, 1963), p. 14. Many of the
quotations from Vico which follow are from this book. The long introductory essay, by Fisch, is one of the most valuable in English.

born from the press" according to its author), Vico grossly underestimated the seminal quality of his work. Hard as was the ground on which it originally fell, the *New Science* thrust down deep roots into the soil of Western culture, gradually flowering into an extraordinarily important and influential work in the developing science of man.

To give some idea of Vico's achievement, the most sweeping claim is simply to say that his work foreshadowed the entire modern approach to the study of man's past. Especially, it anticipated the development of historicism, which the German historian Friedrich Meinecke described as a "fundamental revolution of the Western mind." Even more specifically, in the words of one modern commentator, Vico's work "anticipates not only fundamental ideas of Herder and Hegel, Dilthey and Spengler, but also the more particular discoveries of Roman history by Niebuhr and Mommsen, the theory of Homer by Wolf, the interpretation of mythology by Bachofen, the reconstruction of ancient life through etymology by Grimm, the historical understanding of laws by Savigny, of the ancient city and of feudalism by Fustel de Coulanges, and of the class struggles by Marx and Sorel."[2]

These are awesome claims. What sort of man stands behind them? Vico gives us the answer himself, in his *Autobiography*, the other work which must be read in conjunction with the

---

[2] Karl Löwith, *Meaning in History* (Chicago, 1949), p. 115. Probably the best chapter in this interesting book is the one on Vico. Meinecke's statement is in his *Die Entstehung des Historismus* (Munich, 1936), p. 1. A beginning definition of historicism is offered by Hans Meyerhoff in his anthology *The Philosophy of History in Our Time* (Garden City, N.Y., 1959): "The basic thesis of historicism is quite simple: The subject matter of history is human life in its totality and multiplicity. It is the historian's aim to portray the bewildering, unsystematic variety of historical forms—people, nations, cultures, customs, institutions . . . —in their unique, living expressions and in the process of continuous growth and transformation. . . . The abstract concepts employed in philosophy are not adequate for rendering the concrete realities of history. . . . *Individuum est ineffabile* is the motto of Meinecke's work, expressing an aesthetic rather than a philosophic sentiment. Thus the special quality of history does not consist in the statement of general laws or principles, but in the grasp, so far as possible, of the infinite

New Science. In the *Autobiography,* called by its English translator, "the first application of the generic method by an original thinker to his own writings," Vico attempted to trace the development of his own mind and character in the same way as he had traced the development of humanity in the *New Science:* one mirrored the other. Thus, disdaining both the method of a famous predecessor, Descartes, and the latter's use in the *Discourse on Method* of the first person (with its emphasis on the isolated ego), Vico, in the third person, boasted that "Rather, with the candor proper to a historian, we shall narrate plainly and step by step the entire series of Vico's studies, in order that the proper and natural causes of his particular development as a man of letters may be known." Step by step, then, we are taken through Vico's early education—largely a self-education—through his classical and theological studies, and into his legal and linguistic studies.

Vico's legal studies colored his whole thought, and it is important to emphasize here that Vico, like his contemporary, Montesquieu, was a jurist. From his studies in the law, Vico reported, he had derived two things: an interest in the principles of universal laws, running through all the particular decrees, edicts, and laws; and a close attention to legal terms and their definitions, that is, to words and their meaning (the latter interest, of course, linked directly to his growing skill at comparative linguistics). Vico's approach to legal history also taught him to look behind the dead, mute letters of the law to the loud, vibrant struggle of the oppressed against the oppressor, of the plebs against the patricians. He saw how the swirl of their selfish contentions settled down into a shape unintended by either party; an evolution of law toward a natural

---

variety of particular historical forms immersed in the passage of time." (p. 10.) Other definitions are offered in Dwight E. Lee and Robert N. Beck, "The Meaning of Historicism," *The American Historical Review,* LIX, (April, 1954) 3. More recently, Carlo Antoni has tried to deal with the entire range of the phenomenon in *L'Historisme* (Genève, 1963). In the course of the chapters that follow, I shall have more to say on the subject.

jurisprudence, based on equality.[3] Later, we shall see how this fundamental idea fitted into the framework of the *New Science* as a whole.

Vico, in the *Autobiography*, did not tell only of the positive influences on him. He spoke also of his opposition to and disinterest in the natural sciences. His comment on Robert Boyle's experimental physics exemplifies his scorn: "It contributed nothing to the philosophy of man and had to be expounded in barbarous formulas." Blind to the great creative geniuses of his time in the natural sciences, Vico had an eye only for what contributed to a philosophy of humanity. Yet, cyclopean in his vision, he pretended to universal knowledge. Arrogantly he asserted "that others were concerned with the various parts of knowledge, but his should teach it as an integral whole in which each part accords with every other and gets its meaning from the whole."

Such one-sided boastfulness may repel us. However, before we condemn Vico, we must remember that the narrowing of perspective—and mind—seems almost a prerequisite for the construction of a new science. It is as if the novel mental telescope allowed one to see further ahead, at the expense of what lay on the periphery.

Vico explained it in different terms. He invoked the same Providence to direct his steps as, in the *New Science*, he was to call forth to direct the steps of mankind. Thus, the ways of Providence explained "why even from childhood he had felt an inclination for certain studies and an aversion to others; what opportunities and obstacles had advanced or retarded his progress; and lastly the effect of his own exertions in right directions, which were destined later to bear fruit in those reflections on which he built his final work, the *New Science*, which was to demonstrate that his intellectual life was bound to have been such as it was and not otherwise."

Vico was lucky to have faith in Providence, for his own life

[3] Cf. Giorgio de Santillana, "Vico and Descartes," *Osiris* 9 (1950), 574–575.

was filled with misfortunes, colored over by domestic poverty
and lack of academic success. For nine years a household
tutor, he finally secured a poorly paid chair of rhetoric at the
University of Naples in the year 1697. To eke out his meagre
living, he wrote odes, epithalamiums, panegyrics, and funeral
orations, often obtaining the commissions for them by abject
and humiliating gestures. The demands of his home life, too,
were many, for his wife, while a good woman, was unable to
write and took little care in household matters. The result was
that, as Vico plaintively tells us, "The learned professor was
obliged to plan and provide not only for the clothes but for
whatever else his children might need."

The event which should have rescued him from his penury
and overwork was the competition for the chair of law which
became vacant in 1717, and paid 600 ducats (the chair of
rhetoric had paid only 100). For more than five years, Vico
prepared himself diligently for the competition. Alas, little did
the poor scholar know that the judges who sat on the board in
1723 were already divided into two factions, committed to
other candidates. Vico, far and away the best candidate, received no votes, while the winner received fifteen and the
other loser, fourteen. As the English translator of Vico's *Autobiography* tells us: "The winner, Domenico Gentile, a notori-
ous seducer of servant girls, (he later committed suicide over
one of them) was so incapable of writing a book of any sort
that his one attempt was withdrawn from the press after being
exposed as a plagiarism." Vico's one consolation—surely a
Pyrrhic one for him—was that he could turn all his energies to
working on his new science. His loss was, as it turned out,
humanity's gain.

Knowing the strains and stresses of Vico's life, we can for-
give him much. But it is still necessary to be honest about his
character, and to admit that the pathetic, slightly uncouth
figure which emerges from the *Autobiography*, though arous-
ing our sympathy, is not an admirable one. On his own admission, he was given to melancholy and "choleric to a fault";

unwittingly, he also reveals himself in the *Autobiography* as vain and ambitious. Even his vaunted "candor proper to a historian" is found to be, at best, an exaggeration, and, at worst, a deliberate misrepresentation. There are many errors of fact and of date in the *Autobiography*, and, more importantly, many distortions concerning Vico's intellectual development; for example, his indebtedness and close relations to the Cartesians and epicureans of his time is underplayed badly.[4] Much of this probably reflected his straitened circumstances in an eighteenth-century Naples, where the unhindered expression of thought might have antagonized important religious, political, or academic persons. But much also reflected the fact that Vico was no revolutionary in the ordinary, political sense of the word. His trust in Providence extended easily and supinely to an acceptance of authority.

Sustained by his faith that all had been and was as it must be, Vico could turn from the harsh reality of his own world to an investigation of humanity's past. Craven and fawning in his personal life, he stood proud and erect—even arrogant—in his intellectual work. Thus, Vico's personal existence, while interesting in itself and shedding light on the development of his ideas, is curiously out of tone with the power and sweep of the *New Science*. In the latter, the petty, almost picayune nature of a Neapolitan academician's life is submerged in the onrushing waters of protean thought. Well could Vico have said of his own life and work what he said of the Homer he did so much to discover: "For delicacy is a small virtue and greatness naturally disdains all small things. Indeed, as a great rushing torrent cannot fail to carry turbid waters and roll stones and trunks along in the violence of its course, so his very greatness accounts for the low expressions we so often find in Homer." Vico's contemporaries generally saw only the "low expressions" of an unsuccessful life; posterity has come to appreciate the "great rushing torrent" which is the *New Science*.

[4] Robert Flint, *Vico* (Edinburgh, 1884), follows Vico in this very error.

2

In the *New Science*, Vico put forth two major claims to our attention. The first involved an attempt to work out the epistemology and logic of a human science. This attempt circled about two main points: (1) that "verum=factum," that is, that we know a thing only if we make it; and (2) that the rational and empirical—the philosophy which gives us the true, and the history which gives us the certain—must be fused into one science. These points in Vico's work fall into what nowadays is called the "critical" philosophy of history. The second claim on our attention involved the reconstruction of the past—a theory as to the meaning and pattern of the history which has already unrolled. The latter comprises Vico's great "speculative" philosophy of history.

Central to a consideration of the epistemological part of Vico's work is what may be called the "Descartes Problem." It is extraordinary how divergent are the views on this matter, ranging from Collingwood's sharp "This new attitude toward history is profoundly anti-Cartesian" to the seemingly paradoxical comment of Fisch that "the greatest critic of Descartes was himself the greatest Cartesian of Italy."[5] Much of the problem is created by Vico himself. His blunt disapproval in the *Autobiography* of Descartes, and of Descartes' physics

[5] *Autobiography*, p. 36. R. G. Collingwood argues his position in *The Idea of History* (Oxford, 1946), pp. 59–76. In the *Discourse on Method*, for example, Descartes seems to say that history, by its very nature, cannot give us true and certain knowledge becaue it cannot be approached by his deductive and "geometrical" method. Besides this, Descartes appears to attack the claim of history to offer examples from the past as a guide to present and future behavior. As he comments, "even the most faithful histories, if they do not alter or embroider things to make them more worth reading, almost always omit the meanest and least illustrious circumstances so that the remainder is distorted. Thus it happens that those who regulate their behavior by the examples they find in books are apt to fall into the extravagances of the knights of romances, and undertake projects which it is beyond their ability to complete." In "Antiquity and Authority: A Paradox in the Renaissance Theory of History," *Journal of the History of Ideas*,

and metaphysics would seem to dispose of the matter. But the overt disavowal is undercut by the constant indebtedness to and sympathy with Cartesian ideas which peep through the fabric of Vico's closely woven and repetitive prose.

There is little point, really, in trying to settle the question in terms of whether Vico was Cartesian or anti-Cartesian. The important thing is to ask what was the Cartesian influence on Vico, how did it affect his thought, and how did he attempt to go beyond it? That Vico was fundamentally influenced by Descartes seems beyond question. That he was annoyed, out of professional pique, at the usurpation by Cartesian physics and metaphysics of the place of honor formerly held by humanistic letters is also clear. We hear the voice of a disappointed and poorly paid lecturer on rhetoric when Vico, lamenting the change in taste from letters to science, whined that "as the world by its nature changes in taste from year to year, they [i.e., Vico] later find themselves in their old age strong in such wisdom as no longer pleases and therefore no longer profits." In place of the wisdom which "no longer pleases," there was "the *Meditations* of René Descartes and its companion piece his book *On Method*, wherein he disapproves the study of languages, orators, historians and poets . . . setting up only his metaphysics, physics and mathematics."

Fortunately, however, Vico did not simply complain. Surreptitiously, he also learned. There is little question as to whose voice it is which echoes in the statement: "Thus our science proceeds exactly as does geometry." As the sagacious critic, Jean Le Clerc, commented in a review of Vico's *New Science* in the *Bibliothèque Ancienne et Moderne* (a comment recorded proudly in the *Autobiography*), "it [the *New Science*] is constructed by 'mathematical method,' which 'from

---

XIX, 4 (October, 1958), W. von Leyden argues that the view of Descartes as disdainful toward history is "at best only partially correct." L. Lévy-Bruhl, "The Cartesian Spirit and History," in *Philosophy and History: Essays Presented to Ernst Cassirer*, R. Klibansky and H. J. Paton (eds.) (Oxford, 1936) takes a view opposed to von Leyden.

few principles draws infinite consequences.' " And there is the hum of "cogito ergo sum" in Vico's statement about the "one thing of which we cannot by any means doubt, that is of course . . . thought."

Vico's fundamental response to the challenge of Descartes' method was to pass over to the offensive. The Cartesians had not gone far enough. "These most eminent philosophers," Vico said, talking of Descartes and Malebranche, "if they had been zealous for the common glory of Christendom, not for the private glory of philosophers, ought to have pressed forward the study of philology far enough for philosophers to see whether it could be reduced to philosophical principles." Thereby, Vico added, they would have created a new science: the science of man. For, in fact, as Vico insisted, the world of man was *by its very essence* more susceptible to scientific treatment than the world of nature. At this point, Vico invoked his basic principle: verum=factum. With poetic intensity he cried out that "In the night of thick darkness enveloping the earliest antiquity, so remote from ourselves, there shines the eternal and never-failing light of a truth beyond all question: that the world of civil society has certainly been made by men, and that its principles are therefore to be found within the modifications of our own human mind. Whoever reflects on this cannot but marvel that the philosophers should have bent all their energies to the study of the world of nature, which, since God made it, He alone knows; and that they should have neglected the study of the world of nations or civil world, which, since men had made it, men could hope to know."

The knowledge Vico hoped for about the world of men and nations would be "true and certain" knowledge. It would have the same eternal validity and deductive certainty as Cartesian mathematics. Where Descartes had asserted "But even if God had created several worlds, there would have been none where these [i.e., Descartes' laws] were not observed," Vico contended, in the same rather arrogant tone: "The decisive sort of proof in our science is therefore this: that, once these orders were established by divine providence, the course of the affairs of the nations had to be, must now be and will have to be such as our Science demonstrates, even if infinite worlds were produced from time to time through eternity, which is certainly not the case."

However, in his attempt to justify history—"The course of the affairs of the nations"—as a legitimate form of knowledge, Vico realized that Descartes' belief in clear and distinct ideas equaling the truth was fallacious. In terms later to be echoed by David Hume, the Neapolitan philosopher pointed out that the clear conception of an idea really equals only conviction. The vividness with which we perceive or conceive of something is not a test of its truth, but merely of the ardor with which we believe in it. As early as 1710, in *The Ancient Wisdom of the Italians*, Vico had asserted that "The rule and criterion of truth is to have made it. Hence the clear and distinct idea of the mind not only cannot be the criterion of other truths, but it cannot be the criterion of that of the mind itself; for while the mind apprehends itself, it does not make itself, and because it does not make itself it is ignorant of the form or mode by which it apprehends itself."

Having dismissed this basic misapprehension in Descartes' system, Vico went on to elaborate his justification of history in terms of a very Cartesian notion: that we understand only that which we construct. Instead of points and lines, however, it is the world of nations which we are uniquely able to construct. In words which placed man in almost a Godlike position, Vico lyricized: "Our Science therefore comes to describe at the same time an ideal eternal history traversed in time by the history of every nation in its rise, progress, maturity, decline and fall. Indeed we go so far as to assert that whoever meditates this Science tells himself this ideal eternal history only so far as he makes it by that proof 'it had, has, and will have to be.' For the first indubitable principle above posited [i.e., in #331 previously] is that this world of nations has certainly been made by men, and its guise must therefore be found within the modifications of our own human mind. And history cannot be more certain than when he who creates the things also describes them. Thus our Science proceeds exactly as does geometry, which, while it constructs out of its elements or contemplates the world of quantity, itself creates it; but with a reality greater in proportion to that of the orders having to do with human affairs, in which there are neither points, lines, surfaces, nor figures. And this very fact is an argument, O reader, that these proofs are of a kind divine, and should give thee a divine pleasure; since in God knowledge and creation are one and the same thing."

"Knowledge and creation are one and the same thing." Where Descartes had grounded his method of doubt on the "I doubt, therefore I am," Vico discovered that amidst the "immense ocean of doubt" there is a "single tiny piece of earth" on which to gain a firm footing: verum=factum.[6]

The consequences of Vico's formulation are extended. In one direction, he reached Karl Marx, who, in an important footnote to *Capital*, remarked: "Since, as Vico says, the essence of the distinction between human history and natural history is that the former is made by man and the latter is not, would not the history of human technology be easier to write than the history of natural technology [i.e., Darwin's theory of evolution]?" The next step for Marx was to proceed from the idea of verum=factum to "Man makes himself." Then, to avoid an "undetermined history," Marx hastily added, "Men make their history themselves, only they do so in a given environment which conditions it, and on the basis of actual relations already existing, among which the economic relations are still ultimately the decisive ones." We shall reserve a discussion of the development of verum=factum by Marx for a later chapter.[7]

[6] Cf. Löwith, *op. cit.*, p. 119.
[7] See Chapter VIII, pp. 251, 261. M. Lifshitz, "Giambattista Vico (1668–1744)," translated from the Russian by Henry F. Mins, Jr., *Philosophy*

In another direction, Vico's concept, that we understand
what we make, anticipates the pragmatists of our own time. In
its broadest aspect, as in the pragmatism of William James,
truth is conceived to be that which "works," that is, what we
do in practice proves the truth of what we hold in theory. In
its more narrow vein (and, incidentally, I believe, more acceptable form—instrumentalism—as used by both James and
Peirce), theories are mere tools, or instruments, which we
make, and which are true only insofar as they operate successfully in giving us scientific knowledge. Obviously, these are
extrapolations from Vico's idea; although we cannot explore
their implications here, they are of the utmost philosophical
and historical importance.[8]

Let us turn now, instead, in the other direction, back to
Vico's sources. Four names must be mentioned here: two from
antiquity, and two from Vico's own time. They signal Vico's
exceptional attention to the necessary foundation of any
human *science:* the fusion of the rational and the empirical.
Indeed, what he wished to construct in this part of his new
science was not so much a philosophy of history as a combination of philosophy *and* history. Thus, of Plato and Tacitus, he
remarked in the *Autobiography:* "With an incomparable
metaphysical mind Tacitus contemplates man as he is, Plato as
he should be. And as Plato with his universal knowledge ex-
plores the parts of nobility which constitute the man of intellectual wisdom, so Tacitus descends into all the counsels of
utility whereby, among the infinite irregular chances of malice
and fortune, the man of practical wisdom brings things to
good issue. Now Vico's admiration of these two great authors
from this point of view was a foreshadowing of that plan on

and Phenomenological Research, VIII, 3 (March, 1948) is a most interesting Marxist account of the relations of Vico to Marx. Also consult
Hannah Arendt, "History and Immortality," *Partisan Review* (Winter,
1957).

[8] See further Hannah Arendt, "The Concept of History: Ancient
and Modern," in *Between Past and Future* (New York, 1961).

which he later worked out an ideal eternal history to be traversed by the universal history of all times, carrying out on it,
by certain eternal properties of civil affairs, the development,
acme, and decay of all nations. From this it follows that the
wise man should be formed both of esoteric wisdom such as
Plato's and of common wisdom such as that of Tacitus." In
modern times, Vico's attention was fixed on Francis Bacon, "a
man of incomparable wisdom both common and esoteric, at
one and the same time a universal man in theory and in practice," and on the fourth great figure, Hugo Grotius, who "embraces in a system of universal law the whole of philosophy
and philology including both parts of the latter, the history on
the one hand of facts and events, both fabulous and real, and
on the other of the three languages, Hebrew, Greek and
Latin."[9] In all four cases, what interested Vico was the interplay of the rational and the empirical.

Vico's instinct was perfect. He realized what today still requires emphasis, that the problem of any projected human—as
also natural—science is the problem of relating theory to fact.
For the moment, whether we judge his particular solution
correct or not is immaterial. In his methodology, it would
appear, he was on the right track. And there are few in historical studies we can place next to him in this matter.

3

Before we see in detail how Vico used his insight into the
relationship of the rational and the empirical to construct a
new science, we must go back to a name already cited—
Descartes—and to a name not yet mentioned—Hobbes. They
are the bridge over which Vico threaded his way from the

[9] As Vico tells us in his *Autobiography*, however, he abandoned the
task of writing notes for a new edition of Grotius because the latter
was "a heretical author." (p. 155.)

rational as applied in mathematics to the rational as applied in the real world of facts: the world of history, made by man.

Descartes, as we have noted, stressed the power of pure thought to construct a true and certain geometrical world, and denied the name of science to history because it could not observe or use the simple rules of his method. As Isaiah Berlin has put it succinctly, how could one "find the clear and simple elements of which historical judgments were composed, and into which they could be analyzed; where were the definitions, the logical transformation rules, the rules of inference, the rigorously deduced conclusions?"[10] Without these, history was a pastime, not even fit to amuse serious minds.

It was Hobbes who sought to rescue the civil world from Descartes' doubt and for philosophy. In his youth the translator of Thucydides (the Greek Tacitus?), Hobbes, in his middle age, fell across Euclid and instantly became enamoured. The story of how he chanced upon the geometrical method is a classic, lovingly told by his friend, Aubrey. "He was 40 years old before he looked on geometry; which happened accidentally. Being in a gentleman's library Euclid's Elements lay open, and 'twas the 47 El. libri I. He read the proposition. 'By G—,' sayd he, 'this is impossible!' So he reads the demonstration of it, which referred him back to such a proposition; which proposition he read. That referred him back to another, which he also read. *Et sic deinceps*, that at last he was demonstratively convinced of that trueth. This made him in love with geometry."

Hobbes quickly realized that he could reverse the procedure above, and thus have the axiomatic method working in two directions. Instead of going back from demonstration to demonstration, he could start with the first principle and its demonstration, and then continue on his deductive course. Thus, he could both synthesize and analyze, construct and resolve; and he could do this, not only in geometry, "which is

[10] Isaiah Berlin, "History and Theory: The Concept of Scientific History," *History and Theory*, I, 1 (1960), 1.

the only science that it hath pleased God hitherto to bestow on mankind," but in civil philosophy as well.[11] His conclusion was: "Of arts, some are demonstrable, others indemonstrable; and demonstrable are those the construction of the subject whereof is in the power of the artist himself, who, in his demonstration, does no more but deduce the consequences of his own operation. The reason whereof is this, that the science of every subject is derived from a precognition of the causes, generation, and construction of the same; and consequently where the causes are known, there is place for demonstration, but not where the causes are to seek for. Geometry therefore is demonstrable, for the lines and figures from which we reason are drawn and described by ourselves; and civil philosophy is demonstrable, because we make the commonwealth ourselves." Then, with a gentle condescension towards physics, Hobbes added: "But because of natural bodies we know not the construction, but seek it from the effects, there lies no demonstration of what the causes be we seek for, but only of what they may be."[12]

It is no wonder that, with his novel way of seeing, Hobbes felt himself lifted beyond the ordinary uncertainty of men in these areas. He had glimpsed new, fertile shores in the uncharted sea of knowledge, and, as his friend Cowley, the poet, said, was the "great Columbus of the golden lands of new philosophies." Yet, having discovered one land, Hobbes turned his back on another. He had rescued what he called *Civil Philosophy* from Cartesian skepticism; it was enough. In spite of having translated Thucydides and, later, writing *Bèhemoth*, a history of the English Civil War, Hobbes had nothing but scorn for history, which he deprecatingly called "knowledge

---

[11] Thomas Hobbes, *Leviathan* (Oxford, 1955), pp. 21, 456.
[12] *English Works*, 11 vols., Sir William Molesworth (ed.) (London, 1839–1845), Vol. VII, p. 183. On the question of Vico's familiarity with Hobbes, see the comment in fn. 39, p. 211 of the *Autobiography*. Fisch claims that Vico anticipated Kant in the view of physics outlined above (p. 39); but surely both Hobbes and Locke anticipated Kant before Vico did.

of fact" and "nothing else, but sense and memory." To this he opposed true knowledge, which he called "knowledge of the consequence of one affirmation to another." And this alone, Hobbes contended, "is called science; and is conditional; as when we know, that, if the figure should be a circle, then any straight line through the centre shall divide it into two equal parts. And this is the knowledge required in a philosopher; that is to say, of him that pretends to reasoning."

Vico took up the challenge, and pretended "to reasoning." Hobbes had said that demonstration was possible where construction was in the power of the artist himself. He who can generate or cause a thing, knows it. But man, as Vico patiently repeated, makes, that is, generates or causes, his own history. Hence, history is knowable; it is demonstrable; and it is, in consequence, a science.

Next, however, Vico needed to show how the empirical—the factual—combined with the rational—the universal, eternal, and demonstrable truth. He needed history to take its place next to philosophy. In the words of Flint, it is "The idea of greatest scientific value in the book" [in this case, Flint is talking of the *Universal Law,* an early version of the *New Science*], for "Philosophy investigates and discloses the necessary laws of our natures and the necessary causes of things. History is the record of the results of wills, of human facts themselves, the order of their succession, and the circumstances of their production."[13] It is in this light that we must understand Vico's summary of Principles, in Book I of the *New Science,* where he declared that his propositions five to fifteen

> . . . give us the basis of truth and, will serve for considering this world of nations in its eternal idea, by that property of every science, noted by Aristotle, that 'science has to do with what is universal and eternal' (*scientia debet esse de universalibus et aeternis*). The last propositions, from the fifteenth to the twenty-second, will give us the basis of certitude. By their use we shall be able to see

13 Flint, *op. cit.,* pp. 150–151.

in fact this world of nations which we have studied in idea, following the method of philosophizing made most certain by Francis Bacon, Lord of Verulam, but carrying it over from the things of nature, on which he composed his book *Cogitata et visa,* to the civil affairs of mankind.

Whatever hints and helpful inspirations Vico had from Hobbes or other thinkers, he had, nevertheless, primarily to forge his own tools—such as linguistic analysis and comparative mythology—and to cut his own way to his principles. As he tartly remarked: "For on the one hand the conceit of the nations, each believing itself to have been the first in the world, leaves us no hope of getting principles of our Science from the philologians. And on the other hand the conceit of the scholars, who will have it that what they know must have been eminently understood from the beginning of the world, makes us despair of getting them from the philosophers. So, for purposes of this inquiry, we must reckon as if there were no books in the world." Once again, as in so much else, we hear the echo of Descartes, in this case turning from the world of books to his own Dedalesque contrivances, whereon to fly aloft to new realms of thought.

In this new realm—or science—Vico thought he saw the emergence (or perhaps we should say more correctly the existence) of eternal laws from the matrix of facts. At the end of his *New Science,* Vico proudly declared that

There will then be fully unfolded, not the particular history in time of the laws and deeds of the Romans or the Greeks, but (in virtue of the substantial identity of meaning in the diversity of modes of expression) the ideal of the eternal laws in accordance with which the affairs of all nations proceed in their rise, progress, mature state, decline and fall, and would do so even if (as is certainly not the case) there were infinite worlds being born from time to time throughout eternity. Hence we could not refrain from giving this work the invidious title of a *New Science,* for it was too much to defraud it unjustly of the rightful claim it had over an argument so universal as that concerning the common nature of nations, in virtue of that property which belongs to every science that is perfect in its idea, and which

Seneca has set forth for us in his vast expression: *Pusilla res hic mundus est, nisi id, quod quaerit, omnis mundus habeat*—'This world is a paltry thing unless all the world may find therein what it seeks.' "

Vico, it is clear, did not believe that the world he was offering his readers in the *New Science* was a "paltry thing."

4

It would be a mistake to see in Vico a twentieth-century scientific mind, alive to the fact that the "eternal" ideas derived from philosophy, or the clear and distinct ideas of Descartes were neither innate nor self-evident but, more fittingly, mere logical constructs of the human mind. In this matter, Vico did not always look forward, but more often backward to "the doctrine of Plato who from the very form of our human mind, without any hypothesis, establishes the eternal idea as the principle of all things on the basis of the knowledge and consciousness [*scienza e coscienza*] that we have of ourselves. For in our mind there are certain eternal truths that we cannot mistake or deny, and which are therefore not of our making."

Yet, Vico's instinct was correct, and filled in the deficiencies of his formal epistemology. He operated *as if in fact* his "eternal truths" were hypotheses, to be tested against the facts. Often in practice he went astray, and thought he saw confirmation of his hypotheses—which he called "eternal truths," or axioms, or principles—in areas where today we know better. So confident was he of the power of his "scientific laws" at predicting as yet unobserved fact or of filling in unrecorded gaps in the past that he could boast: "Thus purely by understanding, without benefit of memory, which has nothing to go on where facts are not supplied by the senses, we seem to have filled in the beginnings of universal history both in ancient Egypt and in the East." It was a proud boast, and a noble effort; in reality, however, Vico's views on ancient Egypt were quite misguided. But—and this is the important point—

his *method* was correct. He sought to illuminate the empirical data of the past by the searchlight coming from a rational present, and, in turn, to verify and test his laws or principles by the facts or evidence.

There is one other criticism of Vico, however, which needs to be made at this point. It concerns, specifically, his verum= factum. Even if we grant him his point—and there is much to be said for it—how can we really claim that man consciously "makes" his history? As Vico himself was so keenly aware (indeed, he is perhaps the key figure in this awareness), "man proposes and God disposes." In paragraph after paragraph, as we shall see later, Vico brilliantly illustrated how man intends one thing, for example, the satisfaction of his bestial lust, and makes another, the marriage institution. Can we, then, in all seriousness, say that man "makes" the unintended consequence; and if we perversely insist that he makes it even though he knows not what he makes, is this to say anything more than that the wind makes sand figures and the waves make driftwood sculptures? Is the difference between the two "makings" that man is conscious *afterwards* as to what has emerged? In that case, true though it is, does this argument touch Hobbes' (and Descartes') insistence that we know lines and figures because they "are drawn and described by our-selves," or Hobbes' claim that we know civil philosophy be-cause we have defined, or generated, or caused its elements?

The answer is clearly no. We "make" history in two impor-tant but different senses: (1) we are the actors, the agents involved whose combined behavior "makes up" the unex-pected consequences; (2) we are the thinkers who consciously perceive or "make" a pattern out of the actions spread before us. This, of course, is merely to rephrase the commonly ac-cepted division of history into (1) what has happened; and (2) the reflection on what has happened. In this second part, in reflecting and making a pattern out of our events, we are indeed creating and constructing in the Cartesian and Hobbes-ian sense. Consequently, at least in theory, we are "making" history in the same way as we make geometry or civil philosophy.

Vico did not stress the distinction just made, and indeed he may not even have perceived it. He wished to validate history as a justifiable form of knowledge; and he wished to make the validation in Cartesian terms, by turning Descartes' very weapons upon himself. He thought he had done this successfully in his verum=factum. Whatever criticisms one may make should not obscure the bracing effect on Vico of his "histodicy" (justification of history), or the far-reaching influence of his formula.

5

Girding his loins, Vico plunged into the task of working out in detail his new science. He took as one of his principles: "Philosophy contemplates reason, whence comes knowledge of the true; philology observes the authority of human choice, whence comes consciousness of the certain." "This axiom," he continued, "by its second part defines as philologians all the grammarians, historians, critics, who have occupied themselves with the study of the languages and deeds of peoples: both their domestic affairs, such as customs and laws, and their external affairs, such as wars, peaces, alliances, travels and commerce." Vico's definition of philology, as can readily be seen, was broad. It included both the ordinary meaning of the word—with its stress on linguistics—and the broadest possible interest in ideas, as expressed in customs, myths, laws, and records of deeds.

Philology studied what was certain, that is, what had happened. What had happened, however, was known only through "remains"—the languages, myths, and laws of a people—and these remains required correct interpretation and understanding. At this point, Vico had a great insight: the customs and laws of the ancients were not in the "language" of modern times. Instead, the ancients spoke in a different tongue, whose words could not be accepted literally; their meaning lay hidden behind a secret door. A key was needed. And the key—which Vico called "the master key of this Science"— was simply that the early peoples "were poets who spoke in poetic characters."[14]

Vico had come to realize that mythology was a language. It was neither meaningless, nor a mere intuitive grasp of rational notions. It was simply a different language, expressing reality in a way distinct from the language of eighteenth-century rationalism. In the beginning, Vico explained, fables or myths were "true narratives" delivered in heroic poetry; in the age that followed, they were overlaid by mystical interpretations; and so overlaid and corrupted, they were received into the modern age. The task, Vico asserted, was to reverse this procedure and to "restore to the fables their original historical meanings."

Our purpose here is not to explore the particulars of Vico's effort, nor to point out either how correct or how mistaken he was in his interpretations (often, in practice, Vico himself was far too "liberal" about the myths). However, a few specific illustrations might be useful. For example, by linguistic analysis—and here Vico limited himself to Greek and Latin— he showed how the golden age, when translated, meant the age of grain harvests (grain=gold). He examined the legends of the Chaldeans, Phoenicians, Egyptians, and other early nations, and concluded that they all have a Jove (the name for the thunderclap) and a Hercules, under various names. He dis-

[14] Vico's insight into language is comparable to Kepler and Galileo's inspiration in mathematics. Compare, for example, Galileo's lyric passage: "Philosophy is written in that great book which ever lies before our eyes—I mean the universe—but we cannot understand it if we do not first learn the language and grasp the symbols, in which it is written. This book is written in the mathematical language, and the symbols are triangles, circles, and other geometrical figures, without whose help it is impossible to comprehend a single word of it; without which one wanders in vain through a dark labyrinth." *Dialogues and Mathematical Demonstrations Concerning Two New Sciences*, translated by Henry Crew and Alfonso de Salvio (New York, 1914), p. 52.

cussed the true meaning of Orpheus—who, he tells us, never really existed in the world—and of Hermes and Zoroaster. Turning the key in the lock of Roman history, Vico showed how "the Salic Law, so far as it excludes women from the royal succession, is not, as may appear, contradicted by the statement that Tanaquil, a woman, governed the Roman kingdom. For that was a heroic phrase to describe a weak-spirited king who allowed himself to be dominated by the crafty Servius Tullius." Then, to prove his case, Vico pointed to the story of Pope John who, in "the returned barbarian times" was called a woman for yielding to the Patriarch of Constantinople.

With the key of his new science, Vico attempted to interpret and restore the true meaning of the early Greek and Roman law codes. By replacing them in their original context, when men thought and spoke in poetic characters, he hoped to understand them as the Greeks and Romans had understood them. In the case of Roman history, later scholars, especially Niebuhr and Mommsen, have followed up or confirmed his leads. They have explored and worked out his insights as to the rise of ancient "feudalism," the emergence of agrarian law, and the outbreak of the class struggle in Rome. Perhaps Vico's greatest triumph, however, was in the field of Homeric study. Here, he discovered the "true Homer." Demonstrating from internal evidence of the poems that the Homer of the *Iliad* was not, and could not be, the Homer of the *Odyssey*, Vico went even further. He showed that Homer was not a single poet, but the whole Greek people, expressing itself through a number of rhapsodists, the Homeric poets. It was the latter who "stitched together" the works that have come down to us under the name of Homer. In this ground-breaking work, Vico opened the way to the later researches of men like Wolf.[15]

[15] More recently, many modern scholars have assumed again the opposite opinion to that of Vico. See, for example, George Steiner's account "Homer and the Scholars," *The Atlantic Monthly* (August, 1961), 77–84. This modern reversal, however, does not in any way diminish Vico's contribution; in fact, without the latter, the grounds used in the new decision would probably never have been discovered.

In the broadest sense, Vico, by his restorations, had traversed the road from myth to history. This was not, however, simply to repeat the accomplishment of Thucydides, among the Greeks, or, say, of Pierre Bayle among his contemporaries. These historians had gone beyond myth by simply dismissing it. But this, as Vico was the first to perceive, was to lose the grain with the chaff. The task was to go beyond myth by seizing the kernel of truth which lay inside its mystic wrappings, and to realize that even its "untruth," correctly understood, became a form of the truth revealing what had happened and was "certain." In the process of working out this insight, Vico became a pioneer of comparative mythology. And because he was this, he was also, of necessity, a forerunner of modern anthropology, with its study of primitive cultures, and of modern psychology, with its study of earlier, more childlike and prescientific forms of mentality.

6

Obviously, Vico's insight also had major implications for historical study itself. He pointed out that the poems of Homer, the fables of the gods, and the laws of Solon were a treasure store of Greek history, as were the Roman fables and the law of the twelve tables for Roman history. The "poetic characters," correctly interpreted, became the "first history." And the first history reveals to us the pattern of all future histories. In triumphant tones, Vico proclaimed that his hypothesis about Rome "gives us also the history of all the other cities of the world in times we have so far despaired of knowing. This then is an instance of an ideal eternal history . . . whose course is run in time by the histories of all nations." With this last, of course, we enter upon a narrative philosophy of history. At this point the "speculative" rather than "critical" part of Vico's views on history emerges.

What did Vico wish to do in the application of his new science to a speculative philosophy of history? In part, the answer involves the influence of St. Augustine (to whom Vico attributed the immediate inspiration for his *Universal Law* and his concept of a city of God). In another part, it goes back, behind Augustine, to Vico's pagan master, Plato. Thus, where Augustine could only conceive of a transcendent city of God, standing above and aloof from the earthly cities of men, Vico synthesized a city which was both ideal and material. Meditating on Plato's ideal commonwealth, he envisioned "an ideal eternal law that should be observed in a universal city after the idea or design of providence, upon which idea have since been founded all the commonwealths of all times and all nations."

Plato had lacked the notion of providence; but, unlike Augustine, he had an ideal republic which he projected for *secular* man. Thus, Vico took from Plato the involvement of the ideal with the real and, in heightened form, as we have seen earlier, the intermingling of the rational with the empirical. In consequence, Augustinian as was his inspiration, Vico became part of that great secular onrush which characterized the scientific work of the seventeenth and eighteenth centuries. Without dismissing the "divine" aspect of Vico's "rational civil theology"—in fact, we must discuss it shortly in more detail—we may sat that Vico, like his earlier compatriot, Galileo, wished to read God's message as it was written in the lineaments of existing nature. But in this case it was the nature, not of space, but of time.

7

Before discussing the elements of Vico's treatment of the "ideal eternal history" of the world of nations, we ought to familiarize ourselves with the general outline of his historical picture. What follows, therefore, is a brief précis of his speculative philosophy of history, as offered by a Vico scholar, Max Harold Fisch.

To the first *New Science* Vico prefixed a synopsis beginning as follows:

IDEA OF THE WORK

in which is meditated a Science concerning the nature [=genesis] of the nations, from which [nature] has issued their humanity [=civilization], which in every case began with religion and was completed by sciences, disciplines, and arts.

BOOK ONE

"We wander ignorant of the men and the places": VIRGIL.—Necessity of the end and difficulty of the means of finding this Science within the ferine wandering of Hobbes's licentious and violent men, of Grotius's solitary, weak and needy simpletons, of Pufendorf's vagrants cast into this world without divine care or help, from which the gentile nations have arisen.

His [Vico's] starting point was therefore roughly the state of nature of the natural-law theories. In order to reach it from *Genesis*, as his scruples required, he imagined the descendants of Ham and Japheth, and those of Shem except the Hebraic line, as dispersed after the flood, wandering in "the vast forest of the earth," forgetting the speech and customs of their ancestors, and descending to the level of beasts.

During the two centuries Vico allowed for this process of bestialization, the earth slowly dried, until the first thunderclaps caused by its exhalations startled these brutish men here and there in the act of shameless canine copulation with captured women, and terrified them into the shelter and secrecy of caves for their intercourse. Out of these retreats of fear and shame the first families arose, with a settled life apart in the caves of the earth, sanctioned by "the frightful religions" started in their minds by the thunderbolts of the sky god. With settled habitations came clearing and tilling of the soil, ownership, property, morality, and burial of the dead. Marriage, childbirth, burial, the sowing and reaping of crops, were surrounded with religious ceremonial. The family-father was its king, priest and prophet, sacrificing to the gods to win their favor, and taking auspices to declare their will. He was the arbiter of right and wrong, rewarding the good and punishing the wrongdoer. This "state of the families," "monastic, Cyclopean, monarchic," and not the antecedent chaos, with its "bestial communism of women" and "confusion of human seeds," was the true state of nature from which the civil state emerged; and the three pre-political institutions of religion, marriage, and burial of the dead were the first principles of the new science. This primitive stage of social evolution Vico called "the age of the gods."

The state of nature was one not of static equality, but of differentiation, inequality, and dialectical change. There was inequality between the organized family and the "lawless vagrants" still living in that chaos out of which the family grew; inequality within the family, inequality between family and family, inequality among the vagrants themselves. The more violent and enterprising of the latter raided the homesteads of the settlers and burned or carried off their crops; but they preyed also on the weaker and more helpless of their own kind, who were thereby driven to throw themselves on the mercy of the settlers. "Grotius's simpletons and Pufendorf's waifs, to save themselves from Hobbes's men of violence, fled to the altars of the strong." These refugees were received as dependents, "clients," serfs, tillers of the soil, "hewers of wood and drawers of water." The family unit was thus enlarged and still further differentiated, and the tension between its elements was heightened. To the distinctions of sex and generation there was added a distinction of blood and class.

The serfs of a family had less in common with its blood members than with the serfs of another; the father of a family had more in common with the father of another than with his own serfs. To secure themselves against mutinies of their serfs as well as against outlaw invasions, the fathers formed mutual alliances, patrician orders, "heroic states," with the fathers as citizens and the serfs as plebs. The heroic state was not a monarchy like the earlier family state, for its king was simply one of the fathers, the magistrate of the order; often, in fact, there were two or more such magistrates. It was not a democracy, for the "people" was simply the patrician order, exclusive of the plebs; the only freedom, the only rights, were those of the patricians; the fatherland was the land of the fathers. It was in fact a feudal aristocracy. This second stage of social evolution Vico called "the age of the heroes."

The whole life of these heroic states centered in the conflict between patricians and plebeians. The two classes, as Vico put it, had two eternal contrary properties, the plebeians wishing always to change the state, and the nobles to preserve it as it was. The patricians were better organized; they owned the land; they had the arms and the military discipline; they had a monopoly of public office and knowledge of law; they alone knew how to ascertain the will and win the favor of the gods; the solemn rites of marriage and burial were theirs alone; and they were bound by oath to keep the plebs in subjection. But it was inevitable that the plebs should press successively for land tenure, legal marriage, legitimate children, testamentary succession, citizenship, eligibility to office, and the sharing of the auspices, the key to all the rest. And it was inevitable that the ruling class should be compelled to admit the plebs to one after another of the rights which it had at first so jealously guarded. The heroic states were transformed into democratic or "free popular republics," and the third stage of social evolution, the historical age, "the age of men," began.

It was their economic and social position in relation to each other, and not a difference of mentality, which determined that in the long unfolding of legal change the plebeians should represent reason and the patricians authority. The approximation of law to equity, the gradual establishment of equal rights, was brought about by the struggle of the plebeians to acquire full *humanitas*. The vindication of the rational nature of man as man was an historical process, the same process by which the rationality was achieved; and the main spring of the process was the dialectical opposition of the classes.

But the age of men ran its course too. The discipline, respect for law, and social solidarity of the patrician orders gave way to a humane and easy tolerance. Philosophy took the place of religion. Equality led to license. There was dispersion of private interests and decline of public spirit. Birth was first displaced by wealth as a sign of fitness to rule, since to acquire or retain it implied industry, thrift, and foresight. But in time even the property qualification was swept away, and political power was extended to those who lacked the leisure or the will to exercise it wisely. The meanest citizen could press the public force into the service of his appetites and whims, or sell his vote to the highest bidder among faction leaders and demagogues. The external symptoms of the process of disintegration were abated by the rise of bureaucratic monarchies, for the most part even more "humane" than the democracies, yet relieving nobles and plebeians alike of public responsibility. In this last phase of "the age of men," the humanization and softening of customs and laws continued, until breakdown within or conquest from without brought on a rever-

sion to barbarism, and a new cycle of the three ages began. In
Europe Christianity now took the place of the "frightful religions" of the first "age of the gods"; the later middle age revived
the feudal institutions of the "age of the heroes"; and "the natural law of the philosophers" of the seventeenth century was a
product of the second "age of men."[16]

It is clear from the last part of the synopsis that Vico believed history to proceed in terms of cycles: similar periods
tend to recur in the same order. In fact, the whole of Book V,
short though it is, is devoted to "The Recurrence of Human
Things in the Resurgence of the Nations." It is especially in
this book that Vico developed one of his principal ideas, that
humanity progresses through a series of stages—runs the
course (*corso*), so to speak—and then lapses into a decline and
fall. From this low point, it begins again, in a new barbarism,
and goes through a recurrence (*ricorso*) of the cycle. Up to
his time, Vico indicated, there had been two cycles: one in
antiquity, ended by the fall of Rome; and one started in the
returned barbarism of the middle ages, and now, in the eighteenth century, in its last phase.

Each cycle, as Vico explains, is characterized by three
stages: "(1) The age of the gods, in which the gentiles believed they lived under divine governments, and everything
was commanded them by auspices and oracles . . . (2) the age
of heroes, in which they reigned everywhere in aristocratic
commonwealths, on account of a certain superiority of nature
which they held themselves to have over the plebs. (3) the age
of men, in which all men recognize themselves as equal in
human nature, and therefore there were established first the
popular commonwealths and then the monarchies, both of
which are forms of human government."

It is easily seen from this that each stage corresponds to a
special form of government: theocracy, aristocracy, and a

---

[16] *Autobiography*, pp. 49–53. Fisch's admirable summary—and there
seemed no point in my duplicating his work—is copyright 1944 by
Cornell University and is used by permission of the Cornell University
Press.

republic or monarchy. Vico also attached to each stage a particular kind of language and a prevailing type of jurisprudence. The languages are (1) hieroglyphics, i.e., a mute language of signs; (2) symbolic, i.e., characterized by images and metaphors; and (3) vulgar, i.e., that which serves the common uses of life. As for the types of jurisprudence, we have (1) mystic theology, based on interpreting the mysteries of the oracles; (2) heroic jurisprudence, where all is verbal scrupulosity; and (3) natural equity, relying on universal laws turned to purposes of equal utility.[17] In addition, in a somewhat looser way, a type of human character accompanies the various stages. Thus, as Vico put it, "The nature of peoples is first crude, then severe, then benign, then delicate, finally dissolute."

At this point, there are two important things to note about Vico's theory of cycles. First, it is obvious that he thought in terms of cultural wholes, or what is today called "cultural configurations." At each stage, there is an interlocking way of thought, language, politics, and jurisprudence. One part calls for another, and we cannot have theocratic government at the same time as a legal system based on natural equity. Second, Vico's cyclical theory permitted him to make a suggestion as to historical method. According to Vico, the same general characteristics must color the same stages even when they are found in totally separate cycles: the Homeric period of Greek history and the medieval period of Western history are both heroic periods; hence, a study of the one which is more accessible to us can be used as a guide to the study of the "darker" period. We can move easily, then, from what we know well to what we know less well.[18]

[17] Cf. *The New Science of Giambattista Vico*, translated from the third edition (1744) by Thomas Goddard Bergin and Max Harold Fisch (Ithaca, N.Y., 1948), paragraphs 32–39 for the details. Although Bergin and Fisch have made a few changes in the translation in the Anchor edition of *The New Science* (Garden City, N.Y., 1961), I have preferred to use the original, full 1948 edition for consistency.

[18] As against what we might expect, Vico himself believed that the knowledge of the Homeric period would light up the less well-known

Vico readily admitted that he had derived the theory of the three ages from the Egyptians. He quickly made it his own, however, by the wealth of detail he added, and by the mechanism he devised to make one stage pass into another. Vico made a number of initial assumptions. He assumed that human nature was fixed, that is, the same at all times; that out of this fixed nature, providence made certain institutions; and that these institutions developed in a dialectic fashion. Thus, for example, Vico assumed that "out of ferocity, avarice, and ambition, the three vices which run throughout the human race, providence (in the form of legislation) creates the military, merchant and governing classes." He assumed that there would be class struggle between the patricians and plebeians, and thus a natural and inevitable drift from the age of heroes toward the age of men, characterized, as we have seen, by human equality. And he assumed that, although a change from republic to monarchy or vice versa was possible in the age of men, a direct return from either to an aristocracy and an age of heroes was "almost impossible in the nature of civil things."

It was not imperative that all nations tread the triadic path: some might be destroyed midway, their career cut short by disaster and conquest. Thus, "Carthage, Capua and Numantia, the three cities which caused Rome to fear for her empire of the world, failed to accomplish this course of human civil things." In some ways, however, their fate was less awful than the seemingly successful empire. Arrived at the age of men, the latter necessarily tends to decadence and decay. In almost Spenglerian terms, Vico painted the picture of an oversophisticated, corrupted urban mass: what he called a "disease of cities." Lost in private interests, prey to "desperate civil wars," the people are like beasts. The only remedies are within and without: a strong monarchy (like Augustus'), or conquest by "better nations," for "the world is always governed by those

---

period, in his time, of "recurring barbarism," i.e., the Middle Ages, rather than vice-versa.

who are naturally fittest." If neither of these desperate cures is
at hand, factions and civil war will hold sway, and cities will
be turned "into forests and the forests into dens and lairs of
men. In this way, through long centuries of barbarism, rust
will consume the misbegotten subtleties of malicious wits, that
have turned them into beasts made more inhuman by the barbarism of reflection than the first men had been made by the
barbarism of sense."

It is a depressing scene. Nevertheless, melancholic as was his
vision of the last stage, Vico cannot be counted among the
pessimists. Phoenix-like from the ashes, he thought, mankind
would rise again. His cycle, in truth, is more aptly described as
a spiral, for though each stage is repeated in the next cycle, it
is repeated on a higher level. Thus, though Vico did not believe in straight, linear progress, his work implicitly suggests
that he did believe in an increasingly higher level of human
consciousness: else, why his own new science?

But neither can Vico be counted an optimist. Unlike, for
example, Comte, who was to hold to a similar three-stage division, Vico could not convince himself that the end of mankind's road was the age of positive reason where peace and
happiness would hold sway forever onward. He held too faith-
fully to the dialectic, to the play of human forces which
battled ceaselessly, to be able to accept the end of history. Man
was always the same—a seething mass of ferocity, avarice, and
ambition—made crude, severe, or dissolute by the changing
scene. Historical to his core, Vico welcomed the notion of
constant change and flux around a fixed pole of man's nature.

8

There are certain key points in Vico's historical panorama
which must be noted. First, we encounter the vexing problem
of the role of religion in the *New Science*. This leads immediately to the second problem: the element of theodicy in Vico.

From this we proceed insensibly to the third question: how does Vico employ the notion of providence in his work? And this, in turn, leads to the paradoxical conclusion that the religious elements in Vico's theory have strong, secular overtones and consequences.

Let us start with the first problem: the role of religion in the *New Science*. In his personal life, Vico was a loyal Catholic, educated as such, and retaining his faith throughout his life. One feels that it is not simply a matter of bowing to the watchful eye of the Inquisition in Naples or even the constant constraint of the Austro-Spanish despotism. It is rather a "leaning" on Vico's part, shown by the unrequired coloring of his thought by religious images and the ubiquitous influence of religious concepts on his scientific principles. Yet, directed as he was, Vico could praise the work of a heretic like Grotius and attempt to utilize the ideas of another Protestant, Bacon. Indeed of his four acknowledged masters, two of them, as we have noted earlier, were Protestants, and both of these were the "modern" thinkers.

In Vico's case, then, his religion *combined* with the new, scientific attitude of the seventeenth and eighteenth centuries. Thus, his criticism of the stiff, one-sided position of the Enlightenment, with its overrationalization and its rejection of many areas of human experience (among others, the religious and the poetic), was a forward-looking rather than a reactionary criticism. Perhaps it was too forward-looking; the religious aspect may explain, in part, the neglect of Vico's work by his contemporaries, who tended to see in religion only "l'infâme." But for Vico, religion was an essential part of man's evolution, as well as being the eternal frame of the universe; with this twofold conviction (and I might point out that later times could accept one part without the other), Vico could go on both to investigate mythical thinking and to posit a providential explanation of the world of nations, grounded, however, on the empirical evidence.

Vico started by assuming that the entrance of man into

history is based on a religious experience. It is the clap of
thunder which comes upon brutish men in the act of animal
copulation, and drives them, filled with terror and shame, into
the shelter of caves.[19] From this single encounter with the
divine unrolls the long line of man's development: marriage
and burial, the family and private property, morality and law,
and the state and its dialectic growth.

Again and again, Vico insisted that there can be no society
without religion.[20] If religion is lost among the peoples, they
have no "form by which they may exist in the world at all." In
one of his rare references to Pierre Bayle, Vico remarked
acidly: "Let Bayle consider then whether in fact there can be
nations in the world without any knowledge of God!" Further, willing as Vico was to accept the useful role of "false"
religions at the beginning of history, he insisted on the sole
truth of the Christian religion. It alone "causes" virtuous action by divine grace, "for the sake of an eternal and infinite
good." And, as we shall see when we come to deal with Vico's
providence, one feels that, for him, there was a close connection between providence and Christian divine grace.

With all this said, however, we must also remark that Vico
just as readily treated religion—other than the Christian—as a
projection of man's own character.[21] The Greek people, he
declared, "inasmuch as at their founding they were themselves
pious, religious, chaste, strong, just and magnanimous . . . made
their gods also, as our natural theogony has demonstrated."
Further, by declining to treat of the Hebrews, who by special
creation of God were placed outside history (and thus "natu-

[19] One cannot help thinking in this connection of Luther's climactic
experience in a thunderstorm; naturally there are major differences in
the details. See, for example, the interesting description by Erik Erikson, *Young Man Luther* (New York, 1958), pp. 91–92.
[20] This sort of view was later strongly echoed by conservative
thinkers like Joseph de Maistre. For the connection of Vico and de
Maistre, see Elio Gianturco, *Joseph de Maistre and Giambattista Vico*
(Washington, D.C., 1937).
[21] See the continuation of this idea in Feuerbach and Marx,
pp. 225–226.

ral" development), and devoting his attention only to the "gentiles," Vico almost by default fell into the habit of treating religion in a naturalistic fashion. The startling result is that the faithful Neapolitan ended up largely secularizing religion.

9

Vico's religion also led him to a theodicy which justified secular events in naturalistic terms. This is the second element in Vico with which I promised to deal. It involves what one commentator has called "an 'acquiescence in actuality,' within which he [Vico] discovers its rational course and ineluctable laws."[22] It takes "evil" and shows that, correctly considered, it is really "good." It justifies the "city of man," spurned by Augustine, as part of the city of God, or under the same divine stamp. Thus, Vico argued, since divine providence has infinite wisdom, "whatever it establishes is order . . . whatever it ordains must be directed to a good always superior to that which men have proposed to themselves."

The theodicy of Vico is important in at least two directions. In one, it links logically with his contemporary, Bernard de Mandeville, and the latter's insistence that "Private Vices Made Public Benefits"; and, beyond Mandeville, with Adam Smith and the school of classical economists. And this link is fundamental to the effort at a human science. Without the acceptance of the given, the "acquiescence in actuality," there can be little successful amalgamation of the empirical with the rational. For example, whereas medieval thinkers dismissed the reality of man's selfish economic desires, the classical economists more realistically accepted them as part of the "evidence."[23] Whereas the Enlightened historians, like Voltaire or Condorcet, rejected the medieval experience as irrational, the

[22] Lifschitz, *op. cit.*, p. 396.
[23] For the detailed description of this development, see R. H. Tawney, *Religion and the Rise of Capitalism* (New York, 1947).

romantic school of historians, led by Vico, sought to see them as an ineradicable part of man's past. As Freud has so clearly pointed out, the refusal to accept the "given," as that which has occurred, and *no other*, is the siren call which leads us away from any possible science.[24] Seen, then, in this light, Vico is a pioneer in the effort to make man accept his past "as it happened" and not as he would perhaps have liked it to happen.

In the other direction, Vico's theodicy touches on the development, not of modern science, but of the movement of thought known as historicism. Here, too, although from a romantic rather than an empiricist point of view, there is an acceptance of the given. Indeed, beyond acceptance there is a *sympathy* with all that exists; and because the historian or the poet sympathizes with the products of nature, whatever they may be, he claims to be able to enter their lives and thus to *understand* them from within. Against the cold, indifferent, external knowledge of the scientist, the historicist claims a warm, vibrant, "living" knowledge of his subject. In this direction, too, as we shall see later in more detail, Vico's "acquiescence in actuality" had potentialities for development.[25]

10

Vico's theodicy, at its core, has the idea of providence. And this is the third question with which we must deal. It must be said immediately, of course, that Vico was not original in basing his philosophy of history on this concept: long before him, Augustine had done it, and at about Vico's own time Bossuet was organizing his *Discourse on Universal History*

[24] See, for example, Sigmund Freud, *A General Introduction to Psychoanalysis* (New York, 1953), pp. 31-32.

[25] There are some interesting comments in Erich Heller, "The Conservative Imagination," *Encounter*, X, 2 (February, 1958), especially a quotation from Schopenhauer on page 47, which are relevant in this context.

around the pole of providence. What was new in Vico was his insistence that the workings of providence must be explained in reference to *secondary* causes and exemplified in terms of the *empirical* data. This was a revolutionary turning around of the question: a Copernican revolution in theodicy, wherein providence does not explain the whirling of events, but the events explain the workings of providence.

Vico proceeded as follows: Men (at least after the Fall) start as do the beasts, and are basically selfish. Because of their corrupted nature, they are "under the tyranny of self-love, which compels them to make private utility their chief guide." It is only the providential clap of thunder which makes them seek a settled shelter and start society (in the "civilized" sense). Thus, the creation of humanity is not self-made or spontaneous, but providential; and man's selfish desires are turned into order, into insitutions, and into all kinds of civil relations—marriage, burial, laws, forms of government, class struggles, and so forth—without his wishing it, or knowing it, consciously. This is Vico's great "rational civil theology of divine providence." In one of his most important paragraphs, he set it forth in full view.

It is true that men have themselves made this world of nations (and we took this as the first incontestable principle of our Science, since we despaired of finding it from the philosophers and philologists), but this world without doubt has issued from a mind often diverse, at times quite contrary, and always superior to the particular ends that men had proposed to themselves; which narrow ends, made means to serve wider ends, it has always employed to preserve the human race upon this earth. Men mean to gratify their bestial lust and abandon their offspring, and they inaugurate the chastity of marriage from which the families arise. The fathers mean to exercise without restraint their paternal power over their clients, and they subject them to the civil powers from which the cities arise. The reigning orders of nobles mean to abuse their lordly freedom over the plebeians, and they are obliged to submit to the laws which establish popular liberty. The free peoples mean to shake off the yoke of their laws, and they become subject to monarchs. The monarchs mean to strengthen their own positions by debasing their subjects with all the vices of dissoluteness, and they dispose them to endure slavery at the hands of stronger nations. The nations mean to dissolve themselves, and their remnants flee for safety to the wilderness, whence, like the phoenix, they rise again. That which did all this was mind, for men did it with intelligence; it was not fate, for they did it by choice; not chance, for the results of their always so acting are perpetually the same.[26]

Here we can hear, like overtones to a dominant chord, the voices of Adam Smith, Hegel, and Marx, with their talk of an "invisible hand," the "cunning of reason," and dialectical materialism. In this momentous passage, Vico foreshadowed all the later developments, which will murmur of "unintended consequences," of how "man proposes, and God disposes." And the startling thing is that Vico did it while paying homage to the name of providence, in essentially secular terms, by appealing to secondary causes and to the empirical evidence of history itself. We ourselves, today, can go into the records and see whether it is "certain" that the nobles meant to abuse the plebeians and yet fell unwittingly under the laws. One can hardly overestimate the fecund results of this aspect of Vico's new science.

What, however, has happened to man making his history? If all is determined by providence, by the cunning of reason, where is man's free will to be found? And what did Vico mean by saying that it is not fate or chance that is responsible for history, but choice? There is a certain amount of unsatisfactory wriggling in Vico's handling of this problem. Moreover, it seems to have led him, rather unwittingly, to a secularized statement of the matter. In essence, Vico was concerned to show that, although providence, or God, is responsible for the first cause—the fear-inspiring thunderclap—as well as for the stable characteristics of man—his self-interest—man himself, once launched on his path of development, has free will. The first men, Vico contended, "must have done their thinking

[26] *The New Science*, p. 382.

under the strong impulsion of violent passions, as beasts do."
This was to be in a state of unfreedom. But from the frightful
conception of a divinity sprang "the impulse proper to the
human will, to hold in check the motions impressed on the
mind by the body, so as either to quiet them altogether, as
becomes the sage, or at least to direct them to better use, as
becomes the civil man. This control over the motion of their
bodies is certainly an effect of the freedom of the will, and
thus of free will." In short, Vico seems to be saying, only
when man "knows," that is, when his reason controls his brute
passion, or, to put it even more succinctly, when man is self-
conscious, is he "free" and able to make his own history. We
see this most clearly in Vico's own summation, and it is worth
giving the long passage in its entirety.

In one of its principal aspects, this Science must therefore be a
rational civil theology of divine providence, which seems hitherto
to have been lacking. For the philosophers have either been altogether ignorant of it, as the Stoics and the Epicureans were, the
latter asserting that human affairs are agitated by a blind con-
course of atoms, the former that they are drawn by a deaf inexorable chain of cause and effect; or they have considered it solely
in the order of natural things, giving the name of natural theology
to the metaphysics in which they contemplate this attribute, i.e.,
the providence of God, and in which they confirm it by the
physical order observed in the motions of such bodies as the
spheres and the elements and in the final cause observed in other
and minor natural things. But they ought to have studied it in
the economy of civil things, in keeping with the full meaning of
applying to providence the term divinity, from *divinari*, to
divine; that is, to understand what is hidden from men, the future,
or what is hidden in them, their consciousness. It is this that makes
up the first and principal part of the subject matter of jurisprudence, namely the divine things on which depend the human
things which make up its other and complementary part. Our new
Science must therefore be a demonstration, so to speak, of the
historical fact of providence, for it must be a history of the forms
of order which, without human discernment or intent, and often
against the designs of men, providence has given to this great city
of the human race. For though this world has been created in time

and particular, the orders established therein by providence are universal and eternal.[27]

Divine providence: "to understand what is hidden from men, the future, or what is hidden in them, their consciousness." Is there any doubt that Vico's *New Science* is an exposition of this divine providence? That providence has become scientific explanation? That, whatever the impulse in the beginning, man must proceed now in a lawlike course, although proceeding along it freely? Therefore, in spite of a pious attitude toward providence, Vico gives the impression that he was really talking about the natural laws of human relations, which in some subtle and complicated manner seem to be the outcome (looked at from the other side, they are the governing power) of the interplay of man's own selfish desires.

Can we, now, refrain from exposing the paradox? Vico has proposed and "God" has disposed in a rather strange way! A religiously oriented, providential explanation of history has turned, or been turned, into a secularized, naturalistic new science. God, Vico would have admitted, moves in mysterious ways; but even Vico would have been surprised to realize, consciously, how mysteriously his god had moved in this matter.

11

Vico's work is so broad and so powerful that any summary of it is bound to be a Procrustean bed. Moreover, the diffuse and torrential quality of his book makes such a summary exceedingly difficult. Yet we must attempt to highlight Vico's achievements—and limitations—if we are to reach any sort of conclusion about the *New Science*.

Let us start by admitting Vico's errors and weaknesses. These take a number of forms. The first comprises simple

[27] *Ibid.,* pp. 90–91.

errors of fact. Thus, for example, Vico made the astounding mistake, in the *Autobiography*, of attributing an edition of the *Old Testament* to the wrong Hebrew scholar, Guiseppe Attias of Leghorn, whom he claimed as a friend; in reality, the edition was not by this Attias but by a Guiseppe ben Abraham Attias of Cordova! Close to this type of error is the internal one, of inconsistency: for example, at one point Vico talked of the twelve major gods (beginning with Jove) as really signifying twelve epochs in the chronology of poetic history. But elsewhere he had tried to show that, to the poetic mind, the number twelve actually signifies any large number; Vico cannot have it both ways.

More serious are certain of Vico's erroneous statements, or assumptions. These relate, generally, to his "rational" findings or to his a priori principles. Thus, he believed unquestioningly in the universal flood, and in an age of giants; of the latter, he gave a long explanation as to why they arose, filled with such hopeful phrases as "They must therefore have . . ."[28] One is also surprised that Vico, the "historicist," was often what may be called culture-bound. In this vein, he scorned Chinese painting because of its alleged inability to make shadows, and disparaged Egyptian culture and its achievements to the point of denying its priority or supposed influence on Moses and the Hebrews. The latter judgment, of course, was in the service of Vico's faith that "The first people of the world were the Hebrews, whose prince was Adam," a people who "lived unknown to all the gentile nations."[29]

Here, clearly, Vico was a victim of his preconceived ideas. It was from religion, not history, that he took his belief in the antiquity and uniqueness of the Hebrews. In this matter, he

[28] Vico, of course, was not unusual in his time in believing in giants. See, for example, Percy G. Adams, *Travelers and Travel Liars* (Berkeley, 1962) for some "tall" stories.

[29] Cf. Voltaire's article "Adam," in the *Philosophical Dictionary*, ridiculing the notion of an undetected existence of the father of the human race. In contrast, Vico's position in this matter illustrates the weakness of his "rational" approach when it is divorced from any attempt at empirical verification.

was inferior to Bayle, who discounted the self-evident credibility and trustworthiness of the biblical accounts. Yet, while
there can be no overlooking Vico's weakness in the matter,
something more must be said. Vico avoided Bayle's error of
taking "mythological" writings (in Bayle's case, this included
the Bible) literally; there was no reason, therefore, why later
thinkers—naturalistic historians—should not turn Vico's "master key" in the lock of the biblical stories, and thus translate
them, too, into a secular history, revealed through the interpretation of myth. Indeed, this is exactly what some of the
"higher critics" of the Bible were to attempt in the next
century.

Vico himself, of course, did not apply his method to the
Bible. Nor did he attempt to apply it, in any real sense, to the
period of modern history. Aside from a few vague analogies to
the period of the High Middle Ages, and a few attempts to
equate the age of men of antiquity with that of the seventeenth century, Vico never really spelled out or tested his
theory of the *ricorso*. Thus, at the beginning and the end of
his spectrum of history—with the Hebrews and the moderns—he refused to go into details. We are left, in fact, won-
dering if Vico's method of comparative mythology has any
relevance to modern history. And, looking at the history of
the last 400 years with its spectacular unrolling of a scientific
revolution which Vico disparaged in his own day, we find
ourselves doubting the validity of his specific "speculative"
philosophy of history with its assumption of repetition and
fixity of form.

Lastly, now, we need especially to comment on Vico's use
of the "ideal, eternal laws," and to link it to our criticism of his
treatment of the Hebrews, the moderns, and the question of
repetition in history. Vico's mistake here, I believe, was to
assume that philosophy, a priori, contributes the "rational"
element to historical certainty in the form of "ideal, eternal
laws." This assumption led him, in most of his moods, to the
notion that such laws "determine" history, and work themselves

out in the course of time (or, to use the phrasing of Hegel, who made the same mistake, "The rational is actual, and the actual is rational"). In short, Vico conceived of philosophy as "reason" realizing itself, rather than as a mere formulation of hypotheses, of tentative scientific laws (as, for example, in economics) *created* by man from the observation of data. If he had taken the latter view, he would have eliminated the need for his providential-type explanation. He would also have avoided a Marxist-type determinism in history, for, knowing the "laws" (in the sense we have suggested), man could change things by working in terms of these known laws.[30] Moreover, and more to the present point, Vico would have avoided the errors and weaknesses of fact and theory with which we have just been indicting him.

Let me hastily add: to indict the errors and weaknesses of Vico's work is not to indict Vico, the thinker. While we cannot close our eyes to the blemishes of the *New Science, as it stands in the light of present thought and knowledge,* we cannot treat Vico as if he had not existed in the eighteenth century. Indeed, it is in part *because* of his work that we see far enough today to bring him to task. The greatness of Vico's work is that, like one of his apocryphal giants, it shakes off the chains of error and misguided insight, and goes crashing through the thickets and forests of thought. In essence, then, the *New Science* is not the setting forth of final truth; it is, instead, a work which is, first and foremost, heuristic.

12

We have already touched on some of the fecund results of Vico's attitude and method. In general, they fall into two major areas: (1) the development of the human sciences; and (2) the development of a *Weltanschauung* which may be broadly labeled, "historicism." In the first area, for example,

[30] Cf. Flint, *op. cit.*, pp. 160–161.

Vico's work led to or anticipated certain direct and specific results in historical studies: the researches in Roman history by Niebuhr and Mommsen, in Homer by Wolf, and in the historical treatment of laws by Savigny. More generally, as already stressed, the *New Science* laid the groundwork for the cultivation of comparative linguistics and comparative mythology (comparative literature, too, as we shall see), and had an effect on the development of anthropology and psychology.

In the latter field, there is a striking similarity between some of Vico's insights and the work of Freud in psychoanalysis, which is worth pursuing a bit. First, it may be said that without the existence of comparative linguistics, literature, and mythology, there would be no Freud as we know him; Freud, himself, would have been the readiest to admit this. Second, on numerous specific points, there is startling homogeneity of approach between Vico and Freud. For example, both men, while refraining from Rousseau-like romanticizing, were interested in the minds of children and primitives, and treated them as early stages of the evolution of human thought. Thus, they saw the development of the individual as mirroring the development of society. So, too, both believed in a universal symbol language. In Freud, it was the language of myths and dreams. In Vico's phrasing, "There must in the nature of human things be a mental language common to all nations, which uniformly grasps the substance of things feasible in human social life, and expresses it with as many diverse modifications as these same things may have diverse aspects. A proof of this is afforded by proverbs or maxims of vulgar wisdom, in which substantially the same meanings find as many diverse expressions as there are nations ancient and modern." Then, in an extraordinary anticipation, Vico added that, in all languages, expressions are "formed by metaphor from the human body and its parts or from the human senses and passions. Thus, head for top or beginning; eyes . . . for windows letting light into houses; mouth for any opening; lip for the rim of a vase or of anything else."

Both Vico and Freud were aware that we project our feelings onto the world; what in Freud is called psychic projection. In Vico's phrase, "man in his ignorance makes himself the rule of the universe, for in the examples cited he has made of himself an entire world." A specific consequence of man's extrapolation of himself to the world was, for both Vico and Freud, the creation of the gods in the image of man's psychic desires.

Even in their speculative philosophy of history, the resemblances between the two men are strong. Both saw the origins of society and civilization in a sense of shame and guilt, awakened in man by an early, traumatic experience: for Vico, the thunderclap during carnal relations; for Freud the Oedipal killing of the father by the horde. Different in detail as are the two versions, they share the emphasis on guilt being connected with sex; and this is reinforced by the joint view that society arises with the prohibition of incestuous relations, and can be maintained only by discipline, restraint, and sublimation of the carnal desires.[31] As Vico put it, Socrates was wrong about incest: he had tried to prove that it "was forbidden by nature, whereas it is human nature that forbids it."

It need hardly be said that there are differences as well as similarities between Vico and Freud. Or that Freud goes well beyond Vico in the development of many of the points upon which we have touched. Some of these differences and some of these developments, insofar as they bear on philosophy of history, will be pointed up by the chapter on Freud. Here, I have wished only to suggest a few of the extrapolations of Vico's new science in relation to the coming work in psychoanalysis, and, in back of that, to the work on which the latter in turn stood: comparative linguistics, literature, and mythology.

The other major area into which Vico's ideas can be extrapolated comprises the development of the *Weltanschauung* called "historicism." In part, historicism may be defined as that movement of thought which emphasizes the process of growth and change in historical forms, and sees human life as express-

---

[31] For Vico, see *The New Science*, #17 and especially #336.

ing itself in unique, nonduplicable "moments of time," with these "moments of time" being regarded as wholes, or totalities, or cultural configurations, in which the parts are related in a special integrated fashion. It is obvious that Vico does not square perfectly with this definition. As the leading expositor of historicism, Friedrich Meinecke, pointed out, Vico was not interested especially in the unique, individual aspect of things—a vital part of historicism—but rather in their recurring aspect. He was absorbed by his interest in the collective, in the "type," in the broadest sense, by the abstract concept, humanity.[32]

On the other hand, it was Vico who first stressed the evolutionary aspect of humanity, and who treated each stage in that evolution as a whole, or cultural configuration. As a result, Vico was able to subvert the previous domination of thought by natural law, with its emphasis on a fixed, unchanging, and eternal common humanity, and to substitute for it the main outlines of historicism, *even though Vico himself* tended to think in terms of a generalized unity of mankind.[33] Vico accomplished this break with natural law in a rather interesting way, that is, by his emphasis on theodicy and providence, his "acquiescence in actuality." Thus, defending his analysis of political forms in terms of the three stages, he commented: "Just as the natural law of the philosophers (or moral theologians) is that of reason, so this natural law of nations is that of utility and force which, as the jurisconsults say, is observed by the nations . . . 'as use requires and human necessities demand.'" Markedly present in this passage is Vico's realism and empiricism, his acceptance of human nature and its cruel necessities *as it is* and not as it should be.[34]

[32] Meinecke, *op. cit.*, Book I, chap. I, part 4.

[33] On the relations of natural law and historicism, see especially Ernst Troeltsch, "The Ideas of Natural Law and Humanity in World Politics," translated by Ernest Barker in Otto Gierke, *Natural Law and the Theory of Society: 1500 to 1800* (Boston, 1957). Also, Bruce Mazlish, review-essay of Carlo Antoni, "From History to Sociology: The Transition in German Historical Thought," in *History and Theory*, I, 2 (1961), 219–227.

[34] It is almost as if we hear the echo of Machiavelli, and the prophecy

Vico's break with natural law allowed him to see that humanity had evolved; and he traced this evolution in a naturalistic, empirical manner. As part of his analysis, as we have seen, he introduced his theory of the three ages. Each age was a cultural whole, and Vico coined the phrase "sects of the times" to express its spiritual unity; we, today, use the phrase "climates of opinions," or *Weltanschauungen*. From this part of his work came three emanations: to the history of ideas, to the history of philosophy, and to the development of comparative literature. Let us deal with each of these in order.

First, anticipating the work of Voltaire, who, however, scorned the primitive and barbaric, Vico projected a history of the progress and development of the human mind. Throughout the *New Science*, his emphasis was on what he himself called the "history of human ideas" rather than on heroic exploits and military events.

Second, this new approach to the development of the human mind had important consequences for the history of philosophy, for it tended to transmute philosophy into the history of ideas. Vico was adamant about the sterility of the mere rational, abstract philosophers of his time, with their concern only for pure metaphysical speculation. Of a part of his *New Science*, he remarked, "This may serve as a fragment of the history of philosophy told philosophically," and added that it was a reproof of those philosophers who thought philosophy could have emerged without prior religious thought. In fact, rather than a transmutation of philosophy or the history of philosophy by Vico, one ought perhaps to talk of his transcending philosophy by the history of ideas.

Lastly, for comparative literature, the consequences of Vico's thought were just as great. A work of literature was no longer a work of all time, but of a specific age. It was to be judged and understood in terms of the stage, the "sects of the

---

of Adam Smith to come. Meinecke, *op. cit.*, suggests that Vico undercuts natural law further because his providential view ends the theory of the state as a product of a conscious, rational contract.

times," in which it had originated. To give himself practice, and an eye for the comparative, Vico read, "on successive days . . . Cicero side by side with Boccaccio, Virgil with Dante, and Horace with Petrarch, being curious to see and to judge for himself the difference between them." As a result, Vico realized, unlike many of his rationalist contemporaries of the eighteenth century, that literary values were relative and not absolute; and that the barbaric and imaginative were as valuable in their way as the formal and the constrained.

Historicism then, as we have been seeing, could lead to developments in specific fields: the history of ideas, the history of philosophy, and the study of comparative literature. It could also lead to a philosophic position: the notion that man *is* his history. Ontologically speaking, one could ultimately say with Ortega y Gasset that "Man has no nature; he has only his history." Vico himself would have insisted on the fixed aspect of man's nature, his avarice, ferocity, and ambition. But Vico would also have nullified the antihistorical implications of this by his insistence that the use made of these "givens" is completely a matter of the time and the circumstances. In his first oration, of 1699, Vico had echoed the Socratic command: know thyself. By the time of the *New Science* he had turned this into the precept: to know yourself, you must know your history. In Vico's formulation, man, once given the divine gift of free will, becomes henceforward a creation, as well as a creator, of his history.

13

Unmatched in its scope, its startling poetic intuitions, and its imaginative understanding of the progress of the human mind, Vico's work stands beyond our most extravagent praise. In the *New Science*, Vico threw out lines to the future which have served as a guide for many if not most of the historical-minded philosophers and philosophically-minded historians of the nineteenth and twentieth centuries. It is clear, too, that Vico ought to serve as a fount from which all further attempts to work out a meaningful philosophy of history should draw.

As we have seen, Vico's work took its starting point from Descartes' approach to the natural world; but Vico turned this approach to the use of the historian. Both Descartes and Vico had agreed that man understands what he makes; we know a thing insofar as we understand how it has come into being. Vico's triumph was to insist that it is therefore requisite that we turn to history, for history is the story of origin. Thus, Descartes ends up, not as an opponent to history, but—reinterpreted by Vico—as the foundation stone of the modern philosophy of history. Such is the paradox—and the dialectic play—of the progress of the human mind.

III

Voltaire

*The whole succession of human beings through-
out the whole course of ages must be regarded
as a single individual man, continually living and
continually learning; and this shows how unwarranted is the deference we yield to the philosophers of antiquity; for, as old age is most distant
from infancy, it must be manifest to all that old
age in the universal man should not be sought in
the times near his birth, but in the times most
distant from it. Those whom we call the ancients
are really those who lived in the youth of the
world, and the true infancy of man; and as we
have added the experience of the ages between
us and them to what they knew, it is only in ourselves that is to be found that antiquity which we
venerate in others.*

PASCAL, Pensées

1

VOLTAIRE began writing an "Essay" in history in the 1740s
with the express intention of overcoming the "disgust" his
friend Mme. du Châtelet experienced from reading existing
histories. He promised to forsake useless details, and to write
only about "that which is worth your knowing; the spirit
[*l'esprit*], the customs, the practices of the principal nations,
based on the facts which one cannot ignore." After a number
of partial versions, the first complete edition was published

under the title "Essai sur l'Histoire générale et sur les Moeurs et l'Esprit des nations, depuis Charlemagne jusqu'à nos jours."

Then, in 1765, a work entitled "La Philosophie de l'histoire" appeared, ostensibly from the pen of the Abbé Bazin: it was Voltaire, writing under a pseudonym, and introducing the portentous phrase: philosophy of history. Four years later, in 1769, this work was placed as the Introduction to the *Essai*, and the whole published under the more succinct title, *Essai sur les Moeurs et l'Esprit des Nations.*

What did Voltaire mean by "philosophy of history," and what were his general intentions in writing the *Essai?* His own words can best inform us. "You wish," he said to Mme. du Châtelet, "that philosophers had written ancient history because you wish to read it philosophically [*en philosophe*]. You seek only useful truths, and you have found scarcely anything but useless errors. Let us try to enlighten ourselves together; let us try to disinter a few precious monuments from beneath the ruins of centuries." For Voltaire, then, to be a philosopher of history meant to read history "en philosophe."[1]

What the philosopher of history seeks is the "useful." Voltaire sounded this note repeatedly. Thus, for example, in discussing a clouded point in Greek antiquity, he commented in characteristic fashion, "Let us not lose time in fathoming these useless obscurities." Not for Voltaire the curiosity in history for its own sake! In fact, his conception of history's utility becomes the criteria for selecting, amidst a mass of data, those elements which are worth knowing. Voltaire made no bones about his belief that history entails a point of view, from

---

[1] In order, therefore, to understand fully what Voltaire meant by the philosophy of history, we should have to study the whole complex of thought subsumed under the words "the Enlightenment" and "the *philosophes.*" This task goes beyond the scope of this book, but the interested reader can consult, as a good starting point, Ernst Cassirer, *The Philosophy of the Enlightenment*, translated by Fritz C. A. Koelln and James P. Pettegrove (Princeton, N.J., 1951). Charles Frankel, in *The Case for Modern Man* (Boston, 1959), p. 17, has some very illuminating things to say about Voltaire's intent in using the phrase. For Voltaire's view of the "useful" see further his essay on Bacon, in the *English Letters.*

which certain data is then selected and ordered according to a plan.

By this, however, Voltaire did not mean imposing a *pattern* on history. He was not particularly concerned with discovering a "meaning" in history. As one commentator puts it, "If the phrase 'philosophy of history' implies a coherent view of the nature of historical development, then Voltaire has no philosophy of history."[2] Instead of drawing a meaning from history, Voltaire's task was to give meaning to history; to make history useful. And he made history useful by approaching it "en philosophe." Thus, speaking of his interest in manners and customs, in economic and social organization, he declared: "It seems to me therefore that it would be necessary to incorporate with skill these useful knowledges in the texture of events. I believe that this is the only way to write modern history as a true statesman and a true philosopher [*en vrai politique et en vrai philosophe*]."

It was the voice of the *Encyclopédie*, with its interest in "useful knowledges," speaking through Voltaire. Both the *Encyclopédie* and Voltaire, of course, embraced the desire for reform so ardently felt by the "enlightened" minds of the time. In order to achieve that reform, it was necessary, as Diderot put it in the preface to the *Encyclopédie*, to "change the ordinary way of thinking": to enlighten the people. Voltaire, as is well known, played his part in this change vigorously: he wrote poems, plays, novels, letters, and philosophic dictionaries; and he also wrote history—many volumes of it—in terms of the changed way of thinking. As Meinecke has suggested, Voltaire offered a "new history" to go along with the new *Weltanschauung* of the Enlightenment.[3]

We see the polemical aspect of Voltaire's works clearly in his treatment of antiquity. Here, he wandered in the realm of the past in the same way as he and others had wandered, in novelistic travels, through fictitious or little-known countries;

[2] J. H. Brumfitt, *Voltaire, historian* (London, 1958), p. 127.
[3] Cf. Meinecke, *op. cit.*, the entire chapter on Voltaire.

we think immediately of the famous satiric travel literature of
the eighteenth century, of which Montesquieu's *Persian Letters* is one example and Voltaire's *Candide* another. The interest was in customs and manners, in religious beliefs and political convictions, and the purpose was to use the past or the
exotic as a counterfoil to one's own time and country. Thus,
Voltaire devoted the first chapter of his *Essai* to China, and
extoled its ways and religion directly in comparison with the
"barbarous" Hebrews and indirectly in comparison with
French Christians.

Turning his unique literary gifts fully to the task of effecting a fundamental revolution in man's ways of looking to the
past for guidance, Voltaire tried to show, savagely and ceaselessly, that the ancients—at least, the "bad ones," Hebrews,
Egyptians, and Christians—were unenlightened and barbarous,
uninformed and untrustworthy. They lacked a clear conception of time, and they had no interest in or respect for decent
standards of evidence or induction from evidence. How, then,
Voltaire asked rhetorically, can we draw meaning from such
an irrational and superstitious past? Or from the religions
which base themselves on these fantasies? Voltaire's answer
was to substitute the categories of his "philosophy of history,"
as we have defined it, for the ancient religious ways of seeing
the world.

2

The *Esaai sur les Moeurs*, in its final form, started out in the
long Introduction with a section on "Changes in the globe"
and proceeded quickly to deal with "The different races of
men," "The antiquity of nations," and on to "The religion of
the first men" and "The practices and sentiments common to
almost all the ancient nations." At the end of the Introduction,
about 150 pages long, Voltaire had reached the Romans. In

between, he had dealt primarily with the religious beliefs and customs of primitive and ancient peoples. Upon reaching the book of Zend, of the Parsis, he exclaimed joyfully: "Behold what is perhaps most important in the ancient history of the world: behold a useful religion, based on the dogma of the immortality of the soul and on the knowledge of the Supreme Being."

Then, Voltaire hastened to add: "Let us not leave off noting through how many steps the human spirit must pass in order to conceive of such a system." He was fully aware that "it has required everywhere, not only a prodigious space of time, but favorable circumstances, in order that man might elevate himself above the life of an animal." Thus, Voltaire started with geology, entered into anthropology, and emerged in recorded history in order to show man's development from the animal stage. His geological-anthropological setting for man was of the flimsiest sort: it was sketchy, speculative, and frequently incorrect. But, in spite of all its weaknesses, it was an interesting attempt to provide a genesis, other than the traditional biblical one, for the human race.[4]

Voltaire constantly protested, however, that he was not dealing with theological topics or with the Bible. In mock humility, he pleaded his orthodoxy in accepting revelation, and emphasized that he was dealing only with natural topics and secondary causes. "We reason here," he declared, "only according to natural notions, always submitting the feeble gropings of our limited spirit to the insights of a superior order." But it was only cold comfort that Voltaire's religious opponents could draw from his oft-repeated "conformity." Like his satirical and critical predecessor, Pierre Bayle, he suggested that "if we may examine the historical part of the Jewish books by the same rules which guide us in the critique

[4] Voltaire, however, did not believe in evolution, and rejected monogenesis in his account of the races of mankind. For further details, see the *Essai* or Brumfitt, *op. cit.*, pp. 87 ff.

of other histories," the stories, in this case of Abraham, would occasion difficulties; alas, Voltaire sighed, after indicating what the results would be of such an historical study, all is miraculous in the Bible, and we must dismiss our new speculations. The irony was thinly veiled.

Having restricted himself to natural matters and secondary causal explanations, Voltaire was free to apply "scientific" rules of evidence. These were in direct relation to his fundamental belief, in accord, for example, with Locke and Hume, that "Historical truths are merely probabilities." Or, as Voltaire said in another place, "All certainty which does not consist in mathematical demonstration is nothing more than the highest probability; there is no other historical certainty."

On what grounds, however, do we establish the "highest probability"? In Voltaire's historical work the stress was on the rational rather than the empirical.[5] He was not particularly interested in examining original documents or in unearthing new materials. Instead, he applied his skeptical reasoning to existing accounts. Sometimes, this was quite effective. For example, he questioned the credibility of the Noah's ark story on the grounds of its incompatibility with simple arithmetic: "how many persons were in the ark to feed all the animals for ten whole months, and during the following year in which no food would be produced?" At other times, however, as in his attempt to disprove the authenticity of Richelieu's *Testament Politique*, the weaknesses of his approach showed up.[6]

Voltaire's basic thought was that "That which is not in nature is never true." By nature, he meant both physical and human nature. Physical nature is always the same, everywhere, eternally operating under Newtonian laws. Any account of an episode where these laws are violated is manifestly untrue: there are no miracles in Voltaire's, any more than in Hume's,

---

[5] This is so in spite of the fact that in his more philosophical work Voltaire tends to stress the "empirical way to truth."

[6] For the Noah's ark story, see the whole of Voltaire's article on "Antiquity" in the *Philosophical Dictionary*. For his work on Richelieu's *Testament*, see Brumfitt, *op. cit.*, pp. 147 ff.

world. So, too, human nature is uniform and unchanging, and morality is universal and "one," like geometry.[7] On these grounds, Voltaire rejected Herodotus' story that the Babylonian women, once in their lives, were obliged by law to prostitute themselves to strangers in the temple. "Really," he remarked confidently, "can such an infamy exist in the character of a civilized people?"

Occasionally, Voltaire had second thoughts on this matter, and realized that the criterion of conformity to present experience and unchanging reason might be misleading. Thus, as one commentator puts it, he told the story "of the Siamese king who was willing to believe that the divine Sommona-Codom had straddled the Bay of Bengal (since this was only an exaggerated picture of something within his own experience), but refused to credit the Dutch ambassador who assured him that, in his country, water turned into a hard, solid substance in winter."[8] Even more startling, Voltaire pointed out that "The great misunderstanding about the Chinese rites comes from the fact that we have judged their practices by our own: for we carry to the ends of the earth the prejudices of our contentious spirit. A genuflection, which is with them an ordinary bow, appears to us an act of adoration; we have mistaken a table for an altar: it is thus that we judge everything."

How could Voltaire so contradict and condemn himself? Part of the answer is that he was a polemicist as much as a historian. He used any argument at hand. Another part of the answer is that Voltaire was an eclectic who borrowed ideas from many sources, and did not always bother to synthesize them. Our task, however, is to dismiss this sort of inconsistency and to identify the more fundamental note in his

[7] An interesting confirmation of our interpretation of Voltaire's view of human nature is found in his treatment of the characters in *Candide*. Unchanging in their nature and personalities, however, the puppet-like actors of Voltaire's great philosophical tale do become "enlightened." For a fine analysis of *Candide*, see William F. Bottiglia, *Voltaire's Candide*, 2nd ed. (Geneva, 1964).

[8] Quoted in Brumfitt, *op. cit.*, p. 42.

thought. That fundamental note, as we have remarked, is Voltaire's belief that historical stories must be weighed on the scales of a constant physical and human nature. He believed that the litmus test in history is what is *possible* and *probable* today; in short, what accords with the "reason" of our own time.

On this basis, Voltaire dismissed the myths which had so interested Vico. Discussing the fable which has Jupiter make a eunuch out of his father Saturn, Voltaire remarked sardonically, "Superstition invents ridiculous practices, and the romantic spirit invents absurd reasons." Voltaire disclaimed any interest in how "irrational" men may have thought; their thoughts, he contended, can hardly be useful to present man. Thus, Voltaire lacked completely the historicist sympathy and empathy with past persons and peoples. Cosmopolitan as he was in his concerns and sympathies, he had no desire to "rethink," in a Collingwood fashion, the past.[9] As he deprecatingly remarked, in a revealing phrase: "It is of scant importance to know what idea was passing through the head of a Jew when he was pronouncing Magog or Gog."

It is this same attitude which largely conditioned his treatment of the medieval mind. The *Essai* itself, more or less taking up where the Introduction left off, started with Charlemagne (though not till Voltaire had spent the first 14 chapters on background, beginning with China, and going rapidly through India, Persia, Arabia, the establishment of Christianity, and the fall of Rome), and ended in "modern" times. The main period treated was actually from the accession of Charlemagne to the reign of Louis XIV. In almost all of what related to the barbarous and the feudal past—to what Voltaire called "this chaos of completely bizarre and contradictory customs"—his tone was sharp and unsympathetic. His comment about the Frankish period applied generally to the whole of the Middle Ages: "Too much time has been lost descending into these depths of ruins [*ces abimes de ruines*]." Voltaire

[9] For R. G. Collingwood's theory of "rethinking," see *The Idea of History* (Oxford, 1946), *passim*.

had little desire to deal with these "useless" aspects of an out-dated past.

3

We have already discussed the "history of the human spirit" which Voltaire offered, his view of history as probable truth, and his ways of evaluating that probability. So, too, we have mentioned his approach to human nature as a fixed entity. It remains only to add here a brief comment on his view of causality and then to sum up. Like Hume, Voltaire believed that every effect has its cause, and that the universe is made up of a chain of events. Voltaire's position was quite sophisticated: as he pointed out, "every being has a father, but every being does not always have children." On these grounds, he ridiculed the "For want of a nail the shoe was lost, for want of a shoe the horse was lost, for want of a horse the kingdom was lost" argument (although occasionally erring in this direction in writing his own histories), and pointed out that, as Newton demonstrated,

Every movement is not communicated step by step, until it makes a circuit of the world. . . . Throw into the water a body of like density. . . . You calculate easily that after a short time the movement of this body, and the movement it has communicated to the water, will be destroyed. The movement disappears and is effaced. In the same way, the movement that Magog might have produced by spitting in a well cannot influence what is passing today in Moldavia and Wallachia; therefore present events are not the children of *all* past events: they have their direct lines; but a thousand little collateral lines do not serve them at all. Once more, every being has a father, but every being does not have children.

Fundamentally, however, Voltaire was not interested in offering a causal analysis of historical change. He wished, rather, to offer a "picture of an age," to depict the state of human reason at a given point. True, he frequently used the narrative form.

But this was partly because it came naturally to him as a superb storyteller, and partly because it kept the reader's interest more readily.[10] The central aim of offering a cultural and social "history," however, was never obscured in the *Essai* by the attention to narrative.

Voltaire's achievement, then, was to offer a new sort of history, written from a new point of view. The new kind of history gave, even if fitfully, an extended chronology (as against the orthodox belief in the age of the world dating back only to about 4004 or 4963 B.C.), a greater breadth than usual (China, India, and Arabia, for example, figured in Voltaire's account), and a much wider coverage (including the arts and science) than was commonly attempted. It was, truly, an attempt at a "history of the human spirit," an account, as he had promised Mme. du Châtelet, of the "manners and customs" of mankind.

The purpose of this account, as we have seen, was to offer the reader "some useful truths." In reality, these useful truths boiled down to one: the past was not to serve as an authority for men's actions, institutions, and beliefs in the present. Instead, man, having now in some mysterious way reached a stage of enlightenment, could from that perspective illuminate the record of the past. This was the greatest lesson history could teach. Moreover, man could sit in judgment on the past. While condemning most of it as a record of man's inhumanity to man, he could single out a few bright spots in the darkness. This, basically, was to view history "en philosophe."

One wonders, however, in summing up Voltaire's contribution to historical knowledge, whether the price he paid for his philosophy of history was to forego viewing history "en historien"? Certainly, in one sense of the word, Voltaire had "freed" man from the shackles of his past. This was the "useful" aspect of the Voltairian philosophy of history. But, if it is

---

[10] In his earlier works, while abjuring the rhetorical devices—harangues, portraits, and so forth—of Renaissance historical writing, Voltaire did employ in the main a dramatic form for his histories.

self-consciousness and sympathetic understanding of his history that makes man free, then Voltaire had done little to liberate man from his present moment. In this respect, human reason, "en philosophe," had progressed only a very short way: that that short way—the rejection of unexamined and unreasoned authority—is of great importance is, of course, not to be denied.

IV

Condorcet

> *If humanity marched straight toward some result, there would be no history, only logic.*
>
> ALEXANDER HERZEN,
> From the Other Shore

1

SCHOLARS generally agree that Condorcet was one of the last, if not the last, of the *Encyclopédistes*. As such, he is also presumed to have been "a sort of philosophic résumé of the eighteenth century." This description is given weight by one recent writer on Condorcet who defines an *Encyclopédiste* as one with a universal taste for the sciences and an ambition to embrace and synthesize all human knowledge.[1] We are told further that the *Éloges*, or praises, composed by Condorcet in his position as Secretary of the *Académie des Sciences*, prove

---

[1] For Condorcet as an *Encyclopédiste*, see L. Cahen, *Condorcet et la Révolution française* (Paris, 1904), pp. vii, 24; Alexandre Koyré, "Condorcet," *Journal of the History of Ideas*, IX, 2 (April, 1948), 131; and Gilles-Gaston Granger, *La Mathématique Sociale du Marquis de Condorcet* (Paris, 1956), pp. 13, 16. Granger's, the best recent book on Condorcet, orginal and especially knowledgeable on the mathematical side of Condorcet's work, is essential reading. Granger's one lapse is to repeat all the platitudes about Condorcet as the "last of the *Encyclopédistes*."

his encyclopedic qualities by their attention to chemistry, biology, cartography, and, indeed, to any subject in which his heroes of science worked.

There is a good deal of truth in these claims. In fact, Condorcet contributed an article on mathematics to a Supplement (1776–1777) of the *Encyclopédie,* as well as helping to revise part of the original, and his *Éloges* covered a great deal of ground—Voltaire and Turgot are treated as well as scientists like Buffon—and serve in many ways as a provisional history of science in biographical form. Nevertheless, there is a danger in accepting the characterization of Condorcet as the last and summary figure of the encyclopedists. On two accounts, it gives him far more credit than he deserves: first, there were large gaps in his knowledge, which he would have been the first to acknowledge; and second, his polyhistoric qualities were relatively common in the eighteenth century, a time before the highly specialized growth as well as the unfortunate split of the "two cultures." Worse, however, such a characterization tends to make us see Condorcet in stereotyped and cliché terms. It hides from us the really novel aspect of his "social art."

Nevertheless, one must admit that Condorcet did attempt to synthesize a number of fields—geometry, economics, and morality—in terms of the ideas and spirit of the *Encyclopédie.* Further, the present author is on the side of those who assert that Condorcet's turn from his work in "pure" mathematics to an interest in political matters, theoretical and practical, was part of a unified effort rather than a rupture in his work.[2] Indeed, one might well contend that Condorcet's major achievement was the transformation of his "pure" mathematics into social mathematics.

A glance at Condorcet's life, in the mode of his own *Éloges,* may help us see the elements in his accomplishment. We can

[2] M. F. Arago, one of the editors of the standard edition of the *Oeuvres de Condorcet* (Paris, 1913), sees a break, while Granger emphasizes a continuity. See, however, the long discussion in Cahen, *op. cit.*

skim over some of the early details: his birth in 1743, and the
death of his father immediately thereafter, his mother's queer
idea of dressing him in girl's clothes for the first nine years of
his life, and his Jesuit education about which he talked so little
and hated so much.[3] The first significant item for us is his
decision to abandon the accepted career in his noble family—
the military—and to become a mathematician. His rise in his
chosen field was fairly rapid. At the age of 15, we are told, he
sustained a difficult thesis in analysis, and at the age of 22 he
submitted to the *Académie* his *Essai sur le calcul intégral*,
which earned high praise from both Lagrange and d'Alembert.

In many ways, this was the high point of Condorcet's work
as a pure professional mathematician. Although he continued
throughout his life to publish works on mathematical and scientific subjects, he became increasingly involved in institutional and public matters. His first connections were with the
Académie: elected at the age of 26, he became Secretary four
years later, and perpetual Secretary in 1785. In this capacity he
wrote his *Éloges.* One might say, cynically, that Condorcet
worked his way to scientific eminence as much through com-
mittees as through his own published work. Indeed, he is one
of the first of that flourishing new breed, the scientist-policy-
maker.

Meanwhile, he had become the friend and disciple of many
of the great reformers: Helvétius, Voltaire, and Turgot, to
name a few. From Turgot, especially, he inherited two interests which were powerfully to affect all his future work, an
interest in economics and an interest in the idea of progress.
Turgot offered more than economic theory to his young disciple; in 1774, as Minister of Finance, he tended Condorcet the
post of Inspector of the Mint, a post which Condorcet
accepted and retained until 1776, when he resigned in protest
against the dismissal of Turgot and the appointment of Necker
as finance minister. As for the idea of progress, this Turgot

[3] See Cahen, *op. cit.,* pp. 5 ff., for data on this and the debate about
the date of Condorcet's father's death.

had propounded in two addresses, given at the Sorbonne in
1750, where he declared: "All epochs are connected by a sequence of causes and effects, linking the conditions of the
world to all conditions that have gone before it . . . the human
race, from its origin, appears to the eye of a philosopher one
vast whole which, like the individuals composing it, has had its
infancy and development."[4] We shall hear the echo of these
words in Condorcet's writing.

Marriage in 1786 to Sophie de Grouchy, a woman of 23,
whose salon soon became a meeting place for reformers and
statesmen, accelerated Condorcet's involvement in political
matters. He had already written pamphlets against slavery and
religious intolerance; now he wrote fictitious "Letters from a
bourgeois of New Haven," advocating among other things
woman suffrage and a single-chambered legislature. The cul-
mination of Condorcet's political activity came in the French
Revolution. In 1789, he was elected to the Commune of Paris,
and in 1791 to the Legislative Assembly. With the Abbé Sieyès,
he founded a new club, Le Société de 1789, and edited its
Journal. Undoubtedly, his most important work in the Assembly was his Report on Education, a report which was to have
great influence on the revolutionary remodeling of the French
education system. Elected anew, this time to the National
Convention, Condorcet's major work there was his stillborn
constitution for the Republic.

From this point on, Condorcet and the Jacobins who had
won power in the Revolution began to diverge. Although still
a member of the subcommittee of the Committee of Public
Safety, Condorcet opposed the execution of the King (though
he voted that the King was guilty). His opposition to the
expulsion of the Girondins, and his denunciation in a pamphlet
of the new Jacobin Constitution—a parody of his own constitution—was the last straw. Denounced in the Convention,

---

[4] "Tableau philosophique," *Oeuvres*, Vol. I, p. 215, quoted in Jacob
Salwyn Shapiro, *Condorcet and the Rise of Liberalism* (New York,
1934), p. 239.

Condorcet's name was put on a list of the proscribed.

It is to this event that we owe the composition of the *Sketch for a Historical Picture of the Progress of the Human Mind*. In hiding at a certain Madame Vernet's, Condorcet began to write a "justification" which he intended to plead before his judges. His wife dissuaded him from this personal plea; instead, Condorcet turned to a justification, if we may call it that, of the Revolution itself and of the Progress of the Human Mind. The life of the individual had been superceded by the life of society.

A good deal of nonsense has been written about how Condorcet penned the *Sketch* in the short time from July 1793 to March 1794, without notes or aid, as a sort of spontaneous product. As Cahen correctly puts it, "It has been too frequently believed that Condorcet had written his Sketch without preparation, without notes, without books, from memory: that is not exactly so."[5] In reality, Condorcet had long reflected on the *Sketch*, and had begun to collect notes early in the Revolution. He possessed a wonderful memory, and his wife and friends brought him most of the books and notes that he needed. Perhaps the work would have been fuller and longer under other circumstances, but the essentials of Condorcet's thought are there; indeed, they stand out more clearly and sharply because of the exigencies of circumstances. One result is that the book appears deceptively simple, and thus lends itself to being viewed as a stereotype of the Enlightenment.

There is little left to say about Condorcet's life. Afraid that Madame Vernet would suffer for harboring a fugitive from the law, he slipped out of her house in disguise. For several days he wandered about Paris, half-starved. Entering an inn, his queer appearance attracted attention, and he was arrested for being without identity papers. Still incognito, he was put in prison; the next day he was found dead in his cell. One theory is that

[5] For the view of the *Sketch* as a spontaneous product, see Shapiro, *op. cit.*, p. 105. For the correction to this, see Cahen, *op. cit.*, p. 528.

he had taken poison. The prison medical officer, however, certified that Condorcet had died of a blood congestion brought on by his physical and mental sufferings. There is an ironic conclusion to his death: the Convention which had proscribed him now repented and ordered that his book be published and distributed at public expense.

2

The *Sketch*, as we have seen, was a product of the Revolution. In turn, it can be looked upon both as a justification of the Revolution and as a manifesto of future change. Thus, as Condorcet worked his way through the stages of development of the human mind, he spoke of France's glory and honor in "presiding over a new revolution in the destiny of the human race." In the Tenth Stage, "The future progress of the human mind" is triumphantly heralded and prefigured for us. Probably for the first time, political philosophy is replaced by philosophy of history as justification for a series of events and for a particular political arrangement. A little over half a century before the Communist Manifesto, Condorcet attempted to say not only what the future *should* be, but to predict what it *would* be. Fortunately, in his view, the should and the would coincided.

The basis for Condorcet's confident prediction of a sure and certain future is given in the Introduction. It is a résumé of various points in Locke, Hume, and Voltaire (the last of whom we have already singled out). Now, however, these abstract philosophical points are linked in a line which leads to a definite philosophy of history. In the very first sentence, Condorcet states flatly that "Man is born with the ability to receive sensations; to perceive them and to distinguish between the various simple sensations of which they are composed; to remember, recognize and combine them; to compare these combinations; to apprehend what they have in common and the ways in which they differ; to attach signs to them all in order to recognize them more easily and to allow for the ready production of new combinations." Here we have the sensationalist basis of all knowledge and activity, and the building of the tower of language on this foundation.

According to Condorcet, the first to perceive these truths, but in a vague way, was Aristotle: "We owe him the important truth, the first step in the science of the human mind, that *even our most abstract, as it were our most purely intelligent, ideas have their origin in our sensations.*" The real master in this field, however, was Locke, who "grasped the thread by which philosophy should be guided . . . he proved that all ideas are the result of the operations of our minds upon sensations we have received." (We should remark, however, that the direct source of Condorcet's sensationalist philosophy was his friend, Condillac, who himself elaborated a *Traité des sensations* and developed some of Locke's theories.)[6]

The next important thing, Condorcet tells us, is that "Sensations are attended by pleasure and pain; and man for his part has the capacity to transform such momentary impressions into permanent feelings of an agreeable or disagreeable character, and then to experience these feelings when he either observes or recollects the pleasures and pains of other sentient beings. Finally, as a consequence of this capacity and of his ability to form and combine ideas, there arise between him and his fellow-creatures ties of interest and duty, to which nature herself has wished to attach the most precious portion of our happiness and the most painful of our ills." In short, society, with all its institutions and conventions, arises from our *experience* of pleasure and pain. These experiences are linked for us by memory, and the memory is either personal, defining our *self*, or communal, defining *the human race as a whole.*

If we read Condorcet's own words carefully, we see the link

[6] Ernst Cassirer, *The Philosophy of the Enlightenment,* translated by Fritz C. A Koelln and James P. Pettegrove (Princeton, N.J., 1951), pp. 17 ff.

in his mind between Locke's development of the individual and the social development which can be extrapolated from this position. Condorcet suggests:

If one confines oneself to the study and observation of the general facts and laws about the development of these faculties, considering only what is common to all human beings, this science is called metaphysics. But if one studies this development as it manifests itself in the inhabitants of a certain area at a certain period of time and then traces it on from generation to generation, one has the picture of the progress of the human mind. This progress is subject to the same general laws that can be observed in the development of the faculties of the individual, and it is indeed no more than the sum of that development realized in a large number of individuals joined together in society. What happens at any particular moment is the result of what has happened at all previous moments, and itself has an influence on what will happen in the future.

In the paragraph above, Condorcet has talked of the "general laws" that can be observed in either the development of the individual or of society. These general laws, obviously, are based on the pleasure-pain principle attached to sensation. Unfortunately, this is as far as Condorcet seems to go in his analysis of these general laws. Latent in his thought, however, is an extrapolation which we ought to explore. For the very next thing that Condorcet talks about, after some statements on method, is the development of society in terms of needs: in short, an economic interpretation. The first stage of society, he tells us, is "a small society whose members live by hunting and fishing." Then he traces briefly the changes leading to a primitive form of agricultural society, with a consequent development of surplus property and thus economic exchange. In addition, many of the stages of progress that follow also seem to border on being economic divisions in man's development.

The interesting thing to note is that, with all his sensationalist psychology and his concern for the "material conditions of production," Condorcet is basically not an economic determinist. He is far more interested in the "moral relations" which spring out of increased exchange of surpluses, and in the development of the arts and sciences. Thus, the stages which he marks out in man's progress are primarily intellectual or cultural ones, though they have a strong basis in economic and technical changes. Condorcet never explicitly justifies his "periodization": the stages are simply given us; no attention is even paid to the fact that they are not coordinate in importance. Overwhelmingly clear, however, is the fact that Condorcet is concerned with the changes in man's knowledge—in his total culture—rather than merely with changes in reigning kings or kingdoms. Having abandoned the traditional concern with political history and, consequently, the traditional periodization, Condorcet, however, did stop just short of the future concern with economics and a new periodization based on economic and technological considerations.

Nevertheless, there are hints in Condorcet that the "general laws" of the individual and collective mind embrace a connection between ideas and the social conditions in which they arise. At one point he remarks this about science; at another, about art.[7] But Condorcet's "sociology of knowledge" is extremely vague and general; the conditions embrace political and natural causes, as well as economic and moral ones, and no clear-cut, precise relationship is delineated. Sensations give rise to ideas; but we are never offered any real analysis of how this occurs in society.

Instead, Condorcet bypasses this difficulty, and offers us merely an explanation of his methodology. His starting point is that all events are linked in an "uninterrupted chain." "What happens at any particular moment," he tells us, "is the result of what has happened at all previous moments, and itself has an influence on what will happen in the future." Unlike Voltaire, however, Condorcet does not spend any more time analyzing the chain of cause and effect; we do not know whether "Every

[7] See *Sketch for a Historical Picture of the Progress of the Human Mind,* translated by June Barraclough (London, 1955), pp. 120, 166.

father has a child" or not. In fact, at the very end of the *Sketch*, Condorcet exclaims, "How consoling for the philosopher . . . is this view of the human race, emancipated from its shackles, released from the empire of fate." Then he hastily adds, "He [the philosopher] dares to regard these strivings as part of the eternal chain of human destiny." Which will Condorcet have: release from the shackles, or an eternal chain? Clearly, as a critical philosopher of history, Condorcet has little to offer at this point.

Is there another explanation of Condorcet's position? Was he stumbling toward the idea that man can control his destiny, that is, be free, only if he submits to the laws of nature (in this case, of social development)? I submit that this was Condorcet's vague conception. Thus, after identifying the causal chain in reference to each particular moment, he goes on, "So such a picture is historical, since it is a record of change and is based on the *observation* [italics added] of human societies throughout the different stages of their development. It *ought* [italics added] to reveal the order of this change and the influence that each moment exerts upon the subsequent moment." Then, he concludes, "Such observations upon what man has been and what he is today, will instruct us about the means we should employ to make *certain* [italics added] and rapid the future progress that his nature allows him still to hope for."

Throughout the *Sketch*, Condorcet stresses the methodological basis of his work in *observation*. For example, he bypasses the Adam and Eve story as well as the state of nature abstraction by starting with "the first stage of civilization *observed* [italics added] amongst human beings."; thus, he starts with anthropological "science" rather than with philosophical spec-

---

[8] It is hardly necessary to point out the crude and unscientific nature of Condorcet's anthropology; not that he, of course, is to be blamed for this. Anthropology as a modern science does not begin to develop until the late nineteenth century.

ulation.[8] So, too, he extols the comparative method and asks, "if it is useful to observe the various societies that exist side by side, and to study the relations between them, why should it not also be useful to observe them across the passage of time?" And at one point he chastises the Greeks because "They neglected the observation of facts for the cultivation of the imagination."

It is startling to realize that, with all his talk about observation of facts, Condorcet never once raises the question of what is a "fact" in history and how are we to "observe" it. He is completely blind to this sort of practical historian's sort of problem and to the consequent possibility that he may be building all his castles on sand. So convinced is he that he can pontificate: "The history of man . . . is linked by an uninterrupted chain of facts and observations [notice the shift from a chain of events to a chain of observed facts]; and so at this point the picture of the march and progress of the human mind becomes truly historical. *Philosophy has nothing more to guess, no more hypothetical surmises to make* [italics added]; it is enough to assemble and order the facts and to show the useful truths that can be derived from their connections and from their totality."

"Useful truths"—the cat is out of the bag! As with Voltaire, we now know the code by which we can "assemble and order the facts." Whatever Condorcet may say, we perceive now his guiding principle for selecting his data: it is utility "en philosophe." It is this which permits him, in spite of criticizing the Greeks for their "cultivation of the imagination," to "conjecture the stages by which man living in isolation" came to develop language. "We are therefore," he advises us, "in this matter forced to rely upon *theoretical observations* [italics added] about the development of our intellectual and moral faculties." And Condorcet as much as admits his general bias in the statement that "The history of a group of men must be supported by observations; and to select these observations and to fasten upon their essential features enlightenment is necessary, and to use them to good effect, philosophy in the same measure."[9]

Unlike Voltaire, however, Condorcet thinks these "useful truths" amounted to a science. "If there is to be a science for predicting the progress of the human race," he declares, "for directing and hastening it, the history of the progress already achieved must be its foundation." It is from this science, based on observations, that Condorcet believes we should deduce "the art [i.e., social art] which should be its useful result" and which will allow us to break our shackles. At moments, it is true, Condorcet seems almost to have reduced his "science" to a "decline and fall-type" observation, as when he asks, "Would it then be useless to know how in the past nations have been deceived, corrupted or plunged into misery?" But this is only a relapse on his part into the customary phraseology about the lessons of the past. Fundamentally, he is trying to develop out of the useful truths of history a science of human development. We have already seen the fragile basis—of unexamined observations of facts—on which he has grounded this science.

3

With his new lantern of a useful science held firmly in his hand, Condorcet can now observe the dark past with equanimity. "The human race still revolts the philosopher who contemplates its history," he announces, "but it no longer humiliates him, and now offers him hope for the future." In fact, this "hope" is scientifically certifiable; thus, it becomes a certainty. And the content of this scientific certainty is the indefinite

---

[9] Almost more devastating is the remark by Condorcet, quoted in Cassirer, *op. cit.*, p. 252: "It is not in the positive knowledge of laws established among men that one ought to seek for knowledge which he will adopt; it is in reason alone. And the study of laws instituted among different peoples and in different centuries is useful only in order to give reason the benefit of observation and experience."

perfectibility of man. In Condorcet's words, the result of his *Sketch* is to show that "nature has set no term to the perfection of human faculties; that the perfectibility of man is truly indefinite; and that the progress of this perfectibility from now onwards independent of any power that might wish to halt it, has no other limit than the duration of the globe upon which nature has cast us."

Condorcet's presentation of man's progress in the natural sciences is impressive. A professional mathematician himself, he was well aware of the progress in that field, as well as in astronomy and physics, and throughout the *Sketch* there are paragraphs on the level of development of these sciences at various stages of the past. Indeed, parts of the *Sketch* comprise a prototype of a history of science. But, to employ the useful distinctions of Alfred Weber, did progress in civilization equal progress in culture? Or, to revert to an earlier phrasing of the question: "Has the Restoration [substitute "Progress" here] of the Arts and Sciences Had a Purifying Effect upon Morals?"

In the light of this latter question, we can see that much of the *Sketch* is a polemic against Jean-Jacques Rousseau. As we know, Rousseau's answer to the prize question quoted above of the Academy of Dijon, in 1749, was in the negative. Although not directly named, there can be no question that it is the author of the *Discourse on the Arts and Sciences*, Rousseau, who is being addressed in Condorcet's statement that "We shall prove that the eloquent declamations made against the arts and sciences are founded upon a mistaken application of history." Similarly, after a discussion of the supposed superiority of the "noble savage," Condorcet declares that "we shall see that it is not the growth of knowledge but its decadence that has engendered the vices of civilized peoples, and that knowledge, so far from corrupting man, has always improved him when it could not totally correct or reform him."

Condorcet believed he could refute Rousseau by appealing to an observed progress toward a "science of morality." The first step in this refutation was the elimination in the physical

sciences of false beliefs. "All errors in politics and morals,"
Condorcet asserted, "are based on philosophical errors and
these in turn are connected with scientific errors." Further,
once achieved, progress in the physical sciences provided a
cover under which an attack on general authority could be
carried out. "Advances in the physical sciences are all the more
fatal to these errors [in politics and morals] in that they often
destroy them without appearing to attack them," he pointed
out. What had held up progress in the past was that men had
taken as their authority, "established customs and the beliefs
of antiquity" rather than reason and nature. (This, as we have
seen, was also Voltaire's complaint.) Once freed of these
shackles, Condorcet insisted, men would add a moral science
to the physical ones already reached.

According to Condorcet, the identifying feature of both the
moral and physical sciences is that they be expressed in unambiguous language: in mathematics. It is Descartes, Condorcet tells us, who discovered "the final objective of the
sciences, which is to subject all truths to the rigor of calculation." Implied here, it seems, is the notion that Condorcet's
greatness will consist in extending the rigor of calculation
from the natural to the moral science. Indeed, this is the task
he sets himself in the Tenth Stage, where he outlines the future "social art." Success in this aim will conclusively rebut
Rousseau's dichotomy between progress in the arts and sciences
and in morality.

Let us postpone the full discussion of this most important
topic—Condorcet's social art—until we deal specifically with
the Tenth Stage. By then, too, we shall have worked our way
though the already accomplished stages of man's progress,
which must serve as the basis for predictions about his future
state. Now, we need only notice briefly one other point connected with the progress of the arts and sciences: Malthus'
challenge, in his treatise on Population. Whereas Rousseau had
admitted, by implication, the indefinite progress of the arts and
sciences, Malthus denied it. He based his denial on what we

may loosely call economic grounds: while subsistence may increase arithmetically, population will tend to increase geometrically; the result will be, at best, a very little progress in man's earthly conditions. And Malthus directed his challenge, in 1798, to the then dead Condorcet by name.[10]

As if in direct anticipation of Malthus, however, Condorcet had himself raised the exact same question. "Might there not then come a moment . . . when, the number of people in the world finally exceeding the means of subsistence, there will in consequence ensue a continual diminution of happiness and a true retrogression, or at best an oscillation between good and bad?", he asked. Soberly he answered his own question: "There is doubtless no one who does not think that such a time is still very far from us; but will it ever arrive? It is impossible to pronounce about the likelihood of an event that will occur only when the human species will have necessarily acquired a degree of knowledge of which we can have no inkling. And who would take it upon himself to predict the condition to which the art of converting the elements to the use of man may in time be brought?"

Who, indeed, in a time of atomic energy and space explorations would be so bold as to predict the limits of man's scientific progress? But who, also, would ignore the population explosion danger, and declare against Malthus? One thing, however, is clear. In terms of the recent *observable* past, Condorcet was right in believing that natural science had taken gigantic forward strides; these have continued to our day. Moreover, there seems now to be a built-in factor to modern science and technology which, if we can ignore the cultural factors surrounding it (which, of course, in any full consideration we cannot), makes us sanguine about its future progress. Can we say the same thing about progress in the moral sciences? Was this progress *observable* in the past which lay behind Condorcet? Has it been observable in the time since? And, if pro-

[10] Thomas Robert Malthus, *An Essay on the Principles of Population* (London, 1798).

gress has occurred in knowledge, has it made men more virtuous
and happier? These are complicated questions, and Condorcet
appears now, in our time, to have been unduly optimistic about
the answers to all of them.

4

In the first few pages of the Introduction, Condorcet tells us
that just as the operations of the understanding which lead the
individual into error are part of epistemological theory, so
"the way in which general errors are insinuated amongst peoples and are propagated, transmitted and perpetuated is all part
of the historical picture of the progress of the human mind."
Indeed, "certain prejudices have necessarily come into being at
each stage of our progress." Thus, history for Condorcet is a
history of the struggle between truth and error, knowledge
and superstition, philosophy and religion, with the right gradually winning out. History is not a class struggle, though it is
often related to economic conditions, and it is not dialectical as
in Hegel. It is simply "progressive," though with temporary
setbacks.

   The first stage in this progress, according to Condorcet, is
when "Men are United in Tribes." This is a very short chapter. The second stage is called "Pastoral Peoples: the transition
from this stage to that of agricultural peoples." Of these two
stages, we may remark the following. First, the development
outlined in them is logical, not historical. Condorcet is not
relying on any anthropological knowledge—which hardly
existed—but is reconstructing the past speculatively: as it must
have been. Indeed, throughout these two chapters, as elsewhere, he keeps repeating such phrases as man "must have
produced," "must have discovered," and so on. Second, although a speculative reconstruction, it avoids, as we have already noticed, any mention of a state of nature, or even of any
stage of primitive communism as in the Marxist scheme; in this

respect, Condorcet is *anthropological,* for he speaks of tribal society as the first stage in history "about which we have any direct observation." Third, Condorcet already distinguishes in these early stages the emergence of a priestly caste, whose preeminence (that is, their claim to be above "common nature" and its accompanying ways of reasoning) is based on the maintenance of error. It is these clerical "impostors" who prevent the human race from progressing freely, as it naturally would by experience.

Even at this early stage, then, we see that the struggle is joined. To Condorcet, religion is primarily a negative force. Though he grudgingly concedes it some role in fostering early astronomy and medicine, its adherents then turn this lore into a trade secret, and mask it in secret language. Nor has Condorcet any sympathy with religious myths and legends; unlike Vico, for example, he considers them solely as the work of conscious scoundrels. Thus, as a modern commentator points out, the "eighteenth-century squabble between Philosophers and priests" has been projected into the past "so that it may be regarded as an aspect of a conflict exemplified in all human experience, the conflict between the cosmic forces of good and evil, between the City of Light and the City of Darkness."[11] Whether this projection distorts the past is a question Condorcet never considered.

The third stage contemplates "The progress of agricultural peoples up to the invention of the alphabet." In this chapter, we are introduced to the division of labor, as "necessary in the interest of all," and to the growing division of classes: "to the three existing classes that we can already distinguish in pastoral society, owners, servants attached to the family, and slaves, we must now add workers of every kind, and merchants." Out of these classes arise two new classes: a hereditary nobility and "a common people condemned to toil, dependence and humiliation without actually being slaves." We are in the presence of

[11] Carl L. Becker, *The Heavenly City of the Eighteenth-Century Philosophers* (New Haven, 1932), pp. 105–106.

the feudal system, "a curse not peculiar to our climate but to be found in nearly every part of the globe at a certain stage of civilization."[12]

For feudalism and the period in which if flourished in Western civilization, Condorcet has nothing but scorn. It was a time of "profound darkness," in which "monkish absurdities" dominated. In reality, Condorcet does not call this stage or period the middle ages. He periodizes on other grounds. Thus, the fourth stage deals with "The progress of the human mind in Greece . . .", and the fifth ("the progress of the sciences from their division to their decline") continues this investigation through to the Romans. It is only the sixth stage, "the decadence of knowledge to its restoration about the time of the crusades," and the seventh, "the early progress of science from its revival in the West to the invention of printing," which cover the time period we usually label as "medieval." According to Condorcet, in those "unhappy times," only the Arabs kept the light of science shining.

At last, however, the coming of the printing press shattered the priestly monopoly of learning. A "new enlightenment" (the first had been the Greeks) was now possible, and the "yoke of authority" could be thrown off. This is the burden of the eighth stage, where everywhere "we see reason and authority fighting for supremacy, a battle which prepared and anticipated the triumph of reason." That triumph, which we celebrate in the ninth stage, was begun by Descartes who "commanded man to shake off the yoke of authority, to recognize none save that which was avowed by reason"; it was continued in the realm of thought by the philosophers and scientists, some of whose *Éloges* Condorcet had already composed as Secretary of the *Académie des Sciences*. In the realm of action, the struggle was marked by the American Revolution, where we see "a great people delivered from all its chains." Even more successful and far-reaching, Condorcet

[12] For the controversy over the extent and nature of feudalism cf. Montesquieu's *Spirit of Laws*.

tells us, is the present French Revolution.

In Condorcet's view, a revolution occurs when a new attitude of mind has slowly and imperceptibly developed, and suddenly shows itself out of step with the existing forms of government. At that point, a revolution is inevitable, but whether it comes about peacefully or violently depends upon whether the government anticipates the people's wishes and carries out the revolution "from above" or whether the people themselves have to establish "the reasonable and natural principles that philosophy had taught them to admire." In any case, at the end of the ninth stage, Condorcet welcomes not only the American and French Revolutions but confidently predicts another revolution "that must one day include in its scope the whole of the human race."

Thus ends the historical part of the *Sketch of the Progress of the Human Mind*. To our brief survey of it, let me add two further points. The first concerns its omissions. Striking among these is the complete absence of any treatment or even significant mention of the Jews. Condorcet's detestation of religion has led him so far as to ignore the Hebrew contribution to the progress of the human mind: for him, of course, the prophets had taken a retrograde step. Were they not, however, even to be treated as one of the necessary errors? Condorcet's answer seems to have been "no." It is almost as if he had anticipated the Russian Communists, with their rewriting of history, and made an "unpeople" of the Jews.[13]

So, too, almost all of the Oriental peoples and their history and civilizations are simply neglected. Asia, for Condorcet, is unchanging Asia, and its "history" one of "shameful stagnation." Only China comes in for a few words of praise; like many of the *philosophes*, Condorcet had a touch of the eighteenth-century sinophilism. The only other non-European

[13] For the Russian Communist rewriting of history and the making of "unpersons" and "unpeople," see Bertram D. Wolfe, "Operation Rewrite: The Agony of Soviet Historians," *Foreign Affairs* (October, 1952).

people who seem to have shared in the march to human perfection was, as already mentioned, the Arabs.

The second point we need to make about the *Sketch* is that it is about a hypothetical people: the human race. Condorcet is quite explicit about this. Our task in relation to the "facts transmitted to us in history" is "to select them from the histories of different peoples, to compare them and combine them in order to extract the hypothetical history of a single people and to compare the picture of its progress." These selected facts, in turn, become our chain of events. And these events, mainly mental ones, constitute the progress of the human mind, now presented to us as an historical picture.

It seems that we cannot quarrel with Condorcet's methodology here. He has a perfect right to construct a "hypothetical history of a single people." It is, in many ways, similar to Montesquieu's construction of "ideal types," now made dynamic, and can even be compared to the more recent use of this intellectual device by Max Weber.[14] However, we can legitimately ask how useful, how heuristic, is a "hypothetical history" of the human mind which, for example, has no interest in the religious or mythical categories of thought, even as a mere way of thinking characterizing earlier, more primitive-minded peoples? Which has no room in its pages for the human beings who carried this way of thinking around in their heads? Condorcet's historical construction is a possible one; it is, however, not a very probable one. Surely, it is poor history, and, because it is so far removed from historical reality (taking this term even in its loosest form), it is also bad, that is, non-instrumental or operational science. It may give us a true picture of Condorcet's mind; it tends to offer us only a superficial and distorted picture, from which most of the historical dimension is missing, of the progress of the "human mind."

[14] On Weber's ideal type, see, for example, his *The Theory of Social and Economic Organization*, translated by A. M. Henderson and Talcott Parsons (New York, 1947), especially pp. 12 ff.

5

If the "science" described above were Condorcet's only contribution, we could dismiss him without further ado. But there
is a second, and quite different, science in Condorcet's *Sketch*.
It is the science of the social art, presented to us in the Tenth
Stage. All too often, the distinction between the two versions
of a social science proferred by Condorcet is not remarked
upon sufficiently, and this leads to a gross misunderstanding of
his real achievement. The first science, as we have seen, is
supposed to result from the observation of historical facts; and
we have already expressed doubts about its validity. The second science—the science of calculation—needs to be commented on now, in detail.

Condorcet begins his discussion of the social art by sub-
suming our hopes for the future condition of the human race
under three heads: "The abolition of inequality between nations, the progress of equality within each nation, and the true
perfection of mankind." In reality, the hopes are predictions,
and Condorcet proceeds on the assumption that history has an
inevitable direction.

In dealing with the inequality between nations, Condorcet
has a theory about what we would today call the "underdeveloped nations." He believes that, willy-nilly, the enlightened
and advanced European nations must raise the others—in
many cases, erstwhile colonies—to their own level. The underdeveloped nations "need only assistance from us to become
civilized." Condorcet bases his faith in the "civilizing mission"
of the advanced countries on another faith: that ideas as well
as inventions can simply be exported or imported. Indeed, the
present lesser nations will advance more rapidly and certainly
than their tutors, he tells us, because they can gain from the
latter's experiences and avoid their mistakes.

There is, however, amidst his general optimism on the subject, an ominous warning: the abolition of inequality between

nations is inevitable, but it will come about in either of two ways. Either it will come "of a new-found wisdom on the part of the European nations, or of their obstinate attachment to mercantilist prejudices." Does Condorcet intend by the latter part of this statement a sort of vague dialectical movement? In fact, a hint is present in the surrounding passages that if the European nations continue their unenlightened exploitation of the colonies, they will reap the harvest of an unintended consequence: revolution everywhere. Clearly, one example of the latter way of change is the American Revolution. But this is merely to say in another context what we have already seen Condorcet say about revolutions within a nation.

What about inequality within each nation? There are three main kinds of inequality, Condorcet tells us: in wealth, in status, and in education. All three are inequalities which can be diminished, but they will never disappear because "They are the result of natural and necessary causes which it would be foolish and dangerous to eradicate." No more than his opponent, Malthus, did Condorcet believe in the possibility of a state of complete equality.

What he did believe in was the asymptotic diminution of inequality by means of the "social art." For Condorcet, the social art really takes two forms: one, a matter of practical legislation, and the other a matter of science. In its first form, Condorcet is really aiming at today's welfare state. He asks rhetorically whether the existing inequality in a nation is the result of unchangeable causes, "part of civilization itself," or is due to "the present imperfections of the social art?" Answering in the latter vein, Condorcet both recommends and predicts a whole series of measures. Thus, he sets up a system of social security, by applying the same calculus of life and the investment of money already used in insurance schemes: poverty, he tells us, "can be in great part eradicated by guaranteeing people in old age a means of livelihood produced partly by their own savings and partly by the savings of others who make the same out-lay, but who die before they need to reap

the reward." Condorcet also looks to the spread of birth control, as well as to a gradual increase in the length of the
average life, based on progress in biology. He predicts vastly
increased industrial production, accompanied by the disap-
pearance of dangerous and unsanitary conditions in manufacturing establishments; and he anticipates education for women,
as well as the growing equality of the sexes. All of these predictions—and others—have been justified in recent times.

It is the scientific form of the social art, however, which is
most interesting. The subject is, unfortunately, not clear-cut,
and it is difficult to disentangle from Condorcet's work. This is
largely because he himself was only stumbling toward it, and
rarely grasped clearly what he was trying to do. Our guide in
this matter must be his hints and stabs in the *Sketch*, aided by
our use of his other writings, and by the one indispensable
secondary source, the recent book by Gilles-Gaston Granger,
La Mathématique Sociale du Marquis de Condorcet, which
breaks new ground in this matter.[15]

Condorcet assumes that a moral or social science based on
both practice (that is, the legislation suggested above) and
theory will offer us insight into "the nature and development
of the moral sentiments, the principles of morality, the natural
motives that prompt our actions, and our own true interests
either as individuals or as members of society." As a science, of
course, it will give us this insight and knowledge with "almost
mathematical exactitude." It needs also to be remarked that
Condorcet is not suggesting a psychological science to deal
with "the natural motives that prompt our actions"; he has in
mind a purely social science.

This social science—the social art—will tell us how to reconcile and identify "the interests of each with the interests of
all."[16] "Has the social art," he asks rhetorically, "any other

[15] Granger, *op. cit.*

[16] Condorcet poses the problem in dramatic fashion: "How, with all
the astonishing multifariousness of labour and production, supply and
demand, with all the frightening complexity of conflicting interests
that link the survival and well-being of one individual to the general

aim save that of destroying their apparent opposition?" In this very important formulation Condorcet has linked the work of the economists, for example, Adam Smith's reconciliation of self-love and the social welfare, with Rousseau's views on the general will. In fact, the social art has become the scientific way of determining the general will, as well as of ordering the previously "invisible hand" of the market place.

In its economic aspect, Condorcet's social art bases itself on an unexpected combination of free trade and the application of statistics to social security schemes and their like, to insure the diminution of inequality and the growth of material well-being. Condorcet learned his lessons from Adam Smith, as well as from Turgot and the Physiocrats. The former's "invisible hand" ensures that the pursuit of self-interest is really identical with the pursuit of the general interest. To this Condorcet adds a visible hand—the hand of government—to insure by the same concept of equilibrium mathematics the equitable distribution of income. The extraordinary originality of Condorcet's sketchy suggestions, however, was ignored in his own time, and is, indeed, generally ignored in ours.

So, too, Condorcet's work in the political field has been dismissed as naïve or unimportant. In large part, as we have noted, this is his own fault, for there are only veiled allusions to the subject in the *Sketch*, and the rest of his message is scattered about in odd writings. In the *Sketch*, he starts by asking: "Are we yet in possession of any precise rules for selecting out of the almost infinite variety of possible systems in which the general principles of equality and natural rights are respected, those which will best secure the preservation of

---

organization of societies, that makes his well-being dependent on every accident of nature and every political event, his pain and pleasure on what is happening in the remotest corner of the globe, how, with all this seeming chaos, is it that, by a universal moral law, the efforts made by each individual on his own behalf minister to the welfare of all, and that the interests of society demand that everyone should understand where his own interests lie, and should be able to follow without hindrance?"

these rights, which will afford the freest scope for their exercise and their enjoyment, and which will moreover insure the leisure and welfare of individuals and the strength, prosperity and peace of nations?" Then, he concludes lamely: "The application of the calculus of combinations and probabilities to these sciences promises even greater improvement, since it is the only way of achieving results of an almost mathematical exactitude and of assessing the degree of their probability or likelihood. . . . However, such an application, not withstanding the happy efforts of certain geometers is still in its earliest stages."

Condorcet, in talking of "certain geometers," was talking about himself. In the *Sketch*, he leaves us merely with this vague allusion. Fortunately, Granger has developed this aspect of Condorcet's thought, and put together the pieces of his work. According to Granger, Condorcet's starting point is his analysis of voting, presented for example in the *Essai sur l'application de l'analyse à la probabilité des decisions rendues à la pluralité des voix* (1785). What Condorcet did was to set up a mathematical model, in which voting is considered as a system of betting, and in which it is necessary to minimize the chance of loss. The aim of this betting, in the first version of Condorcet's mathematical model, is to find the truth. "The psychosocial phenomenon of the vote," Granger comments, "is therefore in his view a mode of collective research for the truth."[17] For this reason, Condorcet opposes the system of parties and coalitions, on the grounds that these devices might lead to a balance of interests but not to the general interest, which at this point he identifies with the truth.

One acceptable device for reaching a true judgment is the system of proportional representation: this maximizes the probability of approximating the correct decision. In this model of the first type, according to Granger, Condorcet treats the voters as individual, self-contained atoms, "where

[17] Granger, *op. cit.*, p. 96.

each subject finds himself before an inert world of objects, so to speak in an irenic [*irénique*] situation, to the extent that he does not oppose himself directly to his fellow men." Gradually, however, Condorcet's views changed, and he came to construct mathematical models in which the parameters of the voters were not invariable and equal for all; provision was made for one voter to vary in this respect from another. Finally, Condorcet glimpsed a third stage of his mathematical model, in which his actor was a variable voter, whose vote varied, depending on the votes of others. This is what Granger calls an agonistic [*agonistique*] scheme "where each agent is in the presence not of a kind of nature, but of a group of subjects concerning which he must devise tactics, accept cooperation, and bend behavior by political action [*infléchir le comportement par une action politique*]."[18]

With this model, we are in the presence of what today we call "game theory." The major contemporary strides in this area seem to be in economics rather than politics and the outstanding work in this field, *The Theory of Games and Economic Behavior* by von Neumann and Morgenstern, uses set theory instead of calculus. But the basic idea is the same as in Condorcet. He had glimpsed a new way of dealing with the functioning of social bodies in general: by a social mathematics, or what he called his "social art." Whether it is economic or political functioning, the same mathematical model obtains. As Granger remarks at one point (although referring in this case to the model of the first stage), "Just as the individual action of the marginal *Homo oeconomicus* is thought to concur with an optimal distribution of resources, so the act of *Homo suffragans* would tend to bring forth, on each question placed in debate, the most probable truth."[19]

[18] *Ibid.*, p. 103.
[19] *Ibid.*, p. 97. Cf. John von Neumann and Oskar Morgenstern, *The Theory of Games and Economic Behavior* (Princeton, N.J., 1947). For one of Condorcet's near contemporaries, Jeremy Bentham's effort at a "felicific calculus," see J. Bronowski and Bruce Mazlish, *The Western Intellectual Tradition* (New York, 1960), pp. 436–437.

It does not matter that Condorcet never worked out the mathematics of his second and third stage models; the mathematics of probability were not sufficiently advanced in his time, and he gave up the attempt himself to construct a radically new mathematics for his third stage model. Indeed, when he saw that that model no longer was normative, that is, aimed at the truth, but rather merely described social behavior and laid down practical rules, derived from this description, for decision-making, he recoiled from his own work. But he could not undo the implications of his explorations; and it is the shadow of these which looms over the pages of the *Sketch* and gives real meaning to the second of Condorcet's two sciences.

At the core of Condorcet's second science is the concept of probability. This, as we have seen, was also a term which occupied the thought of Voltaire. For Voltaire (as for Locke and Hume before him), however, it meant a nonmathematical weighing of the historical evidence, and a decision as to the "probability" or "credibility" of the testimony. Condorcet metamorphosed this concept into a truly mathematical form. It is not completely clear from his work whether he thought probability mathematics should be based primarily on the frequency of past occurrences—actual historical experiences—or on an a priori calculation. His work on mortality statistics seems to be of the first genre; but a good deal of his work on voting appears to fall into the second category, the classical probability theory, illustrated in its simplest form by the 50–50 assumptions made about a flipped coin landing heads or tails. In any case, he seems to have used both methods.

Can a science of human behavior be extracted from the past? Or erected on a priori grounds for the future? I have already tried to suggest that in the *Sketch* Condorcet uses one "science" for the past, and another for the future. His first science uses supposed observations of facts, joined together in a deterministic chain: there is no probability here, except in the Lockean-Voltarian sense. His second science seeks to offer man a tool by which to control his future "history," that is, to give man a means of conducting himself rationally in his political and economic decisions. It is of this second science that Granger is talking when he remarks: "The introduction of the contingent [*l'aleatoire*] as a fundamental category of a science of government [*des conduites*], such is without doubt the most fecund contribution of Condorcet to the progress of knowledge."[20]

In sum, then, Condorcet's "social art" is neither based on past experiences—the first nine stages do not really serve as the basis for the tenth—nor used as a tool with which to analyse past experiences. While the social art may serve Condorcet as a means to a sociology, or even a political science, it has very little to do with history, *except in the sense that*, since Condorcet measures the progress of the human mind largely in terms of its ability to express knowledge mathematically, the coming of mathematical exactitude to the knowledge of human behavior marks a new historical stage. We are here, now, in the shadow of Comte, though with an important difference, as we shall see later.[21]

It is important to note, however, that there is a form other than the mathematical which Condorcet's second science may take. It involves an extrapolation of the mathematical form, with its use of signs, as in algebra, to general language. Before Condorcet, many philosophers (Hobbes, Locke, and Hume, to name a few) had complained bitterly that false reasoning was due to the ambiguity and abstruseness of ordinary language. Condorcet now suggests, to remedy this, a "universal language." He defines it as "that which expresses by signs either real objects themselves, or well-defined collections composed of simple and general ideas . . . or the general relations holding between these ideas, the operations of the human mind, or the

[20] Granger, *op. cit.*, pp. 146–147. Did Condorcet give up too easily about applying mathematical probability to the past? One wonders upon reading the interesting attempt of Lewis F. Richardson to apply the statistical method to historical observations, in this case, on war. See Richardson's works, *Arms and Insecurity* (Pittsburgh, 1960) and *Statistics of Deadly Quarrels* (Pittsburgh, 1960), and the stimulating review of these books by Anatol Rapaport in *The Nation*, 13 May, 1961, 414–416.

[21] See Chapter VII on Comte.

operations peculiar to the individual sciences, or the proce-
dures of the arts." Commenting that the chief obstacle to the
development of this new symbolism would be the humiliation
"of having to admit how very few precise ideas and accurate,
unambiguous notions we actually possess," Condorcet goes on
to indicate its beneficial result: "We shall show that this language, ever improving and broadening its scope all the while,
would be the means of giving to every subject embraced by
the human intelligence, a precision and a rigour that would
make knowledge of the truth easy and error almost impossible.
Then the progress of every science would be as sure as that of
mathematics and the propositions that compose it would acquire a geometrical certainty, as far, that is, as is possible
granted the nature of its aim and method."

The name we give today to Condorcet's "universal language" is symbolic logic; or, perhaps, Boolian algebra. The
philosophical school which concerns itself with Condorcet's
problem goes under the name logical analysts or analytic philosophers. In his own time, the conclusion Condorcet drew
from his suggestion of a universal language was that "the perfectibility of man is indefinite." The guarantee for this in
Condorcet's mind was twofold: (1) the record of the past—as
Granger puts it, "He goes so far as to think that the history of
mathematics is the most faithful mirror of the history of
human progress"—and (2) a social art, which in one part was
an art of mathematical calculation and in another part an art
of logical manipulation.[22]

6

It may be, as one commentator suggests, that the result of
Condorcet's social art was to replace divine providence by
human prevision.[23] Did it fall far short, however, of giving
man renewed—or new—vision as to the past? It would seem
that the fruitful aspect *for history* of Condorcet's work is that

[22] Granger, *op. cit.*, p. 91.
[23] Karl Löwith, *Meaning in History* (Chicago, 1949), p. 93.

he invited attention to ideas, and especially to scientific ideas. Thus, the *Sketch* is a rather crude prototype of the history of ideas or, more narrowly, of the history of science. Interestingly enough, it also makes gestures toward being what we may call a history of the masses. As Condorcet remarks, "Up till now, the history of politics, like that of philosophy of science, has been the history of only a few individuals: that which really constitutes the human race, the vast mass of families living for the most part on the fruits of their labour, has been forgotten." In sum, then, Condorcet has tried to replace the conventional political history by a history of the *human*—that is, the mass—mind which is broader even than Voltaire's: Condorcet's will embrace technological, economic, legal, social, and political, as well as religious, philosophical, and scientific history. It also seeks to indicate the pattern prevailing in the past—progress—and its extrapolation to the future.

Certain comments, however, must be made concerning Condorcet's effort. Fruitful as is his attempt at a history of ideas, the execution itself exhibits some glaring weaknesses. Foremost of these is that Condorcet consistently overindulges in abstract speculation and ignores practice. Thus, for example, he remarks deprecatingly that "no Roman work on politics has come down to us," and thereby overlooks entirely the greatness of Roman political practice. Another instance is when he confesses himself puzzled at the existence of slavery in a free America, and admonishes his admired Americans to liberate their slaves. Condorcet is so concerned with ideas that he ignores social and psychological forces in history. One important result is that while he has a clear conception of the progress of the abstraction, humanity, he has no notion at all about the actual, historical transitions—and the ways in which they occurred—which mark this supposed progress.

So, too, he has no real awareness that man develops and changes during his historical evolution.[24] For Condorcet, the aim of man's progress is to realize what is at the beginning: the

---

[24] For Condorcet's nonevolutionary point of view, see his *Sketch*, p. 129.

flavor of his thought is Cartesian, as when he remarks about "the true rights of man and how they can all be *deduced* [italics added] from the single truth, *that man is a sentient being, capable of reasoning and of acquiring moral ideas.*" As a "sentient being," in Condorcet's scheme, man's nature is fixed, just as nature's nature is that of a "fixed chain." In Condorcet's philosophy, pleasure and pain sensations will always be the same, and it is for this reason that a science of morality can be worked out.

It is for a similar reason that Condorcet believes the human race may reach perfection. Man's rights are written in "the book of nature." They are not constructed by him, but given to him to be achieved. Thus, humanity's aspirations being fixed, it is simply a matter of determining whether they can be reached: and Condorcet has "scientific" proof, derived from his "Historical Picture of the Progress of the Human Mind," that they can. It is, therefore, not only the past which Condorcet assumes to share his values of happiness, though in a hampered fashion; it is the future as well. There is no room in Condorcet for man to change his values; he can only achieve them. This is man's fate.

It is a rather ironic conclusion to the Enlightenment's effort to free man from the dead hand of the past, while restoring his "true" history to him. By true history, of course, the *philosophes* meant that which was "most probable," and the "most probable" was that which accorded most, not with received authority, but with the tenets of reason. In turn, reason was grounded on an empirical foundation (though often infiltrated by Cartesian rationalism), which was characterized by a sensationalist psychology. The farthest extrapolation of this position, by Condorcet, as we have observed, was to turn the development of the individual mind into that of the human mind, and to trace its progress over historic time. Seen in this light, then, Condorcet's *Sketch* becomes a sensationalist *Bildungsroman* of the human race.

V

Kant

*. . . this scene of man;
A mighty maze! but not without a plan.*

ALEXANDER POPE,
An Essay on Man,

1

ABOUT ten years before Condorcet wrote his *Sketch*, the German philosopher Immanuel Kant published his one contribution concerned uniquely with the philosophy of history: *Idea
for a Universal History from a Cosmopolitan Point of View*
(1784). As is well known, Kant's major epistemological interest was in providing a philosophical foundation for mathematical and physical knowledge; his work in history was
peripheral. Indeed, aside from the effort mentioned above, it
consisted of a two-part review in the *Jenaische Allgemeine
Litteraturzeitung* (1785) of Herder's *Ideas for a Philosophy of
the History of Mankind* (*Ideen zur Philosophie der Geschichte der Menscheit*), and scattered passages in works such
as *The Critique of Judgment* (1793) and *Eternal Peace*
(1794).[1]

[1] Herder's *Ideen* has been translated by T. Churchill as *Outlines of
a Philosophy of the History of Man*, 2nd ed. (London, 1803). See R. T.
Clark, Jr., *Herder: His Life and Thought* (Berkeley, 1955) and

However, in spite of the paucity of his efforts at a philosophy of history, Kant's contribution is highly significant. In a number of ways, his *Idea* bears a resemblance to Condorcet's *Sketch:* both works are short and packed; both manifest a belief in progress; and both indicate the stages to a desired end. At this point, however, the two diverge. Whereas the end of history for Condorcet is increased equality, for Kant it is greater freedom. Where Condorcet proceeds by ten stages, Kant utilizes nine propositions. And beyond these relatively superficial differences lies a more fundamental one. Whereas Condorcet's philosophy of history is based on the sensationalistic epistemology of Locke and Hume, filtered through Condillac, Kant's idea of universal history is set squarely upon his own work in idealistic epistemology.

The result is that two different streams of influence—real and theoretical—emanate from the two men. If, like the author of the *Sketch*, I may construct a straight line hypothetical history, I would suggest that Condorcet's successor was Auguste Comte, and Kant's was Georg Friedrich Hegel. As we shall see, these two men were the great mid-nineteenth-century figures in philosophy of history; and it is their work which became the basis for the philosophy of history of the third great figure, Karl Marx. Thus, we shall consider Condorcet as the source of positivism, and Kant as a prime inspiration for Hegel's idealistic philosophy of history. Combined, the two help lead to Marx's dialectical materialism.

A. Gillies, *Herder* (Oxford, 1945). For Kant's review of Herder, see Immanuel Kant, *Kleinere Schriften zur Geschichtsphilosophie, Ethik und Politik*, herausgegeben . . . von Karl Vorländer (Leipzig, 1913). Emil L. Fackenheim, "Kant's Concept of History," *Kant-Studien*, Band 48, Heft 3, 1956–1957, adds Kant's short paper, *Conjectural Beginning of Human History (Mutmasslicher Anfang der Menschengeschichte)* to the list above, and gives a short précis of its contents (the article itself is to be found in *Werke*, Vol. VIII, Berlin, 1900–1955, as well as in the Vorländer volume). In general, Fackenheim, in his interesting article, views Kant's ideas on history in a more favorable light than I do but concludes all the same that "his construction of the historical process is a failure."

Was Kant, however, not a man of the Enlightenment? Indeed he was, and he even wrote a short piece entitled *What is Enlightenment?* I have chosen to treat him separately from our other figures of the Enlightenment, Voltaire and Condorcet, however, in order to emphasize my belief that he is really the beginning of a line of influence different from that of his English and French contemporaries. We shall see in detail what that line is if we turn to the *Idea for a Universal History*. Let us do so, however, with one caution: our interest is in the work itself, as well as in the extrapolations it permits.

2

There is a certain irony in the fact that the little philosopher—Kant was only five feet tall—who never left Königsberg wrote a universal history from a cosmopolitan point of view. It corresponds perfectly, however, with Kant's abstracting mind as well as with the content of his philosophy. History, as he tells us, has to be looked at in its full, universal time sweep, for only in history *as a whole* is nature's purpose realized. And history has to be considered from a cosmopolitan point of view because its necessary goal is a "perfect civic association of mankind," a point which Kant stresses not only in the *Idea*, but in *Eternal Peace*, where he defends "the idea of a cosmopolitan world law" against the charge of utopianism.

Kant begins the *Idea* by an assertion that human actions, like any other phenomena, are determined by general laws of nature. What appears accidental in the individual is determinate and predictable in the species. An example is marriage: although a marriage seems freely willed by the individual, yet the annual statistical tables exhibit a consistency which, according to Kant, show that marriages "occur according to stable natural laws." Such a social phenomenon can be compared to the oscillations of the weather: while we cannot predict individual states of affairs, we can rely on a regular support of the growth of plants, the flow of streams, and so forth, "at a uniform, uninterrupted pace."

The conclusion is one to warm the heart of Adam Smith. "Individual men," Kant tells us, "and even whole nations, little think, while they are pursuing their own purposes—each in his own way and often one in direct opposition to another—that they are unintentionally promoting, as if it were their guide, an end of nature which is unknown to them." Nevertheless, since man himself has neither instinct, like the animals, nor a rational plan of his own to guide him to a preconceived end, history, at first glance, seems pointless, like Shakespeare's "tale told by an idiot." Or, as Kant puts it in typical Enlightenment fashion, "It is hard to suppress a certain disgust when contemplating men's actions upon the world stage."[2]

The disgust is relieved only by the discovery that "in this senseless march of human events" nature has a plan and an end. This discovery, however, is the philosopher's task; or rather Kant poses it as a problem for a future Kepler or Newton of the historical world.[3] Kant himself will seek in the *Idea* only to provide a clue, or a guide, to this happy discovery. The whole point about Kant's attempt, however, is that he assumes from the beginning that man's random and free pursuits are to be considered *as if* they were subject to nature's laws—which Kant, as we shall see, equates with an aim or purpose of nature.

One major difficulty in understanding Kant's initial starting point is that it rests on a crucial distinction which he had made

[2] Kant adds that it seems as if the web of human history were woven "out of folly and childish vanity and the frenzy of destruction." Thus, in spite of his admiration for Rousseau, Kant does not appear to share his predecessor's admiration for the childlike state and favors, instead, the notion of the human race growing into reasoned control.

[3] The call for a Kepler of historical science is repeated by Henry Thomas Buckle, in his *History of Civilization in England* (1857); see the first chapter. Compare, however, the view of a contemporary historian, J. H. Hexter, "Personal Retrospect and Postscript," *Reappraisals in History* (Evanston, 1961), p. 202, where he says that "if there should be a historical revolution even remotely comparable in its dimensions to the scientific revolution of three centuries ago, it would be a revolution without Keplers or Galileos or Newtons."

earlier and at great length in his opus, *The Critique of Pure Reason:* the distinction between the phenomenal and noumenal world. It is a distinction to which we shall return later. For the moment we need only note that in the phenomenal world all is under the bonds of necessity and determinism, of causality. In the noumenal world (of which man cannot have sense knowledge) all can be conceived of as free and unconditioned. Thus, Kant is able to retain his belief, conveniently, in man as *essentially* a free agent but as behaving in the phenomenal world of history as a determined being under natural laws.

Having put aside for the moment the all-important question of man's freedom *outside of history*, Kant can proceed in at least a seminaturalistic fashion. His first proposition is, however, a teleological one: "All natural faculties of a creature are destined to unfold completely and according to their end." To support his point, Kant appeals to the evidence of anatomy, and declares that an organ which is not to be used is a contradiction in the teleological theory of nature. Now, with our modern minds, we cannot help but perceive a shadow of the Darwinian theory of natural selection and survival in this proposition; but it is only a shadow, for Kant did not believe in natural evolution and was thinking in terms of a fixed chain of being.

Kant's second proposition establishes man's special natural faculty as reason, and then asserts that "those natural faculties which aim at the use of reason shall be fully developed in the species, not in the individual." Man's reason develops, however, not by instinct but by experience, by trial and error, and must be transmitted through a series of generations. In his own way, then, Kant is saying that man is a cultural or historical animal.

According to Kant in his third proposition, this development of man as a cultural being is *willed by nature*. But it must be brought about by *man* out of his own struggles; he alone must secure the credit for bringing himself up from the crude, savage state to one of natural perfection. It is as if nature had deliberately challenged man by barely providing him with the requisite animal equipment—neither the horns of the bull, nor the claws of the lion—with which to face a harsh environment. All man's necessities, such as shelter from the elements and defence from other creatures, must be brought forth from himself. There is a touch of Vico in this formulation of Kant's.

What are the means which nature employs to achieve its end with man? It is "the antagonism of men in society," Kant answers; it is their "unsocial sociability." With this nice phrase, Kant once again links himself with Smith and the economists, only now in a larger field. By "unsocial sociability" Kant means man's drive to enter the social state as well as his resistance to that tendency; the combination threatens continually to dissolve society. These two tendencies of man— to associate himself and to isolate himself—are, for Kant, innate. Because of the mutual struggle which consequently arises among all men, man avoids falling into a dull "Arcadian" life of harmony and happiness. "Man wants concord; but nature knows better what is good for his kind; she wills discord."

In the single short paragraph which makes up this fourth proposition, Kant places himself at the intersection of a number of paths. Some stretch behind him, and link with moralists like Rochefoucauld and Bernard de Mandeville (the latter with his maxim, "Private Benefits, Public Evils") as well as with economists like Smith whom we have already mentioned. Others suggest a tantalizing trail, leading to Freud and his science of man's ambivalent personality. The most important link, however, is probably the one with theodicy. Like Alexander Pope, for example, who sought in the *Essay on Man* (1744) to "justify the ways of God to man," Kant thought of his universal history with its "unsocial sociability" as showing "the adjusting hand of a wise creator, not that of an evil spirit that has bungled in his own magnificent arrangement, or has spoiled it from envy"; it is a theme that Kant takes up again in the ninth and concluding proposition.

Kant's formulation also means that he has accepted the passions, rather than reason, as the motive force in history. As Collingwood cleverly perceives about Kant's scheme, "If history is the process in which man *becomes* rational, he cannot *be* rational at the beginning of it; therefore the force which serves as mainspring of the process cannot be human reason but must be the opposite of reason, that is, passion: intellectual ignorance and moral baseness."[4] It is, of course, from here only a step to the transmutation of "moral baseness" into moral good since the former serves the progressive purposes of history. This was a step Kant, with his moral freedom outside of history, never took; Smith before him, however, had taken it in economics, and Hegel after him was to take it in the courtroom of history.

One other implication attaches to Kant's "means." It is the recognition that the historical world is not to be thought of as a theatre for man's happiness. If man were happy, he would sink into an Arcadian stupor, and nature's purpose of making him develop his reason would be unfilled. This antihedonism also relates, as we shall see, to Kant's morality, for he insists on the categorical, that is, abstract and independent, rather than utilitarian or happiness aspect of a moral judgment or action. History and morality, then, are the two central foci about which Kant spins the human race; the difficulty is in reconciling the lines that lead from them, and thereby offering a satisfactory theodicy.

In the fifth proposition, Kant sets forth the key problem involved in man's progress from nature to a moral society: it is "the achievement of a civilized society which administers law universally." Starting from the "unsocial sociability" of man, we must devise a civic association which will reconcile freedom and authority. In reality, this is the same problem propounded by Rousseau in the *Social Contract;* and it is Rousseau's inspiration which is obvious in Kant's whole treatment

[4] R. G. Collingwood, *The Idea of History* (Oxford, 1946), pp. 101–102.

of this matter. Kant, however, is not too sanguine about a complete solution to the problem: as he tells us in the sixth proposition, that would be utopian, for "One cannot fashion something absolutely straight from wood which is as crooked as that of which man is made." Nevertheless, nature, having imposed this task on man, intends him to approximate the solution. It will, however, be the problem he solves last.

Before the solution, a perfect civic constitution, can be reached, the *external* relations between the states must be made conformable to law; for without the resolution of this latter problem the domestic commonwealth cannot itself be securely established under law. Kant's answer to the problem is a federal league, a union of nations, wherein even the smallest state could expect legal protection and security of its rights. The means by which this union will be brought about is, paradoxically, the very thing which it seeks to abolish: wars. The destructiveness of war will compel man to give up his "brute freedom" in exchange for peace and security. Even here, however, in the hoped-for "Eternal Peace" Kant appears afraid of man sinking into an Arcadian stupor, and he suggests that the federation itself will not be without disturbances, "else the powers of the human race would go to sleep." One suspects, too, that it is partly for this last reason that Kant wishes a federation of *independent* states rather than a universal state.

What of revolution as a means? Does Kant accept this along with wars? The answer is somewhat complicated. To begin with, Kant obviously prefers gradual and peaceful enlightenment to violent revolution. Indeed, he warns against such a revolution, for through it "the abandonment of personal despotism may be engendered and the end of profit-seeking and domineering oppression may occur, but never a true reform of the state of mind. Instead, new prejudices, just like the old ones, will serve as the guiding reins of the great, unthinking mass."[5] Yet Kant sympathized with the American and

---

[5] The quotation is from *What is Enlightenment?* For more of Kant's strictures against revolution, see his piece, *Eternal Peace*.

then welcomed tentatively the French Revolution. Perhaps the key to his attitude is to be found in a footnote to *Eternal Peace* where he makes the significant comment that political prudence, while effecting reforms, will at the same time "utilize revolutions *where nature produces them of itself*" [italics added]. It is a rather inglorious though judicious evasion of the issue: men ought not to resort to revolution, but where nature produces one, men may avail themselves of it.

It is not only, however, Rousseau's problem of the social contract to which Kant hearkens; it is also the protest in the *Discourse on the Arts and Sciences* to which he responds. Kant admits that in mankind's progress, before the last step is taken of joining the states in a federation, the rise of civilization (i.e., the arts and sciences), does not mean the emergence of culture (i.e., ethics).[6] In fact, Kant says, "Rousseau was not so very wrong when he preferred the condition of savages, if the last stage which our race has yet to surmount be left out of view." This middle stage, civilization, however, is only a temporary one, and will give way to a moral condition, culture, once peace in and among states is achieved. Then states will be free to turn their attention and resources from warlike preparations to the enlightenment and cultivation of their citizens. Thus, Kant's answer to Rousseau is to press on with man's necessary progress, rather than turn back to a state of nature.

Man's progress, for Kant, is assured. In the eighth proposition, he unites his initial assumptions into the conclusion that "the history of mankind viewed as a whole, can be regarded as the realization of a hidden plan of nature to bring about a political constitution, internally, and for this purpose, also externally perfect, as the only state in which all the capacities implanted by her in mankind can be fully developed." (Later, we shall hear the echo of this in Marx's view that the commu-

[6] Here Kant employs the division between culture and civilization which forms such an important element in Western thought from the eighteenth century on. See, for example, Raymond Williams, *Culture and Society: 1780–1950.* (Garden City, N.Y., 1960).

nist is the sole state of society in which the full development of human nature can occur; Kant's political constitution, of course, is quite different from the Marxist one.)

Is there any historical evidence for Kant's conclusion? Can we empirically verify his proposition? To his own question, "whether experience discloses anything of such a movement in the purpose of nature," he answers, "I would say, a little." Resorting to astronomical terms, Kant suggests why we can prove no more by experience: "For this revolution [*Kreislauf*] seems to require so much time that from the small distance which man has so far traversed one can judge only uncertainly the shape of the revolution's course and the relation of the parts to the whole." In the *Idea*, Kant follows this up with a comparison to the incomplete observations on the course of the sun and its satellites. Elsewhere, for example, in the *Prolegomena*, he suggests that "in the structure of an organized body, the end of each member can only be deduced from the full conception of the whole." The fundamental thought here is teleological: we can only judge the parts in terms of the completed whole.

At this point, one might have expcted Kant to hesitate. After all, the path of man's progress was not complete. How can we tell nature's intent with him until the end?[7] Kant, however, blithely skirts this obstacle to his theory, and asserts merely that the indications now available in history are sufficient—though for *this* conclusion he gives no evidence nor, indeed, arguments. Instead, he presses on hastily to the suggestion that we can accelerate "by our own rational efforts" the coming of this necessary progress.[8] To brace us for our task, Kant works out a nice chain of reasonings. State (i.e., military) power, he declares, requires economic power, and this can only be procured at its maximum rate by the fostering of free trade; free trade requires personal liberty of action and

[7] Cf. W. H. Walsh, *Philosophy of History: An Introduction* (New York, 1960), p. 128, for a similar criticism.

[8] We shall hear the echo of this idea, too, in Karl Marx.

even religious freedom; the coming of these freedoms, in turn, leads to general enlightenment, and this leads, gloriously, to the desired political end: the civilized society, internally and externally under universal law. There is an additional item to this cheery, loose "argument": wars will necessarily be eliminated because they interfere with trade, which now connects all states, and because they result in public debts.[9] One wonders what Kant's reaction would be today to the Soviet Union, and to all that its system implies.

Our real insight into Kant's, if not nature's, purpose, however, comes in the ninth proposition. The philosophic attempt to work out a universal history according to a plan of nature, Kant tells us, is possible and, what is more, *useful*. It seems as if we are back again, though in a new form, with the Enlightenment view of history and its stress on "useful truths." But we must be very careful here not to stop at a superficial resemblance. There are two very important additions that Kant makes to the idea of a "useful truth" in history. The first is heuristic; the second is pragmatic; and, combined, they differentiate Kant from the history is "philosophy teaching by examples" school of Voltaire or Condorcet.

The pragmatic aspect of Kant's idea peeps out in quotations like the following from *Eternal Peace*. He is talking about the spirit of commerce entailing the elimination of war: "In this way nature guarantees lasting peace by *the mechanism* of human inclinations; however the certainty that this will come to pass is not sufficient to predict such a future (theoretically). But for *practical* [italics added] purposes the certainty suffices and makes it one's duty to work toward this (not simply chimerical) state." We can piece out the rest of Kant's mes-

---

[9] Kant repeats this notion in *Eternal Peace*. See *The Philosophy of Kant*, edited with an introduction by Carl J. Friedrich (New York, 1949), p. 455, for a convenient translation. Kant, of course, shared the general view that public debt heralded the downfall of a nation, a view which was only discredited by the spectacular success of the British in combining a growing public debt, prosperity, and victory over the French in the Napoleonic Wars.

sage from the *Critique of Judgment*, where he talks of the idea of freedom whose "reality is the reality of a particular kind of causality (whose concept would be transcendent if considered theoretically), and as a causality of that kind it admits of verification by means of practical laws of pure reason and in the actual actions that take place in obedience to them, and, consequently, in experience." If I understand Kant correctly, he is saying that if we act on a belief, the belief becomes true; becomes fact. In sociology, today, this is called a self-fulfilling prophecy. In philosophy, it bears relationship to the pragmatism of William James. However looked upon, it is a highly suggestive—and dangerous—idea.[10]

The heuristic note comes from Kant's suggestion that *if* we assume a plan, for example that human affairs are adjusted to certain reasonable ends, then that assumed plan may serve as a guide through the myriad data of history. In this view, the "plan" is really an hypothesis, to be checked against the evidence. Thus, if one starts with Kant's hypothesis, there appears to be a regular progression toward improvements in constitutional government, from the Greeks, through the Romans, and to ourselves (i.e., Western Europe), who are "probably destined to give laws to all other parts of the world." To the charge that this idea or hypothesis is of an a priori character, Kant responds by disclaiming any intention of supplanting "work on true empirical history." His real intention is only to suggest what "a philosophical mind, who would have to be very knowledgable in history, could attempt from another viewpoint."

In order to judge Kant's "useful" and new "viewpoint" correctly, we must turn to some of his other work for illumination. It is for this reason that the *Idea* in itself is such a frustrating work to read: it seems clear and simple, and thus often

[10] Cf. Hannah Arendt, "History and Immortality," *Partisan Review*, XXIV, 1 (Winter, 1957). For the "self-fulfilling prophecy," see Robert K. Merton, *Social Theory and Social Structure* (New York, 1949), chap. VII.

simpleminded, but at every point Kant is relying on a whole
series of explanations which he is borrowing from or offering
elsewhere. Before entering on these explanations, however, we
might pause for a tentative summary statement about Kant. At
this point then, one might conclude that his main purpose in
contributing to the philosophy of history in the *Idea* appears
more as a call to hope and as an effort at theodicy than as an
attempt to work out there the parameters of historical knowledge.

3

There are four major aspects of Kant's work which we must
single out for especial attention: (1) epistemology; (2) freedom; (3) reason; and (4) teleology. Only if we understand
these more fully, an understanding drawn largely from Kant's
works other than the *Idea*, can we come to any comprehensive
appreciation and judgment of his philosophy of history.

1. *Epistemology.* The revolution in epistemology which
Kant effected was to turn the self from a passive receiver of
sensations into an active participant in the process of knowing.
Where sensationalists or empiricists like Locke and Hume envisioned man as a blank tablet or plate being bombarded by
sense impressions, which are then rather mysteriously arranged
into "ideas," Kant saw man as equipped with certain a priori
forms of sensibility (i.e., space and time) and categories of the
understanding (e.g., causality, substance, etc.). Through these,
experience was then filtered. Although these a priori forms and
categories do not tell us what their content will be—only experience tells us this—they do tell us under what form we will
perceive and conceive of this experience.

The result is that man becomes an integral part of the knowing process. As such, he is creative. He *thinks into nature*
rather than merely receiving her messages. Thus, Kant can
make the remarkable statement in his *Prolegomena to Any*

Future Metaphysics that "the understanding does not derive its laws (a priori) from, but prescribes them to, nature." Without going into further details on this very complicated subject, we can see what is sufficient for our purposes: Kant believes man approaches nature, physical or historical, with a priori concepts and thus, and thus alone, organizes the data which it presents to him. This explains Kant's advocacy of a "plan" in history, which will be supplied beforehand by a philosophical mind; and it is only a short step from this sort of view to Hegel's formula: "To him who looks upon the world rationally, the world looks rationally back."

There is a further, more tentative, extrapolation of Kant's position which should be made here. It is the notion that we not only think into nature, but that we also *act* into nature. This position emerges from what earlier I called Kant's pragmatism, where acting on a belief makes it become true. Thus, before we can *know* something, we must *create* it through our actions. Kant, however, did not particularly develop this notion, and it is better left as merely a suggestive extrapolation. What is certain is that Kant supplied a new basis for our knowing: instead of a sensationalistic epistemology we have his idealistic epistemology. The ramifications of this revolution, as we shall see, were far-reaching, stretching especially through Hegel to Marx, who combined the two epistemologies.

More immediate, however, were the developments in Kant's own philosophical work. On the basis of his new epistemology, Kant could set forth the division of the phenomenalogical and noumenal world which we mentioned earlier. Since we "know" the world only in terms of the forms and categories of our mind, we cannot know things as they really are, that is, before we have shaped them by our a priori. Thus, the noumenal world, the *ding an sich*, will eternally escape our knowing of it. In the phenomenal world, of course, all things are presented to us under the guise of causality, for we cannot perceive anything without imposing causality—one of the categories of our understanding—on it (just as we cannot perceive anything out of space and time). But do causality, space, and time obtain in the noumenal world? Or is that world free and unbounded? This is the next ramification of Kant's thought which we must explore.

2. *Freedom.* On this subject, Kant offers us a paradox. As phenomena we must think of ourselves as subject to necessity; thus, as we have seen, historical man is considered in the *Idea* as under general laws of nature. But as noumena, we must regard ourselves as free. In Kant's terminology, "Nature and freedom therefore can without contradiction be attributed to the very same thing, but in different relations—on one side as an appearance, on the other as a thing in itself." What, however, authorizes us to attribute freedom to man as noumenon when on Kant's own terms we can neither perceive nor conceive in that world? His answer is to turn from what he calls pure reason to the practical reason. On this latter basis, we can assert that freedom is a necessary consequence of the moral law: if man is not noumenally free, he cannot make moral decisions. Thus, though we cannot *really understand* why "Freedom . . . among all the ideas of speculative reason is the only one whose possibility we know a priori," we know it "as the condition of the moral law which we do know."[11]

To be moral, we must be free. And by a similar chain of reasoning, Kant is able to show that though we cannot "know" or prove the existence of God or immortality, nevertheless these are postulates required by the practical reason in the service of morality. (For those not of the Kantian persuasion, the argument is rather tenuous.) What is important for our purposes in all this are the consequences Kant draws from his system, and the use which could be made of these consequences by others, like Fichte and Hegel. What Kant does is

[11] *Critique of Practical Reason,* translated with an introduction by Lewis White Beck (New York, 1951), pp. 3–6; and *Prolegomena to Any Future Metaphysics,* with an introduction by Lewis White Beck (New York, 1951), p. 92.

to define freedom as the state of being unconditioned or un-determined by anything outside our own reason and will. If *we* subject nature to *our* will, then we are free. This, at least, is what I understand Kant to be saying in his rather gobbledy-gook prose: "The difference, therefore, between the laws of a system of nature to which the will is subject and of a system of nature which is subject to a will (as far as the relation of the will to its free actions is concerned) rests on this: in the former, the objects must be the causes of the conceptions which determine the will, and in the latter, the will is the cause of the objects." And just before this, Kant has talked of "the idea of a supersensuous nature, a nature not empirically given yet possible through freedom; to this nature *we give* [italics added] objective reality, at least in a practical context, because we regard it as the object of our will as *pure rational beings* [italics added]."[12]

This "supersensuous nature," it seems to me, Kant identifies as God. At the beginning of the world, as he has informed us, we must posit an "Unmoved mover," that is, a cause which is itself uncaused and therefore free. In Kant's words, "the deter-mination of the causality of beings in the world of sense as such can never be unconditioned, and yet for every series of conditions there must be something unconditioned, and conse-quently a causality which is entirely self-determining." Can we avoid the conclusion that if man becomes free, i.e., "entirely self-determining," as he must be to be moral, he also becomes God, a pure rational being? Kant, of course, would have re-coiled in horror at such a conclusion. As we know from his "crooked wood" metaphor, he thought man would never

---

[12] *Critique of Practical Reason*, pp. 45–46. The following quotation from Adolph Eichmann during his trial for the murder of millions of Jews makes for macabre reading; admittedly, my quoting it is purely *ad hominem*. Professing his belief in the philosophic principles of Im-manuel Kant, Eichmann declared: "I tried as best I could to live accord-ing to Kant's categorical imperative, but this I confess. Man is not a perfect instrument, he cannot always carry out his will 100 per cent." (Homer Bigard, The New York Times News Service, carried in the *Boston Herald*, 25 July, 1961).

become perfect. Yet, the implications in Kant's thought seem to me inescapably to lead in this direction. It is, basically, a religious thought: man partakes of the quality of the divinity.

The other conclusion which emerges from Kant's treatment of freedom is that freedom only prevails when the subject involved exists unconditioned by time. This, however, is as much as to say that Kant's *basic* thought is more mythical than historical. He is more interested in man standing outside of time, as an unvarying moral and rational being, than in man as a phenomenal creature, changing and developing within the confines of history. True, as we have seen, Kant did try to deal with man in time: the *Idea* is his offering on the altar of history. But the fundamental orientation of his thought, as we observe from his treatment of morality, is otherwise directed to a transcendent realm. We shall see this even more clearly if we turn our attention to his handling of reason.

3. *Reason.* In opposition, for example, to Hume with his stress on the passions, Kant views man as *predominantly* rational, and this in spite of his hat-tipping to the passions as a historical force. Further, aside from the *Idea*, he tends to view reason as a divine seed, implanted in man from the beginning, and developing transcendentally by moral exercise rather than through the trials of experience. Thus, talking in this case of metaphysics (equated here with pure reason), Kant declares it "is placed in us by nature itself and cannot be considered the production of an arbitrary choice or a causal enlargement in the progress of experience from which it is quite disparate."[13]

Further, metaphysics, and thus reason, is a completed, fixed thing; like Descartes before him, Kant claimed to be the artificer of the finished product. "For here," he boasts at the end of his *Prolegomena*, "is an advantage upon which, of all possible sciences, metaphysics alone can with certainty reckon: that it can be brought to such completion and fixity as to be in need

[13] *Prolegomena*, p. 102.

of no further change or be subject to any augmentation by new discoveries; because here reason has the sources of knowledge in itself, not in objects and their observation, by which its stock of knowledge could be further increased." The same note is sounded, querulously, toward the end of his life, in 1799, when Kant disclaims identity with one of his self-proclaimed epigoni:

I hold Fichte's *Wissenschaftslehre* to be a wholly untenable system . . . the presumption of crediting me with the intention of giving a mere propaedeutic to transcendental philosophy, and not the very system of such a philosophy, is to me incomprehensible. Such an idea could never have occurred to me, for I myself had declared in the 'Criticism of the Pure Reason' that the completed whole of pure philosophy was the best guarantee of the truth of the 'Criticism.' . . . The Critical philosophy, by its irresistible tendency to satisfy the reason in theory as well as in moral practice, must feel that it has to fear no change of opinions, no amendments, or a different body of doctrine; but that the system of criticism rests on a perfectly sound basis, for ever fortified.[14]

[14] Quoted in William Wallace, *Kant* (Philadelphia, 1896), pp. 81–82. The rejoinder by Schelling and Hegel, in their *Journal of Philosophy*, is most interesting: "It is evident that in this case the language is inseparable from the thing; that if we are to philosophize on Kant's lines, we must use his language; and that any attempt to abandon the letter at once carries us across the narrow line that bounds what may be called his philosophy. Kant, as every one knows, referred all his followers to the clear letter of his writings; and Kantians of the strictest sect have always been on their guard against departing from the master even in the words and outward form. . . . It can be proved by history that Kant had never studied philosophy in its grand and comprehensive type,—that Plato, Spinoza, Leibnitz even, were known to him only through the medium of a metaphysical doctrine, which about fifty years ago was dominant in the German universities—a scholastic metaphysic which, through several intervening stages, derived its origin from Wolf. . . . And thus although, within the circle in which his mode of approaching philosophy has placed him, the persistent tendency of his mind to reach totality in its science may influence our opinion of his personality, and of the high respect he deserves, it cannot alter our estimate of his philosophy. That remains what it was—a secondary derivative, not a native and original growth. His philosophy is a building which at the best rests upon the empirical earth, but in part also on the rubbish-heaps of forgotten systems—no universal system, self-originated and self-subsisting."

How can we reconcile these sentiments with the *Idea?* Obviously, Kant feels that no further development can take place in his system of the pure or the practical reason: in epistemology or ethics. Only the *practical objectification* of this system is possible; that is, its development in the sensuous world. That this is what Kant has in mind, though he tends to hide it from both himself and his readers by that overconscientious attempt at clarity resulting in the almost pure opaqueness which constitutes Kantian prose, can be glimpsed from the first part of the *Critique of Practical Reason*. There, talking of the reality of the moral law, he declares, "The moral law adds to the negative concept [of causality] a positive definition, that of reason which determines the will directly through the condition of a universal lawful form of the maxims of the will. Thus reason, which with its ideas always became transcendent when proceeding in a speculative manner, can be given for the first time an objective, although still only practical reality; its transcendent use is changed into an immanent use, whereby *reason becomes, in the field of experience, an efficient cause through ideas* [italics added]." Disclaim as he might, Kant cannot really avoid the responsibility for having inspired Hegel and Fichte with the notion that reason, and/or the will, create and shape the real world.[15]

In the *Idea* itself, Kant makes certain compromises between his completed system and the developing world. Man does not automatically evolve and make manifest his reason "in the field of experience" through his own rational powers. It is nature which holds the rational purpose, and man fulfills it by the selfish clash of his passional parts. Thus, there is a fundamental ambiguity in Kant's thought, brought on by his arbitrary division of the world into phenomena and noumena, into conditioned action and unconditioned reason and morality. It is an ambiguity which we cannot really resolve, but can only try to understand better by going a little deeper into Kant's belief in nature's rational purpose, i.e., into teleology.

[15] Kant and Hegel, of course, attached different meanings to reason.

4. *Teleology.* By teleology, Kant really means an "As-if" philosophy. We look at things—the world, man, and so forth —*as if* they had been constructed with a purpose in mind. In typical deistic vein, Kant declares, "If I say that we are compelled to consider the world *as if* it were the work of a Supreme Understanding and Will, I really say nothing more than that a watch, a ship, a regiment, bears the same relation to the watchmaker, the shipbuilder, the commanding officer as the world of sense . . . does to the unknown, which I do not hereby know as it is in itself but as it is for me, that is, in relation to the world of which I am a part." In short, "we conceive the world *as if* it came, in its existence and internal plan, from a Supreme Reason."[16]

This Supreme Reason, i.e., God, manifests itself in terms of nature. As early as 1755, in his first important paper, "Universal Natural History and Theory of the Heavens," in which he partially anticipates Laplace's nebular hypothesis as to the origin of the cosmos, Kant asserts that "it is thus evident that the essential properties of matter must spring from one mind, the source and ground of all beings: a mind, in which they belong to a solidarity of plan. All that is in reciprocal relations of harmony must be brought into unity in a single Being, from which it all depends. There is therefore a Being of all beings, an infinite mind and self-subsisting wisdom, from which nature in the full range of all its forms and features derives its origin, even as regards its very possibility."[17]

The production of nature by God is according to a plan which works by means of mechanical laws. And these, men can come to know. "I think," Kant declares, "we may in a sense say without temerity: Give me matter, and I will build a world out of it. I will show how a world comes to be evolved." Even Descartes could claim no more than this.

[16] *Prolegomena,* p. 106.
[17] Wallace, *op. cit.,* p. 17. The full account of Kant's *Universal Natural History and Theory of the Heavens* (*Allgemeine Naturgeschichte und Theorie des Himmels*) can be found in Kant's *Cosmogony,* edited and translated by William Hastie (Glasgow, 1900).

But what of the biological world, could that like the physical be built by man? "Can we truly claim," Kant asks, "such a vantage ground in speaking of the least plant or insect? Are we in a position to say: Give me matter, and I will show you how a caterpillar can be generated? Must we not here stop at the first step, from our ignorance of the real inner constitution of the object, and the intricate complexity which it includes?" Later, in another essay, Kant answered his rhetorical question with definitiveness: the question of how organic matter might have arisen from inorganic matter is "totally beyond any natural philosophy possible for man."[18]

Nevertheless, though we cannot ever know, according to Kant, God's mechanical laws for producing organic beings, and hence man, we can look at nature *as if* it has a plan within each of its creatures and for creation as a whole. No organ is without its use, and no totality of organs without its plan. What that plan may be is never made quite clear, for Kant's views on the organic process seem to waver between a theory of evolutionary change according to a fixed plan and the more stationary concept of the great chain of being.[19] On the question of man's historical and social evolution, however, Kant's views are quite precise. "Nature's mechanical course," Kant announces,

. . . evidently reveals a teleology: to produce harmony from the very disharmony of men even against their will. If this teleology and the laws that effect it is believed to be like an unknown cause compelling us, it is called *fate*. But if it is considered in the light of its usefulness for the evolution of the world, it will be called *providence*—a cause which, responding to a deep wisdom, is directed toward a higher goal, the objective end-in-itself [*Endzweck*] of mankind which predetermines this evolution. We do not really *observe* this providence in the artifices of nature, nor can we *deduce* it from them. But we can and must *add this thought*

[18] It is hardly necessary to point out here, in the light of modern work in biology and biochemistry, the error in Kant's prediction.
[19] Cf. Arthur Lovejoy, *The Great Chain of Being* (Cambridge, Mass., 1953).

(as in all relations of the form of things to ends in general), in order to form any kind of conception of its possibility. We do this in analogy to human artifices.

And Kant caps this explanation by telling us that the term nature is more appropriate and more modest than the term providence, "for by talking of providence we are arrogantly putting the wings of Icarus on our shoulders as if to get closer to the secret of its unfathomable purpose."[20]

Disclaimer aside, there is no mistaking Kant here: nature equals providence. Thus, Kant's teleology of nature is a providential explanation. As such, teleology has also become theodicy, as we have seen earlier from a different point of view.

Yet we must not forget Kant's insistence that teleology is based solely on a *regulative* principle, a matter which he explains more fully in the *Critique of Judgment*, and that we merely operate *as if* there were a Godlike plan. Actually, according to Kant, we can never know for sure about the thing-in-itself, i.e., God or noumenon. To this statement one might add, on the basis of Kant's other work and as an unauthorized extrapolation, the words *except insofar* as our reason partakes of the divinity and becomes itself unconditioned.

At this point I tremble for my own audacity at putting on the wings of Daedalus and soaring through Kant's work in this manner, seeking to rise above his labyrinthian system and to perceive its plan from on high. My only excuse is that, as there is no acceptable scientific means by which to check and evaluate Kant's assumed teleology, I am forced to believe that he wished his "verification" to come from his system of reason, rather than from the empirical data of history. And, as we have seen, that system of reason, with its partner, freedom, lies ultimately in an unconditioned, and therefore unhistorical, sphere. Thus, in the last analysis, in spite of Kant's obeisances in the *Idea* toward "true empirical history," his universal history from a cosmopolitan view is fundamentally a theodicy from an a priori and transcendental view. Whatever heuristic

[20] *Eternal Peace*, in *The Philosophy of Kant*, pp. 448–449.

elements might be present in Kant's epistemology—so that regulative principles might become hypotheses—they are cancelled out by the rest of his work. Looked at in this way, the *Idea* takes on all sorts of meanings which are not present at a first, autonomous reading. The fundamental meaning, as I see it, is that Kant has opened the way for mystical attributions of purpose to God—and, by a cold, proud, and (overtly) unemotional Reason, lured men from the empirical pursuit of historical knowledge.

4

It must be clear by now that I have strong reservations about the Kantian philosophy of history. I share with Nietzsche the feeling that Kant is an old Tartuffe. Thus, where others stress Kant's sweetness of character and nobility of purpose, I see the added hues of a petulant dogmatist, annoyed at public indifference to his great work; of a thin-blooded recluse, whose knowledge of human nature lacks depth and subtlety of insight. Others stress Kant's enlightened political views; I see also the half-hearted courage and the conformity to authority of a careful old man. And instead of the shining figure of the Enlightenment, clothed in love for humanity—a figure set off by most commentators against the villains Hegel and Marx—I see a Kant whose definitions of freedom and reason, whose epistemology, and whose philosophy of history prefigure and prepare the way for the two figures mentioned.[21] In short, my perspective, while I hope not shutting out completely the conventional view of the Königsberg philosopher, allows for a more complete, and illuminating, picture of him and his thought.

Having said this, I wish now to launch even a further charge. Kant was, *for present purposes*, and leaving aside

[21] Naturally, whether this is to Kant's credit or discredit depends also on one's evaluation of Hegel and Marx.

temporarily his evocative work concerning the natural sciences, a surprisingly poor philosopher of science.[22] By his teleology, he brought into the human sciences that old chestnut, nature's purpose, which had just been so painfully excluded from the natural sciences. In the latter, for example, Aristotle had contended that stones dropped because nature willed them to drop. By the seventeenth century, however, Galileo and Newton had rejected this useless anthropomorphism in favor of a functional approach; instead of purpose, they sought after a relationship of forces. In history, however, Kant reintroduces the idea of nature willing events. It is not enough for him to say that men pursue their own selfish ends and come out to unintended consequences, and that the latter *may* be dealt with as if they were a law of nature. Though this thought lurks within Kant's scheme, he pushes it aside with his appeal to the noumenal world. Thus, overlooking the fact that only man (and perhaps other animals) has desires, purpose, and will, Kant moves into the mumbo-jumbo land of attributing personality to nature.

Similarly, though he assumes that man's self-development occurs in history, such a development is really only of man's *reason*. And that reason exists, basically, in a timeless vacuum, autonomous and complete from the beginning. The situation is the same with Kant's definition of freedom: it is not possible in this world, but only in the noumenal (the next?) world.

These aspects of Kant's overall thought are only partially mitigated by the fact that in the *Idea* he ostensibly seeks to justify and understand man's progress on *earth*, in secular terms, and not in some other world, in otherworldly terms. Even so, there remains a fundamental ambiguity between his general metaphysics and his philosophy of history; it relates to morality. For example, in his *Critique of Practical Reason*,

---

[22] This, of course, is a large dismissal. Kant's work in the epistemology of the natural sciences is of momentous importance and worth. It is suggested here only that it ought not to mislead us into too flattering a judgment of his philosophy of history.

Kant insists that a moral action must be taken by an individual irrespective of its end or consequences. However, when he comes to his philosophy of history, he modifies that position. He realizes that, empirically speaking, there is much evil in the world which then produces good; and many good-intentioned actions which produce evil. The result is his theodicy, which, like alchemy, transmutes evil into good. Yet for Kant the initial evil is still defined as evil. It is only with Hegel that we get a new definition of morality: moral action is that which is in accord with the historical process—"Die Weltgeschichte ist das Weltgericht."

The seeds of this last idea, as well as of the ideas concerning reason, freedom, and direction in history, which we have already discussed, are all in Immanuel Kant. He, of course, like a good Tartuffe, was almost completely unconscious of the extrapolations which might, and would, result from his philosophy. Nevertheless, it is in the very heart of the Enlightenment philosophy itself (for Kant was a product of the so-called Age of Reason, as well as the progenitor of the modern idealistic foundation of knowledge) that the new ideas of the nineteenth century in relation to philosophy of history first came to light.

VI

Hegel

> *Know that, by nature, every creature seeks to become like God. Nature's intent is neither food nor drink nor clothing nor comfort, nor anything else in which God is left out. Whether you like it or not, secretly nature seeks, hunts, tries to ferret out the track on which God may be found.*
>
> MEISTER ECKHART

1

THE DIFFICULTIES in the way of understanding Hegel's philosophy of history are manifold. I shall mention three. First, Hegel's philosophy of history is only part of his total system, and it is frequently dependent on what he has said elsewhere, about logic, political philosophy, and so forth. For example, in the *Philosophy of Right*, the section on philosophy of history comes at the very end of the treatment of social ethics, and is obviously supposed to be part of the latter. As Hegel himself claimed, his philosophy is a whole, in which no one part can be correctly comprehended in isolation from the totality. Second, Hegel's language is often a private creation; it is as if in the realm of Hegel's mind only the words of his own coining serve, while all others are counterfeit. Thus, the strain of remembering his definitions may break the back even of the most willing reader. Third, the concepts with which Hegel struggles are of the most abstruse and reified nature, and only occasionally touch the ground from which the reader, like Antaeus, might otherwise draw strength.

Nevertheless, we may take the advice of John Stuart Mill that "A man of clear ideas errs grievously if he imagines that whatever is seen confusedly does not exist: it belongs to him, when he meets with such a thing, to dispel the mist, and fix the outlines of the vague form which is looming through it."[1] Fortunately, we are helped in our effort to dispel the mist surrounding Hegel's philosophy of history by a number of favorable factors. First, among Hegel's various works, the philosophy of history is one of his most readily understandable productions. Unlike Kant, for example, Hegel's treatment of philosophy of history is a full and comprehensive one wherein he sets forth not only his leading concepts but their exemplification in the concrete data of history. Second, in spite of the obscurity of his conceptual language, Hegel's prose abounds with striking images and intense and luminous phrases; on occasion, he is poet as much as philosopher. Third, the subjects which he investigates, such as the state, morality, and the role of the hero, as well as the way in which he approaches them, via a historical dialectic, are interesting and congenial to us; indeed, they are so because Hegel has helped train us to his way of looking at these matters.

If we persevere through Hegel we shall conclude that the effort to comprehend him and his philosophy of history is both possible and well worth making. At the end of our labors we should be able to discern his important achievements as follows. (1) He serves as the transition from religious to philo-

[1] John Stuart Mill, *Dissertations and Discussions*, 3 vols. (Boston, 1865), Vol. I, p. 378. Mill himself, however, seems to have distrusted Hegel. Ought I to add that I make no pretense to a full study of Hegel's philosophy, but only of his philosophy of history, seen in the light of as much of his overall work as seems pertinent?

sophical thinking in modern times; whereas the *philosophes* rejected religious ideas completely, Hegel metamorphosed them into secular creations. (2) He is a bridge in the shift from philosophy to social theory; after Hegel come Marx and a whole host of "scientific" social thinkers. (3) He is a fundamental starting point in the effort to establish the logic and epistemology of the cultural sciences, what the Germans call *Geisteswissenschaften*, and to differentiate them from the natural sciences. In this effort, Hegel, probably more than any other philosopher, "historized" the modern world.[2]

All of these achievements were turned by Hegel to very practical use. On their basis, or, better still, in the course of working them out, he offers new and controversial definitions of such age-old matters as morality and freedom; comments on the nature of society and the state, and on the role of the hero; and weaves a pattern of history out of the chaos of man's past. In the course of this last, he also presents a new solution to the theodicy problem; and, on a less edifying note, while justifying the ways of God to man, he also seems to justify the ways of the Prussian King to his subjects. To understand these matters, however, we had better try to place Hegel against the historical background which he did so much to highlight.

2

It was Hegel himself who claimed that philosophy exists in the actual world and that it is a "child of its times." Comparing it to the individual, he says, "so philosophy too is its own time apprehended in thoughts. It is just as absurd to fancy that a philosophy can transcend its contemporary world as it is to

---

[2] For some of the points listed, see Carl Becker, *The Heavenly City of the Eighteenth-Century Philosophers* (New Haven, 1932), which deals with the shift from religious to philosophical thinking, though not with Hegel's role in this movement; Herbert Marcuse, *Reason and Revolution: Hegel and The Rise of Social Theory* (New York, 1941); and Wilhelm Dilthey, *Einleitung in die Geisteswissenschaften* (1883).

fancy that an individual can overleap his own age." Thus, Hegel implies that he, too, is a product of his period, and that to understand his philosophy, we must grasp at least the outlines of his life in its connection with the historical times in which he lived.

Georg Wilhelm Friedrich Hegel was born in Stuttgart, in the Duchy of Württemberg, in the year 1770. He was a Swabian, a South German, without much initial sympathy for Prussia, a fact often forgotten by those who see in Hegel merely a Prussian nationalist. Indeed, his father was a minor functionary in the Württemberg local fiscal administration, and Hegel's future admiration for the bureaucratic class probably sprang from this source rather than from acquaintance with the Prussian civil service.

At the Stuttgart Gymnasium, Hegel took his schooling till the age of 18. It was during this period that he immersed himself in Greek thought and literature, an influence which permeated all his philosophical and political speculations. At Tübingen University, where Hegel went to study theology, his friendship with the poet Hölderlin fostered his passion for the Greek world. His other close friendship, however, with Schelling, turned him increasingly toward philosophy and away from the arid, abstract theology which was taught at the university. Nevertheless, upon graduation—who can resist telling this story, so encouraging to potential young philosophers today—his report, while characterizing him as average in all other studies, noted that he was below par in one subject: philosophy.

While Hegel was at Tübingen University, aged 19, the French Revolution broke out. The effect on Hegel was profound. Though later he was to turn against the abstract understanding of the *philosophes*, he supported the Revolution itself up until the Reign of Terror, and even that event did not completely disillusion him. Instead, Hegel retained the Revolutionary ideals, of Reason and Freedom, and the Revolution's reforms as the basis upon which his own thoughts might develop; so to speak, as the thesis against which he might play the antithesis of the counterrevolutionary ideas in order to reach his own synthesis. All of this we shall see concretely, when we deal with the last part of his *Philosophy of History*.

On leaving the University, in 1793, Hegel took on tutorial positions to support himself. The first post, not too happy a one, was with an aristocratic family at Bern, Switzerland; the second, with a merchant family in Frankfurt, was more congenial. During this period, stretching up to 1800, Hegel began to develop his own ideas. He read widely—Kant, Fichte, Rousseau, Schelling—and experimented in various manuscripts (which were published only after his death) with a number of different literary styles and philosophic approaches. According to many scholars, this period witnessed a sharp break in Hegel's thinking: from a sympathetic member of the Age of Enlightenment to a romantically oriented member of the Storm and Stress movement.[3] In any case, whatever the truth about his romanticism, Hegel at this time was unquestionably developing his own ideas, and he was doing so in terms largely of *religious* meditation and speculation. It is from this period that his so-called theological works date; but more of this a bit further on.

In 1801, Hegel joined his friend Schelling at the University of Jena. Jena was then the scene of a brilliant scientific and literary culture which, though still flourishing, was beginning to lose its effulgent colors. Locus of the famous meeting of Goethe (Minister of Education for the Duke of Weimar, under whose jurisdiction the town of Jena lay) and Schiller in 1794 at a gathering of the Jena Scientific Society, as well as having been graced by Fichte's occupancy of the chair of

---

[3] A number of other scholars, however, and I place myself in this group, have deep reservations about Hegel's "romanticism." As examples of the debate, see Richard Kroner's Introduction to Hegel's *On Christianity: Early Theological Writings*, translated by T. M. Knox (New York, 1961), pp. 14 ff. for arguments favoring the interpretation of Hegel as a romantic, and Walter Kaufmann, *From Shakespeare to Existentialism* (Garden City, N.Y., 1960), pp. 138–140, for a brief rebuttal.

philosophy at the University (1793–1799), Jena was to serve as Hegel's springboard into public notice. Here he first worked with Schelling, in the writing and editing of a journal of philosophy, and then broke with him over the latter's romanticism and disdain for reasoned as opposed to aesthetic experience.

At last, in 1807, Hegel stood on his own feet, with the publication of his *Phenomenology of Spirit*. In this book, Hegel sounded almost all the themes he was to develop in his subsequent works. It is at once the most literary of his efforts, and perhaps also the most difficult. Striving to bring forth what Josiah Royce called a "logic of passion," Hegel in the *Phenomenology* remade the philosophic world while attempting to remake the world philosophically.[4] At this point Hegel could well have said of himself what he had written a short time before to a friend about Napoleon, who, in 1806, on the eve of a battle in which he would defeat the Prussian army, rode through the streets of Jena, where Hegel saw him in the flesh. Deeply impressed, Hegel wrote: "I saw the Emperor, that World-soul, riding through the city to reconnoitre. It is in truth a strange feeling to see such an individual before one, who here, from one point, as he rides on his horse, is reaching over the world, and remoulding it."[5]

The battle of Jena, transforming the world by the sword while Hegel, writing the *Phenomenology of Spirit*, was transforming it by the pen, temporarily ended Hegel's university career. Forced by the closing of the University to seek a livelihood elsewhere, Hegel took a position first as editor of a newspaper in Bamberg, and then, for eight years (1808–1816) as rector of a gymnasium in Nuremberg. Here he favored his students with a lecture version of his system—what, one wonders, did they make of it all!—and wrote *The Science of Logic*

[4] Cf. Jean Hyppolite, *Genèse et structure de la Phénomenologie de l'esprit de Hegel* (Paris, 1946).

[5] *Briefe von und an Hegel: 1785–1812*, herausgegeben von Johannes Hoffmeister (Hamburg, 1952), Vol. I, p. 120. (Hegel an Niethammer. 13 October, 1806).

(1812–1816). Also, unlike Kant and so many other philosophers, he married.

With the fall of Napoleon in 1815, Hegel's fortunes seem
coincidentally to have improved. In 1816 he was appointed to
the Chair of Philosophy at Heidelberg; and here he published
his *Encyclopedia of the Philosophical Sciences*. Then, in 1818,
he was called to Berlin to fill Fichte's chair at the University,
and from this position he reigned over German philosophy
until his death in the great cholera epidemic of 1831. Before
then, however, he had published his *Philosophy of Right*
(1820) and delivered the lectures on Philosophy of Religion,
Philosophy of Art, History of Philosophy, and, of major interest for us, Philosophy of History, all to be published
posthumously.

Before leaving Hegel's life, however, a brief comment on his
appointment to Berlin in 1818 and a brief summary of the
background factors to his philosophy. It is frequently charged
against Hegel that he was called to Berlin to be the spokesman
for Prussian reactionism or conservatism. (Though these are
quite different, the charge is usually made indiscriminately.)
This, of course, may be so. But it is subject to challenge on
external and internal data.

The external data must revolve around the political situation
in Prussia during and after the Revolutionary and Napoleonic
period. As is well known (though often forgotten in this discussion), in order to defeat the French, Prussia adopted some
of the French reforms. The abolition of serfdom, the opening
of various trades to talent, and universal conscription, all these
borrowings were necessary in order to overcome the enemy.
Many of the reformers, however, wished for the reforms out
of sincere belief as well as out of patriotism. Remembering the
early enthusiasm of Hegel and his friends for the French Revolution, we may call some of these people "liberals."

After the fall of Napoleon, however, a reaction set in in
Prussia, as in so many other countries of Europe. Against the
continuing desire of the liberals for a constitution, with its

guarantees of law and order, and for various freedoms, such as of press and speech, stood conservatives who wished to preserve the status quo, and reactionaries who wished a return to the old regime (or to some idealized version thereof).[6] These factions fought for power around the king. Thus, Hardenberg, a liberal minister, stood next to Marwitz, a reactionary nobleman. Which group called Hegel to Berlin? Surely, it is difficult to believe that the conservatives were able to penetrate the smokescreen of Hegel's prose and to see one of themselves; certainly the reactionaries could not do so. Nor is there much reason to believe that the liberals could have been entirely happy with Hegel's politics. Perhaps all of the groups, in puzzled fashion, believed they would be able to use him for their own ends. And perhaps, although it sounds naïve to say this, Hegel may have been called to Berlin because he was the outstanding philosopher of Germany and had not made himself into a political undesirable.

Hegel, it must be acknowledged, was very careful not to antagonize the powers-that-be. Thus, in the Preface to his *Philosophy of Right* he went to great lengths to show that a state, with a correct knowledge of philosophy and what it seeks to do, which is to comprehend the state *as it is* and not to construct a state *as it ought to be* (we will see later what Hegel really meant by this view, however), would support true philosophy. But this sort of statement and behavior could have been for Hegel, and probably was, simple cautionary camouflage. To anyone who has lived in a state of restrictions and censorships—say, in Franco Spain—it will be understand-

[6] For the German political situation after the French Revolution, see Reinhold Aris, *History of Political Thought in Germany from 1789–1815* (London, 1936); and Karl Mannheim, "Conservative Thought," in *Essays on Sociology and Social Psychology*, P. Kecskemeti (ed.) (New York, 1953). Also, Treitschke's *History of Germany in the Nineteenth Century*, translated by Eden and Cedar Paul (New York, 1916), Vol. II, chaps. III, V. The argument about Hegel's political involvement is carried on with vigor by T. M. Knox, "Hegel and Prussianism," *Philosophy*, XV, 57 (January, 1940), and E. F. Carritt, "Discussion: Hegel and Prussianism," *ibid.*, XV, 58 (April, 1940).

able how an intellectual must resort frequently to double-talk
and pious ambiguity to preserve his position.

The true test of Hegel's intentions regarding the Prussian
government is, therefore, the internal data: his writings. On
this basis, it seems logical that Hegel came to Berlin to pursue
his own purposes. He was trying to synthesize reason and
religion, the Revolution and the counterrevolution, out of the
depths of his own philosophical position. Where this coincided
with the government's wishes, and undoubtedly a number of
such overlaps existed, it was either accident or because Hegel,
out of conviction, shared certain conservative views. One must
remember, however, that in the *Philosophy of Right* he attacked not only Fries, a radical, but von Haller, a reactionary,
and Savigny, a conservative.[7] In short, Hegel's position was his
own, and a rather unique one, as the later emergence of left-
and right-wing Hegelians would seem to suggest. Thus, it can
only be understood in terms of a critical analysis per se and not
by a pejorative attribution of Hegel to the propaganda department of the Prussian state.[8]

Nevertheless, as I have tried to suggest earlier, such a critical
analysis of Hegel must take place against an informed attention
to his background. The influences on Hegel were many, and

[7] It is necessary to call attention once again to the looseness of these
classifications.

[8] One of the worst offenders in this latter view is Karl Popper.
Brilliant in the field of the logic of the physical sciences, Popper allows
his prejudices to lead him astray concerning Hegel and the logic of the
historical sciences. See his *The Open Society and Its Enemies,* 2 vols.
(London, 1945; 4th revised ed. in 1962), Vol. II, "The High Tide of
Prophecy: Hegel, Marx and the Aftermath," and Walter Kaufmann's
criticism of this work in "The Hegel Myth and Its Method," in *From
Shakespeare to Existentialism.* Karl Rosenkranz, *Hegels Leben* (Berlin,
1844), gives the details of Hegel being called to fill Fichte's chair in
Berlin by the Prussian Minister of Education, Baron von Altenstein.
Rosenkranz pictures Altenstein as a reforming minister, and considers
that "the Hegelian philosophy is in truth the completion [*Vollendung*]
of the Kantian," pp. 317–318. R. Haym, *Hegel und seine Zeit* (Berlin,
1857), p. 356 and chap. 15, seems to offer somewhat less support for my
view, but Kuno Fischer, *Hegels Leben, Werke und Lehre* (Heidelberg,
1901), pp. 124–129, reconfirms it with his description of post-1815
Prussia, Altenstein's aims, and the place of Hegel in those aims.

many of them vague; but they were unusually important. For example, he always had in mind the ideal of the Greek polis; he constantly wrestled with the question of Christian belief; and he was a child of the French Revolution and of the Napoleonic and Restoration periods which followed it. Around him, too, were the beginnings of the Industrial Revolution; and, along with his Plato and Aristotle, he read Smith and Ricardo. Perhaps more than any other thinker before Marx, Hegel was *consciously* and *overtly* affected by the historical events occurring about him; but this, after all, is what we might expect from a philosopher of history who recognized so dramatically that he could not "overleap his own age."

3

The approach to Hegel's philosophy of history is probably best made through his religious views. These take their earliest significant form in the youthful, unpublished essays he compiled while a family tutor at Berne and Frankfort, between 1795 and 1799. First brought out in 1907, after Wilhelm Dilthey called attention to them, by Hermann Nohl under the title *Hegels theologische Jugendschriften* (one critic thinks they are better called "anti-theological" essays), they comprise four titles and show the evolution of Hegel's thought and style during this period.[9]

The first thing to be said about Hegel's approach to religion is that it sets itself in opposition to the antihistorical natural religion of the Enlightenment. Hegel conceived of religious belief as rooted in man, not the heavens, and as constantly changing. Where *philosophes* like Voltaire and Condorcet dismissed traditional religion as a mass of outworn superstition,

[9] The English edition, awkwardly titled and which does not include all of the essays, is *On Christianity: Early Theological Writings by Friedrich Hegel, supra.* See the comment on this work by Walter Kaufmann, "The Young Hegel and Religion," *op. cit.* The "anti-theological" phrase is Kaufmann's.

Hegel, with grave irony, asks the more important question: "How is it possible to explain the construction of a fabric which is so repugnant to human reason and so erroneous through and through?" He answers that religion cannot be considered "in *abstraction* from the manners and characters of the nations and epochs which believed it." Religion, in sum, is both a *constant* concern of human beings and a *historically changing* concern.

Specifically, in these youthful essays, Hegel studied the history of the Jews and of the early Christians. In "The Positivity of Christian Religion" he sought an answer to the question of why Jesus had broken with the formal Jewish religion, and why, after his break, Christianity itself lapsed into a positive religion, grounded on law and authority rather than on subjective conviction. Throughout, Hegel directs his attention to the evolution of religious beliefs, and even takes the same attitude to Jesus himself, whom he treats as a developing, historical personality. As Hegel remarks, "Only through the bitter experience of the fruitlessness of his efforts did the ingenious youth fade away and give place to a man who spoke with bitter vehemence, with a heart exasperated by hostile resistance."

Jesus is further viewed as the first "hero" or transgressor against an accepted morality. Later, however, in the essay on "The Spirit of Christianity and Its Fate," Hegel introduces an even earlier "hero," Abraham, for Hegel in effect equates religion with morality, declaring that "the aim and essence of all true religions, our religion included, is human morality." Moreover, since religion and morality are inseparable, Hegel reaffirms his opposition to the Enlightenment idea that religion is a dispensable appendage of man.[10] The problem, instead (for Hegel does not rest with a mere reaffirmation of traditional religion), is to turn religion into philosophy; or, as Hegel would phrase it, to add to the intuition of religion the reason of philosophy.

---

[10] See Hegel's *Philosophy of Mind*, translated from *The Encylopaedia of the Philosophical Sciences* by William Wallace (Oxford, 1894), pp. 154–166, para. 552.

At the center of Hegel's attention to religion is his concern with subjective faith versus positive law. Lutheran to his core, Hegel believed that inner conviction, not outer and formal subservience to ecclesiastical authority, was the essence of religion and thus of morality. Therefore he opposed both the subjection of the individual conscience or will to a "majority vote" or "general will," produced by ecclesiastic "'contract" ("a contract about faith is inherently impossible," he declared), and the separation, as in Kantian morality, of abstract understanding and human passion ("the understanding can never transform principles into practice"). On the basis of these positions, we are well on the way to Hegel's demand regarding the state: The individual must freely and subjectively *will* the right which is posited by *reason*.

In these essays, too, Hegel first talks about the "spirit of the age." Its essence is a people's conception of God. For Hegel, however, this last is no mere abstract dogmatic position; it is rather the result of an interplay between psychological attitudes and political circumstances around the pole of religious ideas and passions. This "spirit," of course, changes. In a revealing and inspired passage, Hegel points out:

The supplanting of paganism by Christianity is one of those remarkable revolutions whose causes the thoughtful historian must labor to discover. Great revolutions which strike the eye at a glance must have been preceded by a still and secret revolution in the spirit of the age, a revolution not visible to every eye, especially imperceptible to contemporaries, and as hard to discern as to describe in words. It is lack of acquaintance with this spiritual revolution which makes the resulting changes astonishing. The supersession of a native and immemorial religion by a foreign one is a revolution which occurs in the spiritual realm itself, and it is thus of a kind whose causes must be found all the more directly in the spirit of the times.[11]

Hegel is concerned, in these early essays, with spiritual changes which involve the traditional religions. When he comes to write his *Phenomenology of Spirit*, it is a similar but

[11] *On Christianity*, p. 152.

different sort of spiritual change he has in mind: the philosophical revolution which has broken through into actuality with the events of 1789. "It is not difficult," he comments, "to see that our epoch is a birth-time, and a period of transition. The spirit of the age has broken with the age as it has hitherto existed, and with the old ways of thinking, and is in the mind to let them all sink into the depths of the past and to set about its own transformation." Hegel is obviously comparing his own period to the "supplanting of paganism by Christianity." His task, when he comes to the *Philosophy of History*, will be to discern and describe both the earlier "supplanting" and the contemporary birth-time, and indeed all such spiritual revolutions throughout the whole course of history.

Clearly, then, the way to understand history is to chart the "spirit of the age" of various periods of time, and to penetrate to the still and secret revolutions which dethroned them. As we have seen, Hegel's "spirit of the age" is largely a religious concept (expanded in the way I have suggested), and it is therefore by a study of the great religious movements that he can approach his subject. Thus, religious insight becomes philosophy of history.

4

Hegel begins his *Philosophy of History* with an explanation of the different types of history. The first is Original History, written by a contemporary of the events described: Thucydides is an example. The second is Reflective History, and comprises four different kinds: (1) universal history, which surveys the entire history of a people or a country; (2) pragmatic history, where we seek to extract "lessons" from history (for example, the Enlightenment approach); (3) critical history, which evaluates historical narratives and examines their truth and trustworthiness; and (4) fragmentary history, which examines one strand of a people's past—art, law, or religion—

from a sweeping, universal point of view. This last sort of history serves as transition to the third type, the Philosophical. Hegel initially defines the latter as "the thoughtful contemplation of history"; then he gives us the additional information that "The sole thought which philosophy brings to the treatment of history is the simple concept of *Reason*." Obviously, the only real definition of what Hegel means by Philosophical History is his whole book.

The first thing to notice about Hegel's types of history is that they revolve about the question of viewpoints. The Original historian shares the spirit of his age; the Reflective historian belongs to another period and spirit, different from the one which he is trying to describe, to use, to criticize, or to examine fragmentarily; and the Philosophical historian, to anticipate a bit, is the one who has penetrated to an understanding of the Spirit which manifests itself in particular spirits of the age. Fragmentary history stands as transition to the latter because it seeks to trace the course of Spirit through the ages in a particular field, such as art. When the various fragmentary histories are seen together, we discover the same spirit of the age permeating *all* the fields, art, law, and religion. From this, it is only a step—but what a giant step—to an awareness of a putative Spirit of history which informs and animates all these spirits of the age (called today, more conventionally, "cultural wholes").

The next thing to state about Hegel's types of history is that with them he rejects the simple approach of the Enlightenment historians—their history is "philosophy teaching by examples." Quite flatly, Hegel declares that we cannot learn from history. "What experience and history teach," he says, "is this—that peoples and governments never have learned anything from history, or acted on principles deduced from it. Each period is involved in such peculiar circumstances, exhibits a condition of things so strictly idiosyncratic, that its conduct must be regulated by considerations connected with itself, and itself alone." Remembering the "cult of antiquity" practiced during the Revolutionary period, Hegel scathingly remarks, "nothing can be shallower than the oft-repeated appeal to Greek and Roman examples during the French Revolution."

What, then, is the purpose and meaning of history? The answer is tied up with the nature of "history" itself. Distinguishing history sharply from myth, Hegel treats it as a stage of conscious reflections reached by man in the course of his development. Only peoples who have reached a certain level of spiritual development *have* history, meaning both the events and the narrative of the events. "We must hold," says Hegel, "that the narration of history and historical deeds and events appear at the same time; a common inner principle brings them forth together." In the ages before the writing of history, although they are ages filled with migrations and upheavals, there is no history, objectively speaking, because there is no subjective historian. This even applies, as we shall see in more detail later, to contemporary peoples: in the eyes of Hegel, the Slavs, the Americans, and the Africans have not arrived at the stage of history.

More positively stated, "History," Hegel declares, "is always of great importance for a people since by means of that it becomes conscious of the path of development taken by its own spirit, which expresses itself in Laws, Manners, Customs, and Deeds. . . . History presents a people with their own image in a condition which thereby becomes objective to them. Without History their existence in time is blindly self-involved—the recurring play of arbitrary volition in manifold forms." In short, the purpose of History—defined as both event and the reflection on that event—is to make man self-conscious. In order to fulfill the Socratic injunction, "Know thyself," we are now told that we must know our past; instead of an unchanging nature, man would seem to have only a developing history.

In tracing that development, Hegel starts neither from a religious paradise nor a philosophic "state of nature." Man does not fall from grace, and he does not start out good and free in a supposed natural condition. Instead, like Hobbes before him, Hegel sees a state of nature (assuming it ever were to have existed) as a "state of violence and wrong, of which nothing truer can be said than that one ought to depart from it." As Hegel remarks, "By nature man is not what he ought to be; only through a transforming process does he arrive at truth." Thus, Hegel partakes of the enlightened idea of progress; yet his starting point, both historically and epistemologically, is markedly different from that of thinkers like Locke and Condorcet.

Hegel, it appears to me, really starts from Descartes' philosophical position, wherein the latter conceives of the "I" which thinks as fully formed and potentially capable of constructing the external world all at once. From Descartes' conception of a free and self-conscious ego (at least potentially), Hegel, however, works out to the construction of the entire social world (as well as of Descartes' natural world). Indeed, for the German thinker, man's development, and thus history, consists in the translation of potential freedom into actuality. "Man is implicitly rational," declares Hegel, "but he must also become explicitly so by struggling to create himself, not only by going forth from himself but also by building himself up within." As a result, what Hegel has added to Descartes is the conviction that man's reason, implicitly there from the beginning, becomes conscious of itself *as it builds the outside world*. Reason, too, develops.

This enormously important thought receives additional coloring from Hegel's insight that the development of mind is involved with the *economic* world which man creates. Concerned, especially in the *Philosophy of Right*, for what he calls civil society and for the theme of alienation, Hegel kindles and then hands the torch of this thought to Marx. In Hegel's difficult terminology, "Mind attains its activity only by creating a dualism within itself, by submitting itself to physical needs and to the chain of these external necessities [i.e., economic life], and so imposing on itself this barrier and this finitude, and finally by maturing itself inwardly even when under this barrier until it overcomes it and attains its objective reality in the finite." To be developed by Marx, none of this conception is in Descartes, with his fixed and unchanging reason, operating outward in the world but suffering no effect in return. Nevertheless, I believe that Descartes (rather than Kant, in this case) is the logical starting point for Hegel's views.[12]

However, having gone beyond Descartes by postulating a developing reason, Hegel also passes beyond Locke and Condorcet, his partial predecessors in this notion, by conceiving of that reason as coming, first, into self-awareness, and, second, into a necessary relation with the will and the passions. Thus, to the *philosophes'* one-dimensional idea of progress, Hegel adds profound depths and shades. It is not only society that changes in the course of history; it is man as well. Man becomes not only a self-conscious being, *realizing* thereby explicitly what he is implicitly, but by *willing* what is rational he becomes *free*. To understand this in detail, however, we must first explore Hegel's other differences from his Enlightenment predecessors: his epistemology and his dialectical method.

5

The starting point for Hegel's epistemology is, of course, the Kantian position. Thus, where *philosophes* like Condorcet begin from sensations and a passive knower, Hegel talks of

[12] Along with Descartes, however, Aristotle's name (and, of course, Kant's) must be added. For the Aristotelian roots of Hegel's thought see, for example, J. N. Findlay, *Hegel: A Re-Examination* (London, 1958), especially pp. 22–23 and 216–217. Popper, *op. cit.*, also has a chapter on "The Aristotelian Roots of Hegelianism." In addition, other statements in Hegel make one think of Vico, without thereby necessarily attributing to the latter thinker an actual influence on Hegel. For example, Hegel asserts that "the genuine truth is the prodigious transfer of the inner into the outer, the building of reason into the real world, and this has been the task of the world during the whole course of its development. It is by working at this task that civilized man has actually given reason an embodiment in law and government and achieved consciousness of the fact." (Hegel's *Philosophy of Right*, translated with notes by T. M. Knox [Oxford, 1942], p. 167.)

intelligence and the active mind. Applied to history, this means for Hegel that the facts do not speak for themselves. "Even the average and mediocre historian," he remarks deprecatingly in the *Philosophy of History*, "who perhaps believes and pretends that he is merely receptive, merely surrendering himself to the data, is not passive in his thinking. He brings his categories with him and sees the data through them. In everything that is supposed to be scientific, Reason must be awake and reflection applied. To him who looks at the world rationally the world looks rationally back. The relation is mutual."

Interestingly enough, Hegel seems to be opposed both to a naïve positivist position, where the facts produce ideas of their own accord, as in Condorcet, and to the later sort of Burckhardt-Croce-Collingwood position, where *Anschauung* mysteriously darts from the historian's eye and suddenly arranges the chaos of material into an artistic pattern. Perhaps he abjures this last because it is too reminiscent of Schelling's romantic and aesthetic emphasis. In any case, Hegel's approach is his own: it is a single-minded concentration on what he calls Reason. But what does he mean by this Reason? How does one look at the world rationally?

Like Kant, Hegel believes that the categories we bring to the task of knowing are empty until experience, and he scornfully rejects the vacant a priori that exists before the encounter with experience. Where Hegel differs from his compatriot is on the issue of phenomena and noumena. Kant, as we recall, did not believe we could ever know reality, the thing-in-itself (noumena), but only the mere world of appearances (phenomena). With one bold and immensely important gesture, Hegel swept away the supposed veil between the two worlds. For him, there is only one world, where appearance *is* reality. And the link establishing this connection is man himself. As a modern commentator has well put it, "behind the curtain of appearance is not an unknown thing-in-itself, but the knowing subject."[13]

What does the knowing subject know? As I interpret

[13] Marcuse, *op. cit.*, p. 112.

Hegel, it is simply that—he knows. As we have seen, for Hegel man's knowing is a developing thing, growing as man develops the external world. The relation is mutual. Thus, so to speak, as man becomes self-conscious, he creates the world in his knowing image, and the created world then calls forth increased self-consciousness in man. In fact, this, in its shortest definition, is the meaning of history.

Such, I believe, is what Hegel had in mind when he makes the seemingly cryptic statement that "the only thought which Philosophy brings with it to the contemplation of History, is the simple conception of Reason." We have already identified Descartes as the source of Hegel's convictions that Reason is the starting point, which then creates the world.[14] We can see now that, for Hegel, what makes this creation possible is that the logic of the mind (which, as we shall see in a moment, is dialectical) corresponds to the logic of the world. And, he suggests, we deduce this latter, the logic of the world, from the very way in which we come to know it.

Behind this, of course, stands an initial assumption on Hegel's part: that at the beginning is Reason, which, like a seed, will unfold what is in it potentially and come into self-realization. Hegel knows this for the simple reason that he is the end product of this development. *Because* he is self-aware and conscious, he knows that this is the direction intended from the beginning. His notion is basically a religious one: Reason is God. It is that which exists, realized *ahead of time*, but only as potential; it must gradually realize itself *actually*, in space (Nature) and over time (History).[15]

Now, perhaps, we can understand the famous oracular pronouncement of Hegel that "What is rational is actual and what is actual is rational." Often, this is translated as "What is rational is real" (for Hegel's word *wirklich* is open to a number

[14] To fully interpret this particular idea, most scholars correctly emphasize Aristotle as the source of Hegel's belief in entelechy, i.e., the realization of that which a thing is by virtue of its form.

[15] When talking of history, Hegel will refer to Reason as Spirit or the Idea.

of interpretations), and when so translated is taken to mean a defense of the existing order, that is, that which is real, or has existence, is therefore rational. On my interpretation, however, Hegel is saying that when the potentiality involved in one of the moments of Reason (for as we shall see, Reason develops by means of a dialectic which contains individual moments of the whole) is realized—made actual—then, of course, it is a manifestation of the rational. For example, as one modern scholar helpfully explains, "If we say of a statesman who accomplishes nothing that he is not a 'real' statesman, then we mean by 'real' what Hegel calls 'actual.' The statesman exists as a man in office, but he lacks the essence constitutive of what statesmanship ought to be, say effectiveness."[16] Or, to take Hegel's own words, "A thing is not actual even though it may have acquired existence. A bad state is one which merely exists [i.e., it is "bad" because it does not represent the existing stage of consciousness, and thus what a state should be on any present *rational* basis, to which Reason has come]; a sick body exists too, but it has no genuine reality. A hand which is cut off still looks like a hand, and it exists, but without being actual. Genuine actuality is necessity; what is actual is inherently necessary."[17]

If I understand him correctly—his ideas are often most ambiguous—Hegel is saying that amidst the chaotic array of the existing, the mass of empirical data, Reason can tell us which elements (or moments), which structures or creations of Spirit, are actual, and therefore rational (and vice versa). Reason cannot tell us this a priori, but only *after* reality has been created (i.e., after Spirit has realized itself actually), and, in turn, has created our self-consciousness concerning Reason. Thus, like Vico, Hegel has sought to reconcile the empirical and the rational and to eliminate the dichotomy between

---

[16] T. M. Knox, *Philosophy of Right*, p. 302. Throughout this work, Knox's notes are of the greatest assistance in the understanding of Hegel's meaning.

[17] *Ibid.*, p. 283.

them; and he has sought to do this by means of a dialectical relationship between the two.

6

At last, now, we must deal with Hegel's dialectic. The dialectic is the *way* in which the predetermined end comes into actuality. Though Reason realizing itself as self-consciousness is predetermined, it also brings man his *Freedom*. To be free, in Hegel's system (and here we need only a brief glimpse at what Hegel means by Freedom, reserving a fuller discussion for later), is to will freely what is necessary and rational. In short, it is Kantian freedom. With this provisional definition, we can perhaps comprehend the following statement concerning History and the dialectic:

> Universal history . . . shows the development of the consciousness of Freedom on the part of Spirit, and of the consequent realization of that Freedom. This development implies a gradation—a series of increasingly adequate expressions or manifestations of Freedom, which result from its Idea. The logical and—as still more prominent—the *dialectical* nature of the Idea in general, viz. that it is self-determined—that it assumes successive forms which it successively transcends; and by this process of transcending its earlier stages, gains an affirmative, and, in fact, a richer and more concrete shape; this necessity of its nature, and the necessary series of pure abstract forms which the Idea successively assumes —is exhibited in the department of *Logic*.

The dialectical as a method of Logic was not new; and, as Hegel gratefully acknowledges, it had been used by philosophers from Socrates to Kant.[18] What is new is Hegel's particular use of the dialectic. For him, the dialectic of the mind is matched by a dialectic of the world. Hence, the inner and outer development proceed together; and, to repeat, "To him who looks upon the world rationally the world looks ration-

---

[18] On some of the anticipations, see Findlay, *op. cit.*, pp. 64–65, 69.

ally back." Now, however, we see too that the rational look is
a dialectical look.

According to Hegel, all thought is dialectical, that is, a matter of Becoming. All thinking is thinking a contradiction.
Thus, we know a light is *on*, only if we know what it is for a
light to be *off*. The mind *synthesizes* the two moments—on
and off (to use the technical terms, Being and Naught)—into a
conscious union of these opposites: Becoming. Hegel sets himself against the "sound common sense" view which "will not
admit the union of Being and Naught," and which declares
"Either it is Being, or it is not. There is no third." Instead,
Hegel asserts that "Being is the simple empty immediateness
which has its opposite in *pure Naught*, and whose union
therewith is the Becoming."[19]

Hence, against Parmenidean fixity, Hegel postulates Heraclitean process. Within any given whole, there will be partial
moments, succeeding one another and developing toward the
totality which is involved in the concept of the thing from the
beginning. We can see this best, not in the matter of our light
switch, but in the example given by Hegel of a plant's existence:

The bud disappears when the blossom breaks through and
we might say that the former is refuted by the latter; in the same
way when the fruit comes, the blossom may be explained to be
a false form of the plant's existence, for the fruit appears as its
true nature in place of the blossom. These stages are not merely
differentiated; they supplant one another as being incompatible
with one another. But the ceaseless activity of their own inherent
nature makes them at the same time moments of an organic unity,
where they not merely do not contradict one another, but where
one is as necessary as the other; and this equal necessity of all
moments constitutes from the outset the life of the whole.

The same process outlined in the development of the plant
holds good for the development of man and his institutions—

[19] The translation is from *Outlines of Hegel's Phenomenology*, translated by William T. Harris from Hegel's *Philosophische Propadeutik*,
Karl Rosencranz (ed.) (1840).

but with a significant difference. The plant goes through its stages of developing, and then, at the end, merely turns into another seed and recapitulates its development. Moreover, it is totally unconscious of its development. Man has a different fate. "Development," Hegel tells us, "which in nature is a quiet unfolding, is in Spirit a hard, infinite struggle against itself. What Spirit wants is to attain its own concept. But it hides it from itself and is proud and full of enjoyment in this alienation from itself. Historical development, therefore, is not the harmless and unopposed simple growth of organic life but hard, unwilling labor against itself." Then, with a glance at the implications of this view for the way in which historians introduce the rational Idea into the empirical data, Hegel adds: "Furthermore, it is not mere formal self-development in general, but the production of an end of determined content. This end we have stated from the beginning: it is Spirit in its essence, the concept of freedom. This is the fundamental object and hence the leading principle of development. Through it the development receives meaning and significance—just as in Roman history Rome is the object and hence the guiding principle of the inquiry into past events. At the same time, however, the events arise out of this object and have meaning and content only with reference to it."

Thus, development for Hegel is the unfolding of what is already present in the concept of a thing—a plant or man— from the beginning. (Of course, we only know this after it has unfolded.) The unfolding takes place by means of a dialectical movement—"The concept's moving principle, which alike engenders and dissolves the particularizations of the universal, I call 'dialectic,' " is Hegel's pronouncement—which occurs both in the logic of thought and in the logic of the actual world.

Two observations ought to be made about this development. The first is that the actual stages need *not* necessarily occur in the same order as the logical stages. What we have, Hegel tells us "is a series of thoughts and another series of existent shapes of experience; to which I may add that the time order in which the latter actually appear is other than the logical order. Thus, for example, we cannot say that property *existed* before the family, yet, in spite of that, property must be dealt with first."[20]

The second observation concerns the famous thesis-antithesis-synthesis conception of Hegel. In fact, it appears that Hegel never used these terms together in his own work, and, though he used the triadic scheme itself often, he handled it with flexibility and imagination.[21] A formal, mechanical triadic procession would have violated the poetic nature of Hegel's dialectic, and been especially inappropriate to the nuances of change traced by him in the course of universal history.

In any case, the dialectic method obviously fitted hand-in-glove with the contents of Hegel's philosophy, and there would seem to be no need for further justification of its use. However, I should like to suggest three other aspects of Hegel's employment of the dialectic—nonphilosophical aspects, so to speak. The first springs from Hegel's political position. It is simply that in a situation like that of early nineteenth-century Prussia, as described earlier, the dialectic was the perfect way of "politique" reasoning. Hegel could attack or defend almost any idea or institution, and then take shelter under the assertion that it was a necessary "moment" in the development of Spirit. Indeed, part of the ambiguity as to Hegel's political position stems from this slippery nature of the dialectic.

The second aspect we ought to notice is the usefulness of the dialectic for Hegel's theodicy. How better to justify the ways of God to man than by asserting that what looks like a particular evil is merely a necessary "moment" on the way to a greater good; and hence not evil at all? Specifically, for ex-

[20] *Philosophy of Right*, p. 233; see also p. 35.
[21] See Findlay, *op. cit.*, pp. 68–70; and Gustav E. Mueller, "The Hegel Legend of 'Thesis-Antithesis,'" *Journal of the History of Ideas*, XIX, 3 (June, 1958). George Lichtheim, *Marxism: An Historical and Critical Study* (New York, 1961) credits Fichte with the use of the terms and claims that "they occur nowhere in Hegel's writings" (p. 7, fn. 2).

ample, Hegel could attack the medieval Catholic Church and yet justify it as a necessary step toward later, purer Christianity. Therefore, unlike the *philosophes*, Hegel is not compelled to reject religion because religious institutions have seemed so frequently to behave badly. Hence, where Alexander Pope could say, "Whatever is, is good," Hegel could amend this to read, "Whatever is *actual*, is good." Thus Hegel could have his cake and eat it too; that is, he could justify whatever he wished while remaining able to criticize as merely existent and not actual what he disliked. It is an enviable position.

The third aspect regarding Hegel's use of the dialectic is more subtle and more difficult to present. It involves his psychological insight. I believe that the latter is directly linked to his dialectic, so that the dialectic shiftings—the synthesis of opposites, the resolving of contradictions—are psychological changes in mood and outlook. (One is reminded of Stendhal's lightning-like shifts from love to hate, in *The Red and the Black*.) Thus, Hegel brilliantly treats Abraham as a man who, psychologically, "wanted to be free by not loving," and thus set himself over against the whole world "as simply his opposite" to which his only possible relationship was mastery. Pursuing this insight, Hegel then analyzes the dialectical-psychological changes which this brought about in the Jewish people. So, too, talking of the loss of martial fervor in the Roman Empire, Hegel remarks, "A nation in this mood must have welcomed a religion which branded the dominant spirit of the age, i.e., moral impotence and the dishonor of being trampled underfoot, with the name of passive obedience and then made it an honor and the supreme virtue. This operation gave men a pleasant surprise because it transformed the contempt felt by others and their own sense of disgrace into a glory and a pride."[22] If we recall the earlier statements by

---

[22] *On Christianity,* pp. 165, 187. There is an interesting comparison in the Abraham example with Freud's view of the primal horde leader as free of libidinal ties. See p. 415.

Hegel, of a "silent revolution" in the "spirit of an age," it is now possible to identify that revolution as a revolution in psychological attitude. The dialectic movement of Spirit, for example, from the Roman world via Christianity to the German world, is a movement which takes its origin from the spiritual, which is to say psychological, changes in man.

7

When he came to compose his *Philosophy of History*, Hegel apparently forgot the detailed psychological analyses of his early theological writings. Instead, he talks of rather indeterminate "Passions, private aims, and the satisfaction of selfish desires" as the springs of action. According to Hegel, these passions and desires are then taken in hand by the "cunning of Reason" and used for ends unintended by the actors in the human drama. One way of phrasing this concept is "Man proposes, God disposes." Another, more revealing way is to compare it to Adam Smith's notion of an "invisible hand" guiding man's selfish acts to a favorable end. In fact, it may well have been under the influence of the economic analysis of Smith and Ricardo that Hegel laid aside his initial psychological analysis. He even uses an image from the textile industry—so crucial in the Industrial Revolution—to make his point, and, although I do not want to overplay the analogy, it is provocative. As Hegel declares: "Two elements, therefore, enter into the object of our investigation; the first the Idea, the second the complex of human passions; the one the warp, the other the woof of the vast arras-web of Universal History."[23]

Thus, while Hegel makes central the role of Reason in history, as the Idea realizing itself, he, like Kant, realizes that the *means* by which this realization takes place is the passions. The passions, not rationality, are the springs of action which pro-

[23] Cf. Robert C. Tucker, "The Cunning of Reason in Hegel and Marx," *Review of Politics*, 18, 3 (July, 1956).

duce the dialectic movement of history. The reason for this is that "Their power lies in the fact that they respect none of the limitations which justice and morality would impose on them; that those natural impulses have a more direct influence over man than the artificial and tedious discipline that tends to order and self-restraint, law and morality." Especially is this so for the world-hero. While for the ordinary citizen Hegel reserves the unrestrained exercise of selfish passions for the economic arena (the scene of free competition; elsewhere the citizen is to obey the customary law and morality), the hero, on the other hand, is a hero because he overrides existing morality. He does this in pursuit of his own selfish aims, as in the example of Caesar or Alexander the Great. "Such individuals," Hegel remarks, "had no consciousness of the general Idea they were unfolding, while prosecuting those aims of theirs." Was Hegel, for example, remembering his sight of Napoleon riding through the streets of Jena as a conqueror, both destroying and creating a Germany?

Strictly speaking, for Hegel heroes as such can only exist when a state is first being founded.[24] "World-Historical persons," however, "soul-leaders" who embody Spirit in its movement through the world, while few in number, can exist during each of the revolutions which ushers in a new stage of development. The task of these soul-leaders is to transcend the previous spirit, or morality. As we have seen, in doing so they must override great and sacred interests. Hegel admits that, judged from the existing code, "Such conduct is indeed morally reprehensible, but so mighty a form must trample down many an innocent flower, and crush to pieces many an object in its path." Then, in a well-known formulation, Hegel acidly disposes of the pedagogue's claim to sit in judgment on the great men of this world. He insists, instead, that "The World's History is the World's Court."

This formula, taken from a line in Schiller's poem, "Resigna-

[24] *Philosophy of Right*, p. 245. Cf. Vico's views on the hero, pp. 37, 38.

tion," has often been interpreted to mean that "might makes right" or that success is all that matters. On two counts, it is doubtful if this is what Hegel meant. First, as we have seen, only what is *actual*, that is, fulfilling itself rationally, and not what is merely existing, wins Hegel's esteem. Second, the world historical persons to be judged in the court of world history are "soul-leaders," not successful butchers like Tamerlane, who embody nothing of Spirit in them. This last may not be obvious when Hegel is talking of political and military men like Caesar or Napoleon, who literally trampled over men as well as morals. It is made clearer, however, when we see that Hegel treats Jesus Christ in the same fashion as Alexander the Great. Thus, Christ shattered the existing bonds of morality—the Jewish faith in which he had been raised—by claiming that his doctrine transcended all previous duties and moral bonds. As Hegel points out, Christ insisted that men follow him even if they had to desert their father and mother: " 'Think not that I am come to send peace on the Earth. . . . I am come to set a man against his father, and the daughter against her mother, and the mother-in-law against her daughter-in-law.' " Then, in a quiet tone, Hegel sums up this revolution, perhaps the greatest of all, in the spirit of the age: "We may say that nowhere are to be found such revolutionary utterances as in the Gospels; for everything that had been respected, is treated as a matter of indifference—as worthy of no regard."

8

Important, however, as is the leader—Christ or Caesar—as the means by which history propels itself, the leader is not the subject of history. That role is reserved for the state. As Hegel tells us, "In the history of the world, only those people can come under our notice which form a state." But by the state, Hegel means something quite special; his language, here as almost everywhere else, is his own unique creation.

The first thing to be noticed is that a real state and a real government can arise "only after a distinction of classes has arisen, when wealth and poverty become extreme." By this Hegel means, I believe, that without economic pressure man would be in a sort of state of nature situation, that is, he would escape to the woods and thus out from under civil society and an organized state.[25] Class, however, does not mean caste. Hegel believes in the free movement of the individual from class to class according to his ability, as a result of free competition in the sphere of civil society (i.e., the economic world based on the necessary division of labor). Nor does class mean class conflict. Unlike Marx, who saw the state simply as an instrument of coercion used by one class in its struggle with another, Hegel conceived of the state as the ideal reconciliation of particular interests and functions.[26]

The basis of any state must be the distinction between those who command and those who obey. The forms which this distinction may take are, in the abstract, Monarchy, Aristocracy, and Democracy. Which constitutional form is best, however, Hegel cautions us, ought not to be dealt with as an abstract question, for the constitution of a people is not a matter of free choice but only of the stage of history at which they find themselves. On this question, Hegel's dialectic allows him to be very *politique*. With much hemming and hawing, he says,

[25] See the discussion in Hegel's *Philosophy of History*, with prefaces by Charles Hegel and the translator, J. Sibree (New York, 1900), pp. 85–86; and *Philosophy of Right*, p. 13. One might argue that it is the *Volk* rather than the state which is the central actor in Hegel's drama, and that in fact the state only appears with the Greeks and Romans (disappearing again with feudalism and reappearing with enlightened absolutism). As I read Hegel's philosophy of history, however, a *Volk* without a state does not "come under our notice" in the history of the world. For details on Hegel's purely political views, see *Hegel's Political Writings*, translated by T. M. Knox and with an introduction by Z. Pelczynski (Oxford, 1964).

[26] *Philosophy of Right*, p. 180. Moreover, Hegel viewed the middle class, by which he really meant the civil servants rather than the businessmen, as being most conscious of the "right" embodied in the existing form of the state. See *ibid.*, p. 193.

The fundamental but abstractly (and therefore imperfectly) entertained conception of Freedom, has resulted in the Republic being very generally regarded—in *theory*—as the only just and true political constitution. Many men, who occupy elevated official positions under monarchial constitutions—so far from being opposed to this idea—are actually its supporters; only they see that such a constitution, though the best, cannot be realized under all circumstances; and that—while men are what they are—we must be satisfied with less freedom; the monarchical constitution—under the given circumstances, and the present moral condition of the people—being even regarded as the most advantageous.[27]

No wonder the conservatives and reactionaries around Frederick William III were uneasy about Hegel, in spite of his fulsome praises and obsequious adulations of hereditary monarchy.

Nevertheless, "under the given circumstances," Hegel defended hereditary monarchy as offering an impartial judge above the civil strife. To this support of hereditary monarchy, he then joined the whole paraphernalia of conservative belief, much along the line of Edmund Burke. Thus, Hegel reserves a chamber of the legislature for the class of landed gentry, based on primogeniture (elsewhere he severely attacks primogeniture), on the grounds that their "independent" position uniquely suits them for political position. He has the individual represented, not as such, but only as a member of a class or corporation. And he dismisses the notion of checks, such as the right to vote yearly taxes, as unnecessary because they are based on the false notion of a divergence of spirit between the ruler and the ruled. In all of this, the servile rather than the liberal parts of Hegel seem to show through.

On the other hand, it must be pointed out, against those who go to the other extreme and see Hegel as the forerunner of fascism, that he *never* diverges from an opposition to despotism and tyranny. His centralized state is always under law; there is no arbitrary element in his government. Free speech

[27] *Philosophy of History*, p. 45. Cf. Rousseau's similar formulation in *The Social Contract*, Book III, chaps. IV–IX.

and free trade both exist, largely unhampered. In fact, the monarch is merely to exist; he is not to legislate. Ideally, Hegel believes, there would be no need for "new" laws. The duty of the monarch is "but to say 'yes' and to put the dot upon the 'i'." Once again, it is difficult to believe that the Prussian King, Frederick William, could have been too pleased with the i-dotting role assigned to him in Hegel's system.

In reality, Hegel was not too concerned with the abstract *form* of the state. This is so because by *state* he means the totality of a people's spiritual life rather than a mere political mechanism. Thus, as he declares, "The constitution adopted by a people makes one substance—one spirit—with its religion, its art and philosophy, or, at least, with its conceptions and thoughts—its culture generally." (Therefore, as against, say, Condorcet, Hegel does not believe a people can import a new constitution as they might import a new piece of technology.) In fact, in his total system, Hegel, on a different tack, carefully differentiates the state from culture. Treating the former as Objective Mind, he places it below Absolute Mind, that is, art, religion, and philosophy. Only in the sense indicated, then, can we understand what Hegel means by the statement, "The state is the divine Idea as it exists on earth."

Living today in an era of totalitarian states, it is difficult for us to enter sympathetically upon Hegel's conception of the state. His language tends to repel us. Therefore, it is especially necessary for us to guard against our preconceived definitions in this area, and, at least for the nonce, to suspend our disbelief in order to understand him. We must realize that Hegel's ideal, especially in his early years, is not the modern dictatorial regimes but the Greek polis (without its slaves, however). What Hegel adds to the Greek polis is the subjective freedom of the Christian; the ideal goal now is to will the rational, knowingly and self-consciously, without external coercion. When we have done this, we have achieved the right. Thus, we can understand Hegel's statement (similar to Rousseau's belief that the individual is really free only when he submits to the general will) that "the state is the actually existing realized moral life. For it is the unity of the universal, essential Will, with that of the individual; and this is 'Morality.' "[28]

Indeed, the individual without the state, i.e., his culture, would not really be human: he would lack the attributes of freedom and morality and simply be an animal creature of unconscious sensations. "All the worth which the human being possesses," Hegel contends, "all spiritual reality, he posseses only through the state. For his spiritual reality consists in this, that his own essence—Reason—is objectively present to him, that it possesses objective immediate existence for him." We are back from where we have begun. Man develops his implicit reason by creating it explicitly in the form of the state—defined in the extended manner of Hegel—and this external realization of reason, the divine Idea on earth, in turn gives spiritual reality to the individual man.

The spiritual reality, as we have seen, is a developing thing, and here Hegel departs sharply from Rousseau's static conception. Spiritual reality develops, dialectically, by Reason cunningly realizing itself. In this process, Reason uses the passions of men, especially world-historical persons, in the form of successive states which embody a particular "spirit of a people." According to Hegel, "each particular National genius is to be treated as only One Individual in the process of Universal History. For that history is the exhibition of the divine, absolute development of Spirit in its highest form—that gradation by which it attains its truth and consciousness of itself. The forms which these grades of progress assume are the characteristic 'National Spirits' of History; the peculiar tenor of their moral life, of their Government, their Art, Religion, and Science." Proof that Hegel often, though not always, means by the state a cultural whole rather than simply a political arrangement comes from a glance at his *Philosophy of His-*

---

[28] But see *Philosophy of Right*, p. 33, for Hegel's criticism of Rousseau's scheme. Also, Isaiah Berlin, *Two Concepts of Liberty* (Oxford, 1959).

tory. There he deals with Spirit's progress through the Oriental, Greek, Roman, and German "Worlds"—i.e., "world-views"—in terms primarily of their *religious*, that is, spiritual, nature rather than in terms of their political form (though this is, of course, touched upon).

9

Before turning in detail to the progress of Spirit through Universal History, we need to consider one more *means* by which Spirit realizes itself. Earlier, we have seen that Hegel stressed the passions, and not mere thought, as being the woof to be threaded with the warp of the Idea. Now, we must in part unweave this connection and make room for the golden strand of *thought* running through the arras-web of history. The mist surrounding Hegel at this point is particularly thick; and it makes especially for the ambiguity as to whether he is conservative or liberal, reactionary or revolutionary.

If we start with certain formulations such as are to be found in the *Philosophy of Right*, then the task of thought (which Hegel frequently identifies with philosophy) is not to change the existing world but merely to comprehend it. Thus, according to Hegel in this mood, "The instruction which it [philosophy] may contain cannot consist in teaching the state what it ought to be; it can only show how the state, the ethical universe, is to be understood." In the same vein, at the end of the preface to the *Philosophy of Right*, he declares in an oft-quoted passage: "When philosophy paints its grey in grey, then has a shape of life grown old. By philosophy's grey in grey it cannot be rejuvenated but only understood. The owl of Minerva spreads its wings only with the falling of the dusk."[29]

But what, then, are we to make of statements in the same

[29] *Philosophy of Right*, p. 13.

book, such as that of Hegel about the Stoics, that "the tendency to look deeper into oneself and to know and determine from within oneself what is right and good appears in ages when what is recognized as right and good in contemporary manners cannot satisfy the will of better men. When the existing world of freedom has become faithless to the will of better men, that will fails to find itself in the duties there recognized and must try to find in the ideal world of the inner life alone the harmony which actuality has lost"? Or about Socrates, that he "lived at the time of the ruin of the Athenian democracy. His thought vaporized the world around him and he withdrew into himself to search there for the right and the good"?[30]

Clearly, on the basis of these quotations we can say only that a few thinkers like Socrates may occasionally vaporize the world around them by thought and then retreat into their own inner world. Still, while such vaporizing thought may undermine belief in the existing morality, it does not seem to change the world, dead as the latter is. In the *Philosophy of History*, however, Hegel seems to contradict, or better yet, transcend his previous statements. Now, thought, or philosophy, causes the dissolution of the existing by setting against it the image of the better. Along with the hero, an even more powerful dissolvant of the old order has been introduced on the stage of history: Thought. In this mood, talking of the Sophists, Hegel declares that they "began the process of reflection on the existing state of things, and of ratiocination"; as a result, "Parallel with the advance in the development of Religious Art and with political growth, we find a progressive strengthening of Thought, *its enemy and destroyer* [italics added]."

For Hegel, in this mood, there have been two major steps toward the awareness of the power of thought, where the philosophical ideal of what the real should be negates the existing, and, in the resultant conflict of these two moments, leads

[30] *Ibid.*, p. 255.

to a synthesis on a higher level: one by the Greeks, and the other by the French revolutionists. Speaking of the French Revolution, toward the end of the *Philosophy of History*, he announces:

> Never since the sun had stood in the firmament and the planets revolved around him had it been perceived that man's existence centres in his head, i.e. in Thought, inspired by which he builds up the world of reality. Anaxagoras had been the first to say that *nous* governs the World; but not until now [i.e., the French Revolution] had man advanced to the recognition of the principle that Thought ought to govern spiritual reality. This was accordingly a glorious mental dawn. All thinking beings shared in the jubilation of this epoch.[31]

Hegel, however (for example, in the *Philosophy of Right*), qualified his admiration for the revolutionary thought which had sought to govern spiritual reality. This thought, he now asserted, had been merely abstract understanding, not reason. True, "when these abstract conclusions came into power, they afforded for the first time in human history the prodigious spectacle of the overthrow of the constitution of a great actual state and its complete reconstruction *ab initio* on the basis of pure thought alone, after the destruction of all existing and given material." Alas, "The will of its re-founders was to give it what they alleged was a purely rational basis, but it was only abstractions that were being used; the Idea was lacking; and the experiment ended in the maximum of frightfulness and terror."

"The Idea was lacking"; but this is exactly what Hegel's philosophy could provide. Only by studying the way in which the Idea—Reason—has come into realization can we understand the Idea itself. Or, to phrase it another way, only when Reason actualizes itself in our self-consciousness, that is, reaches a certain level of *historical* awareness, which means we

---

[31] *Philosophy of History*, p. 447. There can be no doubt that this is the Hegel who is followed, naturally with modifications, by the left-Hegelians and by the Marxists. Cf. Marcuse, *op. cit.*, pp. 48 and 51.

then understand it, is it in turn then actualized. And this is precisely what Hegel's philosophy of history allows—he would say provides for. We now turn to the details of his philosophy of history itself.

10

The basis of history, according to Hegel, is geography. Although it is only one factor, Nature plays an original role in the germination of the spirit of a people. It is the soil from which spirit springs. Specifically, it affects the religious conceptions of a people. Thus, talking of the Nile and its physical cycle, Hegel remarks, "This basis of the life of the Egyptians determines moreover the particular tenor of their religious views." Where natural conditions are too severe, however, as in the Frigid and Torrid zones, spirit is stillborn. "The true theatre of History," Hegel tells us, "is therefore the temperate zone."[32]

In this part of his work, and it should be noticed that he begins his discussion of each national spirit with a characterization of its geographical setting, Hegel offers us both a typological classification and a particular description of the major continents. To take the classification first, within each continent and indeed each nation there exists the possibility of three types of geography: the Upland; the valley-plains; and the seacoast. These three areas have different sorts of economies: respectively, the rearing of cattle; the pursuit of agriculture and industry; and commerce and navigation. They also have different political forms, or stages of social development: thus, "Patriarchal independence is strictly bound up with the first condition of society; property and the relation of lord and serf with the second; civil freedom with the third." One cannot help comparing this, of course, with Marx and his "the wind-

[32] *Philosophy of History*, p. 80. Cf. Arnold Toynbee, p. 359.

mill brings feudalism, and the steam-engine, capitalism" type of classification.

Passing to the particular, Hegel delivers himself of some broad generalizations. The New World is inferior, as are almost all its flora and fauna; so, too, are its aboriginals.[33] Colonized as it is now by Europeans, it is the land of the future; but as yet it has no history. Africa is a benighted continent, lost in isolation: it is "the land of childhood, which lying beyond the day of self-conscious history, is enveloped in the dark mantle of Night." Its primitive, childlike Negroes are really outside humanity, as well as history: "The Negro . . . exhibits the natural man in his completely wild and untamed state. We must lay aside all thought of reverence and morality—all that we call feeling—if we would rightly comprehend him; there is nothing harmonious with humanity to be found in this type of character." The only relation of the Negro to European man is slavery which, though in itself an injustice, is also a form of education. Without a history, Africa, alas, is also denied a future by Hegel.

Even in Europe, Hegel finds a people without a history: the Slavs. They have not yet played a part "in the series of phases that Reason has assumed in the World." Whether they ever will play a role is a question that does not concern him, "for in History we have to do with the Past."

What is to be said about Hegel's views here? One might try to show that they are of a piece with his ideas concerning self-consciousness as the defining quality of man. Or one could try to excuse them on the grounds of his deficient knowledge of anthropology—a deficiency which he shared with many eminent scientists of his time. Renouncing these attempts at mitiga-

---

[33] Hegel cites as evidence of their inferiority that they are "small" in size. His remarks, however, must be seen in the light of similar ones by such contemporaries as Buffon and the Abbé Corneille de Pauw. For a most interesting treatment of this problem, see Antonello Gerbi, *La Disputa del Nuovo Mondo, Storia di Una Polemica, 1750–1900* (Milan and Naples, 1957), and the review of this book in *The Times Literary Supplement*, 1 February, 1957. For Hegel, the motive for his remarks may have been the desire to quash the "noble savage" myth.

tion, we can simply say that they represent the prejudices of a great man, gone astray in this particular area. They also stand for bad history.

In Hegel's scheme, Asia and Europe are the only continents to manifest any history. Fittingly, the light of Spirit rises where the sun does, in the east, and sets in the west. Pursuing his metaphor, Hegel declares that "The History of the world travels from East to West, for Europe is absolutely the end of History, Asia the beginning." With the sun travels Freedom, for "the East knew and to the present day knows only that *One* is Free [i.e., Despotism]; the Greek and Roman world, that *some* are free [i.e., Aristocratic Democracy (on a slave basis)]; the German World knows that *All* are free [i.e., Monarchy].[34]

Back of these large generalizations and periodizations is Hegel's effort to trace, in the empirical data of history, the development of self-consciousness, the coming into actuality of Reason. He finds, as we have already noted, that the spirit of a people is primarily concentrated in their religious conceptions (that is, in their views about Spirit), which then permeate all other aspects of their culture. Thus, his *Philosophy of History* is to a large extent a work in comparative religions: Confucianism, Hinduism, Buddhism, Zoroastrianism, Judaism, Christianity, and Mohammedanism figure prominently in Hegel's account. (And for this reason, of course, Americans, Africans, and Slavs are "outside" history, for they have never produced a new religion, i.e., a manifestation of Spirit.) Whatever one's judgment as to Hegel's scheme in general, one cannot help but be impressed by the range and depth of insight which he demonstrates in his long journey through cultural-religious history.

We can only touch on the highlights here. In the Oriental world as a whole, man has separated himself from nature, but

[34] Herbert Butterfield, in *Man on His Past* (Cambridge, 1955), as well as others have pointed out that Hegel's four worlds bear a suspicious resemblance to the old four monarchies classification.

he is not yet fully *conscious* of this division.[35] Hegel calls this substantial, but not yet subjective, freedom. "The substantial world is distinct from the individual, but the antithesis has not yet created a schism between [absolute and subjective] Spirit." Thus, man obeys the laws of the state as outside forces to which he must conform, and not because they accord with his conscience. So, too, there is no division between Religion and the State, and the constitution is generally a theocracy.

The starting point for Hegel's discussion of the Oriental world, and thus of universal history, is China.[36] He then proceeds to India, Persia, Phoenicia, Judaea, and Egypt. China is really the first nation, according to Hegel, to keep a written history, and we have already seen that this is the first step toward self-consciousness. India has imagination; an intuitive reach toward Spirit. Persia is the "first Historical People," for whereas China and India still exist as nations, the Persian Empire "was the first Empire that passed away." Zoroaster and Cyrus are both praised, respectively, as perhaps the first thinker and the first "soul-leader" in history. The Phoenicians introduce a new principle: Industry. The Jews rise to the realization that Spirit occupies the first place, before Nature, and thus raise the possibility for the first time of a truly *historical* view. The individual, however, is still unfree before the laws; he does not obey out of inner consciousness.[37] Egypt's contribution is that of being the first "to express the thought that the soul of man is *immortal*," which involves the view that "the human individual inherently possesses infinite value."

Earlier, I said that Hegel could be as much a poet as a philosopher. It is this side of him that emerges in his treatment of the Sphinx as a symbol of the Egyptian spirit, which he sees as emerging from the merely natural but still connected with it. "*The Sphinx*," he lyricizes,

[35] Cf. Henri Frankfort *et al.*, *Before Philosophy* (Chicago, 1946), chap. I.

[36] Cf. Voltaire, p. 62.

[37] Cf. Hegel's earlier work, "The Positivity of the Christian Religion," in *On Christianity*.

in itself a riddle—an ambiguous form, half brute, half human. The Sphinx may be regarded as a symbol of the Egyptian Spirit. The human head looking out from the brute body, exhibits Spirit as it begins to emerge from the merely Natural—to tear itself loose therefrom and already to look more freely around it; without, however, entirely freeing itself from the fetters Nature had imposed. The innumerable edifices of the Egyptians are half below the ground, and half rise above it into the air. The whole land is divided into a kingdom of life and a kingdom of death. The colossal statue of *Memnon* resounds at the first glance of the young morning Sun; though it is not yet the free light of Spirit with which it vibrates. Written language is still a hieroglyphic; and its basis is only the sensuous image, not the letter itself.

The transition from Egypt to the Greek world comes with Hegel pursuing his metaphorical thought. The solution to the riddle is in the utterance: "Man, know thyself." Thus, Hegel tells us,

Wonderfully, then, must the Greek legend surprise us, which relates, that the Sphinx—the great Egyptian symbol—appeared in Thebes, uttering the words: "What is that which in the morning goes on four legs, at midday on two, and in the evening on three?" Oedipus, giving the solution, *Man*, precipitated the Sphinx from the rock. The solution and liberation of that Oriental Spirit, which in Egypt had advanced so far as to propose the problem, is certainly this: that the Inner Being [the Essence] of Nature is Thought, which has its existence only in the human consciousness.

The connection of Oedipus with the unriddling of the Sphinx must arouse our especial interest for, as Hegel continues, "that time-honored antique solution given by Oedipus—who thus shows himself possessed of knowledge—is connected with a dire ignorance of the character of his own actions." The metaphor and the insight shown in this passage is something we shall wish to pursue when we come to Freud and his philosophy of history.

With the Greek world, we feel ourselves at home; we are in the region of the European spirit. Indeed, we are halfway to spiritual freedom; yet, because we still start with Nature,

"Spirituality is therefore not yet absolutely free; not yet absolutely *self*-produced—is not self-stimulation." Noteworthy, too, for the light it sheds on Hegel's political position is his emphatic preference for Athens over Sparta, though he recognizes that both share in the overall Greek spirit.

Passing on to the Roman world, Hegel gives credit to it for setting up the freedom of an abstract Ego over against an abstract, universal state. Here, however, all is constraint and obedience to external law. The major function of Rome seems to be as a stage setting—a "world sunk in melancholy," where Spirit is unhappy—for the rise of the supersensuous, free spirit of Jesus Christ.

With the coming of Christ, man recognizes that God is Spirit, though only in its triadic aspect. By this Hegel means that the Father-Son-Holy Ghost relationship is a dialectic one in which Spirit—Pure Identity—sets up its opposite—"existence for and in self as contrasted with the Universal"—and then, annulling this separation, comes to its synthesis in self-consciousness, i.e., Freedom. "This new principle," Hegel tells us, "is the axis on which the History of the World turns. This is *the goal* and the *starting point* of History." In bringing this new principle to the world, Christ, as we have seen, is a revolutionary who has overridden and transgressed the previous morality.

How revolutionary Christ really is can be seen if we pursue Hegel's interpretation of his message. The message, according to Hegel, is that man can become God: "The unity of man with God is posited in the Christian Religion. . . . But this unity must not be superficially conceived, as if God were only Man, and Man, without further condition, were God. Man, on the contrary, is God only in so far as he annuls the merely Natural and Limited in his spirit and elevates himself to God."[38] As we have seen, man annuls the merely natural and

[38] Cf. what Hegel says in a letter to Schelling: "I hold it one of the best signs of the times, that humanity has been presented to its own eyes as worthy of reverence. It is a proof that the nimbus is vanishing from

limited in himself through the development of thought and self-consciousness, that is, of Freedom. As Hegel emphasizes, this development must be expressed conceretely, in the world, and not merely as an inner, abstract Freedom. And this, exactly, is the content of History after Christ: "The whole sequel of History," Hegel says, "is occupied with the realization of this concrete Freedom."

At the very beginning of our treatment of Hegel, it was suggested that one of his claims on our attention is that he marks a transition from religious to philosophical thinking in modern times; or, better still, a *synthesis* of the opposed claims of Feeling and Reason. Here, now, we see the way in which he goes about achieving this feat. "The process displayed in History," Hegel informs us, "is only the manifestation of Religion as Human Reason—the production of the religious principle which dwells in the heart of man, under the form of secular freedom. Thus the discord between the inner life of the heart and the actual world is removed." To realize this concretely, a new Chosen People (my phrase, not Hegel's,) is needed; viz., the German.

By German, Hegel does not mean the German state, either of 1830 or of 1870; he means the Germanic peoples who inhabit Western Europe after the decline of the Roman Empire, from about the fifth century. It is really a "period" rather than a racial or national concept he has in mind. Thus, talking of the stage of development at which the *German* world appears as "The fourth phase of World History," he remarks, "This would answer in the comparison with the periods of human life to its *Old Age*." But that which in the Natural world would entail weakness and decrepitude, in the world of Spirit is "perfect maturity and *strength*."[39]

---

the heads of the oppressors and gods of the earth. Philosophers are now proving the dignity of man. . . ." (Quoted in Edward Caird, *Hegel* [Philadelphia, 1896], pp. 21–22.)

[39] Cf. Hegel's formulation with the similar view of time held by Francis Bacon and others, and described in W. von Leyden, "Antiquity and Authority," *Journal of the History of Ideas*, XIX, 4 (October, 1958).

Taking the large view first, Hegel tells us that there are really two phases in the development of this German world: one ecclesiastical, and one secular. These take concrete form in the Church and in the State. It is only when the antithesis between these two vanish that we enter upon the true, concrete realization of the Ideal; and this, of course, is Freedom. With this realization, we are at the end of history. "For the Christian world," Hegel enunciates, "is the world of completion; the grand principle of being realized, consequently the end of days is come.

At this point, too, we have realized a new definition of Freedom. Abjuring both the supposed Teutonic freedom of the forests (as presented by Tacitus and others) and Rousseau's unfettered noble savage, Hegel emphasizes against these mere associations of private interests an acknowledged Kantian freedom. He reasons as follows: Man's task is to comprehend Reason as it makes its way through the world. By doing so, he comprehends God or Spirit and thereby makes himself one with God. Once man attains to his self-consciousness he is, like God, unconditioned and free. In the words of Hegel, in the *Philosophy of History:*

The nature of Spirit may be understood by a glance at its direct opposite—*Matter.* As the essence of Matter is Gravity, so, on the other hand, we may affirm that the substance, the essence of Spirit is Freedom. All will readily assent to the doctrine that Spirit, among other properties, is also endowed with Freedom; but philosophy teaches that all the qualities of Spirit exist only through Freedom; that all are but means for attaining Freedom; that all seek and produce this and this alone. It is a result of speculative Philosophy, that Freedom is the sole truth of Spirit. Matter possesses gravity in virtue of its tendency toward a central point. It is essentially composite; consisting of parts that *exclude* each other. It seeks its Unity; and therefore exhibits itself as self-

---

Hegel, however, solves the problem posed by von Leyden by differentiating between a natural periodization and a spiritual one; thus, Hegel's solution points to a significant difference between man and natural creatures.

destructive, as verging toward its opposite [an indivisible point].
If it could attain this, it would be matter no longer, it would have
perished. It strives after the realization of its Idea; for in Unity it
exists *ideally*. Spirit, on the contrary, may be defined as that
which has its centre in itself. It has not a unity outside itself, but
has already found it; it exists *in* and *with itself*. Matter has its
essence out of itself; Spirit is *self-contained existence* (Bei-sich-
selbst-seyn). Now this is Freedom, exactly. For if I am dependent,
my being is referred to something else which I am not; I cannot
exist independently of something external. I am free, on the
contrary, when my existence depends upon myself. This self-
contained existence of Spirit is none other than self-consciousness
—consciousness of one's own being. Two things must be distinguished in consciousness; first, the fact *that I know;* secondly,
what I know. In *self* consciousness these are merged in one; for
Spirit *knows itself*. It involves an appreciation of its own nature,
as also an energy enabling it to realize itself; to make itself *actually*
that which it is *potentially*. According to this abstract definition it
may be said of Universal History, that it is the exhibition of Spirit
in the process of working out the knowledge of that which it is
potentially. And as the germ bears in itself the whole nature of
the tree, and the taste and form of its fruits, so do the first traces
of Spirit virtually contain the whole of that History.

Concretely expressed, Freedom—Hegel now calls it subjective freedom—exists when the individual wills, consciously,
what is rational and actual. This last, of course, is embodied in
the state. Thus, as I have stated before, Hegel has really taken
Rousseau's insight into the general will and dynamicized it, for
the state is now a changing, developing entity which possesses
and then loses the vital impulse of Spirit as the latter makes its
way through the history of the world.

If we abandon our lofty station above the course of history
in its German phase, having now perceived there the general
trend to Freedom, and descend for a closer look at the details,
we are offered the following panorama by Hegel. The Frankish Empire is the "first consolidation of Christianity into a
political form proceeding from itself," and hence a step forward. However, feudalism itself does not win Hegel's ap-

proval. In fact, rather surprisingly, he shares the disdain of the
philosophes for the medieval period—he calls it "the long,
eventful, and terrible night of the Middle Ages"—and discerns
in it disunity rather than, for example, a Comtean unity. Further, Hegel disdains the romantic praise of that disunity as a
manifestation of variety and life, and scathingly indicts the
feudal period for its private interests and unequal privileges.[40]

For Hegel, as for Jacob Burckhardt, the Renaissance,
marked by the revival of learning, the flourishing of the fine
arts, and the discovery of America as well as of the passage to
India by the Cape, is the "blush of dawn" which "betokens the
return [sic] of a bright and glorious day. This day is the day
of Universality." Thus, we are on the threshold of "The
Modern Time," and, with the Reformation, we pass into the
modern period itself. Here, our hero is Luther and not Calvin.
Indeed, Hegel seems to regard the German reformer as his
true predecessor, one who perceived intuitively (that is, by
religious feeling) what the author of the *Philosophy of History* has come to know rationally—by philosophical thought.
Thus we are told that "In the Lutheran Church the subjective
feeling and the conviction of the individual is regarded as
equally necessary with the objective side of Truth. Truth with
Lutherans is not a finished and completed thing; the subject
himself must be imbued with Truth, surrendering his particular being in exchange for the substantial Truth, and making
that Truth his own. . . . Thus Christian Freedom is actualized."

In discussing Lutheranism, Hegel eulogizes activity in the
world and anticipates the Weber thesis concerning Protestantism (although with the important difference that Weber
placed his emphasis on Calvinism rather than Lutheranism) as
the driving power of capitalism. According to Max Weber,
Protestantism sanctified economic activity as a form of doing
God's work; it became the new "calling." Moreover, Weber
tells us, Protestantism repudiated the view that charity to beg-
gars was a virtue and also attacked the monastic withdrawal

---

[40] *Philosophy of History*, p. 371. The truth is that Hegel never wavers
in his preference for a centralized state.

from the world. Hegel, in discussing Luther, says much the same thing: "The repudiation of work no longer earned the reputation of sanctity; it was acknowledged to be more commendable for man to rise from a state of dependence by *activity*, intelligence, and industry, and make themselves independent. . . . Industry, crafts and trades now have their moral validity recognized, and the obstacles to their prosperity which originated with the Church, have vanished."[41]

The specific way in which God's work is done in history unfolds directly from the work of Luther. As a result of the Reformation, the Germans (and now Hegel means his own people) rose to a correct knowledge of speculative Freedom; but they held this as a "tranquil theory." The French, on the other hand, wished to give it practical effect. The result was the Revolution of 1789. At this point, Hegel becomes his most *politique* and dialectic self. He approves of the Revolution, and even admits that its violence was justified, because the French government would do nothing to bring about the necessary change itself. The various freedoms instituted by the Revolution—freedoms of trade and profession, of access to offices of state, and so forth—all earn Hegel's praise, and so, indeed, does the regime of Napoleon which helped spread these reforms to Europe.

Alas, however, according to Hegel the Revolution was *bound* to be a failure, at least spiritually, for it was vitiated from the beginning by its occurrence in a Catholic state. Thus, in a France where there was still separation of Church and State, as well as a reliance on abstract Understanding instead of Reason, a people whose spirit was unilluminated by the Lutheran revelation could not hope to attain to subjective freedom. The result had to be anarchy and terror, and at best an abstract, formal Freedom.

Hegel's conclusion is paradoxical. The Revolution could

[41] *Ibid.*, p. 423. Naturally, the comparison with Weber must not be pushed too far. See, however, his *Protestant Ethic and the Spirit of Capitalism;* also R. H. Tawney, *Religion and the Rise of Capitalism* (New York, 1947). It must also be noted that Hegel, while praising the Lutherans, disparaged the Puritans; see *Philosophy of History*, p. 435.

only have been successful in a Protestant state—"For it is a false principle that the fetters which bind Right and Freedom can be broken without the emancipation of conscience—that there can be a Revolution without a Reformation"—yet in a Protestant state, which has already reached speculative freedom, it is unnecessary. Thus, while justifying the French Revolution in a left-handed way, Hegel ends up with his famous paean of praise for the Prussian constitution, where he sees the Protestant disposition successfully fused with the essential freedoms and reforms of political life. "In the Protestant world," Hegel informs us, "there is no sacred, no religious conscience in a state of separation from, or perhaps even hostility to Secular Right." We are, then, finally in the realm of Freedom, where the individual will accords with the rational law.

With a sigh, Hegel tells us that at this point, "Philosophy escapes from the weary strife of passions that agitate the surface of society into the calm region of contemplation." We are at the "end of days" and thus of the history of the world.

11

Before we seek a final evaluation of Hegel's philosophy of history, we ought to consider his thought in relation to what is called "historicism," and to view the latter in relation to the theodicy problem. The very last paragraph of the *Philosophy of History* informs us that the "process of development and the realization of Spirit" which Hegel has traced for us is "the true *Theodicae,* the justification of God in History." This, in fact, echoes Hegel's views in the introduction to his work, where he informs us that religion has anticipated his views about Reason ruling the world, only in the form of Providence. The upshot of the providential view is that everything that happens is necessary. (The one fault, however, with the providential explanation, Hegel explains, is that, while it tells us that the world is not abandoned to chance and external accident, it considers the *plan* behind the appearances of history to be hidden from us.)

From this two conclusions follow. The first, in Hegel's words, is "That harmony [of Objective and Subjective Will; of matter and mind] which has resulted from the painful struggles of History, involves the recognition of the *Secular as capable of being an embodiment of Truth* [italics added]; whereas it had been formerly regarded as evil only, as incapable of Good—the latter being considered essentially ultramundane." The second conclusion, connected with this, is that we must pay attention to "despised Reality." In sum, like Vico before him, Hegel has come by way of theodicy to accept the "given"—all of it—as data for his philosophy of history.

Now, it would seem that this links directly with Hegel's version of historicism. By historicism, I mean here five things (although Hegel does not accord with all of them): (1) a sympathetic identification with all historical phenomena; (2) as a further development of this first point, the acceptance of the equal worth of all stages of history and all cultures instead of the imputation of superiority to a given culture, say, to Enlightened France; (3) a realization that the parts have meaning only in terms of the whole; (4) a conviction that the individual phenomenon itself, in its unique, living expressions, should be the object of our attention (this may seem a contradiction of number three, but it is not); and (5) a belief that the historian's aim is to portray the variety of historical forms in terms of their growth and transformation. Out of these five traits, Hegel makes his own, unique synthesis of historicism.

Point one applies to Hegel especially in his early theological works, where he seems to come to an historicist position through what he has to say about love. Love, he tells us, "is no universal opposed to a particular, no unity of the concept, but a unity of spirit, divinity. To love God is to feel one's self in the 'all' of life, with no restrictions, in the infinite."[42]

[42] *On Christianity*, p. 247.

Love of God, of course, becomes love of Reason in the *Philosophy of History* and thus an identification with all the historical phenomena through which Reason realizes itself. In practice, however, as we have seen, Hegel appears to have had little love for either Roman law or the Catholic Church, to take only a couple of examples; and as a result point one applies to Hegel's total work only with severe qualifications.

Point two would seem to follow directly from Hegel's theodicy; but it does not. For Hegel, the Middle Ages, while as *necessary* as the Renaissance, are not of equal worth with it. Similarly, he asserts that Chinese art does not measure up to European standards.[43] Further, he claims that those who hold that there has been no progress in history or culture, no increase in morality, are in the wrong. In short, like the *philosophes,* Hegel believes in critical judgment grounded in a notion about progress (his version of progress is, of course, dialectical as opposed to lineal).

Point three lies at the heart of Hegel's work. He admits as his predecessor here, Montesquieu, who "proclaimed the true historical view, the genuinely philosophical position, namely that legislation both in general and in its particular provisions is to be treated not as something isolated and abstract but rather as a subordinate movement in a whole, interconnected with all the other features which make up the character of a nation and an epoch."[44] Where Hegel goes beyond Montesquieu—and almost all present-day "cultural holists"—is in giving motion to this concept. Not only is the part a subordinate moment in the whole culture or epoch; the whole culture or epoch, in turn, becomes only a subordinate moment—a part —in the whole of history. This is Hegel's grand contribution, his really daring extension of the notion of *Gestalt* which he now ties firmly to his general position, rooted as it is in Aristotelian entelechy and in his own rather unique form of teleology.

[43] *Philosophy of History*, p. 137.
[44] *Ibid.*, p. 16.

Point four, in this light, does not contradict point three (though it may violate Hegel's version of point two): we can only come to know the whole through a tender consideration of the individual moments or parts. This, of course, fits in perfectly with Hegel's epistemology, where he pushes aside an empty, a priori knowledge of the course of universal history.

Point five is self-evident: Hegel throughout is concerned with growth and transformation. For him, of course, this is not formless, chaotic change but a process which is informed by a definite purpose—the actualization of Reason in the world—and by a definite method—the dialectic.

In sum, then, Hegel has taken the traditional theodicy position and set it on its head. In place of justifying the ways of God to man, what he has really done is to justify the ways of man to God, i.e., to himself. It is under this peculiar guise that we must understand what I have called Hegel's historicism.

12

How shall we evaluate Hegel's philosophy of history? For good or for bad, it is an impressive kaleidoscope of thought, which has given many men and peoples a peephole on history. It has supplied the categories, either in itself or in its Marxist garb, which many of us bring to a consideration of the phenomena of the past. The glowing phrases of Hegel's *Philosophy of History* have become part of our general inheritance. How valid is the thought and how illuminating the phrases?

The major flaw in Hegel, in my judgment, is that he over-synthesized and underanalyzed. By this, I mean that he unnecessarily treated Reason, in its guise of national spirits, as a mystical, transcendental force shaping the institutions of a people, rather than as a purely descriptive term summing up the character of a culture. In similar vein, he looked at the great religions largely as abstractions—ideal-types—and ignored the internal struggles and discords which characterized

them in reality. Next, in his political thinking, he showed a
certain amount of naïveté (although it was a fairly traditional
view in his time) in assuming that the hereditary monarch
would synthesize the antagonisms of his people in an impartial
rule "above passions," as if history had not shown that the
major conflict is often between ruler and ruled. Finally, I must
point out, as so many others before me, that there is a basic
conflict between Hegel's method and content.

Let me go into a bit more detail on these charges. By always
thinking of Reason as "cunningly" using events for its own
purposes, Hegel undercuts his own deepest insight: that man
comes to know himself as his activity in the world—his history
—interacts with his mind. Instead of this being a natural process, emerging in an evolving world, Hegel's terminology leads
us to view it as a supernatural unfolding of a predetermined
development. And this last is an "unnecessary" view, for
which there is no evidence. Obviously, however, this is the
price which must be paid for Hegel's achievement, remarked
upon earlier, of transmuting religious conceptions into philosophical ones. Still, extenuating as this may be, we must not
forget that it allowed Hegel to neglect the analysis of the
mechanics by which his cunning of Reason—today we would
call it "unintended consequence"—worked itself out; and this
analysis is the difference between mere speculation and true
science.

Similarly, he neglected an analysis of religion as a sociological phenomenon, and merely *asserted* its social role, that is, the
effect of religious ideas on the culture and history of a people.
The same charges that can be made against Max Weber's handling of the Protestant ethic can be brought against Hegel's
treatment of the great religious movements—we are not really
given much proof that the ideas had the effect attributed to
them. (This is not necessarily to deny their effect; only to
claim insufficient evidence for proof of this effect.) Weber,
however, at least tries to understand Confucianism, or Hinduism, as a complex of competing forces—doctrinal and social—

and to treat these forces as an inner dialectic working out to an "unintended consequence."[45] Hegel has time in his *Philosophy of History* only for a brief, frozen glimpse of an abstract Oriental world-view.

Politically, Hegel is at his most uninspired. We shall consider only two examples of his superficiality. First, we must ask on what grounds he assumes that there will be no conflict between the ruler and the ruled. Hegel claims that the prince "must will what is just and reasonable." But what if he does not? Surely, Hegel had sufficient evidence around him to note that the concrete political world exhibited a conflict between ruler and ruled rather than a community of interest (and Hegel has insisted in his *Philosophy of Right* that he will concentrate on "what is" and not "what should be"—though of course he violates this vow). Ferdinand VII in Spain, Alexander I in Russia, the Austrians in Northern Italy, all ruled their subjects in a fashion that was not "just and reasonable." Even Hegel's own pet monarch, the Prussian King Frederick William, was having trouble with his subjects. Simply to ignore the reality about him and to offer on this score only a pious solution by definition is hardly commendable.

Nor is his statement that "it is absolutely essential that the constitution should not be regarded as something made, even though it has come into being."[46] The point is that constitutions *are* made, and that their being made can be as much a part of the culture as any other development. Conveniently, Hegel ignores the American Constitution, but the whole point of the American experience is that a people, in tune with its culture, can *make* a constitution, and make it on the very grounds of *thought* so highly praised by Hegel in another context.[47]

And, finally, how does Hegel reconcile his praise of both

---

[45] For Weber's dependence on Hegel, see Reinhard Bendix, *Max Weber* (Garden City, N.Y., 1962), pp. 387–388.

[46] *Philosophy of Right*, p. 178.

[47] For the significance of American constitution making, see, for ex-

Napoleon I and a monarchy such as that of Frederick William III? In a state like the latter, all is under law, and there is obviously no room for the world-history person to trample on the existing moral life. Is this life, then, so perfect? Yet Hegel elsewhere praises wars and "trial by ordeal," negations and antitheses, and damns with faint praise the state which has realized the task of Spirit and now exists without opposition. As he asserts,

A Nation is moral—virtuous—vigorous—while it is engaged in realizing its grand objects, and defends its work against external violence during the process of giving to its purposes an objective existence. The contradiction between its potential, subjective being —its inner aim and life—and its *actual* being is removed; it has attained full reality, has itself objectively present to it. But this having been attained, the activity displayed by the Spirit of the people in question is no longer needed; it has its desire. The Nation can still accomplish much in war and peace at home and abroad; but the living substantial soul itself may be said to have ceased its activity.

At this point, the life of the state has become a mere *customary life*, an activity without opposition. In Hegel's unenthusiastic words, "Thus perish individuals, thus perish peoples by a natural death; and though the latter may continue in being, it is an existence without intellect or vitality; having no need of its institutions, because the need for them is satisfied—a political nullity and tedium."

Is this Hegel's ideal state: a political "nullity and tedium"? It would seem rather that Hegel's dialectic method, ceaselessly dissolving the existent, conflicts sharply with the content expressed at the end of his philosophy of history, where the wheels of history seem hardly to move. Surely, it is at this point that Hegel leaves us with a mere paradox instead of a synthesis.

---

ample, R. R. Palmer, *The Age of the Democratic Revolution: A Political History of Europe and America, 1760–1800* (Princeton, N.J., 1959), Vol. I.

All of the examples so far touched on—and obviously our discussion has been brief and necessarily somewhat superficial —illustrate the ground on which Hegel is most open to attack: his reliance on an overabstract, reified, transcendental Reason which allows him, when necessary, to avoid the hard confrontation with the detail of reality. Thus, in spite of his obeisances to empirical phenomena, he was not always successfully able to incorporate them in his rational framework.

What, then, has he contributed to philosophy of history and to the development of the cultural sciences? The answer is simple: in spite of all his deficiencies, Hegel supplied a large part of the metaphysical foundations of the subsequent *Geisteswissenschaften*, the cultural sciences. Moreover, by insisting that they needed new techniques and different attitudes or perspectives, he tried to mark off their boundaries from the natural sciences.[48] Thus, Hegel insists that the only way to understand scientifically the spirit of a people is from the "inside"; the methods of the natural sciences, with their measuring and abstraction and dissection into parts will not work.[49] Instead, according to Hegel, only a knowledge of the "whole," of a restless, changing "life" of forms, deserves to be called a science of culture. And Hegel, as we have seen, sought to give this knowledge of the whole in his *Philosophy of History*.

The key problem in this effort, as Hegel saw it, was to distinguish two kinds of laws: the laws of nature and the "laws of the land" (as he called it in the *Philosophy of Right*), i.e., customs, mores, and laws. The first (the laws of nature) "are what they are and are valid as they are." Our ideas about them may be false, we may transgress them, but we cannot *change* them. The laws of the second kind are initially presented to us,

[48] Cf. Ernst Cassirer, *The Myth of the State* (Garden City, N.Y., 1955), p. 338.
[49] See Hegel's *The Phenomenology of Mind*, 2nd ed., translated by J. B. Baillie (London and New York, 1949), pp. 100–104, for his comments on the methods of mathematics. Hegel is obviously like the romantics in his approach here; it is his addition of a dialectical Reason which differentiates him most sharply from them.

too, as what they are, outside ourselves, and valid. However, as we develop to maturity and reason (and here I am extrapolating a bit from the text of Hegel), we realize that the laws of the land are created by man, and can be *changed* by him. Thus, man raises the problem of the *rightness* of the laws. He passes judgment on whether "what is" is "what should be," that is, accords with his inner convictions. In this, man does something which is completely absent from the terrain of the natural sciences. As Hegel puts it, "A schism and a conflict of this sort is to be found only in the territory of the mind."[50] So, too, this action distinguishes man from the animals, for the latter exist without that unique combination of will and thought which makes up human self-consciousness.

The equivalent of the individual's coming to reason is mankind's progress toward the same goal. With all of Hegel's hedging in the power of thought, he is really saying, as I interpret him, that man's developing reason allows him to pass judgment on the laws of the land—his culture—and to change them. The primary form this judgment has hitherto taken is the great religions. In their name and by their perspective, men have trampled on existing moralities and laws, and erected new spiritual and physical entities, i.e., cultures.[51] Hegel's great revelation at this point is that Philosophy has taken the place of Religion; in the new "birth time" of our epoch, cultural change will be attended by the midwife of Reason.

All of this insight is the work of history. History tells us that it has happened, and only because it has happened can we understand this history. Without history, there would be no development (and Hegel's emphasis on *historical* development

[50] *Philosophy of Right*, p. 224. Looking ahead, might we view this as Freud's conflict of the ego and the super-ego, a conflict which serves as the origin of tension in the realm of human law?

[51] On the powerful role of religion in social change, see, for example, Anthony F. C. Wallace, "Religious Revitalization: A Function of Religion in Human History and Evolution" (a paper presented at the 8th Institute on Religion in an Age of Science at Star Island, off Portsmouth, N. H., 26 July 1961), and "Revitalization Movements," *American Anthropologist*, 58 (1956).

is one of his major achievements) and no rise in the level of self-consciousness.

We can best understand Hegel here, I believe, by a quick example. Man in the twentieth century is no different, *naturally*, according to the laws of nature, than man in the first century. He is, however, vastly different *historically*, that is, according to the laws of the land. This is not simply a result of the passage of time: a twentieth-century Hottentot is *not*, historically, the contemporary of a twentieth-century Western man, although, *potentially*, he is akin to the latter. What distinguishes Hegelian man is his *self-consciousness*. He is conscious of the passage of time—cultural time—and this historical consciousness defines his being. He is what he is because he, and his fellow men, have incorporated into their internal mind and external society such happenings as the Reformation, the scientific revolution of the seventeenth century, and the French Revolution, to cite only a few instances. In this fashion, man, as Hegel tells us, can be said to be his history.

There is no point in claiming that Hegel has given us a science of man. His satellite of Reason orbits much too far above the empirical data to be of any scientific use. It gives us very little information as to either the "what" or "how" of concrete historical phenomena. What Hegel does offer us is a philosophy of history, a metaphysical *Weltanschauung* in this case, which can provide the framework within which scientific investigation into man's cultural life can take place.[52] With all its grandiose faults and flaws, Hegel's philosophy of history has braced subsequent thinkers with the firm conviction that man is a historical as well as natural animal, who develops his self-consciousness through his construction of the external world, both social and physical. (The exact relationship between the developing self-consciousness and the external world, however, is a puzzling one, and Hegel's explanation in

[52] Cf. for a treatment of this same phenomenon in the natural sciences, Edwin Arthur Burtt's pioneering work, *The Metaphysical Foundations of Modern Physical Science* (London, 1924, rev. ed. 1932).

terms of the elaborate drama played out by the dialectic of Reason is one which I personally find unacceptable.) In any event, we ought at least to be grateful to Hegel that, though he himself never entered the Promised Land of the cultural or human sciences, he at least glimpsed its major features from afar.

VII

Comte

If we trace the history of the progress of the human mind, and of its errors, we shall observe final causes perpetually receding, according as the boundaries of our knowledge are extended.

LAPLACE,
The System of the World

1

IN FRANCE, the spirit of the age seems to have produced a fitting counterpart to the philosopher of Berlin. At first glance at least, Comte and Hegel appear to be one of those rare double stars which light up the horizon of thought together: like Leibnitz and Newton with the differential calculus, and Darwin and Wallace with the theory of evolution, Comte and Hegel can be said to have developed the same general philosophy of history at the same time.

Certainly this is what one of Comte's friends, Gustave d'Eichtal, concluded after becoming acquainted with Hegel's lectures on the philosophy of history during a trip to Germany in 1824. He wrote to Comte: "There is a marvelous agreement between your results, even though the principles are different, at least in appearance." Having inserted the quali-

fication "at least in appearance," d'Eichtal added: "The identity of results exists even in the practical principles, as Hegel is
a defender of the governments, that is to say, an enemy of the
liberals." Going still further, d'Eichtal presented Hegel with a
copy of Comte's early work and was able to report that the
German philosopher had been pleased with it, especially the
first part, reserving judgment only on the meaning of the
method of observation recommended in the second part. On
the basis of this report, Comte decided that Hegel was probably the best man in Germany to push the positive philosophy
of history there.[1]

Many later commentators have agreed with this interpretation. Thus, in a striking passage, one modern scholar, Frank
Manuel, has declared, "Stripped of the thick hide of their private language, these philosophical dinosaurs stand revealed as
belonging to the same species. . . . Hegel and Comte are two
nation-culture versions of idealist historical philosophies of
spirit." Similarly another scholar, F. A. Hayek, has argued that
Comte and Hegel are fundamentally in agreement.[2] Moreover,
support for this view can easily be derived from the background factors: both Comte and Hegel stood in the shadow of
the French Revolution, were influenced by the counterrevolution, and sought to effect a synthesis of the two movements.
As Comte (like Hegel before him) remarked, "The schemes of
philosophers are always a reflection of the genius of their
time."

Nevertheless, with all this impressive evidence for the veiw
that Comte and Hegel are alike, I shall take the position that
their differences are more important than their likenesses.

---

[1] G. d'Eichtal à Auguste Comte, 18 November, 1824 and 12 January,
1825, in Pierre Lafitte, "Matériaux Pour Servir à la Biographie D'Auguste
Comte": Correspondence d'Auguste Comte et Gustave d'Eichtal, *La
Revue Occidental*, 2nd°, XII (Paris, 1896), 257–272; and Auguste Comte
to Monsieur d'Eichtal, 6 April, 1825, in *Lettres d'Auguste Comte à
Divers* (Paris, 1905), Vol. II, p. 86. Cf. F. A. Hayek, "Comte and Hegel,"
Measure, II, 3 (Summer, 1951), 326.

[2] Frank E. Manuel, *The Prophets of Paris* (Cambridge, Mass., 1962),
p. 287, and F. A. Hayek, *op. cit.*

Comte's positivism is quite removed from Hegel's idealism, and traces back logically through Condorcet to a Humean empiricism, whereas Hegel harks back to Kant's idealistic epistemology. From these bases, the two thinkers press on in vastly different ways. Without exploring these paths further at the moment, I shall simply put forth here the following hypothesis: Comte and Hegel, rather than being fundamentally in agreement, are better thought of as standing in a rather loose thesis-antithesis relationship; and, to pursue the metaphor all the way, they find their synthesis in Karl Marx. What is mere assertion here can only be tested by a scrutiny of Comte's philosophy of history.

2

Comte's philosophy of history is, of course, rooted in that genius of the time upon which he remarked. It is also rooted in his personal life. As might be expected, the interplay of these two elements, his life and times, go far to explain, and thus to illuminate, the details of his thought.

He was born Isidore Auguste Marie François Comte in January, 1798. Like many a young man before and since, Comte selected his own name, dropping the Isidore and giving first place to the Auguste by the time he was 21.[3] Perhaps there were aesthetic elements to his decision; but it marked the assertion of independence from his family as well.

The Comte family were vigorous Catholics from Montpellier, whose Catholicism had been made more active by "persecution" during the Revolution. Comte's picture of them is a bitter one. He accused them of nagging at him, of circumscribing his life, and of not helping him in his financial distress. (In return, he occasionally lied to them, as when he pretended to

[3] Thus, for example, David Hume changed the spelling of his name from David Home, and Thomas Woodrow Wilson decided to be Woodrow Wilson.

be trying to re-enter the École Polytechnique in 1817, while actually serving as Saint-Simon's secretary.) Though unjust in part—for example, Comte's family apparently was unable to help him financially—his accusations do rest on numerous grains of truth. Parts of the family portrait are not pleasant. Both the father and the mother, who was 12 years older than her husband, were constantly complaining of bad health. Comte's younger sister, Alix, whom he considered a covetous and hypocritical fanatic, suffered from hysteria, as well as a nervous inflamation of the stomach. One need only read some of the mother's letters to realize the psychological tone of Comte's relation to his family. In 1820, she wrote, "my tranquillity is lost for ever, my adored son, far from me and needing my care, which nothing, I dare say it, could replace. . . . give me your news accurately and punctually, I beg you; otherwise you are the death of me"; and, typically, "I ask you for your news the way a beggar asks for a crust of bread to sustain his painful life; you will only understand all that you have lost when I will be no more."[4]

Much of Comte's early life, then, seems to have been an effort to escape emotionally from his family. At an early age, 9, when he entered the lycée of Montpellier, he tells us that he felt the beginning of an affective rupture with his family; by the age of 14, he had ceased believing in God and also rejected the royalism of his parents. In short, he had become a complete republican. Entering the École Polytechnique (founded in 1794, originally to train military engineers, and then rapidly transformed into a general school for advanced science) in 1814, Comte seems at last to have found his true home. "Ah," he exclaimed, "if the spirit [*l'esprit*] everywhere were like that at the École!"[5] Here, in this school, the joint influences of the

[4] Quoted in Henri Gouhier, *La Jeunesse D'Auguste Comte et la formation du positivisme*, 3 vols. (Paris, 1933, 1936, 1941), Vol. I, p. 39. This is the outstanding biography of Comte.

[5] Ibid., pp. 63–71, 99. On the École Polytechnique and French education, see for example, L. Pearce Williams, "Science, Education, and Napoleon I," *Isis*, XXXXVII, 4 (December, 1956).

French Revolution and modern science conspired to produce the basic outlines of Comte's positivist philosophy. The École, offering much of the reality of positivist education, also became a model for positivist society.

One major ingredient of Comte's philosophy, however, is missing from the description just given: the Catholic religion in its relation to counterrevolutionary ideas. We shall see this element re-entering his thought in 1821, when, along with the Condorcet and the Lagrange he had been reading, he was to take up De Maistre's *Du Pape*. Thus, while Comte's interests appear to have been mainly philosophic and scientific in his early years, he gradually became increasingly religious (in a very special sense, for he never took up again either Catholic dogma or a belief in God), eventually assuming the position of high priest of his new religion of humanity. At this point, his religion was not merely an effusion of religious feeling: it was also endowed with its holy days, a calendar of saints (a weird collection, including Adam Smith and Frederick the Great, Dante and Shakespeare), and a positive catechism.

Some writers have contended that Comte's religiosity was with him all through the early writings; others, that it only emerged later, after his nervous breakdowns and his involvement in a love affair with Clothilde de Vaux. The first group cite the *Opuscules*, which, originally published under the cover of Saint-Simon's work, were openly appended by Comte to his four-volume *Système de politique positive* (1851–1854) to prove the continuity of his thought. Among these opuscules, the fifth, "Considérations sur le pouvoir spirituel," seems to prove the point. The second group rest their argument on his major work, *Cours de philosophie positive* (1830–1842), whose six volumes established the positivist philosophy but not the religion of humanity. In this group are to be found most of Comte's initial disciples or admirers, men like Émile Littré and John Stuart Mill, who clearly saw in him a nonreligious thinker.

What judicious position shall we take on this matter? It

seems to me that at this point Comte's personal life crisscrosses decisively with his philosophy. He, who was aware that during his mental illness of 1826 his mind regressed through the stages of metaphysics and theology (and in the latter through the phases of monotheism, polytheism, and fetishism) and then, recovering, back to positivism, might well have understood, too, what Freud meant by the "return of the repressed."[6] Overtly repudiating his family and all that they stood for, Comte's mind latently played its trick upon him and brought back the material in a different form. The past enacted its price from him in a way he did not understand.

Emerging, however, from this brief excursion into depth psychology, I would conclude that the religious element in Comte is a matter of degree. Never completely absent, the tone grows increasingly loud as his later volumes fall from the press. Gouhier, the author of the classic account of Comte's life, points out quite rightly that the French Revolution, by demonstrating the failure of Catholicism to become a national church (as envisioned in the Civil Constitution of the Clergy), opened the way for an attempt at a new religion: the cult of reason in 1793, of the Supreme Being in 1794, and of theo-philanthropie in 1796–1799.[7] Comte could no more avoid the religious challenge than he could avoid the challenge to create a new society based on modern science. Positivism, then, would at least have to acknowledge the past existence of religion and deal with its role in the present and future stages of society.[8] We shall not understand Comte's treatment of

[6] For Comte's comment on his mental experience, see his *Système de politique positive*, 4 vols. (Paris, 1851–1854), Vol. III, p. 75; also Manuel, *op. cit.*, p. 281, to whom I am indebted for this notice.

[7] Cf. Gouhier, *op. cit.*, p. 5.

[8] Part of the problem in this debate, I believe, lies in what Comte meant by religion. In his early years, it would seem, the stress was on the functional role of religion, its institutional aspect. Thus, Comte could recognize that religion in the Middle Ages played a worthwhile role as the basis of morality, while also recognizing that science had now taken over this function from religion. Even in his later outburst of religious fervor, in the *Catéchisme Positiviste* (Paris, 1852; 2nd ed., 1874), where he and his beloved Clothilde talked as "père" and "fille," he could

religion, however, unless we see it in the context of his whole
life and of his positivist philosophy of history. Therefore,
deferring further treatment of this problem here, we pick up
the threads of his intellectual existence as it weaves itself in and
out of the period of the post-1815 Restoration.

Comte's vantage point for viewing the troubled times,
which included the return of Napoleon from Elba and his
subsequent defeat at Waterloo, was, as we have seen, the École
Polytechnique, that unique institutional fusion of the scientific, technological, and revolutionary ideas of some of the
philosophes. First on the list of candidates for the École from
his area, Comte showed not only brilliance—he had a marvelous
memory—but disobedience as well. Although at first opposed
to Napoleon, he supported his cause during the 100 days (only
later turning against him again). In the subsequent royalist
reorganization of the École, Comte was among the students
ousted. The course of his relations with the École authorities
at this point is cloudy—Comte's own account in the *Cours* is
untrustworthy—but, for whatever reasons, Comte did not return to the school. Instead, after a brief sojourn in Montpellier,
he went to Paris.

During his two years at the École (1814–1816), Comte had
been immersed in the attitudes of mind of such scientists as
Carnot, Monge, Lagrange, and Laplace. Lagrange, indeed, was
the first to precede Comte, as Comte acknowledged, and to
rise to the level of a philosopher of science. In his *Analytical
Mechanics*, Lagrange realized that it was necessary before
presenting the problems of statics and dynamics per se to ex-

still hold to some such view. Thus, when Clothilde asks why he calls
his doctrine a "religion" while rejecting all supernatural belief, he answers
by defining religion as "The state of complete *unity* which distinguishes
our nature . . . this term being equivalent to the word *synthesis* . . .
religion, therefore, consists in *regulating* each individual nature and
rejoining all individuals [to one another]" (p. 42). Earlier, however,
when his friend d'Eichtal succumbed to the religious enthusiasms of the
Saint-Simonian sect, Comte sarcastically disassociated himself from such
nonsense. See Manuel, *op. cit.*, p. 256.

pose the principles animating his science, an exposition which could only take place by a historical account. In Comte's words, Lagrange was "The only geometer who has justly perceived the further alliance of the historical spirit with the scientific, destined to characterize the highest perfection of positive speculations."[9]

Once in Paris, however, Comte appears to have subjected himself increasingly to the spell of the *idéologues:* Volney, Cabanis, and Destutt de Tracy. The latter was regarded by Comte as the metaphysician closest to the positivist state; the school as a whole he appears to have valued as supplying the physiological basis for the development of a complete human science—sociology. It is interesting to note, too, that the *idéologues*, and especially Destutt de Tracy, favored the formation of an École Polytechnique for the "moral and political sciences" as well as for the natural sciences.[10]

Along with the *idéologues*, Comte now read a wide variety of authors whom we can only touch on briefly. He meditated on Condorcet, "my immediate predecessor" (reading five volumes of the *Éloges des Académiciens* as well as the *Sketch*), and on Montesquieu, whom he credited with being the first to consider social phenomena as falling under invariable laws. He read the histories of Hume and of Robertson, and the works of political economy by Smith and Jean-Baptiste Say. Spurning the latter's abstract and unhistorical political economy, Comte, however, always retained his admiration for the Scottish thinker (Smith, in fact, was included in the positive calendar, and one of his books selected for the 150-volume Positive Bibliography—the book however was Smith's *Essay on the History of Astronomy* and not the *Wealth of Nations!*). Not until 1821, however, as we have already noted, did Comte turn to the counterrevolutionary thinkers, Bonald and De

[9] *Cours de philosophie positive*, 6 vols. (Paris, 1830–1842), Vol. VI, p. 383. Here a comparison with Hegel's "fragmentary history" is also in order.

[10] Cf. Georges Gusdorf, "For a History of the Science of Man," *Diogenes* (Spring, 1957). See, too, Gouhier, *op. cit.*, p. 151, fn. 36.

Maistre, who were to have such increasing influence on him.[11]

Before that, after flirting with the idea of emigrating to America, and modelling himself on Benjamin Franklin, the new culture-hero who combined science and virtue, Comte had entered on his decisive connection with Saint-Simon. In August of 1817, he became the latter's secretary. This crucial relationship was to last seven years, when it exploded in hatred and repudiation.

On this relationship alone, a book could be (and has been) written. The question is always asked: how original is Comte; how much does he owe to Saint-Simon? Gouhier, for example, in his book on Comte, claims that Comte owed almost nothing to his employer: Saint-Simon was merely the personification of the American and French Revolutions, in both of which he had partaken; as for ideas, Comte and his patron shared the same climate of opinion, and it is this which inspired similar intellectual attitudes. Another writer, writing primarily on Saint-Simon, makes the same point, but this time to play down Comte's originality: "It is difficult to detect any fundamental difference between the master and the pupil, after allowing for the fact that Saint-Simon was an amateur in philosophy and Comte a trained professional."[12]

At first, Comte lavished fulsome praise on his new mentor. In 1818, he wrote to his friend Valat: "My mind has gone further in the 6 months that our relationship has lasted than it would have in 3 years if I had been alone. . . . He is a singular

[11] For some of the broader reasons why Comte might have been interested in Adam Smith, see my introduction to *The Wealth of Nations: Representative Selections* (New York, 1961), where Smith is treated as a philosopher of history. For details on the influence of the various thinkers named above, in addition to Smith, see Gouhier, *op. cit.*, pp. 124–230.

[12] *Henri Comte de Saint-Simon: Selected Writings*, edited and translated with an introduction by F. M. H. Markham (New York, 1952), p. xxxiv. Markham then goes on to qualify his remarks; but the flavor of his original comments remains. This volume is a good place to read Saint-Simon in English. The magisterial treatment of Saint-Simon is Frank E. Manuel, *The New World of Henri Saint-Simon* (Cambridge, Mass., 1956), but see also his chapter on Saint-Simon in *The Prophets of Paris*.

being in every respect. . . . I have vowed to him an eternal friendship; and, in return, he loves me as if I were his son." Alas and alack, the father-son relationship broke down, as had Comte's original familial situation, and the eternal friendship consumed itself in bitter reproaches. Now, Comte saw in Saint-Simon only a senile old man, who was expropriating or else repressing his secretary's talents. By 1824, the break was open and complete.

In many ways, Comte had been an ungrateful "son." Saint-Simon, admittedly in unphilosophical fashion, had first announced what came to be Comte's law of the three stages, first focused attention on the succession of organic and critical periods, and first called for a positive science of human behavior, a "social physiology." On the basis of this new knowledge, Saint-Simon called for a new order of society, founded on the rule of a scientific-industrial elite, and for a new international community to replace the universal papacy. Into this general framework of ideas, Comte fitted his early work. Thus, his initial Opuscules, including the prototypic "Plan des travaux scientifique nécessaires pour réorganiser la société," appeared as part of the Saint-Simonian publications; indeed, it was in this form, rather than in the form of the *Cours*, that the Comtean ideas probably had their greatest influence on thinkers like Marx.[13]

With this said, however, we must suspend further judgment. It presumably always takes two to make a quarrel, and Saint-Simon's hands were not clean in the matter.[14] To preserve his individuality and affirm his own genius, Comte probably had to cut the umbilical cord; it is only unfortunate that the knife was so dirty. As for the question of originality, as might be expected, it is a question of degree. By the quantity of scientific and historical detail which Comte gave to the law of the three stages, he made it qualitatively his own. Saint-Simon's emphasis was on industry; Comte's on science. Saint-Simonian-

[13] Cf. Hayek, *op. cit.*, p. 325.
[14] Cf. Manuel's account, *The Prophets of Paris*, pp. 251–260.

ism drifted toward socialism; Comtean positivism eventuated in sociology. Whereas Saint-Simon sought, at least in one phase, to reduce the social sciences to mathematics and believed that from the law of gravitation all knowledge could be deduced, Comte realized that each science must develop its own method (the more complex the phenomenon, the more repugnant it would be to mathematical treatment) and that the emergence of sociology could not be as a deduction from some universal concept but only as a development in the historical progress of the human mind.

Whatever final judgment we might make in this matter, it remains true that, by the time of his break with Saint-Simon, the outlines of Comte's mentality and of his system were fully shaped. Thus, while the rest of his life is filled with fascinating episodes, they were not particularly to affect his basic ideas (although the relation with Clothilde de Vaux fostered his religious turn). In brief, however, after his break with Saint-Simon, Comte supported himself, badly, by writing and by tutoring in mathematics; he never became a professor at the university (perhaps because he quarrelled with most of his perspective backers). Instead, he lectured privately on his philosophy to a select audience (at one point, it included Dr. Esquirol, the famous psychologist, who had treated Comte during his first attack of madness, as well as Alexander von Humboldt, the naturalist, Fourier, the mathematician, and Blainville, the physiologist).

Meanwhile, Comte's private life went its erratic way. In 1823, he entered into a common-law marriage to a former prostitute and kept woman; later it was formalized in an eerie religious ceremony which Comte's mother had insisted upon. Although Comte was not happy with his wife, it was she who nursed him through the nervous breakdown of 1826 (part of her ordeal was his flinging knives at her) and back to sanity. Finally, in 1842, the unhappy marriage was terminated, when Mme. Comte walked out for the last time. Two years later, Comte fell in love with Mme. Clothilde de Vaux, the deserted wife of a petty official. Alternately sensual (unsuccessfully so) and platonic in his pleas, Comte's love for her ultimately clothed itself in the universal religion of humanity, where, to the earlier watchwords of Order and Progress, he now added the principle of Love. Alas, his beloved Virgin-Mother, for Comte treated her as this as well as his "mére subjective" and "fille objective" (he entertained the notion of adopting her as his legal daughter), died within a year.[15] Desolate, Comte lived on in wretchedness and isolation until 1857, cherishing her memory, praying to her relics, and writing annual confessions to her.

It is a pathetic picture. But it must not be allowed to obscure the solid work Comte accomplished during this time. Astoundingly, during all his domestic anguish and mental breakdowns, Comte found time to write the six-volume *Cours de philosophie positive*, the four-volume *Système de politique positive*, and numerous other works, including the various religious and devotional writings of his later years.[16] Of these, only the *Cours* and the *Système* (along with the *Opuscules*) are important for understanding the positivist philosophy of history which Comte wove out of the varied experiences and mental stimuli of his life and times. From the Revolution and the Restoration, the *philosophes* and the *idéologues*, the political economists and the natural scientists, from the works of Montesquieu and de Maistre, Condorcet and Destutt de Tracy, Adam Smith and Lagrange, he fashioned his own figure of the tapestry of history. It is a unique work of synthesis, offering us a novel encyclopedic panorama of the past and the future.

3

In essence, Comte's law of the three stages is Condorcet's progress of the human mind analyzed and divided more

[15] See *Catéchisme Positiviste*, 2nd ed. (Paris, 1874), p. 20.
[16] For a bibliography of Comte's works, see, for example, Manuel, *The Prophets of Paris*, pp. 337–338.

closely. Comte admits as much. The chain of influence, he claims, started with Pascal, who posed the "first satisfactory view of general progression" and "was animated by a sense of the progress of the sciences when he uttered the immortal aphorism: 'The entire succession of men, through the whole course of ages, must be regarded as one man, always living and incessantly learning.'" Then came Montesquieu, who perceived that political and social phenomena were subject to invariable laws. Unfortunately, he lacked awareness of the idea of progress, but this was made good by Condorcet, following the views of Turgot. Excellent as were Condorcet's ideas, however, Comte points out, their execution was weak, and the whole scheme was vitiated by the undervaluation of previous ages. It is, therefore, by fusing the invariable laws of Montesquieu with the progress of Condorcet, in the correct manner, that Comte could found sociology, which, as he tells us, "is the term I may be allowed to invent to designate Social Physics."[17]

According to Comte, it is only by viewing the progress of the human mind historically that we can come to understand the stages of mental development. In point of fact, the historical human mind Comte studies is really the Western European mind; he is quite frank in narrowing his focus to the "vanguard of the human race": Italy, France, England, Germany, and Spain. To study India and China, he tells us, would be a waste of time, for they have not aided the process of development. In short, by universal history Comte does not mean mere coverage but significant development. His history is "essentially abstract"; ideally, "It would, in fact, be history, without the names of men, or even of nations, if it were not neces-

---

[17] *The Positive Philosophy of Auguste Comte*, 3 vols., freely translated and condensed by Harriet Martineau (London, 1896; first published 1853) Vol. II, p. 210. Where possible, I shall make my footnote references to this condensation, which, approved by Comte, is probably most available to most readers. For an interesting treatment of Montesquieu as a forerunner of sociology, see the essay by Émile Durkheim in *Montesquieu et Rousseau: Précurseurs de la Sociologie* (Paris, 1953).

sary to avoid all such puerile affectation as there would be in depriving ourselves of the use of names which may elucidate our exposition, or consolidate our thought."

This "dehumanization of history," as I shall call it, comes about because Comte is really interested only in the sciences and their development. The sciences are Astronomy, Physics, Chemistry, and Physiology (or what we should call Biology) —Mathematics is a logical tool and not a science per se—and now Sociology. A close study of each of these fields shows that it proceeds through three stages: the theological, metaphysical, and positive. This is the fundamental law of mental evolution, and while this progress to complete positive knowledge is asypmtotic, that is, we are "forever approaching and never attaining" it, it is also inevitable and irreversible.

Not only the sciences, however, but the human race itself goes through these three stages. Thus, in the beginning, the human mind proceeds theologically. All things are viewed as animated by a will and a life analogous to man's own, though in different intensities, which he can try to propitiate or control by prayer and magic. Within this general theological view, however, there are also distinct phases to be perceived. Man starts with fetishism (or animism), where each object is perceived as having an independent will, and then proceeds through polytheism to monotheism, where all objects are still imbued with will, but now the will of one God. From this last phase of the theological view, mind progresses to metaphysical thought, where objects are viewed in terms of abstractions, such as cause or force (in the political sphere, Comte mentions "sovereignty of the people" as an example), and where the attempt is ultimately made to subsume them under one great entity, Nature (which replaces God's will by invariable law). Finally, the vain search for absolute knowledge, for final causes, is abandoned in the positive stage, and we look only for laws which indicate relations of succession and resemblance.

Corresponding to each mental stage is a form of material development. The theological coexists with military life and primitive slavery; the metaphysical with lawyers and efforts at legal government; and the positive with industrialism. In fact, the great aim of history and especially the European polity seems to be "the gradual transformation of the military into the industrial life" which, when accomplished by the slow rise of humanity's faculties above animality, lifts "by one degree, the primitive type of social Man." Thus, history is the story of changes in mind and society which match and mirror each other. Like Hegel, Comte's approach can be called "holistic."

Complicated as is Comte's philosophical view of history up to this point, it receives further "refinements." To his special periodization, where each of the three great divides, theological, metaphysical, and positive, tends to be triadically divided again, he now adds a further division into organic and critical periods.[18] (And this new division, I might add, comes on top of Comte's admission that the three fundamental world-views themselves can and do coexist.) The organic period, as its name implies, is one in which certain fundamental principles are accepted by all members of society; this consensus of opinion, seen as based on true knowledge, makes for a stable social order in which all parts are informed with the same spirit and organically related to one another. The example Comte offers is the Catholic Middle Ages. It overlaps, of course, the theological stage of man's progress. The critical period, which Comte often also calls the negative period, is characterized, to put it in its simplest terms, by "the absolute dogma of individual free inquiry." It dissolves the old harmonious order in a wave of negative, critical questioning. Incidentally, the critical period turns out to be coexistent with Protestantism, and with the metaphysical stage (which is also labelled the Enlightenment).[19]

[18] See, for example, *The Positive Philosophy*, Vol. III, p. 218.
[19] It is clear that Comte derived his view of the Enlightenment, as well as of Protestantism, being "negative" from Joseph de Maistre. Thus, for example, claiming that from Protestantism Locke had learned only to deny and to protest, de Maistre says of the English empiricist: "It is he who denies everything, shakes everything, *protests* against every-

Comte's real animus is directed against this latter stage. He calls the metaphysical stage "that temporary chronic malady," and denies it any power whatever to organize society. That is a task reserved only for theology and positive science. Nevertheless, Comte informs us, the critical, metaphysical stage was necessary to dissolve the old Catholic order which, while based on fundamental principles, was based on outdated, unscientific ones. Thus, in a rather dialectic fashion, Comte grudgingly admits the metaphysical stage as a way station on the road to positive knowledge. The latter, of course, will revive the organic, settled nature of society, a society, however, now based on the final, correct scientific principles.

Even this complicated arrangement (to which Comte does not always adhere rigorously; we are never sure whether organic and critical periods keep succeeding each other in every stage or occur only once in the development of the three stages) is not left alone. Comte also talks about "Order" and "Progress." The former he describes as a Catholic-feudal idea and equates it with the "theological state of social science." The latter he sees as the idea of progress derived from the purely negative philosophy issuing from Protestantism, and ties it to the metaphysical state of politics. Both must be transcended, in a science which links order and progress: this is positivism.

At this crucial point, Comte passes over from a *description* of historical stages and phases to an *analysis* of sociology in terms of statics and dynamics. The master-thought of social statics is that all existing political-social systems can be studied relative to their existing level of civilization, that is, as functioning cultural wholes. Social dynamics, on the other hand, is concerned with a study of the changing levels of civilization.

---

thing: on his brazen face is written NO! and this is the real title of Locke's book, which, in its turn, can be considered as the preface to all the philosophy of the eighteenth century, which is completely negative and consequently worthless." (Joseph de Maistre, *Oeuvres Complètes de J. De Maistre,* Nouvelle Édition [Lyon, 1884], Vol. IV, p. 373.)

This division, Comte is at pains to point out, is merely for analytic purposes. In reality, the science of sociology is unitary; the distinction is not between two classes of facts, but between two aspects of a theory.[20] Most important to note, however, is Comte's comment that the distinction between social statics and social dynamics "corresponds with the double conception of order and progress."

Of what value is all this periodization and divisioning? The initial fact that must be remarked is that Comte is actually engaged on two tasks which he more or less disguises as one: in this, he is comparable to Condorcet, with his two social arts. First, Comte is working out a history of the natural sciences, in which he *traces* progress in each field in a very knowledgeable and detailed fashion. While naturally he makes some mistakes, as in overrating Gall's phrenology or in misjudging the possibility of introspective psychology, his treatment is unusually competent and impressive for his times. Moreover, his division of this progress into the three stages, of theological, metaphysical, and positive attitudes or world-views, is quite compelling. In one form or another it has influenced many later students of the history of scientific thought.[21] Indeed, the strength of his work in this field cannot be conveyed here; the actual passages must be read in order to see what he has added to Saint-Simon's glittering generality.

Secondly, however, Comte seeks to *establish* a science of man. He does this by making two important extrapolations from his discovery that the natural sciences have progressed from the theological to the positive stage. First, he assumes that not only the history of these sciences but the history of mankind as well, which he equates with the progress of the

[20] The counterpart would be, perhaps, the division between the study of anatomic organization and of evolution in biology (although Comte did not, in fact, accept the notion of evolution).

[21] See, for example, the classic work by A. D. White, *A History of the Warfare of Science with Theology in Christendom* (1896). In Ernst Cassirer, *The Myth of the State* (Garden City, N.Y., 1955), a fairly common division between mythical and logical thought is traced out.

human mind, can be correctly regarded as evolving through these stages. Thus, as we have seen, he equates the Catholic Middle Ages with order and the theological attitude; the Protestant Reformation and the Enlightenment with progress and the metaphysical attitude; and the Post-Revolutionary industrial era with a positive synthesis of the preceding periods. On this Procrustean bed, he has then sought to fit the concrete data of society's history.

Next, and connected with this first extrapolation, Comte has assumed that the science of sociology must go through the same stages as the other, natural sciences. Indeed, his own great task is to bring "sociology" into the positive stage. This, he believes, can be done because the way has been prepared by both the actual history of modern man and by the antecedent development of the other sciences (the latter an absolute necessity in his scheme as shortly we shall see in more detail).

Now, according to Comte, once a positive sociology has been worked out, society will once again emerge from the anarchy and disorganization of the French Revolution and base itself on true and, this time, scientific knowledge. "Liberty of conscience," he tells us, will no more be accepted in the field of sociology than it is in the field of astronomy.[22] Freely arrived at, for Comte insists that unity of thought must result from open discussion, this consensus of opinion—nay, knowledge—will constitute true liberty, for freedom is the rational submission to the laws of nature. Hence, Comte claims, a science of sociology must free us from the false notion that we can govern at will in this class of phenomena. With Comte's sociology, we are supposed to perceive that not only Montesquieu's static social phenomena are under invariable laws, but that so are dynamic social phenomena (i.e., the

---

[22] As Bonald points out, there is no "tolerance" in mathematics; tolerance of divergent opinions simply indicates lack of correct knowledge. Bonald declares, "Therefore, far from growing, tolerance ought to diminish and disappear in proportion as there is more enlightenment in society. Therefore, the most enlightened man would be, *about opinions*, the least indifferent and the least tolerant." (Quoted in Henri Moulinié, *De Bonald* [Paris, 1915], p. 109.)

necessary progress of man's mind and social organization).

It is Comte's political desires, I believe, arising as a compound of his life and times, that betray his scientific good sense. His analysis of the natural sciences and his plea for a scientific sociology are worth our serious attention. Contrariwise, his treatment of the concrete historical development of society—primarily European—while filled with sudden insights and unusual analogies, is warped and distorted by a priori conviction out of any convincing rapprochement with the data.[23] Nevertheless, though honored perhaps only in name, it is Comte's desire for a scientific method and a philosophy of science which distinguishes him quite acutely from Hegel and which constitutes the essence of positivism.[24]

4

Comte dissociates the positive method sharply from two things: the inquiry into first causes, and the use of mathematics in all the sciences. "The Positive philosophy," he tells us, "is distinguished from the ancient by nothing so much as its rejection of all inquiring into causes, first and final; and its confining research to the invariable relations which constitute natural laws."[25] To do otherwise, for Comte, would be metaphysical.

More surprising is Comte's objection to the overextended

[23] For examples, see further pp. 211–212.
[24] For a more critical view of Comte's failings as a scientific thinker, see John Stuart Mill, *The Positive Philosophy of Auguste Comte* (Boston, 1866), p. 51.
[25] *The Positive Philosophy*, Vol. III, p. 360. J. S. Mill's strong comment on this is: "He sees no difference between such generalizations as Kepler's laws, and such as the theory of gravitation. He fails to perceive the real distinction between the laws of succession and co-existence which thinkers of a different school call Laws of Phenomena, and those of what they call the action of Causes: the former exemplified by the succession of day and night, the latter by the earth's rotation which causes it. The succession of day and night is as much an invariable sequence, as the alternate exposure of opposite sides of the earth to the sun. . . . There are thus two kinds of uniformities of succession, the one unconditional, the other conditional on the first: laws of causation, and

use of mathematics. Mathematics (which, after all, was his own special field), he believes to be only an instrument. While in principle, he contends, all phenomena might be subject to mathematical treatment, in practice phenomena far up the scale in complexity, like biology or sociology, are repugnant to manipulation by mathematics. Thus, efforts by men like Bernoulli and Condorcet to subject sociology to "a fanciful mathematical theory of chances" are doomed to failure.[26] Instead, Comte praises "the eminent logical superiority of the sociological over the mathematical point of view." By sociological, as we have seen, he primarily means historical, i.e., social dynamics. Game-theory, because it neglects the historical approach, is not positive.

Comte believes that the historical study of the sciences themselves alone teaches us the logic proper to each science. The logic of the mind cannot be explained apart from its applications, and the only way to know what the mind can do is to see what it has done in the past.[27] Thus, Comte concludes that "the philosophy of the sciences cannot be properly studied apart from their history." Conversely, however, he also realizes that this history, apart from the philosophy, "would be idle and unintelligible."

By this latter conviction, Comte means that the history of the sciences will reveal their first principles; and that these first

---

other successions dependent on those laws. All ultimate laws are laws of causation, and the only universal law beyond the pale of mathematics is the law of universal causation, namely, that every phenomenon has a phenomenal cause." (Mill, *op. cit.*, p. 54.)

[26] See *The Positive Philosophy*, Vol. II, pp. 267–268; and Vol. III, p. 349.

[27] As part of this belief, Comte also holds that psychology, which pretends to discover the laws of the human mind by contemplating mind itself, has an impossible and useless task.

As for Comte's contribution in the field of history of science, see the comment by George Sarton, founder of the journal *Isis*, that he was one of the "great precursors of our discipline." According to Sarton, the task of *Isis* would be "to improve on Comte's work on deeper and more solid scientific and historical foundations." ("L'histoire de la science," *Isis*, I [1913].)

principles—the philosophy of the sciences—will then reveal to us the historical progress of the human mind (and, as we have seen, by Comte's false extrapolation, of society as well). This was what Lagrange had seen with the field of analytical mechanics; and behind Lagrange stood the even more significant figure of Descartes. As early as 1819, in a letter to his friend Valat, Comte had declared: "It is solely by well executed observations on the general manner of proceeding in each science, on the various ways one follows to arrive at discoveries, on the *methods*, in short, that we can reach sure and useful rules on the manner of guiding one's mind. These rules, methods, skills, comprise in each science what I call *its philosophy*. Let us suppose the philosophy of each science worked out; in taking that which would be common to each, one would have the general philosophy of all the sciences, the only reasonable logic."[28]

What, however, is the general philosophy of all the sciences revealed to us by history? First, history shows that the earliest sciences to go through the three stages and become positive are those whose phenomena are most general, simple, and remote, that is, affect all others without being affected. Astronomy, of course, has the first place in this classification; thus, for example, astronomy shows a solar system subject to unvarying laws; without this fixed solar system, there could be no chemistry; and without a fixed chemistry (for example, stable conditions of water and soil), no human life. On the other hand, the fixed laws of chemistry persist even with changes in human life, and chemical changes do not affect the solar system.

Second, each science is dependent on the development of the preceding science. Before astronomy, there could be no physics; before chemistry, no biology. To illustrate by taking the most widely separated sciences, astronomy and sociology, only a knowledge of astronomical *laws* can free us from super-

[28] 24 September, 1819. From *Lettres d'Auguste Comte . . . à M. Valat . . . 1815–1844* (Paris, 1870), pp. 90–91.

stitions about comets and final causes and thus permit us to see
human existence as under invariable astronomical conditions;
with such knowledge as a basis, we can rise to the conception
of human existence under invariable social conditions. It is
Comte's great glory to have demonstrated this dependence of
each science upon its predecessor by a mass of details, which
occupy the first three volumes of the *Cours.*[29] He also shows
that, before his own time, the development of the last science,
sociology, was impossible because the anterior sciences were
not sufficiently developed. To this insight, he adds the interesting thought that the necessary phenomena of social life did not
yet exist in sufficient dimensions, until the French Revolution
proved the insufficiency of the old polity for progress, to
allow for a science of man. Thus, Montesquieu and Condorcet
were not simply misguided; they lived too soon.

Third, the history of the sciences produces a law, that "The
complication of the phenomena coincides with the extension
of our means of inquiry." It is on this topic, which he treats at
various places throughout his work, that Comte demonstrates
the real power of his thought. He is imaginative and sophisticated, and he avoids the temptation to be dogmatic. There is
almost nothing, for example, in Hegel to match this part of
Comte.

Comte starts out with observation as the first means of investigation. What we observe are facts; and like the logical
positivists of our day, Comte would agree that a proposition
not reducible to a simple enunciation of fact can have no intelligible meaning. In this respect, Comte traces back to the
empiricism of Locke and Hume. But Comte is far too sophisticated to rest content with such a simple assertion. By a "fact"
he does not mean a Humean sensation or series of such sensations. Instead, he declares that an empirical observation is idle

[29] It is interesting to note that even before Comte, Pierre Bayle had
intuited the necessary relationship between ideas about comets and ideas
about human affairs. See his progression from *Miscellaneous Thoughts on
the Comet of 1680* to his *Historical and Critical Dictionary.*

unless connected with some law useful for science. Admitting that the simultaneous creation of observations and laws is a "sort of vicious circle" and that the danger that "the observer may sometimes pervert facts, by erroneously supposing them to verify some ill-grounded speculative prejudices of his own must be guarded against," Comte still insists on the need for hypotheses which would admit of verification at some future time by further observations and reasoning, and which then become laws. As we have seen, Comte wants hypotheses about invariable relations of phenomena, not about essences or first causes; the former alone can be verified; and this verification alone makes for "positive science.[30]

We can see how wide Comte intended his definition of observation of "facts" to be in his advice to the future historian-sociologist. "It is not only the immediate inspection or direct description of events that affords useful means of positive exploration; but the consideration of apparently insignificant customs, the appreciation of various kinds of monuments, the analysis and comparison of languages, and a multitude of other resources. In short, a mind suitably trained becomes able by exercise to convert almost all impressions from the events of life into sociological indications, *when once the connection of all indications with the leading ideas of the science is understood* (italics added)."[31]

To observation, understood in this sense, Comte next adds experimentation. This is possible when the regular course of a phenomenon can be interfered with in a determinate and artificial manner. For Comte, of course, this method cannot be applied to astronomical phenomena; it finds its true scope in physics, and then chemistry. Interestingly enough, he considers biology and sociology to have equivalents to experimentation, in disease in the one case, and revolution in the other; these "pathological" cases, while not determined beforehand,

[30] See *The Positive Philosophy*, Vol. II, pp. 243, 244.
[31] *Ibid.*, Vol. II, p. 245. Cf., in this connection, similar comments by Vico and Freud in relation to their particular sciences.

can substitute for pure experimentation.

The method par excellence for the more complex phenomena of biology and sociology, however, is comparison. For Comte, this takes three forms. The first would be, for example, comparative anatomy, or, to take another instance, the comparing of voluntary cooperation in animal societies with cooperation in human groups, such as the family or tribe. The second involves comparing coexisting states of society. We can study all types of social organization (in this case, human) "from the wretched inhabitants of Tierra del Fuego to the most advanced nations of Western Europe." It involves what today we would call anthropology. But, as Comte points out, this comparison gives us no idea of the order of succession, for we observe all these different societies coexisting. Thus, we must also engage in a third form of comparison, that of consecutive states. This study comprises history, which Comte describes as a "new department of the comparative method." For him, the influence of human generations upon the generations that follow accumulates continuously, *till it constitutes the preponderating consideration in the direct study of social development* (italics added)."

Here, then, is the kernel of Comte's positive system. Social phenomena can only be understood historically, that is, by the comparison of consecutive states. Comparison, in this sense, is really only observation of moving states. While biologically man may remain the same (in fact, Comte forbids any sociological view which contradicts the known and fixed laws of human nature), intellectually and socially he moves through various stages, the three stages of Comte's philosophy of history. Only as a developing creature, then, can man be correctly understood, and no part or stage of that development can be understood apart from the whole, that is, from the positive knowledge of all the sciences, including sociology. As Comte remarked in another context, a "sort of vicious circle."

By his work, however, Comte thought he had completed the

task originally set by Descartes' methodological excursion. Summing up his achievement toward the end of the *Cours*, Comte boasts, "What I have done in this direction must be considered as a natural equivalent of the discourse of Descartes on method, allowing for the diversities resulting from the new situation of modern mind, and the new corresponding wants. Descartes had for his subject the introductory evolution which had been for two centuries preparing for the ascendancy of rational positivism; while I have had to examine the fulfilment of that preparation, in order to determine the final constitution of a sound philosophy in connection with social objects,—a view which Descartes avoided, but which Bacon already anticipated." Continuing in this vein, he adds that, whereas Descartes, after a positive, scientific study of the physical functions of the animal organism, stopped abruptly "when he arrived at the functions of the affections and the intellect . . . and expressly constituted from them a special study, as an appurtenance of the metaphysico-theological philosophy," Bacon carried on to a positive study of man as well.[32]

Seen in this light, Comte is the synthesis of Descartes and Bacon. He has cut across the rational-empirical division *in relation to the study of man* and thereby sought to lay the true methodological basis for a social science. For this, he deserves full credit, even if he was generally not sufficiently aware of what he was doing.[33] Nonetheless, though seen dimly, Comte had discerned the true shape of sociology.

[32] See *The Positive Philosophy*, Vol. III, p. 385; and Vol. II, p. 113. Also, cf. Vol. III, p. 265 for a view more favorable to Descartes and less so to Bacon.

[33] Comte, for example, was not really clear whether it was the addition of social phenomena as a field of scientific inquiry to Descartes' original scheme, or of empiricism to rationalism, which was decisive for the emergence of a science of man. This ambiguity is shown by his listing of Hobbes, for Comte was always eager to link himself with precursors, along with Bacon as one who supplemented Descartes by bringing to light "the germs of true social science." (*The Positive Philosophy*, Vol. III, p. 358.) As we have seen, however, Hobbes was a rationalistic social scientist (cf. pp. 23–26).

5

At the core of Comte's sociology stand two assumptions: (1) that social phenomena are subject to investigation by the positive method, as outlined above; and (2) that the positive method must be looked at historically. Descartes had abolished the past; Comte assumes it. As Gouhier points out, Comte takes Descartes' "I think" and turns it into the statement that "All men think—and have thought."[34] Thus, Comte's task, and the task of the social scientist who recognizes that men *change* the way in which they think at different stages of history, is to study the way man has thought in the past.

Nevertheless, like Descartes, Comte speaks of science as mere extended and refined common sense; and both men consider common sense *common* to all men. The difference, however, is that Descartes appeals always to *individual* common sense in his *Discourse*, whereas in Comte the emphasis—probably borrowed from traditionalists like De Maistre and Lamennais—is on the common experience of mankind. Thus, where Descartes believes he could create the world (purely physical, of course), a second time, *alone*, imitating thereby God's first creation, Comte knows that only all men together have created and are creating the social world. The difference is major.

6

Now, what if we shift our main focus of comparison from Descartes, and return to the suggestion posed at the beginning of our treatment of Comte: that Comte's differences outweigh his similarities with Hegel? What do we have when we cast up accounts in this matter?

Let us start with the similarities. Both men are opposed to

[34] Gouhier, *op. cit.*, p. 246. See the similar views of Vico, and of R. G. Collingwood, *The Idea of History* (Oxford, 1946), *passim*.

the individualism implicit in Descartes' thought; both are more or less revolutionary in their philosophy and conservative in their politics (Descartes was like them in this aspect); both are European-oriented in their perspective; both are against the doctrine of the balance and separation of powers; both use what can be called a dialectic approach to social phenomena, though Comte's is far less formal and consistent than Hegel's; and, most important of all, both emphasize the historical development of the human mind. As for the way to study that development, they agree that it must be "philosophical," or, in other words, that, as Comte puts it, echoing Hegel's strictures in the first pages of the *Philosophy of History*, the historian, "now so lost in the laborious acquisition of a conscientious but barren learning," must learn to bring hypotheses (Hegel might have said "categories") to his data. Both Comte and Hegel *do* bring hypotheses or categories from philosophy to their study of the progress of the human mind; thus, both are philosophers of history.

Here the similarities end, and the differences predominate. Whereas Hegel extolls Protestantism as fostering inner freedom, Comte condemns it as inevitably leading to intellectual anarchy. Correspondingly, he praises Catholicism. Whereas Hegel favors the fusion of the secular and the religious in the state, Comte insists on the absolute necessity of a separation of church and state. Where Hegel dislikes the Middle Ages, Comte lauds them as an organic period. Where Hegel speaks glowingly of world-historical personages, and especially of Napoleon, Comte offers them no role, and pointedly characterizes Napoleon as a charlatan (although for a brief time in 1814, as remarked earlier, he had fallen under Napoleon's spell).

Comte has no room for theodicy in his philosophy of history—how can he allow for it when he openly disavows a belief in God? Indeed, whereas Hegel's work in general is permeated by religious warmth and imagery, there is a religious coldness in Comte's philosophy of history. Catholic in essence as the *Cours* indeed is, its Catholicism is that of a hierarchically organized social order; it is the Catholicism of the Grand Inquisitor.

In place of the Catholic religion, Comte offers the new religion: Science. The latter is, of course, *not* the same as Hegel's Reason; and the difference between the two marks the profound difference between Comte and Hegel. Hegel starts from a Kantian epistemology and terminology, and never really breaks away from Kant's transcendentalism. There is no clear verification procedure for Hegel's Reason; it floats where the spirit moves it. Comte, on the other hand, starts from a Humean sensationalism and rises to the positive scientific method. Sociology *is* a science—or at least an attempt at one—and is, at least in principle, subject to empirical verification, though of a rather special kind.[35]

It follows from the scientific nature (or attempt thereat) of Comte's work, just as it does not follow from Hegel's, that Comte's sociology attempts to predict future social phenomena. (Concerning the success of this effort, I have grave reservations, as I shall demonstrate shortly.) Speaking of his new science, Comte declares that it "asks from history something more than counsel and instruction to perfect conceptions which are derived from another source: it seeks its own general direction, through the whole system of historical conclusions." Not for Comte the polite Enlightenment notion that history is "philosophy teaching by examples," that is, an instruction in moral or political behavior (Hegel, of course, also scorned this). For Comte history teaches us the general direction taken by the human development, and by so doing gives us scientific laws by which to discern the necessary shape of man's future progress. Instead of Hegel's owl, a more appropriate image for Comte would be the far-sighted hawk.

---

[35] In practice, as we have noted, Comte tends to betray his own new science. See p. 201.

7

With all this praise of Comte's pioneering work in sociology, as well as in the history of science, I retain severe reservations about his general work. On one level, this criticism relates to his data—the empirical part of Comte. On another, it relates to his assumptions and theories—the rational aspect of his work.

The first part, the data, is often warped by Comte's polemical needs. Thus, for example, he defies all evidence to the contrary, and, in talking of the Crusades, sweepingly asserts as a *matter of fact* that "All great expeditions common to the Catholic nations were in fact of a defensive character."[36] Similarly, he describes the decline of the Roman Empire in the usual cliché terms (for example, as "exhibiting a moral corruption without parallel in the history of society"), without the slightest effort at verification of his assertion.

Closely connected with this sort of erroneous data is what I shall call his sweeping general statements, another form of factual inaccuracy. Thus, discussing the development of religious tolerance, Comte declares that "the forcible repression of religious liberty was, in Catholicism, simply a consequence of its modern disorganization; whereas, it is inherent in the very nature of Protestantism." This may be so, although most modern scholars see the relationship the other way; but Comte does not even deign to deal with the concrete historical data which, on the surface at least, seem to show a high, even if accidental, correlation of Protestantism with toleration.[37] We must take his statement on his mere word. Of this same character is his claim that the "metaphysical" polity, that is, the

[36] *The Positive Philosophy*, Vol. III, p. 110. De Maistre, as in so much else, serves as the original of this thought in Comte.

[37] See J. Bronowski and Bruce Mazlish, *The Western Intellectual Tradition: From Leonardo to Hegel* (New York, 1960), for some of the arguments and data concerning the rise of religious tolerance. In this matter, Comte's Catholic bias, of course, can be viewed simply as the counterpart of Hegel's Protestant bias.

right of free inquiry, "can produce nothing but anarchy." Was nineteenth-century England really an anarchic nation? Comte igores such questions (or would answer that England must be anarchic by definition).

Sheer prejudice seems to account for some of his remarks. Thus, he castigates "The accomodating temper of the founders of the English Church towards the shocking weaknesses of their strange national pope," while adding that "Catholicism was never thus openly degraded." Were the bastard children of Pope Alexander VI not open degradation? Similarly, he chastises the "anti-scientific tendencies of Protestantism," and claims that only Catholicism provides a favorable climate for men of science. Thus, it was in France, Comte tells us, "That science flourished most." One wonders how much Comte knew of the Royal Society in England and of the influence of Protestantism in its work.[38]

In more polite terms, it might be contended that Comte was "present-minded" rather than prejudiced. He was certainly aware of his contemporary situation and his mission. He believed his age to be one of "great crisis," in which the most civilized nations were experiencing the tension occasioned by the coexistence of two movements: one of disorganization and one of organization. Comte's task was clear: "We come therefore openly to liberate the West from an anarchic democracy and a reactionary aristocracy, in order to constitute, as much as possible, a true sociocracy [*sociocratie*], which ought wisely to make all human forces contribute to the common regeneration."[39] From this missionary vantage point, Comte could argue, he secured his perspective on the facts of history. (Many a historian since has taken the same stand.)

[38] For a discussion of this relationship, and citations to the literature, see *ibid*. Comte claims that Protestant scientists, as in the case of Newton whom he cites, were not involved with the positive spirit, which arose only in France; instead, he charges, they turned to the vagaries of theology, or, at best, of metaphysics.

[39] *Catéchisme Positiviste*, pp. 3–4. For Comte's views on his age as one of crisis, see *Opuscules de Philosophie Sociale, 1819–1828* (Paris, 1883), p. 60 (Opuscule 3).

How does Comte's "present-mindedness" sit with his vaunted relativism, which often seems almost a species of historicism? As early as 1817, he wrote to his friend, Valat, "Your political ideas are tainted with the vice of the absolute. . . . I myself am passed beyond that." Later, in the *Système*, he announced: "Everything is relative, that is the only absolute principle."[40] We learn, Comte tells us in the *Cours*, "of the efficiency of the positive philosophy in transferring us to the successive points of view from which the phases of human development may be understood . . . it will be easy to show henceforth that the spirit of each period has been not only the most suitable to the corresponding situation, but accordant with the special accomplishment of a determinate process, essential to the development of human nature." Thus, for example, Comte points out, there is no ideal, immutable political type but only different ones "according to the variable state of civilization."

It would be a mistake, however, to accept Comte in this mood of sweet-minded charitableness toward all periods as the typical Comte. We have already seen his "present-minded" verdicts. Now we shall see that his relativism does not mean an historicist acceptance of all that exists, but rather a belief in relative knowledge as against absolute knowledge. In place of the metaphysical interest in the fixed nature of being, Comte substitutes the scientific concern with the mere laws of phenomena, which is relative "since it supposes a continuous progress of speculation subject to the gradual improvement of observation, without the precise reality being ever fully disclosed." This, of course, is positivism. Therefore, the end of philosophical absolutism does not mean the emergence of an arbitrary or skeptical philosophy but of scientific knowledge. Part of our scientific knowledge is the awareness that phenomena are relative to the whole in which they find their

[40] The line to Valat is quoted in Gouhier, *op. cit.*, p. 218. The second quotation is in Comte's *Système de politique positive*, Vol. IV, Appendice, p. II.

place, and that our knowledge of this relationship is itself relative in the sense of being extended and refined by further
observations; in short, Comte's relativism must be taken in two
senses.

In practice, Comte frequently passes dual judgments on a
given historical phenomenon: one judgment from the point of
view of social statics, and the other from that of social dynamics. An example will give us the full flavor of his thought.
Talking of the Greeks and Romans and of the moral inferiority of their polytheism, Comte suggests that "If we take the
point of view of the ancients regarding their morality in its
relation to their polity, we cannot but admire its aptitude as an
aid to their military activity: and in this direction, it has shared
the general human progression, which could not have taken
place in any other way." Then, having delivered himself of
this praise, Comte adds, "But it is no less strikingly imperfect,
if regarded as a necessary phase of the moral education of
mankind."

Passing now from Comte's attitudes about his data, we come
to the validity of his assumptions and theories. The first charge
here is that some of his assumptions seem rather naïve. Let us
take one important example. According to Comte, the organic,
positive polity must be based on the separation of his scientific
elite from the secular, political power. As in Catholic society,
Comte insists upon the separation of the spiritual power, devoted to education, and the temporal power, devoted to action; only now the educators, instead of being priests, will be
scientists. These, by influencing opinion will influence the
state; for all political power, according to Comte, rests on
opinion. And when opinions cohere on matters of fundamental
principles—which with scientific knowledge will no longer be
a matter of sheer opinion—the body politic is stable. Thus, an
independent scientific elite, and Comte carefully distinguishes
them from wrangling, metaphysical "intellectuals," insures
unity and order.

Comte's example of his independent elite was influenced not

only by the Catholic priesthood but by his admiration for the Jacobins. Thus, he states that "The positivists are the successors of the Jacobins." In his view, "The society of Jacobins, placed outside of the government properly speaking, spontaneously constituted at that time a sort of spiritual power in that combination so remarkable and so little understood which characterized the revolutionary regime."[41] Catholic Church and Jacobins—a rather strange combination! Together, they represent the two forces whose synthesis Comte discerns in his scientific elite. "Above politics," or so Comte saw them, they alone were placed at the true point of view of the general interest. It is Comte's version, of course, of Hegel's impartial hereditary monarchy, though in a striking new guise.

Now, I have called this view of Comte's naïve. With three or four centuries of European polity showing the gradual absorption of the hitherto "independent" clergy into the power of the state, and with the even more present and obvious failure of the Jacobins to guide the state from outside, one may ask on what grounds Comte saw any real chance for his polity to come into existence. (If he had merely recommended his scheme as, theoretically, a good one, it could not be condemned in this fashion; it is because he considers the progress to his polity as immediately necessary that he is open to criticism.) Why assume that the political power will graciously let itself be guided by the scientific elite, whose findings might well remove political power from its existing holders? All that Comte really offers us here are the pious postulates of his system.

In the form Comte proffers it to us, his elite polity is not only naïve; it is based on a fundamental misconception of the true spirit of scientific inquiry. Comte actually knew better: in

[41] See to M. Hadéry, 20 January, 1853, in *Correspondence inédite d'Auguste Comte*, 4 ser. (Paris, 1903, 1904), Vol. II, p. 246. See Gouhier, *op. cit.*, p. 18; and to Mill, 4 March, 1842, in *Lettres d'Auguste Comte à John Stuart Mill, 1841–1846* (Paris, 1877), pp. 20–29.

his best moments he was fully aware that free inquiry was the heart of science. But his wishes and his hopes for a stable, ordered polity made him stress, time and again, his distrust or even hatred of free inquiry, which he equated with metaphysical speculation. While in one breath Comte speaks of the relativity of scientific knowledge, in another he mouths phrases about its fixed and stable nature. Positive science demands free inquiry and changing knowledge; positive polity requires obedient opinion and fixed dogma (incidentally, had Comte never heard of the heresies of the Middle Ages?). Polity all too often uttered the commands to Comte's strange, two-headed beast of society, and, while praising "free inquiry" in science, scathingly condemned "liberty of conscience" in politics.

There are other criticisms to be made of Comte's theories. For example: how can we be sure that the positive stage is the last one? As Comte himself claims, we only know about the human mind and the logical laws by which it operates in terms of its application; thus, it is at least theoretically possible that another stage might be reached.[42] Even if we grant Comte's point about the ultimate stage, another question arises along the same lines: how can we be sure that because the positive method has been extended to all natural phenomena, it can be extended to human phenomena? The belief that it can is a faith upon Comte's part.[43] But faith is not proof (although I would agree that faith in the regularity of social phenomena is abso-

[42] Cf. H. B. Acton, "Comte's Positivism and the Science of Society," *Philosophy*, XXVI, 99 (October, 1951). Sir James George Frazer, the anthropologist and author of the *Golden Bough*, commented about the possible movement of thought: "So far as we can trace it, [it] has on the whole been from magic through religion to science. Science is not the end, however. As science has supplanted its predecessors, so it may hereafter be itself superseded by some more perfect hypothesis, perhaps by some totally different way of looking at the phenomena—of registering the shadows on the screen—of which we in this generation can form no idea." (Quoted in Stanley Edgar Hyman, *The Tangled Bank* [New York, 1962], p. 238.)

[43] Indeed, it is exactly this problem which has been perplexing the modern critical philosophers of history who seek to answer the question whether history is or can be a science.

lutely necessary in order to amass data leading to proof).
Then, even granted that we can discover laws regulating social
phenomena, are we in possession of a final human science?
After all, as H. B. Acton points out, the social sciences can be
misused just as the natural sciences have been.[44] Do we have a
science of morality—that is, a science which will tell us with
utter positive certainty what ends to pursue?

John Stuart Mill, who, though he fell under Comte's spell,
always retained a keen critical attitude to the system and, indeed, broke with Comte on his later religiosity, offers another
important criticism of Comte's efforts at a social science. According to Mill, Comte's omission of a place in his hierarchy of
sciences for Psychology, and his rejection of psychological
observation (of internal consciousness) as a field of study—in
favor of Phrenology!—was "not a mere hiatus in M. Comte's
system, but the parent of serious errors in his attempt to create
a Social Science."[45] Pursuing this thought we can ask whether,
if Comte had paid more attention to introspective psychology,
he might have raised for himself the question whether the
pursuit of science necessarily improves man's moral disposition.

Lastly, our faith in Comte's prophecy of the immediate
coming of a positive science of human behavior suffers from
the failure of some of his more mundane prophecies. Two
examples will serve. On the basis of his system, Comte predicted both a continued European political supremacy and the
abolition of war. The recent colonial rebellions, not to mention the rise of Communist China, plus World War II and the
present atomic arms race make us less than sanguine about
these two predictions. Did Comte leave out something in his
system? Did his "dehumanization of history," coupled with his

---

[44] Action, *op. cit.*, p. 308. In many ways, Dostoevsky's novel, *Notes from
Underground*, is a protest on exactly this point; it is interesting to
remember, too, that Dostoevsky was originally a member of the
Petrashevsky circle, where readings of the Saint-Simonians (and thus
of Comtean ideas as well) flourished.

[45] Mill, *op. cit.*, p. 62.

superficial psychology, leave him with a science of human development in which the principal subject, man, was missing?

8

With all these criticisms of Comte's work, we must not lose sight of his lasting claims to importance. The overwhelming claim is that from philosophy of history he created positive sociology. The new subject officially emerged into life in the fourth volume of the *Cours*, 47th lesson, when Comte proposed the word "sociologie" for the previous "physique sociale." Comte coined the new term in order to differentiate his work from the mathematics of chance of Condorcet and the statistical method of the Belgian, Quételet, who described his own work as social physics.[46] What really distinguishes Comte's success in fissioning sociology out of philosophy of history from, say, Condorcet's development of the social art out of the same source is Comte's attempted retention of the historical dimension in the new science.[47] Any possible sociology, Comte tells us, must be historical in nature.

Comte's new historical sociology, as we have seen, places both static and dynamic social phenomena under invariable laws. According to Comte, the submission to these laws constitutes true freedom, and the wise legislator recognizes that he cannot govern society at will. Thus, Comte puts his knowledge of social phenomena to a social purpose, that of outlining a society which would order itself according to positive knowledge by taking its lead from a scientific elite. In short, his second claim to achievement is his projection from the philosophy of history to the true polity.

Paradoxically, the final effect of Comte's work in this last area is a playing down of the importance of politics. This may

[46] See Jean Lacroix, *La Sociologie D'Auguste Comte* (Paris, 1956), p. 9. This is an interesting book, worth consulting in general.

[47] See, for example, pp. 90–98 for Condorcet's social art.

be somewhat disguised by his attention to polity. But just as the eighteenth-century French physiocrats eliminated politics by subordinating an enlightened despot to the laws of nature (that is, to economic laws), so Comte did it by subordinating his polity to the laws of society. The difference is in the social, rather than economic, nature of his laws.[48] So, too, Comte's attention to scientifically based opinion as the mistress of political life and his insistence on the supremacy of moral forces (*not* intellectual forces, for Comte had no illusions as to the power of abstract ideas to influence men, whom he saw as largely controlled by their passions)—these also undercut the power of politics. As Comte remarked, "The disposition to seek in political institutions the solution of all difficulties whatever is a disastrous tendency of our time."

Indeed, part of the merit of Comte's social solution is that, while it ignored the psychological, it embraced a wider group of interrelated phenomena than did the merely political thinking of his time. Comte constantly emphasized the necessity for unity of thought. He opposed the rampant specialization of his day, which he discerned both in practice and in theory. (To offer one piquant example, he asserted that the worker who specializes in pins' heads—shades of Adam Smith!—and the intellectual "classifying insects" suffer from an analogous evil moral effect.) Instead, Comte wished to link the findings of various fields, for the phenomena they studied were interconnected in reality and in a chain of unified knowledge.

The "chain," as we can now see, is hierarchical rather than holistic in essence. Each field in Comte's system is dependent upon another field (because, according to him, the dependence of the science itself is a reflection of the dependence between the corresponding phenomena). Whereas the *Encyclopedia* of Diderot was a mere "equalitarian" compilation, the new en-

---

[48] Actually, Comte looked upon political economists, with the exception of Adam Smith, as metaphysicians, tied to a negative effort by their idea of liberty. For Comte, laissez faire meant simply systematized anarchy. Cf. Gouhier, *op. cit.*, p. 220.

cyclopedia of Comte is a ladder of knowledge, reaching up ultimately to the most complicated phenomenon and to the science of that phenomenon: sociology. Traced out as such, the encyclopedic *Cours* becomes an extended history of science, one of the first ever to be attempted. Finally, an historical overview of the sciences allows us to establish a major position in the philosophy of science: positivism.

In the light of these claims, Comte's work hardly needs the additional praise of having us say that it was to influence many important thinkers in the future; we shall explore its effect on Marx, who, like Comte with Saint-Simon, disdained to acknowledge the debt.[49] Comte's positive philosophy of history, with its emphasis on a science of society, on the history of science, on a new philosophy of science, on the superiority of social to political arrangements, and on the need for unified knowledge, throws out its own broad beam, spectacularly lighting up the horizon of thought.

[49] For a discussion of the effect on Marx, see pp. 227–230. Donald Geoffrey Charlton, *Positivist Thought in France During the Second Empire* (Oxford, 1959), by its title, speaks for itself. W. M. Simon, *European Positivism in the Nineteenth Century* (Ithaca, N.Y., 1963), is the latest effort to assess Comte's influence. It is a painstaking work of scholarship, with a splendid bibliography; the latter should be consulted for numerous items. Simon's concern, however, is largely with Comte's direct disciples, and with positive (if I may pun) evidence of Comte's influence. He is not concerned with probing the entity known as "climate of opinion," nor with the possible influence of Comte's ideas on thinkers such as Frazer or Freud. In fact, he is opposed to this sort of attribution. His position emerges clearly from a remark such as the following: "It is rather pathetic to be given long lists of books said to derive from Comte which contain nothing specifically from him and sometimes, indeed, contain explicit rejections of him and of his system" (p. 269).

VIII

Marx

Have you not heard of that madman who, in the broad light of the forenoon, lit a lantern and ran into the market-place, crying incessantly: "I am looking for God!" . . . As it happened, many were standing there who did not believe in God, and so he aroused great laughter. . . . The madman leapt right among them. . . . "Where is God?" he cried. "Well, I will tell you. We have murdered him—you and I. . . . But how did we do this deed? . . . Who gave us the sponge with which to wipe out the whole horizon? How did we set about unchaining our earth from her sun? Whither is it moving now? Whither are we moving? . . . Are we not falling incessantly? . . . Is night not approaching, and more and more night? Must we not light lanterns in the forenoon? Behold the noise of the grave-diggers, busy to bury God. . . . And we have killed him! What possible comfort is there for us? . . . Is not the greatness of this deed too great for us? To appear worthy of it, must not we ourselves become gods?"—At this point the madman fell silent and looked once more at those around him: "Oh," he said, "I am too early. My time has not yet come. The news of this tremendous event is still on its way. . . . Lighting and thunder take time, the light of the stars takes time to get to us, deeds take time to be seen and heard . . . and this deed is still farther from them than the farthest stars—and yet it was they themselves who did it!"
NIETZSCHE, The Gay Science

1

KARL MARX is a protean as well as a Promethean figure. We shall try to seize him primarily in his character as a philosopher of history. While this will be our main interest, we shall not understand him or his historical system well unless we have some idea of the challenges he issued in his other shapes.

Much of Marx's strength springs from the fact that he linked together so many strands of thought and analyzed so many drives for power present in nineteenth-century Western society. On the level of power, Marx offered a unified analysis of the interests of the capitalists against a declining and now defeated feudal order, and, at the same time, of the needs of the proletariat called into being by that victory and destined in turn to overthrow the capitalist order. In the sphere of thought he combined at least the following elements: (1) German, Hegelian philosophy, with its emphasis on historical change, especially in consciousness, by means of the dialectic; (2) French socialist doctrine and example, with its desire for a new society, most probably brought into being by revolutionary class action; (3) English political economic theory, with its interest in the mechanism by which the emerging capitalist and industrial society worked; and (4) almost as part of English political economics, the Scottish philosophical-historical outlook with its sweeping concern for an understanding of all parts of man's social and moral life.[1]

Marx the revolutionary; the professional economic analyist; and the socialist leader of an international workers' movement: these are all involved studies which, while they would illuminate our subject, must be passed by. Our focus will be on the Marx who sought to fulfill Vico's desire for a union of true philosophy and certain history by combining the rational necessity found in German metaphysical speculation with the empirical certainty of English economics via the catalyst of French political action—the famous Marxian "union of theory and practice."

I shall take the position that, in seeking to achieve this synthesis, Marx brought forth a new science of his own, wherein, like two pioneers from another field, Copernicus and Galileo

[1] For the last named, see Gladys Bryson, *Man and Society: The Scottish Inquiry of the Eighteenth Century* (Princeton, N.J., 1945).

(and the comparisons are apt in terms of the images Marx uses), he sought to go behind the veil of appearances and to reveal another, more real, more scientific, cosmos. In the course of this effort, he created a new language to translate his perceived reality, and he then used that language to transvalue all past values. Finally, having offered men a novel way of looking at the world, he then enticed them, on the basis of that vision, to construct a brave new world for themselves. In this last, of course, he took the decisive step beyond Vico and Hegel. It is the sum of these achievements which comprise his true genius; his is a revolution in thought which has affected even those who are most opposed to his revolution in action. In this sense only, then, shall I be dealing with Marx the revolutionary.

2

In a previous chapter it was suggested that Marx's greatness, as viewed from the philosophy of history, was that he synthesized the insights of Hegel and Comte. Let me put this in exaggerated and simplified form. On one side, he found the tradition of thought running up from Descartes, through Vico, to Kant and Hegel. In general, this tradition, as it emerged in its German guise, emphasized the constructing power of reason, a reason which it saw as informing and giving shape to material ·objects rather than merely reflecting or copying them. The epistemology is that of Kantian idealism. On the other side, Marx appropriated the body of doctrine which, starting again with Descartes, runs from Locke, Hume, and Condorcet, to Comte. In this doctrine, the emphasis is antimetaphysical. There is distrust of a supposedly pure reason, and the stress is on discovering a natural science by investigating material objects. The epistemology is Lockean empiricism.

In the case of Hegel, Marx's debt is clear and acknowledged.

Comte, he deliberately scorned. Now, while dealing briefly with the external evidence of Marx's relation to the two men, our real concern is *not* with their actual, direct influence on him, but rather with the *logical* relationships that can be perceived as existing among the three. Some of this relationship, I shall now state explicitly; much of it emerges implicitly from the previous chapters on the two earlier thinkers.

The direct connection of Marx to Hegel is so obvious, and has been dealt with by so many writers, that little needs to be said here.[2] Although he did not study personally under Hegel, who was dead when he attended the University of Berlin, Marx practiced his philosophical apprenticeship with the young Hegelians, especially Bruno Bauer, who had sought to take up the old man's legacy. Turning from law (begun at his father's request) to metaphysics, Marx read Hegel to such purpose and with such intensity that he appears to have gone through all of his works in a short space of time: the result was a permanent infection, which, while it brought its own immunization, left ineradicable traces and occasionally flared anew into virulence. Thus, working on the material which was to take form as his *Critique of Political Economy*, Marx wrote to Engels in 1858, "I have thrown overboard the whole doctrine of profit as it has existed up to now." Then he added, in an odd juxtaposition, "In the method of treatment the fact that by mere accident I again glanced through Hegel's *Logic* has been of great service to me."[3] Even at the end of his life, Marx, in his letters and writings, is constantly making reference to Hegel.

What Hegel gave to Marx was insight into the *rational*, into the necessary. As part of this insight, he also presented Marx

---

[2] See, for example, Sidney Hook, *From Hegel to Marx* (Ann Arbor, 1962); Herbert Marcuse, *Reason and Revolution: Hegel and the Rise of Social Theory* (New York, 1941); and Auguste Cornu, *Karl Marx: De l'hégélianisme au matérialisme historique* (Paris, 1934).

[3] Karl Marx and Frederick Engels, *Selected Correspondence (1843–1895)* (Moscow, no date given, but follows Russian edition of 1953). Marx to Engels, London, 14 January, 1858.

with the way or method by which rational necessity both developed and could be understood: the dialectic. Once stripped of the mystical form which Hegel had given it, the dialectic stood revealed as the only right method—and now Marx's method—of penetrating rational reality. All that was needed, as Marx reiterated in the preface to the second edition of *Capital*, was to turn Hegel's dialectic, which was standing on its head, the right way up again. Instead of starting from the ideal and proceeding to the material world, we reverse the operation, for "the ideal is nothing other than the material when it has been transposed and translated inside the human head."[4]

Hegel's emphasis on "consciousness," on what was "inside the human head," was correct. What was wrong was his attribution of consciousness to ideal rather than material forces and movements. Thus, according to Marx, the problem was to discover the real causes of human consciousness, and this entailed research into the empirical world which gave rise to the ideas.

In this latter effort, Marx's guide was Ludwig Feuerbach. Where Hegel, as we have seen, had effected the transition from religious to philosophical ideas, Feuerbach took the next step. He demonstrated that both religion and philosophy were "illusions" reflecting man's emotional needs.

Feuerbach was a keen psychologist, and his analysis of religious phenomena was more subtle than the usual Young-Hegelian effort. In his view, the kernel of religion is man and not god. Instead of a theology, Feuerbach offered an anthropology, in which the forms of religious worship are

---

[4] Karl Marx, *Capital*, 2 vols., translated from the 4th German edition by Eden and Cedar Paul (London, 1951), Vol. II, p. 873. In connection with Marx's turning Hegel right side up, there is a pleasant little verse, which goes as follows:

> Long ago in London town
> Marx turned Hegel upside-down,
> Revealing him as *sans-culotte*.
>
> Bernard Crick

Quoted from *Encounter* magazine, 117 (June, 1963), 65.

treated as fetishistic expressions of human needs. Where Hegel saw man cunningly manipulated by Spirit, Feuerbach saw the spirits as cunning psychic projections of self-deceiving men. The task was for men *consciously* to free themselves from their illusions.

Now, just as Feuerbach had gone beyond Hegel, so Marx went beyond Feuerbach. The latter had said, "In place of the illusory, fantastic, heavenly position of man which in actual life leads to the degradation of man, I substitute the tangible, actual, and consequently also the political and social position of mankind."[5] But Feuerbach had never really pursued his research into the "actual" conditions of man. Instead, neglecting the study of the changing "political and social position" which underlay man's psychic processes, he merely postulated an abstract, unchanging human being, who could free himself from his "heavenly position" by mere self-enlightenment: "Know Thyself" was the original title of Feuerbach's book, *Essence of Christianity*. Against this latter view, Marx turned quite savagely in his *Theses on Feuerbach*. The main burden of his attack was that Feuerbach, materialist as he was, overlooked completely the "human sensuous activity, practice" whch underlies all perception of external reality.

Fortunately, however, according to Marx, "the *active* side, in contradiction to materialism, was developed by idealism [i.e., Hegel]—but only abstractly, since, of course, idealism does not know real, sensuous activity as such."[6] Thus, the problem was to combine Hegel and Feuerbach. Obviously, one of the main appeals of Hegel for Marx was that the former's dialectics dissolved the existent. However, although Hegel supplied an active, changing element, he did so only in relation

---

[5] Ludwig Feuerbach, *Sammtliche Werke* (1846), Preface to Vol. I, pp. xiv–xv, as quoted in Hook, *op. cit.*, pp. 222–223.

[6] Karl Marx and Friedrich Engels, *Basic Writings on Politics and Philosophy*, Lewis S. Feuer (ed.) (Garden City, N.Y., 1959), p. 243. (Where possible I have tried to quote from this handy collection.) As Engels put it, "Therein lay the true significance and the revolutionary character of the Hegelian philosophy . . . that it once for all dealt the deathblow to the finality of all products of human thought and action" (p. 199).

to an ideal world. On the other hand, Feuerbach grounded this idealism in man, on this earth; but in an abstract man, on an unchanging earth. Marx sought to apply Hegel's principle of *active* perception and dialectic change to a Feuerbachian man involved in *actual* social relations. Marx's famous conclusion to the theses was that "the philosophers have only *interpreted* the world, in various ways; the point, however, is to *change* it."

Where in all this development of Marx's ideas does Comte fit? Ostensibly, nowhere. Marx's comments on the French positivist are few and disparaging. Thus, in 1866, when he appears to have read him for the first time, Marx remarked to Engels, "I am studying Comte on the side because the British and French make so much fuss over that fellow. What captivates them is the encyclopaedic about him, the synthesis. But compared with Hegel it is wretched (in spite of the fact that Comte as a professional mathematician and physicist is superior to him, i.e., superior in details; but even here Hegel is infinitely greater on the whole)." Then, with Hegel's death date in mind, Marx snapped "And this trashy positivism appeared in 1832!" Clearly, Marx did not consider Hegel and Comte as belonging to the same species.[7]

Part of Marx's distaste, surely, was grounded in his dislike for Comte's reactionary Catholic polity. Thus, writing in 1871 to his friend E. S. Beesly, one of the outstanding English positivists of the period, Marx declared that "as a Party man I entertain a thoroughly hostile attitude towards Comtism." Then he added, "as a scientific man I have a very poor opinion of it." Interestingly enough, as Marx himself tells us in the Preface to the second edition of *Capital*, the positivists returned the favor by reproaching him "for having treated economics metaphysically."[8]

[7] Marx to Engels, London, 7 July, 1866, *Selected Correspondence*, p. 218. On the "species" question, cf. my comments on pp. 184–185. Especially good as a comparison of Comte and Marx is Lucie Prenant, "Karl Marx et Auguste Comte," *A la lumière du Marxisme* (Paris, Cercle de la Russie Neuve, 1937), Vol. II, Part I. (This work, peculiarly, may be listed in library catalogues under *Cercle* rather than *A la lumière*.)

[8] Marx to E. S. Beesly, London, 12 June, 1871, *Selected Correspondence*, p. 322; *Capital*, Vol. II, p. 870.

There seems little doubt, therefore, that Comte did not consciously influence Marx's thinking. On the unacknowledged
level, however, Comte may have touched the young Marx's
mind through the Saint-Simonian movement. We know, for
example, that a Saint-Simonian, Ludwig Gall, apparently connected with a liberal circle which included Marx's father and
the headmaster of the local school, attracted attention in Trier
while Marx was a high-school pupil there; that Marx spoke of
his highly revered father-in-law, Ludwig von Westphalen, as a
disciple of Saint-Simon; and that Eduard Gans, whose course
on jurisprudence at the University of Berlin had a profound
influence on Marx, was a convinced Saint-Simonian.[9] Indeed,
the evidence is strong that Marx was exposed to Saint-Simonian doctrines, and therefore probably Comtean ideas, before
his headlong rush into Hegelian studies.

The point to be made here, however, is not that Comte did
or did not seriously influence the young Marx, and that, later
in life, he was rejected in much the way that Comte had
spurned Saint-Simon. Rather it is that the logic of their two
systems is more intimately related than Marx or most commentators will allow. It is because Marx synthesized certain
crucial elements present in Comtean positivism (whether Marx
derived them from it or not is immaterial here) with Hegelian
idealism, as refined into materialism by way of Feuerbach, that
he achieved his tremendous power over the modern imagination.

There are three crucial beliefs held in common by the
Comtean and the Marxist systems. First, that thought itself
develops along with the material world thought about. For
Comte, of course, this idea took the form that the logic of the
mind cannot be explained apart from its applications; only the
historical study of the sciences teaches us the logic proper to

[9] See the comments in Karl Marx: *Selected Writings in Sociology and
Social Philosophy*, T. B. Bottomore and Maximilien Rubel (eds.) (London, 1961), pp. 9, 13–14. See also Isaiah Berlin, *Karl Marx* (New York,
1952), and his comment that while Marx was studying under Gans,
"Hegelianism at first repelled his natural positivist intelligence" (p. 67).

each science. Marx made other use of this concept. Declaring that "the thought process itself grows out of conditions, is itself a *natural process* [Der Denkprozess selbst ein *Natur-prozess* ist]," he focused (as we shall see in detail later) on analysing the conditions and the consciousness which "corresponded" to or was "determined" by these conditions.[10]

Second, that social relations exist independent of men's will, and, as such, are subject to invariant laws. We have already seen this faith as the basis of Comte's science of sociology. In Marx's phraseology (although at various times he seemed to modify his position), we are told that "In the social production which men carry on they enter into definite relations that are indispensable and independent of their will."[11] To investigate these necessary relations during one particular stage of social production, capitalism, Marx wrote both his *Critique of Political Economy*, and *Capital*.

Third, and connected with the preceding two points, both Comte and Marx believed that they were ending the long reign of philosophy and metaphysics and were ushering in a new period of positive knowledge in the field of social phenomena. Thus, in the *German Ideology* (1845), Marx and Engels declared that "Where speculation ends—in real life—there real, positive science begins. . . . Empty talk about consciousness ceases, and real knowledge has to take its place. When reality is depicted, philosophy as an independent branch of activity loses its medium of existence."[12]

We must not gloss over the really major differences between Comte and Marx. These leap to the eye at once. By the same token, however, we must not overlook the fact that both men were seeking a social science, in the form of a historical sociology. Together reflecting the changed conditions of a world which had been rocked by a series of revolutions, polit-

[10] Marx to L. Kugelmann, London, 11 July, 1868, *Selected Correspondence*, p. 252.
[11] *Basic Writings*, p. 43.
[12] *Ibid.*, p. 248.

ical, economic, technological, and scientific, both thought they knew how to solve the growing social chaos, and both thought they knew how to do this "scientifically." Comte had perhaps a better grasp of the natural sciences than did Marx and his mentor Hegel; Marx admitted as much. What he lacked was the depths and heights of Marx's soaring flight through the past, the "Divine Comedy" quality of Marx's vision of the human condition. Comtean positivism might appeal to a small elite of scientists and industrialists. Marxism sought to speak to mankind (conceived as soon to break the fetters and bonds of class differences) at large. Comte had wished to found a religion of humanity, and ended up fathering only a sect. Where Comte had failed, Marx succeeded. As a result, Marx gave to the world its new, secular religion, that is, a "scientific" philosophy of history.

3

Certain aspects of Marx's life may shed useful light on our inquiry into his system of thought. In this area, however, I shall mainly be pointing up problems for research, rather than making final assessments. With that fact carefully underlined, let us touch on a few important items.

The first involves the relations of Marx and Engels. Our concern is with this relationship primarily as it affected the development and enunciation of the Marxist philosophy of history.[13] According to Engels himself, the entire credit for the historical approach belongs to Marx. The *Manifesto*, for

[13] There are, of course, many fascinating personal aspects to the relations of Marx and Engels, such as Engels' labelling Marx as the "Moor" (as, in fact, did Marx's children); Marx's rather callous disregard, at least initially, of Engels' feelings at the death of his mistress, Mary Burns; and so forth. The book to consult on Engels is Gustav Mayer, *Friedrich Engels*, 2 vols. (The Hague, 1934). (Incidentally, Freud was also labelled "Moor" by his mother, because of his tangle of black hair as a child. See *The Interpretation of Dreams*, translated by James Strachey [London, 1961], p. 337, fn. 1.)

example, was originally drawn up by Engels in the form of a catechism. It was Marx who rewrote it, admittedly at Engels' suggestion, as the scenario of a great historical drama to be played out on the world's stage. Reminiscing about the *Manifesto*'s conception, Engels summed up the matter in his Preface to the German edition of 1883:

The basic thought running through the Manifesto—that economic production and the structure of society of every histurical epoch necessarily arising therefrom constitute the foundation for the political and intellectual history of that epoch; that consequently (ever since the dissolution of the primeval communal ownership of land) all history has been a history of class struggles, of struggles between exploited and exploiting, between dominated and dominating classes at various stages of social development; that this struggle, however, has now reached a stage where the exploited and oppressed class (the proletariat) can no longer emancipate itself from the class which exploits and oppresses it (the bourgeoisie), without at the same time forever freeing the whole of society from exploitation, oppression and class struggles—this basic thought belongs solely and exclusively to Marx.

It was a judgment he repeated in 1888, in the foreword to an edition of "Ludwig Feuerbach and the End of Classical German Philosophy."[14] We can hardly do otherwise than to accept Engels' verdict in the matter.

While giving Marx the single credit for the philosophy of

[14] Speaking of the passage from Hegelian idealism to the materialist philosophy of history, Engels says: "Here I may be permitted to make a personal explanation. Lately repeated reference has been made to my share in this theory, and so I can hardly avoid saying a few words here to settle this point. I cannot deny that both before and during my forty-year collaboration with Marx I had a certain independent share in laying the foundations of the theory, and more particularly in its elaboration. But the greater part of its leading basic principles, especially in the realm of economics and history, and, above all, their final trenchant formulation, belong to Marx. What I contributed—at any rate, with the exception of my work in a few special fields—Marx could very well have done without me. What Marx accomplished, I would not have achieved. Marx stood higher, saw further, and took a wider and quicker view than all the rest of us. Marx was a genius; we others were at best talented. Without him the theory would not be by far what it is today. It therefore rightly bears his name." (*Basic Writings*, pp. 224-225, fn. 1.)

history, for most other purposes we can talk of Marx and
Engels in one breath. There were differences of emphasis, of
course. Engels, with his greater *bonhomie* and open nature,
was less sharply polemical than Marx (on the other hand, Marx
had a much better sense of humor, and could often be extremely funny and gay); he was more interested in the natural
sciences and quicker to see the dialectic supposedly at work in
such fields as chemistry and biology; and he was probably
more interested in changing, even ameliorating gradually, the
economic conditions of the working class than he was in transforming the nature of man.[15] Such divergencies, however,
never amounted to differences of principle. Therefore, quotations from Engels can be considered here as fully representative of the Marxist position.

With this granted, our task is simplified. Further, we can now
single out aspects of Marx's life, without having to do the same
for Engels, and assume their connection with the philosophy
of history which is here our primary concern. The first thing
to note about Marx's existence is its general marginality. Born
in 1818, in Trier (Trèves), Germany, the young Marx grew up
in the Rhineland, on the borderland between German and
French culture. Descended from a long line of rabbis on both
sides of his family, Marx was at least formally initiated into
Christianity at the age of 6 (although his father, a prosperous
bourgeois lawyer, had actually converted to Protestantism a
year before his son's birth). As a nominal Protestant, Marx was
one of about 300, living among something like 11,000 Catholics
in Trier.[16] One of his Protestant neighbors was the aristo-

[15] Cf. George Lichtheim, *Marxism: An Historical and Critical Study*
(New York, 1961), pp. 60–61.
[16] Cf. Edmund Wilson, *To The Finland Station* (Garden City, N.Y.,
1940), p. 113. Two short biographies of Marx are Berlin, *op. cit.*, and
Cecil J. S. Sprigge, *Karl Marx* (London, 1938). Franz Mehring, *Karl
Marx*, translated by Edward Fitzgerald (Ann Arbor, 1962) is standard.
Otto Rühle, *Karl Marx: His Life and Work*, translated by Eden and
Cedar Paul (London, 1929) is interesting for its psychological specula-
tions. See also the biographies by E. H. Carr, *Karl Marx: A Study in
Fanaticism* (London, 1934); and B. Nicolaievsky and O. Maenchen-
Helfen, *Karl Marx: Man and Fighter* (Philadelphia, 1936).

cratic von Westphalen family, and the young Karl eventually married the beautiful Jenny von Westphalen, four years older than himself. Although Marx always retained bourgeois tastes and habits, he was later to take the lovely Jenny to live with him temporarily in lower-class conditions (the lot, of course, of most political refugees of the period).

At the university, first Bonn and then Berlin, Marx, as we have already noted, studied law at his father's request, and then switched to philosophy. Although he took his doctorate in philosophy, he was prevented from becoming a professional philosopher by the hostile attitude of the Prussian government. Instead, in 1842 he became a journalist with the *Rheinische Zeitung* in Cologne, and then, for a short while, its editor. If Marx can be said to have pursued any career other than that of a professional revolutionist, it was that of a journalist. One result of this latter sort of work was that it involved him in practical and detailed everyday phenomena which would have probably escaped the attention of a lofty academic philosopher.

In fact, Marx's transition from a liberal to a communist is marked by his articles on the proceedings of the Rhenish Diet concerning a law for punishing the picking up of wood in the forests. On this issue, which involved the attempt by the government to deprive the peasants of one of their few remaining communal privileges, Marx confessed himself ignorant; Hegel had not prepared him for such material questions. What we can see intertwined in this incident is Marx's interests as a journalist, law student, and philosopher. The last interest, philosophy, is in part what distinguishes the young Marx from another observer of a contemporary parliamentary body debating economic and social conditions, Charles Dickens in England. Instead of novels, the result in Marx's case is the *Communist Manifesto*.

With the suppression of the *Rheinische Zeitung*, after five months under Marx's editorship, the newly married journalist, feeling "sick of the hypocrisy, the stupidity, the brutal authority, and of our cringing and complying and quibbling and tergiversation," and convinced that there was no possible further career for him in Germany, started with his bride on the life of exile which was to characterize his remaining existence. By November of 1843, he and Jenny were in Paris. Then, a sojourn in Brussels, necessitated by expulsion from Paris by Guizot, was eventually followed by settlement in London from 1849 to 1883.

It was in Paris that Marx first got down to serious study of the "material questions." It was here, too, that he and Friedrich Engels, whom he had first met briefly and unpromisingly in 1842, when Engels was on his way to Manchester to take up the textile manufacturing business of his father, began their astonishing and fecund collaboration. Where Marx was learning about the class struggle by reading the French historians Thierry and Guizot, Engels had experienced it first-hand in the factory of Ermen and Engels.[17]

Paris saw Marx turn into a communist. London, the heart of bourgeois, capitalist England, where the British Museum offered untold treasures to be mined and wrought into explosives for use against the society which had endowed it, witnessed his evolution into an economist. Each capital—Berlin, Paris, London—marks a step in expansion of thought: philosophy, revolutionary socialism, economics. Indeed, at the end of his wanderings, Marx had turned into an internationalist, whose vision transcended the narrow boundaries of the prevalent nationalism of his day, and whose theories cut across traditional dividing lines. In fact, within a few years of 1845, when Marx formally abandoned Prussian citizenship, he seemed to have achieved as an exile the precious marginal view which could leave him free of all ties and chains, whether of thought or of interest.

[17] Thus, while Engels' 1843 essay for the *Deutsch-Französische Jahrbücher* discussed the English political economists and called attention to Carlyle's passionate description of the situation in England, his *Condition of the Working Class in England in 1844* (1845) supplied the black hues of empirical data for the material question.

4

Now, having noticed Marx's marginality, a sociological observation, I want to turn to more personal, psychological considerations. I enter upon this task with great trepidation. Marx,
himself, offers no assistance. Although, like Hegel and Feuerbach, he is much concerned with man's self-consciousness, this
last is more a social or historical than a personal consciousness.
Feuerbach had seen the human essence or personality as an
"abstraction inherent in each single individual." Marx dismisses
both the individual and the abstraction, and defined the human
essence as, in reality, "the ensemble of the social relations."
Thus, when talking of the capitalist, he points out that he is
not describing a unique, particular individual, but a product of
social relations who reacts in an externally determined fashion.[18]

Marx never critically examined himself (admittedly, not an
unusual state of affairs for someone as active as Marx, especially in the mid-nineteenth century). There is no introspec-
tion, no plunge into the self à la Nietzsche. And Marx's neglect
of his own psyche is mirrored by his neglect of psychological
processes in his economic interpretation of history. Thus, the
personal factor—or ostensible lack of it—in Marx has significant ramifications in his theory. By understanding this fact, we
may go on to two important consequences of our concern
with his psyche.

The first is that we can attempt to differentiate those elements of Marx's system which reflect primarily his own psychological needs from those which seem to rest more on an
objective analysis of the social reality surrounding him in the
nineteenth century. Thus, while carefully avoiding the view
that a comprehension of the psychological origin of a state-

[18] *Basic Writings*, p. 244. Looked at objectively, Marx's formulation
seems just as "abstract" as Feuerbach's. See further *Capital*, Vol. I, p. 138;
and Vol. II, p. 650.

ment is a substitute for the consideration of its logical validity,
I stress the value, for our purposes, of understanding why,
psychologically, certain elements of Marx's system exist in a
given place.[19]

The second consequence of note is that the *emotional* impact of Marx's work, which comes from the heightened charge
he places on certain metaphors, is often far more important
than the intellectual effect. Thus, exactly the same ideas about
capitalists and laborers which are to be found comfortably and
quietly residing in Adam Smith's *Wealth of Nations* are
awakened into revolutionary feelings by Marx's incendiary
phrasing of them. If we learn to comprehend this correctly,
we might better be able to understand the appeal of Marxism
to his followers.[20]

Any such study of Marx's psyche as recommended here
would have to involve a careful analysis of many items. For
example, Marx's youthful poems, not to mention his novels and
dramas, offer a whole array of symbols; they are filled with
allusions to the sea, storms, and men's bones, images generally
not used in his later writings. Next, of course, his relations
with his parents and his brothers and sisters need to be studied
closely, and while there is little material on this subject, what

[19] Cf. Robert Tucker, *Philosophy and Myth in Karl Marx* (Cambridge,
England, 1961). While many of the specific interpretations must be
sharply questioned, the effort Tucker makes to look at Marx in a new
way requires admiration. For a typically negative review of Tucker, see
Eugene Kamenka's in the *Australasian Journal of Philosophy*, 40, 2
(August, 1962). I should also add, indeed stress, that a full treatment of
Marx ought to be informed by the knowledge that his psychological
needs—as those of any individual—cannot in fact be isolated from the
social reality with which they interacted and by which, in large part,
they were formed. On the sort of general psychoanalytic approach I
have in mind, see Erik H. Erikson, *Childhood and Society*, 2nd ed. (New
York, 1963).

[20] A psychoanalytically informed study of Marx might link significantly with an inquiry such as Nathan Leites' *Study of Bolshevism*
(New York, 1954), where content analysis is used to probe the psychological processes of th Bolshevik leaders. It would be interesting to discover whether the results of the two inquiries would be the same. In the
general area of psychoanalysis and history, a splendid model is provided
by Erik H. Erikson, *Young Man Luther* (New York, 1958).

there is must be studied in the most expert and illuminating manner. Perhaps Marx's relations with his father were as simple or affectionate as almost all his biographers would have it (a typical statement is that the relations of Marx and his father were always "warm, intimate and grave"), but, in the light of modern theory, the subject needs to be re-examined; for example the oft-cited fact that Marx carried his father's portrait around with him at the end of his life proves nothing against the smoldering feelings that may have existed in the young boy, Karl Marx.[21] So, too, Marx's "Jewishness," and all its subtle relations to his family background as well as to society at large, requires more perceptive treatment than it has hitherto received. Then there are his relations with Engels, the lifelong friend who addressed him in many of the letters as "Dear Moor"—did he have in mind the dark Othello, who had married the fair Desdemona? Or the relations with his own immediate family: the more or less uncomplaining Jenny, who gave him self-effacing devotion, the children with whom he romped and played (his son affectionately called him "Devil", and all the children called him "Moor"), and one of whom came to such a sad ending (two daughters committed suicide, but one did so only at the age of 70, when her husband died). And what of Marx's carbuncles, headaches, and other illnesses? Were they, like Darwin's somewhat similar symptoms, protections against society's intrusion on the creative thinker?[22]

[21] Berlin, *op. cit.*, p. 29. For suggestive efforts at understanding this type of father-son relations, see Alexander L. George and Juliette L. George, *Woodrow Wilson and Colonel House* (New York, 1956). Charles Darwin's relations with his father seem to have been of a similar nature; a description, though not an analysis is provided in Gertrude Himmelfarb's excellent example of intellectual history, *Darwin and the Darwinian Revolution* (Garden City, N.Y., 1962), *passim*. The point here is not that overt fondness for one's father is necessarily proof of latent antagonism—far from it—but rather that latent antagonism *may* exist *in spite of* overt fondness; and only an open-minded look at the total evidence can supply a useful answer. For Marx's youthful writings, see the collected edition of his works, *Marx-Engels Gesamtausgabe* (MEGA), Erste Abteilung, Band I, Zweiter Halbband (1929); and Wilson, *op. cit.*, p. 114.

[22] See Lewis S. Feuer, "Marxian Tragedians," *Encounter* (November,

Uncomfortable and amateurish as some of these questions are, they should not be shrugged aside. Correctly approached, they will help in a task Marx constantly set himself: the "revealing" of reality. Indeed, for brief moments, Marx touched, unknowingly, on what Freud was to concern himself with throughout his life. Thus, Marx commented that "as in private life one differentiates between what a man thinks and says of himself and what he really is and does, so in historical struggles one must distinguish still more the phrases and fancies of parties from their real organism and their real interests, their conception of themselves from their reality."[23] Marx was thinking only of social reality, and of personality as a reflection of social relations; Freud would go deeper into psychology.

However, a word of caution is badly needed here. Any such study as I have suggested must carefully distinguish between what is unique to Marx's psyche and what is common to the thought of his time. If Marx talks constantly about "fetters," it may be a reflection of his own fear of dependency, but it is as likely to be a philosophical concept borrowed from Hegel, and before him, perhaps from Epicurus. Freud's own attribution to Leonardo da Vinci's character of certain traits which were actually commonplace elements of the art of his time, is a warning.[24]

1962), which, while suggestive, must be read with caution. (Incidentally, the difficulties in determining the source of Darwin's symptoms—an insect bite or neurosis—should serve as a caution to the overeager analytically-minded investigator.) For some of the debate, see "Darwin's Illness," *New Statesman*, 3 April, 1964, and the letter by Douglas Hubble in the *New Statesman* of 10 April, 1964.

[23] Karl Marx and Frederick Engels, *Selected Works*, 2 vols. (London, 1950), Vol. I, p. 247.

[24] Cf. Hook, *op. cit.*, p. 70; and J. N. Findlay, *Hegel: A Re-Examination* (London, 1958), p. 99. Freud's essay, of course, is his *Leonardo da Vinci and a Memory of his Childhood* (1910). See the discussion of this by Meyer Schapiro, "Leonardo and Freud: An Art Historical Study," *Journal of the History of Ideas* (April, 1956); and, in turn, of the latter by K. R. Eissler, *Leonardo da Vinci: Psychoanalytic Notes on the Enigma* (New York, 1961).

Unqualified, or at least unable here, as I am to engage in a
psychological study of Marx, what may be suggested, however, and even this in an all too superficial way, is a sort of
"stylistic" analysis of a few traits in Marx's writings; that is, a
study of three or four important motifs or metaphors whch
run through his work.[25] The first of these is one remarked
upon by many commentators. It is the Promethean note in
Marx.

This note is sounded in the early poems, and is made completely manifest when Marx placed at the beginning of his
doctoral dissertation (*Differenz der demokritischen und
epikureischen Naturphilosophie*) the speech delivered by
Aeschylus' Prometheus: "Know well I would never be willing
to exchange my misfortune for that bondage of yours. Far
better do I deem it to be bound to this rock than to spend my
life as Father Zeus's faithful messenger." Later, when the government suppressed the *Rheinische Zeitung* which Marx was
editing, a contemporary cartoon showed him chained to the
press with a Prussian eagle tearing at his liver.

This image of defiance is taken up in a number of key
places, and persists all through Marx's writings. Thus, as late as
1879, Marx is still scornful about the petty bourgeois because
"instead of defiant resistance to ill-treatment from above,"
they offered only "humble submission and confession that the
punishment was deserved." Now, intimately connected with
this note of defiance is the concept of alienation in Marx, and
it is well at this point to hint at its relation to the Prometheus
theme (reserving a fuller treatment of the concept itself till
later). Thus, in the doctoral thesis, Marx quotes Epicurus to
the effect that: "Not he is Godless who scorns the Gods of the
multitude, but he who accepts the opinions of the multitude
concerning the Gods." This note persists into 1871, and Marx's
injunction to his friend Kugelmann about the Paris Commune:
"Compare these Parisians, *storming heaven*, with the *slaves to*

[25] Cf. Stanley Edger Hyman, *The Tangled Bank: Darwin, Marx, Frazer
and Freud as Imaginative Writers* (New York, 1962).

heaven of the German-Prussian Holy Roman Empire, with its posthumous masquerades reeking of the barracks, the Church, cabbage-junkerdom and *above all, of the philistine* (italics added)." The Gods, as we shall see later, represent alienated men; to end alienation, we must "storm heaven."[26]

The second major note in Marx's writing is part and parcel of the Promethean: it is the emphasis on the necessity of struggle and conflict, on hardness and force. Bourgeois society is "unheroic" and supine, although it had originated in "sacrifice, terror, civil war and battles of people." Scathingly, Marx comments that "the German philistine is cowardice incarnate. He respects only those who inspire him with fear." In the "Confessions," recorded by his daughter, Laura, Marx apparently responded to the following questions in the following way: "Your favorite virtue in man. . . . Strength [it is revealing that his response to the same question about woman was 'Weakness']; your idea of happiness. . . . To fight; your idea of misery. . . . Submission; the vice you detest most. . . . Servility."[27]

Marx's picture of the world was of a hostile environment, against which he had to strive. "I . . . am engaged in the bitterest conflict with the whole world," he confessed (and his parenthetical, "the official one," does not really convince us). The effect of his structuring the social world in this fashion on the whole socialist movement which he created and shaped ought not to be underestimated. Left to himself, for example, Engels tended to lapse into a less aggressive attitude to life. Although he would remember to admonish the revisionist,

[26] Marx and Engels, "Circular Letter," 17–18 September, 1879, *Selected Correspondence*, p. 392; Mehring, *op. cit.*, p. 31; and Marx to Kugelmann, London, 12 April, 1871, *Selected Correspondence*, p. 319.

[27] *Selected Works*, Vol. I, p. 226; and *Reminiscences of Marx and Engels* (Moscow, no date), p. 266. Shall I let myself be tempted by a bit of amateur psychologizing? Is the German philistine Marx's father, Heinrich Marx, who, when Marx was 16 in 1834, supposedly backed down in abject humiliation from a plea for a real parliament, in the face of the authorities' displeasure? Alas, real life is undoubtedly more complicated than this. For an account of the putative episode, see Berlin, *op. cit.*, p. 28.

Eduard Bernstein, "Hit back, that's what you have to do, two or three blows for every one the enemy strikes," Engels' "softness" came creeping through; thus, he qualified his insistence on struggle by remarking at another time, "I cannot agree . . . that the *bellum omnium contra omnes* was the first phase of human development. In my opinion, the social instinct was one of the most essential levers of the evolution of man from the ape." For Marx, other images were constant and more characteristic. Talking of the petty-bourgeois penetration of the German Social Democratic Party, he said curtly, "How the Party can tolerate the authors of this article in its midst any longer is incomprehensible . . . if . . . the leadership of the Party should fall more or less into the hands of such people, the Party would simply be castrated [so wird die Partei einfach entmannt] and there would be an end of proletarian snap."[28] The link of philistines, weakness, and castration is too clear to be doubted or ignored.

Closely connected with Marx's Promethean defiance is a third, related group of images. Like Prometheus, Marx felt himself bound and fettered, tied down by servitude out of which he had to break. There is some basis for believing that he hypostatized his personal feelings, and projected them as a condition of both the working class and of industrial society in its capitalist phase. The link is made obvious for us in *Capital;* speaking of a "law" concerning relative surplus population, or the industrial reserve army, Marx declares that it "chains the worker to capital even more effectually than Prometheus was fastened to the rock by the fetters forged by Hephaestus." In numerous places, the proletariat are enjoined to rise up and, so to speak, to storm heaven, for they "have nothing to lose but their chains." Economic forces, too, are prevented from their

[28] Marx to S. Meyer, Hanover, 30 April, 1867, *Selected Correspondence*, p. 224; Engels to E. Bernstein, London, 18 January, 1883, *ibid.*, p. 431; Engels to P. L. Lavrov, London, 12–17 November, 1875, *ibid.*, p. 369; Marx and Engels "Circular Letter," *ibid.*, p. 395 (although this letter is signed by both Marx and Engels, we can be sure the imagery is Marx's).

full development by incompatible relations of property: thus, in the feudal period the latter "became so many fetters. They had to be burst asunder; they were burst asunder"; and the same situation, we are told, now obtains under bourgeois society.[29]

While it is true that the imagery of "chains" and "fetters" was a commonplace of eighteenth-century thought—one thinks immediately of Rousseau's "Men are born free; everywhere they are in chains," and of the *philosophes'* attack on the fetters of ignorance holding back the progress of the human mind—the savage and constant preoccupation by Marx with these metaphors is especially noticeable. He even talks of "the fetters that the towns had imposed on the will of the countryside." In combination with the Promethean preoccupation, the ubiquity of the "fetter" image justifies the view that it is special and personal to Marx.

As it develops, the breaking of the fetters is metamorphosed into the image of tearing the veil. Before we can act, we must *see* the reality of life. To anyone who has read the *Manifesto,* examples leap to mind. Interestingly enough, Marx credits the bourgeoisie itself with the initial rending of the veil: it has "torn away from the family its sentimental veil"; "stripped of its halo every occupation"; and "for exploitation, veiled by religious and political illusions, it has substituted naked, shameless, direct, brutal exploitation." The note of "tearing" and "stripping" is strong. Thus, the bourgeoisie has "pitilessly torn asunder the motley feudal ties"; in *Capital* we are told that "large-scale industry has torn away the veil which used to hide from human beings their own social process of production"; and even Louis Bonaparte is credited with having "stripped its halo from the entire state machine."[30]

"Illusions," in Marx's poetic imagination, hide "nakedness."[31] And while he will develop his concept of "illusion"

[29] *Capital*, Vol. II, p. 714; and *Basic Writings*, p. 12.
[30] *Selected Works*, Vol. I, pp. 305, 311; and *Capital*, Vol. I, p. 525.
[31] See Marx to A. Ruge, March, 1843, *Selected Correspondence*, p. 25.

into a serious and important piece of analysis (his treatment of "ideology," as we shall see), its frequent connection with the images of "veil" and "nakedness" underlines for us the personal aspect of the concept for Marx.

Lastly, and somewhat more tenuously connected with the group of images I have just set forth, is Marx's stress on passion. The breaking of the chains, the tearing of the veil is effected by passion, what Marx, perhaps following Hegel here, at one place describes as "blind, unbridled passion." Men act blindly—they are "not free to chose their *productive* forces" —and they act out of a disreputable passion—" the only wheels that set political economy in motion are *greed*." For Marx, it would seem that the riddle of reality appears capable of solution only by men acting blindly, tearing apart the veils, and perceiving the naked truth. Has Prometheus, perhaps, also become Oedipus Rex?[32]

5

Whatever speculations we may indulge in concerning Marx's personal psychological processes, and I have emphasized my tentative approach to it as a "problem area," we must never forget that he functioned in a real, external world. Two events within that world were of critical importance, and serve as landmarks in Marx's development.

The first was the Revolution of 1848. It seems obvious that, in the early 1840s, Marx's primary concern was Germany. He started out, as a "liberal," wanting the French Revolutionary reforms for his own country. Very quickly, probably by 1842–1843, he became convinced that revolution at the hands of the "cowardly philistines," i.e., the bourgeoisie, was out of

[32] Here I restrict myself rigorously to the Greek play; while the psychological overtones cannot be avoided, I prefer to remain in the world of myth from which Marx drew his own image of Prometheus. See *Capital*, Vol. I, p. 269; Marx to P. V. Annenkov, Brussels, 28 December, 1846, *Selected Correspondence*, p. 40; and Tucker, *op. cit.*, p. 138.

the question. They had been scared by the example of 1793, when the "people" took over. Hence, at about this time, Marx changed from a liberal to a communist. His journey to the *Manifesto* and its vibrant challenge now led through the road indicated in the dying years of the French Revolution by Babeuf and the Conspiracy of the Equals.[33] In fact, the origin of the *Manifesto* can be traced back to a splinter group from the conspiratorial Société des Saisons headed by Blanqui (one of Babeuf's epigoni) which in 1836 formed itself into the League of the Just. Moving to London from Paris, and changing its name to the League of the Communists, the group invited Marx and Engels to draft "a complete theoretical and practical party program." The program, written in 1847, and published at the beginning of 1848 (just after the outbreak of revolution in Paris in February), bore the name, *Communist Manifesto*.[34]

The *Manifesto* had no effect on the revolution of 1848. However, when the revolution spread to Germany, Marx went to Cologne, where he helped edit a newspaper. On the failure of the revolution and the suppression of the paper, he returned to Paris and then to London. The arrest and trial of the League members still in Cologne marked the end of the Communist organization. Marx, who realized that the failure of 1848 meant the end of revolution à la Babeuf and Blanqui, at least for the time being (although he still suffered recurrent fits of unwarranted optimism, the chiliastic hope refusing to die completely), turned after 1850 from the barricades to the British Museum.

The period from 1850 to, say, 1864, was a true scholarly moratorium for Marx. It made him into a professional eco-

[33] Note, too, that the clarion call to revolution issued by the Conspiracy of Equals was called a Manifesto. The tradition of "Declarations"— of independence or the rights of man—is superseded by the new "Manifestoes." On Babeuf, see David Thomson, *The Babeuf Plot* (London, 1947).

[34] The authoritative edition of the Communist Manifesto is that edited by D. Ryazanov. See also Engels' Preface to the English edition of 1888, in *Basic Writings*, pp. 1–6.

nomic analyst, and into the author of *Capital*.[35] To the bare
outlines of the economic interpretation of history, which he
had already sketched in the *Manifesto*, he could now add the
detailed drawing of the nerves and muscles by which the process, in its captalist form took on animation. During his life-
time, he published one volume of *Capital*, of about 800 pages.
He also left notes for two other volumes which were put
together and published posthumously by Engels.

According to Marx, one reason why he was unable to finish
Capital was his involvement in the International Working-
men's Association.[36] This is the second major event to be
noted in Marx's career.

Formed in 1864, the International came into being over a
"national" problem, the Polish question, which was perceived
by Marx and others to have "International" consequences for
the workers. As Marx remarked in his Inaugural Address, the
encroachment of "that barbarous power," Russia, on Poland,
had "taught the working classes the duty to master themselves
the mysteries of international politics." So long as the feudal
power of Russia existed, local emancipation in Europe was
impossible. The revolution had to be both permanent and
worldwide. With these statements, Marx had risen far above
his 1848 commitment to Germany (and France).[37]

In fact, however, the revolution had first to occur in the
most advanced country, England, and under the influence of
the English working-class movement. Marx, for politic reasons
as much as anything else, even modulated his stress on force
and violence, and conceded that the change might be gradual

---

[35] See the comments by Joseph Schumpeter, *The History of Economic
Analysis* (New York, 1954), *passim*.

[36] Some scholars believe that Marx never completed his work on
Capital because of the theoretical difficulties he ran into with his concept
of surplus value.

[37] Cf. Marx to Engels, London, 4 November, 1864, *Selected Correspondence*, pp. 179–182; and *Selected Works*, Vol. I, p. 349. In theory,
of course, Marx's position was international from the beginning; now it
had become so in practice (although the International of 1864 really
embraced only Europe and America).

and parliamentary. We cannot bog down here in the notoriously involved problem of Marx's views on the method of change, peaceable or violent; he changed his mind and tone a number of times. Generally, however, we can say that in his early writings he seems to have assumed the necessity of violence (with the Paris Commune of 1871 reawakening this conviction). However, Engels and scholarship appear often to have mellowed his views, and, for example, in a remarkable speech at Amsterdam, in 1872, he admitted that different methods might apply to democratic and autocratic countries: while force, he declared, was the "lever of our revolution" in the latter, "we do not deny that there are countries, such as America, England, and—if I understand your institutions correctly—Holland where the workers can attain their goal by peaceful means."[38]

The International became the focus of Marx's practical activity, and it served as a means by which to capture the nascent labor movement for his theories. In turn, the demands of day-to-day "administrative" decisions, for Marx soon became the guiding figure of the organization, as well as his polemics with Bakunin and others who contested his views, took their very subtle toll in moderating and reshaping his views. Changed circumstances also, for the European world of 1864 and thereafter was quite different from that of 1848, found their reflection in Marx's letters and writings. Thus, while he did not lose the force of his personal motives, the strength of his principles, or the acidity of his literary style, he did broaden his perception of reality. Nevertheless, his later development, while it had very important consequences for the international socialist movement and also casts interesting shadows on his theories, must not be accounted to have significantly affected his basic philosophy of history.

[38] Cf. Carl Landauer, *European Socialism*, 2 vols. (Berkeley, 1959), Vol. I, pp. 132–133.

6

Important as are the psychological and political aspects of
Marx, they serve merely as background for understanding his
vision of man's development in time. Let us now turn directly
to Marx's interpretation of history. This last depicts a tremendous panorama, in which parts of the picture are left in
the sketchiest possible shape—mere cartoons—while other
parts are shaded in with smouldering, Goyesque-like realism,
and still other parts in tortuous, Breugel-like detail. It is a
canvas, lit with queer and wavering lights, on which a great
divine comedy is portrayed. As Marx himself remarks at one
point, aware of the analogy of his description of a part of the
capitalist system, "Dante would have found the worst horrors
of his Inferno surpassed in this manufacture."

Putting aside now, however, the dramatic aspects of Marx's
work, and looking at it more coldly and analytically, we shall
see that the essential form of his philosophy of history is as a
critique. Whereas English thinkers of the eighteenth century
tended to place in the title of their works the word "Inquiry"
—we think immediately of Hume's *Inquiry Concerning
Human Understanding* (and before that, Locke's) and of
Adam Smith's *Inquiry Concerning the Wealth of Nations*—a
German thinker like Kant labeled his works *Critique of Pure
Reason* and *Critique of Practical Reason*. And while Hegel did
not generally use the term as a title for his books (though he
did write a *Kritik der Verfassung Deutschlands*), a Young
Hegelian like Bruno Bauer wrote a *Kritik der evangelischen
Geschichte der Synoptiker*, dealing with the "higher criti-
cism" of the Bible, and in turn was attacked by his former
pupil, Karl Marx, under the heading *Kritik der kritischen
Kritik*. Marx also used the term in such works as his *Kritik des
Hegelschen Staatsrecht, Zur Kritik der politischen Okonomie*,
and many others. Choice of words by a writer is not accidental, and the uses of the terms "inquiry" and "critique"

point to different states of mind; implicit in the two words are references to an empirical and an idealist epistemology.

Marx made explicit his use of the word in his very first serious attempt to synthesize his readings in economics and philosophy, in the so-called *Economic and Philosophic Manuscripts of 1844* (sometimes also called the "Paris Manuscripts," unpublished until a partial edition in Russian in 1927, a full text in German in 1932, and in English in 1959). He begins by noting that his critical labors had already commenced with a "critique of jurisprudence and political science in the form of a critique of the *Hegelian* Philosophy of Right" (in the *Deutsch-Französische Jahrbücher* of 1844), and that he will now "issue the critique of law, ethics, politics, etc., in a series of distinct, independent pamphlets, and at the end try in a special work to present them as a connected whole . . . and finally, shall make a critique of the speculative elaboration of that material." The interesting adjective Marx uses to describe himself is *positive;* he is a positive critic.[39]

Now, by criticism Marx means what Kant meant: the examination *by reason* of what has hitherto itself been taken for granted. In Kant's case, this centers on the very possibility of metaphysics, which his British predecessor, David Hume, had simply assumed as the given. For Marx, concern centers on two major problems: (1) religion and its uncritical acceptance as the basis on which then to explain the nature of man; and (2) classical political economy which "proceeds from the fact of private property, but does not explain it to us . . . i.e., it takes for granted what it is supposed to evolve." Correctly viewed, from a critical standpoint, the answer to the first problem is that "*Man makes religion*, religion does not make man" (this statement, Marx tells us, is "The basis of irreligious criticism"); and to the second problem, that "Private property . . . results by analysis from the concept of *alienated labour*." As

---

[39] Karl Marx, *Economic and Philosophic Manuscripts of 1844*, translated by Martin Milligan (Moscow, 1961). (Hereafter referred to as *E-P*, pp. 14–15, 16–17.

Marx remarks decisively, summing up the two critical endeavors, "it becomes clear that though private property appears to be the source, the cause of alienated labor, it is really its consequence, just as the gods *in the beginning* are not the cause but the effect of man's intellectual confusion."[40]

In his *Contribution to a Critique of Hegel's Philosophy of Right* (*Zur Kritik der Hegelschen Rechtsphilosophie*), Marx has already stated that "criticism of religion is the premise of all criticism." Criticizing Hegel, Marx yet acknowledges him as the true source of the fundamental criticism. "The *Phenomenology* is . . . an occult criticism—still to itself obscure and mystifying criticism; but inasmuch as it keeps steadily in view man's *estrangement*, even though man appears only in the shape of mind, there lie concealed in it *all* the elements of criticism, already *prepared* and *elaborated* in a manner often rising far above the Hegelian standpoint." To substitute material man for man appearing only in the "shape of mind," and thus to make Hegel's criticism positive was Feuerbach's accomplishment. It is to the latter that "positive criticism as a whole—and therefore also German positive criticism of political economy—owes its true foundation. . . . It is only with Feuerbach that *positive*, humanistic and naturalistic criticism begins. . . . The only writings since Hegel's *Phänomenologie* and *Logik* to contain a real theoretical revolution."[41]

As we have already noted, Marx soon discovered that Feuerbach's "theoretical revolution" was not enough. It was necessary for Marx to bring about another "theoretical revolution" beyond the beginner of positive criticism. He indicates its tenets in his *Theses on Feuerbach*. In the fourth thesis Marx says of Feuerbach, "His achievement consists in dissolving the religious world and revealing its secular foundation. He overlooks the fact, however, that after completing this work *the chief thing still remains to be accomplished* [italics added]."

[40] *Ibid.*, pp. 67–68, 80; and *Basic Writings*, p. 262.
[41] *E-P*, p. 150 (this whole passage is worth close reading), and pp. 16–17.

Put another way, "the task of history," Marx declares, "once the world beyond the truth has disappeared is to establish the truth of this world. The immediate task of philosophy, *which is at the service of history* [italics added], once the *saintly form* of human self-alienation has been unmasked, is to unmask self-alienation in its *unholy forms*. Thus the criticism of heaven turns into the criticism of the earth, the *criticism of religion* into the *criticism of right*, and the *criticism of theology* into the *criticism of politics*." According to Marx, therefore, what is missing in Feuerbach is the yoking of philosophy to the chariot of history (or change), as well as a critical analysis of the secular foundation which underlies the religious world (in other words, an analysis of the material world). The task ahead, Marx declares, is that "once the earthly family is discovered to be the secret of the holy family it must be *theoretically criticised* and *practically transformed* [italics added]." Then, again writing about Feuerbach, in *The German Ideology*, Marx adds a final ingredient, "It is not criticism but revolution which is the driving force of history—as well as of religion, philosophy and every other theory."[42]

This, then, is the final meaning of Marx's *positive critique*. In terms reminiscent of Vico, he has informed us that "the task of history . . . is to establish the truth of this world." In doing so, history, with the help of philosophy (soon, however, to be ended "in the hitherto accepted sense of the word"), will critically transform and revolutionize both the world and the men whom that world conditions and circumscribes.

7

What, however, does Marx really mean by "history," or the "critique of history," to which he assigns such important tasks? And how are we to understand and interpret it? In the

---

[42] *Basic Writings*, p. 263; and Hook, *op. cit.*, pp. 290–291.

briefest compass possible, the salient features of Marx's philosophy of history may be summarized as follows. We start with man, who "makes" history. However, in order for man to make history, he must first live; and to live, he must produce. Thus, man must produce himself—procreation—and the material world. Both forms of production involve the division of labor, and the division of labor involves private property and the conflict of the particular interest with other interests. It also gives rise, as we shall see, to the state of being which Marx calls "alienation."

Concentrating on man's production of the material world, Marx emphasizes the crucial role of "tools." It is by means of tools or instruments that man works away at his material environment. Further, it is the nature of the tools themselves which "determines" the particular form taken by the division of labor. The latter form *in all its complexity* can then be described as the "economic relations of production." Corresponding to this last, however, are also all the social relations occasioned by the division of labor; for example, the class structure of society; the legal code which regulates the relation of the classes (as well as the economic process of production); and the political constitution which is the official expression of these various relationships. Whereas the economic relations constitute what Marx calls the "real foundation," the social relations which arise on their basis are "superstructures." To the latter, moreover, correspond forms of social consciousness: spiritual processes of life, which may be summed under the rubric "ideologies" (and include art, religion, and philosophy, as well as political and social doctrines).

The history made by man falls into various stages, or epochs, and these are based on a particular conglomeration of tools, economic relations, social relations, and level of consciousness which coexist at one time. Change takes place via the dialectic. When, in a given epoch, the tools change, then the existing economic relations of production and the social and ideological relations become so many fetters and bonds on the full utilization of the new productive forces. The result is conflict. This conflict is not between abstract and disembodied "ideas" or "spirits," but between classes; for new classes are "produced'" by the tools and economic relations, and like the material goods themselves, later find themselves in straited circumstances, unable to develop fully. Out of the class struggle comes a new synthesis, a new epoch, with characteristic tools, relations of production, social relations, and ideology. This in turn then becomes, to shift our metaphor to another characteristic Marxian image, the "womb" in which new productive forces will develop, and the dialectic process begins anew.

According to Marx, however, from this dialectic, this play of forces beyond his control, man must now free himself. He must substitute his *will* for the hitherto blind process. This he does by coming to *understand* the process, by realizing that the productive relations, like the gods of religion, are really only products of his own imagination. At this point, Marx seems to flit nimbly past the contradiction latent between a process hitherto presumed to be "independent" of the will of man and this new, voluntarist consciousness of man. To put it in the boldest terms, Marxian man will now end the domination of his own alien powers, by a last turn of the dialectic. The result will be a "communist regulation of production," where division of labor, classes—and history!—will be abolished. Or so it seems.

Now Marx himself has supplied a more limited, though equally long, sketch of his economic interpretation of history, one that requires and has been given much quotation, in the Preface to his *Contribution to the Critique of Political Economy*. In spite of its length, as the classic statement of Marx's philosophy of history it demands reprinting.

To begin with, he tells us that from his "*critical* [italics added] revision of Hegel's *Philosophy of Right*" he was led to the conclusion that "legal relations as well as forms of state could be neither understood by themselves nor explained by the so-called general progress of the human mind." Passing, then, beyond the restricted views of men like Condorcet and Comte (though he does not mention them by name), Marx realized that the legal and political forms were "rooted in the material conditions of life, which are summed up by Hegel after the fashion of the English and French of the eighteenth century under the name 'civil society'; the anatomy of that civil society is to be sought in political economy."

Grasping firmly the Ariadne thread which would lead him through the labyrinth of history, Marx continues:

The general conclusion at which I arrived and which, once reached, continued to serve as the leading thread in my studies may be briefly summed up as follows: In the social production which men carry on they enter into definite relations that are indispensable and independent of their will; these relations of production correspond to a definite stage of development of their material powers of production. The sum total of these relations of production constitutes the economic structure of society— the real foundation, on which rise legal and political super-structures and to which correspond definite forms of social consciousness. The mode of production in material life determines the general character of the social, political, and spiritual processes of life. It is not the consciousness of men that determines their existence, but, on the contrary, their social existence determines their consciousness. At a certain stage of their development the material forces of production in society come into conflict with the existing relations of production, or—what is but a legal expression for the same thing—with the property relations within which they had been at work before. From forms of development of the forces of production these relations turn into their fetters. Then comes the period of social revolution. With the change of the economic foundations the entire immense super-structure is more or less rapidly transformed. In considering such transformations the distinction should always be made between the material transformation of the economic conditions of production, which can be determined with the precision of natural science, and the legal, political, religious, aesthetic, or philosophic—in short, ideological—forms in which men become conscious of this conflict and fight it out. Just as our opinion of an individual is not based on what he thinks of himself, so can we not judge such a period of transformation by its own consciousness; on the contrary, this consciousness must rather be explained from the contradictions of material life, from the existing conflict between the social forces of production and the relations of production. No social order ever disappears before all the productive forces for which there is room in it have been developed, and new, higher relations of production never appear before the material conditions of their existence have matured in the womb of the old society.

Clearly, Marx's powerful formulation, even in the oversimplified précis of his theories offered here, presents an awesome though perplexing interpretation of man's past. It is our task now to swoop down once again, from our Daedalus heights, to the labyrinth of history, and, with Karl Marx as our guide, to study more closely the mazelike construction of this human prison.

8

If Hegel is Marx's starting point in philosophy, Adam Smith is certainly his starting point in political economy. This is so, in spite of the fact that Ricardo's theoretical apparatus probably had the greater effect in the area of economic analysis per se. Smith is the central link in Marx's synthesis of philosophy and economics, and, as such, supplies Marx with the all-important emphasis on labor and production, as well as spreading before him a general scheme for the economic epochs and movements of history.[43] Both Smith and Marx started out as philosophers, and ended up as self-taught economists. Both took the widest possible view of economics, and studied it in its connection with morality, polity, and history.

In the *Economic and Philosophic Manuscripts of 1844*, page after page is devoted to extracts or quotations from Smith; and

[43] See my introduction to *Adam Smith: The Wealth of Nations: Representative Selections* (New York, 1961); and Robert C. Tucker, "The Cunning of Reason in Hegel and Marx," *The Review of Politics* (July, 1956).

the opening words of *Capital* are "The wealth of societies." However, as with all his predecessors—Hegel, Feuerbach, Bauer, and a host of others—Marx transmutes and transvalues his heritage from Smith into almost unrecognizable shape. Thus, he substitutes for Smith's rather static division of labor the notion of division of labor as a relative arrangement, taking many historical forms, and evolving with the changing tools and relations of production.[44] So, too, in place of Smith's view of capitalism turning labor into a commodity, Marx projects the image of labor being transformed into a machine.

Passing well beyond Smith, and entering upon thorny philosophical paths, Marx defines labor as "a process going on between man and nature, a process in which man, through his own activity, institutes, regulates, and controls the material reactions between himself and nature. . . . By thus acting on the external world and changing it, he at the same time changes his own nature. He develops the potentialities that slumber within him, and subjects these inner forces to his own control." Thus, "What happens is, not merely that the worker brings about a change of form in natural objects; at the same time, in the nature that exists apart from himself, he realizes his own purpose, the purpose which gives the law to his activities, the purpose to which he has to subordinate his own will."[45] Clearly, though these words are in *Capital,* an economic treatise, they are philosophical in importance. Marx has set up as his hero the "sensuous practical man" whom he found missing in Hegel and Feuerbach. This man is the new philosopher, who must "change" the world by the very nature of his productive labor; until now he has been insufficiently conscious of his own purpose. In sum, labor, *in the very important sense just indicated,* a point often overlooked by commentators on Marx, is the materialistic basis of history.

[44] Marx to P. V. Annenkov, Brussels, 28 December, 1846, *Selected Correspondence,* p. 42. His polemic here is directed against Proudhon, but it could as well be against Adam Smith.

[45] *Capital,* Vol. I, p. 170.

The next thing to note is that man, in seeking to realize his potentialities and purpose, calls into existence new purposes. To adopt the phraseology of *The German Ideology* (written by Marx and Engels in 1846), "as soon as a need is satisfied . . . new needs are made; and this production of new needs is the first historical act." Conjoined with this "first historical act" is the circumstance that men "who daily remake their own life, begin to make other men, to propagate their kind: the relation between man and wife, parents and children, the *family*."

At the beginning, the family is the first social relationship. As such, it already embraces the fatal division of labor, "which was originally nothing but the division of labor in the sexual act." Marx then continues to startle us by saying that the natural division of labor in the family is the basis of private property, for in the family we have "unequal distribution . . . of labor and its products, hence property: the nucleus, the first form . . . where wife and children are the slaves of the husband. This latent slavery in the family, though still very crude, is the first property." It is a short step from this to larger social units, based on families or several individuals cooperating in productive labor. Indeed, with each "mode of production or industrial stage is always combined . . . a certain mode of cooperation, or social stage, and this mode of cooperation is itself a 'productive force.'"

It follows that each "mode of cooperation" involves in an expanding fashion division of labor and hence private property. In turn, this implies a growing "contradiction between the interest of the separate individual or the individual family and the communal interest of all individuals who have intercourse with one another." As long as this cleavage, which is based on the division of labor, exists, "as long, therefore, as activity is not *voluntarily* but naturally divided, man's own deed becomes an *alien* power opposed to him, which enslaves him instead of being controlled by him [italics added]." Then Marx adds a lyric contrast between life in the enslaved state and life in communist society: "For as soon as labor is distributed, each man has a particular, exclusive sphere of activity which is forced upon him and from which he cannot escape. He is a hunter, a fisherman, a shepherd, or a critical critic, and must remain so if he does not want to lose his means of livelihood; while in communist society, where nobody has one exclusive sphere of activity but each can become accomplished in any branch he wishes, society regulates the general production and thus makes it possible for me to do one thing today and another tomorrow, to hunt in the morning, fish in the afternoon, rear cattle in the evening, criticize after dinner, just as I have a mind, without ever becoming hunter, fisherman, shepherd, or critic." In short, Marx seems to be saying, only by *abolishing* division of labor can we free ourselves from the "alien power" and enjoy the idyllic existence.[46]

Now much has been made in recent scholarship of the concept of alienation in Marx.[47] There is no question that it is an important concept. Marx found the notion in Hegel, studied its development in Feuerbach, and embodied it in his own work.

Essentially, the alienation theme is related to the use of critique, and this operates in the following way. When man believes himself under the control of the very powers that he himself has produced, the gods of the temple and the gods of the market place, and conceives of them as objective powers, outside and above himself, he is alienated from his own essence. He allows himself, blindly, to be propelled to unintended consequences by the very forces he himself has set in motion. He permits his labor, for example, to become es-

---

[46] *Basic Writings*, pp. 249-254.

[47] Marx uses two terms that can be translated as "to alienate": "entaussern," meaning "to sell" or "to alienate" (a right, or one's property); and "entfremden," meaning "to estrange" or "to alienate." See *E-P*, pp. 11-12. The literature on Marx's concept of alienation has been growing apace. For example, see Heinrich Popitz, *Der entfremdete Mensch, Zeitkritik und Geschichtsphilosophie des jungen Marx* (Basle, 1953); Tucker, *op. cit.*; and, for a provocative treatment, Daniel Bell, "Two Roads from Marx: The Themes of Alienation and Exploitation and Workers' Control in Socialist Thought," *The End of Ideology* (New York, 1961).

tranged, alienated labor, and to rule over him in the form of private property. He takes for causes what are really effects.[48]

All this illusory world is *dissolved* by the acid of critique (the veil is torn asunder, to use the other image), and man sees his real condition for the first time. In seeing his condition, however, man sees it at the end of a development which has already occurred in blind, unperceived fashion. Marx accepts this development, all of it. He is not an intellectual Luddite who wants to smash the machinery of history; he wishes, instead, to harness its power for his own purposes. We may secure from two quotations the flavor of his approach to the related problems of alienation and critical dissolution. The first is from the *Economic and Philosophic Manuscripts of 1844* and has a definitely mystical Hegelian air to it. "*Communism,*" Marx declares exultantly, "as the *positive* transcendence of *private property* [is] . . . the complete return of man to himself as a *social* (i.e., human) being—a return become conscious, and accomplished within the entire wealth of previous development. This communism . . . is the *genuine* resolution of the conflict between man and nature and between man and man—the true resolution of the strife between existence and essence, between objectification and self-confirmation, be-

---

[48] *E–P*, p. 80. An interesting light is thrown on Marx's ideas by some of the statements made by people trying to cope with the depression of 1929. Thus, Donald R. Richberg, testifying at the Hearings of the Subcommittee of the Committee on Manufacturers, United States Senate, January, 1933, declared:

"Public physicians who urged us to let an epidemic run its course would be universally condemned. Economic illness is primarily man made and can be cured by the use of human intelligence or aggravated by human timidity and folly.

"I do not pretend to be an economist in the sense of one having a series of university degrees in such subjects to my credit, but I have long been a student of political economy and a student of the law, and it seems to me quite obvious that our economic conditions are all man made. This is a kind of social structure and business structure which we have built up in which we live. It is not a creation of Providence—something found in the world; it is not a natural product; it is man made and if it is not working correctly, it is subject to correction by the men who made it. The idea of saying that the system is going badly and therefore we must wait until it begins to go rightly is a type and

tween freedom and necessity, between the individual and the species." Then, in a cryptic phrase, Marx concludes, "Communism is the riddle of history solved, and it knows itself to be this solution."[49]

By the time of writing *The German Ideology*, Marx was ready to substitute a more sober economic content for his metaphysical vision. He asks rhetorically,

How does it happen that trade, which after all is nothing more than the exchange of products of various individuals and countries, rules the whole world through the relation of supply and demand —a relation which, as an English economist says, hovers over the earth like the Fate of the ancients, and with invisible hand allots fortune and misfortune to men, sets up empires and overthrows empires, causes nations to rise and disappear—while with the abolition of the basis of private property, with the communistic regulation of production (and, implicit in this, the destruction of the alien relation between men and what they themselves produce), the power of the relation of supply and demand is dissolved into nothing, and men get exchange, production, the mode of their mutual relation, under their own control again?[50]

Here, Marx has linked his concept of alienation with Adam Smith's "invisible hand." What he has done is to give apocalyptic overtones to the Scottish economist's desire to understand, and thus to control, the laws governing the productive forces of a laboring society. Marx has also added two all-important elements to the classical economic position. He has stated that the laws of supply and demand are not eternal

kind of logic I can not follow. It is simply our own system that is not going rightly. It is as though a man whose office gets in such a mess that he can not do business, should then sit down and say, 'If I wait long enough it will straighten itself out and everything will be all right.'

"That is the whole situation, as I see it, in regard to our economic conditions. We created society and created, by law, the corporate forms of activities which permit this tremendous mass organization of our resources and therefore permit mass destructive policies. All these factors in our system are man created and certainly the remedy for them lies in new systems . . ."

[49] *E–P*, p. 102.
[50] *Basic Writings*, p. 257.

verities, but mere modes of production created by men, and he has insisted that man can *under certain circumstances, will* these modes to be otherwise.

9

In the presentation of Marx up to now, I have pictured him as stressing will and consciousness. This is a very Hegel-like, rather romantic Marx, from the "storm and stress" period of his life. It is time to shade and balance the portrait. While reserving till later a full discussion of how "men make their history," it is necessary here to add that they make it under certain conditions which are "given"; and these given conditions are basically economic in character.

As we have seen, man in history seeks to realize certain purposes and needs. In so doing, he calls into being the division of labor and its concomitant aspects of property, class, and so forth. Man also utilizes what Marx calls "instruments of labor." Marx gives this a very wide definition, one which includes the earth itself (in the form of stone missiles) and domesticated animals, as well as the more usual wood, bone, and shell objects. In fact, Marx claims that it is not the traditional attribute of reason but the fabrication of instruments of production which distinguishes man from the other animals (although, as he points out, the first beginnings of the making of tools can be found among certain other animal species), and he quotes approvingly Benjamin Franklin's definition of man as "a toolmaking animal."[51]

At this point, Marx more or less creates a new branch of historical study: history of technology. "The relics of the instruments of labor," he suggests, "are of no less importance in the study of vanished socio-economic forms, than fossil bones are in the study of the organisation of extinct species. The various economic epochs are distinguished one from another,

[51] *Capital*, Vol. I, pp. 172, and 341, fn. 3.

not by differences in what is actually made, so much as by differences in the instruments of labor."[52] Pointing out that prehistoric times are classified according to the materials from which tools and weapons were made—the stone age, the bronze age, and the iron age—he chides historians for neglecting the development of material products, "which is the basis of all social life, and therefore of real history." Later on, in an extremely important footnote, Marx underlines the need for "a critical history of technology," and makes a direct comparison to Darwin and a significant allusion to Vico.

Darwin has aroused our interest in the history of natural technology, that is to say in the origin of the organs of plants and animals as productive instruments utilised for the life purposes of these creatures. Does not the history of the origin of the productive organs of men in society, the organs which form the material basis of every kind of social organisation, deserve equal attention? Since, as Vico says, the essence of the distinction between human history and natural history is that the former is the work of man and the latter is not, would not the history of human technology be easier to write than the history of natural technology? Technology reveals man's dealings with nature, discloses the direct productive activities of his life, thus throwing light upon social relations and the resultant mental conceptions. Even the history of religion is uncritical unless this material basis be taken into account.[53]

What Marx has done is to take Vico's "verum=factum," his "man makes history," and turn it into "man makes his history by means of tools." Darwin did not influence Marx—that can be stated categorically—and his name is invoked mainly for propaganda reasons. It is rather the thread leading from Descartes through Vico which, passed on to Hegel and Feuerbach, has guided Marx to the "material basis" of man's constructing and creative activity.

[52] *Ibid.*, p. 172. Francis Bacon, it may be noted, had earlier called for a "History of Trades," but he wanted it in order to understand nature, whereas Marx wanted it in order to understand man. For Bacon, see Walter E. Houghton, Jr., "The History of Trades: Its Relation to Seventeenth-Century Thought," *Journal of the History of Ideas*, II (1941).

[53] *Capital*, Vol. I, p. 172, fn. 3; and p. 392, fn. 2.

Marx, it must be added, does not leave his concept of the material basis of all social life and history in a simple and unanalysed form. It is not *simply* a matter of tools. The history of technology must be *critical;* and a *critical* history will lead us through all the epochs of the past, through all the complex "relations of production" which surround the changing material basis, and, finally, to a rigorous, detailed analysis of the present epoch, capitalism, and to a forecast of its necessary outcome. Marx's eye is like a moving picture camera, which first presents the wide horizon, then moves down to the middle view, and then pans in for a close shot. Let us try to follow him.

10

Marx identifies four epochs in the progress of the economic formation of society: the Asiatic, the ancient, the feudal, and the modern bourgeois. The similarity to Hegel's periodization is apparent, but the basis of the classification and the dialectic force which causes development from one epoch to another is quite different. In place of Hegel's Spirit, coming into increasing self-consciousness by means of the dialectic war of ideal contradictions, Marx presents us with a materialist dialectic, based on technological change. Epochal shifts in the relations of production, he tells us, are "always due to a revolutionary change in the instruments of production." Or, as he puts it in one of his catchy phrases: "the wind-mill gives you society with the feudal lord," while the steam engine implies the bourgeois capitalist.[54]

Nevertheless, while instruments of labor certainly form the basis of Marx's analysis of historical epochs, this is not the whole story. In practice, Marx had a keen eye for the various

[54] *Basic Writings*, p. 44; *Capital*, Vol. I, p. 385; and cf. H. B. Acton, *The Illusion of the Epoch: Marxism-Leninism as a Philosophical Creed* (London, 1955), p. 136.

elements producing a particular epoch. He was also fully aware that the epochs had not automatically succeeded one another everywhere, like a worm adding rings to its body. All four epochs were still coexisting. To put it succinctly, while Marx appears to be talking of time periods, he is really talking of forms of social relations, which, naturally, have had to make their appearance over time. In this sense, he is talking of "ideal types" rather than offering empirical descriptions of historical phenomena.

The Asiatic epoch is, thus, a society characterized by *Oriental despotism*. Such a society is marked by the absence of private property in land. Typical examples are Turkey, Persia, Hindustan—indeed, the whole area extending from the Sahara to the most elevated Asiatic highlands—and includes even Russia. Its basis is in climate and the nature of the soil. When these, taken together, make large-scale artificial irrigation the first condition of agriculture we have a situation where there is no private property, where individual communities are completely isolated from one another, and where Oriental despotism must prevail. In a nice example, we see how Marx stands Hegel on his head concerning the Asiatic epoch, when he says: ". . . *the absence of private property in land*. This is the real key, even to the Oriental heaven."[55]

What causes change in Asiatic society? Basically, nothing. The conditions circumscribing men in this situation are so fettering that he cannot, even if he wills to, break loose; moreover, the conditions prevent him from even becoming conscious of his own will. The Asiatic is an unchanging, dead form which can only have development imposed on it from the outside. The example Marx offers is that of British rule in India. It is probably the first sociological analysis of the impact of a mature economy on an underdeveloped nation. According

[55] *Basic Writings*, p. 471; Marx to Engels, London, 2 June, 1853, *Selected Correspondence*, p. 99. On the general subject, see the interesting treatment by Karl A. Wittfogel, *Oriental Despotism: A Comparative Study of Total Power* (New Haven, 1957).

to Marx, what the British have done is to break up the isolated, individual communities which form the basis of Oriental despotism. "These small stereotype forms of social organism have been to the greater part *dissolved* [italics added]," Marx informs us, through "the working of English steam and English free trade. Those family-communities were based on domestic industry, in that peculiar combination of hand-weaving, hand-spinning and hand-tilling agriculture which gave them self-supporting power." Into this scene swept the English spinning industry, "and thus produced the greatest, and to speak the truth, the only *social* revolution ever heard of in Asia." Marx then adds significantly that, in causing this social revolution, England "was actuated only by the vilest interests, and was stupid in her manner of enforcing them . . . she was the unconscious tool of history in bringing about that revolution."[56] We shall hear this theme sounded again, when we study the bourgeois revolution in Europe itself.

It is worth noting along the same lines the comments by Marx and Engels on Russian development. Marx, himself, toward the end of his life became increasingly interested in Russian society, and even acquired the language in order to learn about Russian conditions as directly as possible. He began to realize that tsarist Russia, hitherto the bulwark of counterrevolution (compare Marx's 1848 orientation), might be on the verge of revolutionary change. The fundamental issue was whether or not Russia, as an Oriental despotism, had to pass through the intermediate stage of private property, of bourgeois small ownership. Quoting the Russian novelist and philosopher of history, Chernyshevsky (who, incidentally, was a disciple of Feuerbach), Marx asks whether "Russia must begin by destroying the village community in order to pass to the capitalist regime, or whether, on the contrary, she can without experiencing the tortures of this regime appropriate all its fruits by developing the historical conditions specifically

[56] *Selected Works*, Vol. I, pp. 316–317. Cf. Lichtheim, *op. cit.*, p. 145; and R. P. Dutt, *Articles on India* (Bombay, 1957).

her own [i.e., pass to socialism directly, without experiencing capitalism]." He never arrived at a clear answer. However, amidst his many vacillations, Marx forcefully rejects the attempt to "metamorphose my historical sketch of the genesis of capitalism in Western Europe into an historico-philosophic theory of the general path every people is fated to tread, whatever the historical circumstances in which it finds itself."[57]

Leaving aside now, in this tantalizing fashion, the problem of the impact of a more developed "epoch" or social form on Oriental despotism—an impact which presupposes the existence of a developed epoch—we return to the question of how epochs other than the Asiatic arose in the first place. Marx was never wholly of one mind on his historical epochs, and his remarks on the subject are frequently sketchy.[58] Nevertheless, the general picture which seems to emerge concerning the ancient epoch is as follows. According to Marx, the families, wherein division of labor and slavery first appear, group together into larger, tribal units. These, in turn, enter into a higher social organization on either the Asiatic or the ancient model. In both, there is communal ownership of property. In the Asiatic, as we have seen, the communities are isolated villages, ruled over by a despot who supplies artificial irrigation and appropriates the peasants' "surplus" production. In ancient society, several tribes unite into a city, a polis, which possesses property (including slaves) in a communal or public fashion. Alongside and subordinate to this communal property, however, some private property develops. The increasing devel-

---

[57] Marx to "Otechestvenniye Zapiski," London, November, 1877, *Selected Correspondence*, pp. 377, 379. Cf. Leon Trotsky's views, as expressed in his *History of the Russian Revolution* (New York, 1932), especially Vol. I, chap. 1.

[58] The best source for Marx's discussion of epochs are his *The German Ideology* and the draft of *Capital* eventually published as *Grundrisse der Kritik der Politischen Oekonomie* (see the Berlin, 1953, one-volume edition). Unfortunately, the latter has not yet been translated into English. A good treatment of the subject is George Lichtheim, "Marx and the 'Asiatic Mode of Production,'" *St. Anthony's Studies*, 14 (1963).

opment of the latter brings about the decay of the social order
established on the basis of communal property.[59]

Before this, however, these small city-states, existing free
from any central or despotic power above them all, come into
necessary warlike conflict with one another. Thus, Marx tells
us, "War is therefore the great common task, the great joint
effort required to occupy the objective conditions of living
existence, or to guard and perpetuate their occupation. . . .
The urban concentration of dwellings is the foundation of this
military organization." The backbone of this war effort is the
independent farmer, possessing his own property; in turn, the
city safeguards the individual against the outside world. In
contrast to the Asiatic epoch and its village base, "the history
of classical antiquity is the history of the cities; but of cities
founded on land ownership and agriculture."[60]

Two weaknesses lurk within this system, Marx informs us,
and they will eventually cause its decay. The first is that only
constant military expansion can provide the growing body of
citizens with landed property. Unfortunately, "the effect of
war and conquest, which for example in Rome was among the
essential economic pre-conditions of the community, eliminates the real tie binding it together." The second defect is
that the classical cities regarded only farming as a legitimate
occupation, and conferred citizenship only on landowners.
Trade and industry were turned over to foreign artisans and
former slaves. As Marx points out, the ancients sought, not to
create wealth, but to produce model citizens. But this very
fact meant that the development of the productive forces
needed to maintain the constant expansion of the city-state was
limited and fettered. Marx's conclusion, after a more complicated analysis than I have offered here, is "Hence the maintenance of the commonwealth leads to the destruction of the

[59] See *The German Ideology*, in *Marx-Engels Gesamtausgabe*
(MEGA), 1/5, pp. 11–15, and cf. Plato's lament about this same situation
in Book VIII of *The Republic*.

[60] The translation of these passages from the *Grundrisse* is from
Lichtheim, *Marxism*, pp. 149–150.

conditions on which it is based. . . . If it be argued that productivity could be raised within the same area by developing
the productive forces etc., (which in the case of traditional
farming takes longest of all) this would necessitate new forms
of organising labor . . . thus once more doing away with the
old economic conditions of the commonwealth. . . . Reproduction until a given point. Then . . . dissolution." In *Capital*, he
phrases it as follows: "In the ancient Asiatic mode of production, in that of classical antiquity, etc., we find that the conversion of products into commodities, and therefore the conversion
of men into producers of commodities, holds a subordinate
place, which however, increases in importance as the
primitive communities approach nearer and nearer to their dissolution." Then he adds rather condescendingly, "Those ancient social organisms of production are, as compared with
bourgeois society, extremely simple and transparent."[61]

I find myself singularly unimpressed by Marx's analysis of
the ancient epoch. While it is made wothwhile by his usual
aperçus and by his stress on the production aspect of antiquity,
it cannot be considered as either a major historical treatment
or interpretation of the classical epoch. Comparison with Gibbon's *Decline and Fall*, or even with Montesquieu's *Grandeur
and Decadence*, is not particularly in its favor. Lacking in
fullness, Marx's treatment of the ancient epoch is merely an
effort to fill in with a dab here and there a lacuna in his general
economic interpretation of history. It ought not to be taken
more seriously than that.

The same judgment, I fear, holds true for his work on the
feudal epoch. Here, it is interesting to note that the very conception of a feudal society had only arisen in the century
before Marx. According to the best evidence available, it was
the Comte de Boulainvilliers who first used the term *féodalité*
(in his *Lettres Historiques sur les Parlemens*, published post-

---

[61] *Ibid.*, pp. 150–152; and *Capital*, Vol. I, p. 53, although here I have
preferred to use the translation from Bottomore and Rubel, *op. cit.*,
p. 107.

humously in 1727) to mean a state of society rather than a mere legal description of a form of real property. As Marc Bloch comments: "In the study of history there have been few stages so decisive as the moment when 'Empires,' dynasties, famous periods identified with some great names—in a word, all the old arbitrary divisions born of a monarchical and oratorical tradition—began to give place to *another system of classification, based on the observation of social phenomena* [italics added]."[62] Then, taken up by Montesquieu, the new classification came to its glorious apogee in 1789. At that point, the French Revolution, in presumed rebellion against the institutions enshrined in the concept, feudal society, declared in the famous decree of 11 August that "the National Assembly totally abolishes the feudal regime."

Marx, in referring to feudal society, is within this tradition. His description, however, both of the origins and nature of the feudal order, is vague and sketchy. The seeds of feudalism, he informs us, are to be found in the decay of the Roman Empire. At that time there was added, to the internal elements of developing private property and the transformation of the small peasantry into a proletariat, the external and "accidental" element of the barbarian conquests. The time period for the feudal society itself is the European Middle Ages. The form of the society, Marx tells us, arises from the fact that

The last centuries of the declining Roman Empire and its conquest by the barbarians destroyed a number of productive forces; agriculture had declined, industry had decayed for lack of markets, trade had died out or had been violently interrupted, and the rural and urban population had diminished. These conditions and the mode of organization of the conquest determined by them gave rise, under the influence of the Teutonic military constitution, to feudal property. Like tribal and communal property it is also based on a community, but the directly producing class which confronts it is not, as in the case of the ancient community, the slaves, but the enserfed small peasantry.

[62] Marc Bloch, *Feudal Society*, translated by L. A. Manyon (Chicago, 1962), p. xvii.

It is best to let Marx continue the story in his own words:

This feudal structure of landownership had its counterpart in the *towns* in the form of guild property, the feudal organization of trades. Here property consisted chiefly in the labor of each individual. The necessity for association against the organized robber nobility, the need for communal market-halls . . . the feudal structure of the whole country, combined to bring about the *guilds*. The gradually accumulated capital of individual craftsmen, and their stable numbers in an increasing population, gave rise to the relation of journeyman and apprentice, which brought into being in the towns a hierarchy similar to that in the country.

Thus, in the feudal period, the chief forms of property consisted on the one hand of landed property with serf labor chained to it, and on the other hand of individual labor with small capital commanding the labor of journeymen. The structure of both was determined by the narrow conditions of production—small-scale and primitive cultivation of the land, and handicraft industry.

Marx's comment is that "This feudal structure was, just as much as the communal property of antiquity, an association against a subject producing class, but the form of association and the relation to the direct producers were different because of the different conditions of production."[63]

Two things must now be noted in Marx's account. The first is his emphasis on social rank and class struggle. While later we shall consider this subject in more detail, we need to remark here Marx's juxtaposition of the landed and guilded property holders against the "subject producing class" (i.e., serfs and journeymen, whereas in antiquity it was against the slaves and proletariat). "The history of all hitherto existing society," as the *Manifesto* dramatically proclaims, "is the history of class struggles." The second point of interest concerns the "narrow conditions of production." These were unable to accommodate the new demands arising from "the discovery of America, the rounding of the Cape . . . The East Indian and Chinese markets, the colonization of America, trade with the colonies, the increase in the means of exchange and in commodities gen-

[63] Bottomore and Rubel, *op. cit.*, pp. 117–119.

erally." As Marx puts it, "The conditions under which feudal
society produced and exchanged, the feudal organization of
agriculture and manufacturing industry, in one word, the
feudal relations of property, became no longer compatible with
the already developing productive forces; they became so
many fetters."[64]

Marx's account is familiar, without for that reason being
worthy of contempt (though by now it has almost become the
catechism it was originally intended to be). Indeed, there is no
need to spend time (nor does Marx) describing the death
throes of feudal society. The *coup de main* is dealt by an
emerging new class. "From the serfs of the Middle Ages
sprang the chartered burghers of the earliest towns. From
these burgesses the first elements of the bourgeoisie were developed." It is this bourgeoisie which, with revolutionary activity, bursts asunder the fetters of the old conditions of production, tears away the veil of illusion hiding the feudal social
relations, and brings into existence the new conditions and
relations of production: capitalism. Marx's account is the
Horatio Alger story of a whole class.

Before our camera pans in for the close, detailed picture of
the capitalist epoch, what are we to say of Marx's history of
the early epochs? The first thing to remark is that it is really
not a *history* of these epochs, but a vision of history. As such,
it is powerful and inspiring. Secondly, Marx's "history" consists of a series of assertions, rather than of hypotheses tested
against a mass of evidence. And, partly for this reason, thirdly,
Marx is really offering us some "ideal types," a sort of "Ur-
form," of economic-social organizations which he then claims
to perceive as arising in historical time. We have, in short, a
historical sociology, and not a history of societies; it is in these
terms, then, that Marx's work in this area must finally be
judged.

[64] *Basic Writings*, pp. 8, 12.

11

In dealing with Marx's detailed critique of capitalist society, we must once again return to the fundamentals of his philosophy of history. The difficulty here, however, is that we pass rapidly from philosophical and historical presuppositions to largely economic considerations and analysis: a matter for experts. Nevertheless, we must make the effort to seize upon certain features of Marx's economic analysis pertinent to our interests, while realizing that we are greatly oversimplifying and possibly distorting his work. For in this area, unlike the Asiatic, ancient, and feudal, Marx cannot be accused of superficiality of data or lack of sustained analysis.

Marx's starting point as always is critique. Much of the imagery is Darwinian. "Man's thought about the forms of social life," Marx announces in the first chapter of *Capital*, "his scientific analysis of these forms, runs counter to the actual course of social evolution. He begins by an examination of the finished product, the extant result of the evolutionary process. The characters which stamp labor products as commodities, the characters which they must possess before they can circulate as commodities, have already acquired the fixity of the natural forms of social life, when economists begin to study, not indeed their history (for they are regarded as immutable), but their meaning."[65]

The task of the "historical" economist, however, is to go back to the beginning, but in the light of the development which has already occurred. In this way, once the capitalist relations of production is critically understood, man can shake off his alienated condition. "The life process of society, this meaning the material process of production, will not lose its veil of mystery until it becomes a process carried on by a free association of producers, under their conscious and purposive

[65] *Capital*, Vol. I, p. 382, fn. 2, and p. 49.

control. For this, however, an indispensible requisite is that there should exist a specific material groundwork (or a series of material conditions of existence) which can only come into being as the *spontaneous outcome* [italics added] of a long and painful process of evolution."[66]

That evolution, as we have already seen, has gone through four epochs. In the beginning of that evolution, before the four epochs unfold, man labors. He works under the conditions of division of labor, with the help of instruments of labor, and on what Marx calls the subject matter of labor (i.e., the soil, water, timber, ores, etc.). The result is that in the labor process, "man's activity, with the help of the instruments of labor, brings about changes in the subject matter of labor, changes intentionally effected. The process disappears in the product. The product is a use-value, materially supplied by nature, and adopted to human wants by a change of form. The labor has become incorporated with the subject matter of labor. Labor has been materialised."[67]

The use-value of materialized labor, Marx informs us, is its utility. When use-values of one kind are exchanged for use-values of another kind, and owing to the division of labor this is bound to occur, a ratio is established which Marx calls exchange-value. He devotes the whole of his first chapter of *Capital* to explaining the nature of commodities in terms of their "value." Indeed, this is the key to all that follows. In Marx's imaginative prose: "Value changes all labor products into social hieroglyphs. Subsequently, people try to decipher these hieroglyphs, to solve the riddle of their own social product. . . . The recent scientific discovery that labor products as values are but the material expressions of the human labor expended in their production, marks an epoch in the evolutionary history of mankind."[68]

The reason why this discovery has not occurred before is

[66] *Ibid.*, p. 54.
[67] *Ibid.*, p. 173.
[68] *Ibid.*, p. 47.

that, hitherto, the commodity form has hidden the labor product which lurks within it. What it hides is the fact that behind the social relation of the commodities—their exchange value—must necessarily be the social relations of the original producers. In other words, labor can only be *social* labor, labor as part of the *division* of labor. But it is exactly the forms of the division of labor, of social labor, which assume different shapes throughout history: the Asiatic, the ancient, the feudal, and the capitalist. (And we have already seen that the specific form of the division of labor to be found in a given society corresponds to the tools it uses.) Now, Marx adds another element to his analysis of the labor process. Commodities themselves, he tells us, take on during their circulatio.1 the mask of money (itself a commodity). Next, the latter itself is transformed into capital. Capital is simply money that expands during the course of its circulation by adding to itself a surplus value. (As such, incidentally, capital confronts landed property; and the capitalist the feudal owner.) But what is surplus value? Ah, says Marx, let us go past the commodity-money form, let us "leave this noisy region of the market, where all that goes on is done in full view of every one's eyes, where everything seems open and above board. We will follow the owner of money and the owner of labor power into the hidden foci of production, crossing the threshold of the portal above which is written: 'No admittance except on business.' Here we shall discover, not only how capital produces, but also how it is itself produced. We shall at last discover the secret of the making of surplus value."[69]

What is this holy of holies (leaving aside any psychological or stylistic interpretation)? It is simply the production of a commodity "whose value will exceed the total of the values of the commodities used up in producing it; the total value of the means of production and the labor power for which, in the commodity market, he [the capitalist] has advanced money."

[69] *Ibid.*, pp. 44–47, 136, 164.

This is capitalist surplus value. In the boldest possible terms, surplus value anywhere and anytime is that part of the laborer's work which is not absolutely necessary to keep him alive (i.e., feed him and allow him to reproduce his kind), and which can therefore be expropriated from him because the social forms regulating the division of labor permit, and indeed enforce, this expropriation. Marx's conclusion is that "What distinguishes the various economic types of society one from another (distinguishes, for instance, a society based upon slavery from a society based upon wage labor), is *nothing other* [italics added] than the way in which surplus labor is extorted from the actual producer, from the worker."[70]

In essence, this is the one economic law which applies to *all* forms of society, at least up until the present: the law concerning the extortion, in some form or other, of surplus labor. Now, this raises an interesting problem. Elsewhere, Marx (and Engels) has insisted that the so-called economic laws of the classical economists are not eternal laws of nature, but historical laws which arise and disappear; we have already seen Marx's views on the law of supply and demand.[71] On the surface, therefore, there may seem to be a contradiction between the view expressed in the sentence above and another statement by Marx to the effect that the "*necessity* of the *distribution* of social labor in definite proportions cannot possibly be done away with by a *particular form* of social production but can only change the *mode* of its *appearance*, [this] is self-evident. No natural laws can be done away with." The solution to our problem is the realization that Marx, when he speaks of "historical laws," is talking about the form in which the expropriation of surplus labor takes place; when he speaks of "natural law" he is referring to the always-present expropriation itself. Thus, "What can change in historically

[70] *Ibid.*, pp. 179, 214.
[71] Cf. Engels to F. A. Lange, Manchester, 29 March, 1865, *Selected Correspondence*, p. 208.

different circumstances is only the *form* in which these laws assert themselves." Then he adds, thinking particularly of capitalism, "And the form in which this proportional distribution of labor asserts itself, in a state of society where the interconnection of social labor is manifested in the *private exchange* of the individual products of labor, is precisely the *exchange value* of these products."[72]

To sum up Marx's position: the *form* in which society organizes its labor is not eternal—capitalism, for example, is merely one effanescent shape—but within that form, as Marx in *Capital* explains in great detail, change must take place according to fixed economic laws. These are independent of the individual wills. Thus, in Marx's analysis of capitalism, certain developments must inexorably occur: for example, the division into constant capital (i.e., the means of production) and variable capital (i.e., the labor which produces surplus value) must widen, with the proportion of the former growing constantly greater. Capital will grow larger, in general, and will be increasingly centralized; business cycles will grow increasingly acute, and the rate of profit will decline. The fate of the worker, in a growing relative surplus industrial army, will be one of increasing misery (and if not of *absolute* misery, for Marx did wrestle with the possibility of some improvement, then at least of *relative* deprivation); the class division will become increasingly polarized into the haves and the have-nots; and so forth. After a while, of course, the contradictions will be so glaring, the existing social form of extortion so fettering on the productive capacities of the society, that dissolution of capitalism must inevitably ensue. In fact, capitalist society will have called into being, with the sureness of inescapable fate, the conditions of its own destruction.

There is, fortunately, no need for us to grasp the economic nettles of Marx's *Capital*.[73] Nor is this the place to arrange the

---

[72] Marx to L. Kugelmann, London, 11 July, 1868, *Selected Correspondence*, pp. 251–252. See too, *Capital*, Vol. I, p. 156.

[73] Good treatments of Marx's economics can be found in Landauer,

final confrontation in Marx of man's free will against nature's inevitable laws; that we shall deal with later. In order, however, more fully to understand Marx's view of history and of the capitalist epoch, we must here briefly tackle two further problems: the question of primary accumulation, and the question of the epoch after capitalism.

As a historian of capitalism, and Marx deserves that title, he wished to know from whence capital originally came. His formulation of the problem and its solution has had an enormous influence on the professional historians who have come after him.[74] Marx calls it the problem of primary accumulation, which "is not the historical result of the specifically capitalist method of production, but the historical foundation of that system." According to Marx, capital must originate independently of the unpaid labor of other persons, for it is exactly the *primary* accumulation (which first permits the capitalist to step into the market as a purchaser of labor power) into which we are inquiring.[75]

Marx's enumeration of the factors involved is as follows: "The spoliation of the property of the Church, the fraudulent alienation of the State domains, the theft of the common lands, the transformation of feudal property and clan property into modern private property (an usurpation effected by a system of ruthless terrorism)—these were the idyllic methods of primary accumulation. They cleared the ground for capitalist agriculture, made the land part and parcel of capital, while providing for the needs of urban industrialization the requisite supply of masterless proletarians." To this list, Marx later added "the colonial system, the national debt system, the

---

op. cit.; Lichtheim, *op. cit.;* and Schumpeter, *op. cit.* One of the more interesting, though difficult, debates has been that between Eugen von Böhm-Bawerk and Rudolf Hilferding over the key topics of surplus value and a uniform, or social, rate of profit.

[74] As examples, see the various articles and books by Earl Hamilton on American treasure as a source of capital; and P. Vilar, "Problems of the Formation of Capital," *Past and Present,* No. 10 (November, 1956).

[75] *Capital,* Vol. II, pp. 689, 625.

modern system of taxation, and the modern system of production."[76] As we can see, primary accumulation is perhaps more complicated than it sounds at first. It covers a good deal of territory.

In essence, Marx tells us, primary accumulation "is nothing other than the historical process whereby the producer is divorced from the means of production. It assumes a 'primary' aspect because it belongs to the primary phase that is traversed immediately before the history of capitalism begins, immediately before the establishment of the methods of production proper to capitalism." Further, all the factors involved in this process reduce finally to "brute force": "One and all, they relied upon the power of the state, upon the concentrated and organized force of society, in order to stimulate the transformation of feudal production into capitalist production, and in order to shorten the period of transition. Force is the midwife of every old society pregnant with a new one. It is itself an economic power." Then, in a rather overdramatized fashion, Marx concludes his Grand Guignol portrayal of primary accumulation with the phrase: "capital comes into the world soiled with mire from top to toe, and oozing blood from every pore."[77]

Raising our eye from this brutal and bloody accumulation, we are informed that, with capital now available, its modern history "begins in the 16th century with the establishment of a worldwide commercial system and the opening of a world market." To supply this market, we need a new form of production, and "alike historically and conceptually, the starting-point of capitalist production is where a large number of workers are aggregated at one time and in one place . . . under the command of one capitalist, for the production of one and the same kind of commodity." This form of production is itself divided by Marx into a period of manufacturing per se, extending from the middle of the sixteenth century to the last

[76] *Ibid.*, pp. 812–813, 832–833.
[77] *Ibid.*, pp. 792, 837, 843.

The Riddle of History

third of the eighteenth century, and a period after that of what he calls "machinofacture," marked by the large-scale use of machinery in the division of labor. The point to remember in all this, however, is that for Marx, capital in any of its phases has "outsoared all earlier systems of production, those that were based upon forced labor," in its ability ruthlessly and efficiently to extract surplus value and to exploit labor power.[78]

12

Primary accumulation, then, is the origin of capitalism, and exploitation is its essence. Inexorably, in the way we have briefly indicated, it works toward its own dissolution. What is the epoch to follow? Earlier in this work, we have seen that Hegel refused to go beyond the boundary of the present; the Owl of Minerva, he insisted, does not fly into the future. As a revolutionary, Marx rejects this view. Willy-nilly, he has to offer his followers at least a vision of the promised land. He, himself, is aware of the difficulties. In a revealing letter of 1881, he confesses that "The thing to be done at any definite, given moment of the future . . . depends of course entirely on the given historical conditions in which one has to act. But this question is posed in the *clouds* and therefore is really a phantom problem to which the only answer can be—a *criticism of the question* itself." Barely suppressing his annoyance, Marx continues, "Had any eighteenth-century Frenchman the faintest idea beforehand, *a priori*, of the manner in which the demands of the French bourgeoisie would be forced through? The doctrinaire and necessarily fantastic anticipation of the programme of action for a revolution of the future only diverts one from the struggle of the present." Abjuring this fantastic anticipation, Marx contents himself with an interest-

[78] *Ibid.*, Vol. I, pp. 131, 320, 336, 353, 366ff.

ing analogy. "The dream that the end of the world was near inspired the early Christians in their struggle with the Roman Empire and gave them confidence in victory."[79] Today, he concludes, "Scientific insight into the inevitable disintegration of the dominant order of society continually proceeding before our eyes and the ever-growing fury into which the masses are lashed by the old ghostly governments, while at the same time the positive development of the means of production advances with gigantic strides—all this is a sufficient guarantee that the moment a real proletarian revolution breaks out the conditions" (and Marx adds ominously, "these are certain not to be idyllic")—"of its immediately next *modus operandi* will be in existence."[80]

Nevertheless, while Marx refused to go into details concerning the "historical conditions" of the post-capitalist epoch, certain features emerge logically from his critical analysis of earlier epochs.[81] First, in communist society there will be, by definition, no extracting of surplus value and exploiting of labor power. Borrowing the phrase from Proudhon, Marx stands the capitalist relationship on its head by declaring "From each according to his ability, to each according to his need." The elimination of the extracting and exploiting relationship can only come about with the abolition of division of labor, the basis on which it rests. Marx abolishes the division of labor. Communist man, as we have already seen, will "hunt in the morning, fish in the afternoon, rear cattle in the evening," and, a characteristic Marxian activity, "criticize after dinner." With division of labor eliminated, the class structure which has arisen from it comes crashing down. Indeed, as the one class whose interests correspond to the interests of society

[79] From this passage, Georges Sorel could well have—and might have—taken his inspiration for his theory of myth. See his *Reflections on Violence* (1908).

[80] Marx to F. Domela-Nieuwenhuis, London, 22 February, 1881, *Selected Correspondence*, pp. 410–411.

[81] Note that whereas the French Revolution experience could serve as a guide to the forthcoming revolution of the proletariat against the bourgeoisie, it could offer no guidance to the postcapitalist epoch.

as a whole, the proletariats' triumph can only introduce the classless society.[82]

The end of classes, so the syllogism continues, will also witness the end of the state. Earlier, Saint-Simon and Comte had declared politics to be the science of production and had foretold the complete absorption of politics by economics. Now, Marx and Engels predict the "future conversion of political rule over men into an administration of things and a direction of processes of production—that is to say, the 'abolition of the state.'" In reality, the state is abolished *by definition* when classes are abolished, for the state is simply the instrument by which a ruling class extracts surplus value from the original producers: no ruling class, no state. A transitional stage, called the "dictatorship of the proletariat," will intervene between the revolutionary dissolution of capitalism and the withering away of the state, but this is temporary and does not affect the eventual outcome, according to Marx.[83]

In this new epoch, where things are administered, man will be free to develop his individual self. This development, however, will be a *social* development as well, for the individual does not exist and cannot develop outside the historical conditions surrounding him. As the *Manifesto* declares, "In place of the old bourgeois society, with its classes and class antagonisms, we shall have an association in which the free development of each is the condition for the free development of all." Only in these circumstances, then, can man end the alienated state in which he has previously existed and come into repossession of himself. Thus, the communist epoch produces not only a new society but a new man.

Momentarily at least, Engels seems to have brushed against a harsher reality and to have permitted himself some doubts. Writing around 1874, Engels investigates the anarchists' attack

[82] *Basic Writings*, pp. 254, 264–265.
[83] *Basic Writings*, pp. 75–76. Cf. Engels to A. Bebel, London, 18–28 March, 1875, *Selected Correspondence*, p. 357. While I have greatly oversimplified Marx and Engels' soul-searching about these matters, I have not, I believe, oversimplified their conclusions.

on the principle of authority. Reminding them that "whoever mentions combined action speaks of organization," he asks, "now is it possible to have organization without authority?" Of course not, Engels replies to his own question, and what is more, he adds, "authority presupposes subordination." Calling upon his own personal experiences, Engels offers the example of a cotton-spinning mill.[84] Here, "All these workers, men, women, and children, are obliged to begin and finish their work at the hours fixed by the authority of the steam, which cares nothing for individual autonomy." Even if particular questions about production—and Engels suggests the impossibility of this—were to be settled by an elected delegate or, better yet, by majority vote, "the will of the single individual will always have to subordinate itself, which means that questions are settled in an authoritarian way." Engels' conclusion is a piece of good, pre-Communist epoch Marxian analysis: "A certain authority, no matter how delegated, and, on the other hand, a certain subordination are things which, *independent of all social organization* [italics added], are imposed upon us together with the material conditions under which we produce and make products circulate." Continuing in this realistic vein, Engels remarks significantly, "The automatic machinery of a big factory is much more despotic than the small capitalists who employ workers ever have been." The last comment of his I shall quote is of surprising irony: "These gentlemen think that when they have changed the names of things they have changed the things themselves. This is how these profound thinkers mock at the whole world."[85]

Marx and Engels push aside these sobering considerations and go on with their dream. Effectively, in projecting the communist epoch, they abolish not only the division of labor, exploitation, authority, classes, the political aspects of man, etc.; they also abolish history. Important and searching as is

---

[84] It is characteristic, of course, that Engels would use the example of a textile mill, while a pin factory served as the model for Adam Smith.

[85] *Basic Writings,* pp. 481–484.

their investigation of the past, and this needs underlining here and later in our treatment, their horror at the nightmare of the nineteenth-century industrial present causes them to leap into a future which was really "out of time" as well as place. In place of reality, they put fantasies, although fantasies of immense practical power. For historical analysis, they substitute an apocalyptic religious vision. In this sense, then, Marx, who scathingly attacked others on these same grounds, can be called the last of the great utopians. The fifth epoch in his philosophy of history is not a historic, i.e., scientific, but a chiliastic construct.[86]

13

Severe as are these strictures on Marx's utopian speculations, we must not let them obscure our view of his other contributions. One of the foremost of these is his stress on the role of classes in history. The class for Marx is the real actor in history. Where other thinkers might be concerned with individuals or "spirits of the age" moving through history, Marx keeps his eye on classes of men.

Marx freely and frequently admits that his idea of classes, and indeed of class struggles, is not original. Scottish thinkers, like Dugald Stewart, Adam Ferguson, John Millar, and Adam Smith, had all emphasized the "difference of ranks" which they saw accompanying the progress of society. French "bourgeois historians," like Thierry, whom Marx calls "the

---

[86] The sense in which Marx, for example, can be blamed for events in the Soviet Union is because he aroused passions for sweeping changes without any real indication of what was to follow, i.e., the forms and requirements of economic planning in a modern society. For this utopianism, the price paid in Russia has been the reality of "forced" organization. On the other hand, perhaps, sweeping changes, such as inaugurated by the 1917 Revolution, can only occur through blind passion. Hegel, of course, had said as much. For modern chiliastic movements, see the interesting book by E. J. Hobsbawm, *Primitive Rebels* (Manchester, 1959).

father of the 'class struggle' in French historiography,"
Mignet, and Guizot, had seen the class struggle as the key to
French history since the Middle Ages. And above all, David
Ricardo, the great economist, emphasized the origin of class in
the conditions of production, and pointed out the antagonism
between landowners and manufacturers (although asserting
the identity of interest between capitalists and workers).[87]

What did Marx add? First of all, he placed the class conflict
squarely in the center of nineteenth-century consciousness.
The cutting edge of his critique sliced through the catchword
of the French Revolution: *"Fraternité* . . . This pleasant abstraction from class antagonisms, this sentimental reconciliation of contradictory class interests, this visionary elevation
above the class struggle." In its place, on the dusty battle fields
of reality, Marx claims the existence of a struggle between
what men like Disraeli called the "two nations." Further,
"What I did that was new," Marx declares, "was to prove: (1)
that the *existence of classes* is only bound up with *particular
historical phases in the development of production*, (2) that
the class struggle necessarily leads to the *dictatorship of the
proletariat*, (3) that this dictatorship itself only constitutes the
transition to the *abolition of all classes* and to a *classless society*."[88]

Claims two and three we have already dealt with as parts of
Marx's chiliastic vision. His first claim merits additional attention. As is well known, Marx views all of past history in terms
of class struggles. The classes might be different—"in ancient
Rome we have patricians, knights, plebians, slaves; in the Middle Ages, feudal lords, vassals, guild masters, journeymen, ap-
prentices, serfs; in almost all of these classes, again subordinate
gradations"—but the conflict was always between oppressor

[87] Marx to Engels, London, 27 July, 1854, *Selected Correspondence*,
p. 105; Marx to J. Weydemeyer, London, 5 March, 1852, *ibid.*, p. 85;
and cf. Lichtheim, *op. cit.* Adam Smith saw the conflict as between
manufacturers and laborers.

[88] *Selected Works*, Vol. I, p. 138; and Marx to J. Weydemeyer, cited
above, p. 86.

and oppressed. Ignoring other forms of oppression, such as religious, ethnic, psychological, and so forth, for these he subsumes under his major category, Marx sees oppression as *fundamentally* connected with the conditions of production.[89]

Marx also claims that, as the conditions of production change in the capitalistic epoch, a novel class situation is brought about. For the first time, only two classes exist, in polarized fashion: the capitalists, or possessing class, and the workers, or nonpossessing class. In this situation, the proletariat, which has really only emerged around 1848, becomes the world-historical hero. In terms reminiscent of Hegel, Marx tells us in *The German Ideology* that "the proletariat can thus exist only *world historically*, just as communism, its movement, can only have a 'world-historical' existence. World-historical existence of individuals, i.e., existence of individuals which is directly linked up with world history."[90]

Antiphilistine and antibourgeois to the core, Marx makes the proletariat his chosen people. In the struggle which is to ensue beween the now sharply polarized powers of light and dark, of positive and negative forces, the outcome is certain. With the victory of the proletariat, the class struggle will be ended, the motor of history stilled. To use another image, there will be no more actors left on the stage of history, for, as we have seen, classes and not individuals are at the center of Marx's vision of the decisive movements of time.

Nonetheless, in spite of the utopian way in which he ultimately undercuts his own insight about the role of classes in history, we cannot deny to Marx the credit for magnificently placing this particular social grouping in the forefront of the

[89] At this point, Marx defines class as follows: "In so far as millions of families live under economic conditions of existence that separate their mode of life, their interests and their culture from those of other classes, and put them in hostile opposition to the latter, they form a class." (*Selected Works*, Vol. I, p. 303.)

[90] *Basic Writings*, p. 257. It is interesting, in this connection, to note Marx's scorn for the peasants, who, in 1848, still comprised by far the largest proportion of the world's population. See *Selected Works*, Vol. I, pp. 159, 302.

modern historian's perspective. Just as, with all his fumbling errors of data and theory, he calls into existence alongside feudal society a new classification of modern social phenomena, capitalism, so he conjures into being a novel way of analyzing that social phenomena, the study of social-economic class divisions. The present-day multiplicity of social-stratification studies, to take one example, is a vigorous offshoot of the seed he planted so deeply in the modern mind, and a testimony of the success of his polemic and erratic critique.[91]

14

Let us now put aside the details of Marx's system and turn to a critique of his critique of history. The fundamental thought in Marx is that "man makes his history." This is more a Vico-like than a Hegel-like formulation, for Marx deliberately states that "History does nothing. . . . It is by no means 'History' which uses man as a means to carry out its ends as if it were a person apart; rather History is nothing but the activity of man in pursuit of his ends."[92]

As Marx has already told us, at the beginning of time man pursues his immediate end—life and survival—by laboring and producing. In the course of this activity, he "makes," not only

[91] Marx, however, does not distinguish between economic classes and the status groups familiar to modern sociologists. For a refreshing investigation of the notion of "class," see J. H. Hexter, "The Myth of the Middle Class in Tudor England," *Reappraisals in History* (Evanston, 1961). At one point, Hexter makes the interesting remark that "The Tudor middle class is no threat to aristocracy or monarchy because it has no ideology of class war or even of class rivalry" (p. 113). This suggests that it is consciousness that makes for class in the Marxian sense. It might also be pointed out that acceptance of Marx's lead concerning the existence and importance of class phenomena in history does not entail an acceptance of the particular dialectic which he sees animating class struggle. One last comment on Marx's use of class: it allows him to set up a new "decline and fall" model in history, where now, instead of empires, it is classes that rise and fall.

[92] Quoted from F. Mehring's *Aus dem literarischen Nachlass Marx-Engels* (1902), Vol. II, p. 179, in Hook, *op. cit.*, p. 38.

the family, but larger social arrangements, which include ideological superstructures like religion and politics, as well as the more fundamental economic relations of production. These become, in some malignant and unintended fashion, alien powers which man has set over himself. They become, in fact, the very "conditions" which then shape his future making. Thus, we must now reformulate our initial statement and say with Marx, "Men make their own history, but they do not make it just as they please; they do not make it under circumstances chosen by themselves, but under circumstances directly encountered, given and transmitted from the past. The tradition of all the dead generations weighs like a nightmare on the brain of the living."[93]

The task which presents itself is, obviously, to throw off the nightmare, the incubus of the past which weighs upon us. This we can do, Marx suggests, only by becoming *conscious* of our ends and of the mechanism by which our activity has hitherto worked to unintended ends. We must come to understand the conditions surrounding us.

Fortunately, Hegel and Feuerbach have already shown us the way to regain control of our religious conditions, by means of the critique of religion. Now Marx has added to this a critique of political economy. In both cases, religious and economic, he points out, the cause of these conditions is man's activity, but an activity which takes place within conditions which have existed even earlier; and so on. Writing against Proudhon, who did not see this "real movement of history," Marx asks rhetorically:

What is society, whatever its form may be? The product of men's reciprocal action. Are men free to choose this or that form of society? By no means. Assume a particular state of development in the productive faculties of man and you will get a particular form of commerce and consumption. Assume particular stages of development in production, commerce and consumption and you will have a corresponding social constitution, a corresponding

[93] *Selected Works*, Vol. I, p. 225. A comparison with Freud leaps immediately to mind.

organization of the family, of orders or of classes, in a word, a corresponding civil society. Assume a particular civil society and you will get particular political conditions which are only the official expression of civil society. . . .

It is superfluous to add that men are not free to choose their *productive forces*—which are the basis of all their history—for every productive force is an acquired force, the product of former activity. The productive forces are therefore the result of practical human energy; but this energy is itself conditioned by the circumstances in which men find themselves, by the productive forces already acquired, by the social form which exists before they do, which they do not create, which is the product of the preceding generation. Because of this simple fact that every succeeding generation finds itself in possession of the productive forces acquired by the previous generation, which serve it as the raw material for new production, a coherence arises in human history, a history of humanity takes shape which is all the more a history of humanity as the productive forces of man and therefore his social relations have been more developed.[94]

Let us examine these assertions more closely. The basis of all history is the productive forces, which men are not free to choose (or so we are told here). To these forces, we are informed, *correspond* various social, political, etc., conditions. If we go back to the Preface to *The Critique of Political Economy*, however, we shall find not only the word "correspond" used frequently, but also the word "determines." What is meant by these two words?: "Definite forms of social consciousness" *correspond* to "the economic structures of society —the *real* foundation"; "The mode of production in material life *determines* the general character of the social, political, and spiritual processes of life [italics added]." How does this correspondence take place? How is this determination effected? Marx is, perforce, vague on these details.[95] Further, do

[94] Marx to P. V. Annenkov, Brussels, 28 December, 1846, *Selected Correspondence*, pp. 40–41.

[95] For inquiries along these lines, devoted to what is now called the sociology of knowledge, see, for example, Robert Merton, *Social Theory and Social Structure* (New York, 1949), chaps. VIII, IX; and Karl Mannheim, *Ideology and Utopia*, translated by Louis Wirth and Edward Shils (New York, 1952).

the spiritual processes of life have a reciprocal effect on the economic structure of society? In most of Marx's writings, this, too, is left vague, though the implication of his explicit statements is that the effect is minor. (As I shall try to demonstrate in a moment, the implication of Marx's *logic* is quite opposite.)

Engels, as late as 1890, is still wrestling, in a fumbling though revealing way, with this problem. There he phrases it that "According to the materialist conception of history, the *ultimately* determining element in history is the production and reproduction," and here Engels adds a significant note, "of real life. More than this neither Marx nor I have ever asserted." The rest of the paragraph is equally revealing, and needs to be quoted in full:

> . . . Hence if somebody twists this into saying that the economic element is the *only* determining one, he transforms that proposition into a meaningless, abstract, senseless phrase. The economic situation is the basis, but the various elements of the superstructure —political forms of the class struggle and its results, to wit: constitutions established by the victorious class after a successful battle, etc., juridical forms, and even the reflexes of all these actual struggles in the brains of the participants, political, juristic, philosophical theories, religious views and their further development into systems of dogmas—also exercise their influence upon the course of their *form*. There is an interaction of all these elements in which, amid all the endless host of accidents (that is, of things and events whose inner interconnection is so remote or so impossible of proof that we can regard it as non-existent, as negligible) the economic movement finally asserts itself as necessary. Otherwise the application of the theory to any period of history would be easier than the solution of a simple equation of the first degree.

"Reflexes" which "exercise their *influence* [italics added]" and an economic movement which "finally asserts itself as necessary": these are vague, through perhaps persuasive, statements. So, too, are Engels' additional comments that "the economic ones [assumptions and conditions] are *ultimately decisive*. But the political ones, etc., and indeed even the traditions which haunt human minds also *play a part, although not the decisive one* [italics added]" and, in a later letter, "If therefore Barth [a German bourgeois socialist and opponent of Marxism] supposes that we deny any and every reaction of the political, etc., reflexes of the economic movement upon the movement itself, he is simply tilting at windmills."[96]

What are we to make of all this? First, of course, we can remark that it shows a nice lack of dogmatism or of an unduly limited perspective. Other factors than the purely economic or "material" are acknowledged to play a part in history. Next, even the vagueness could be forgiven. After all, Marx and Engels are merely the pioneers in this new area, and they cannot be expected to map with complete precision every detail of the unknown continent of knowledge which they have discerned in the mists. Others can investigate more closely the exact way in which economic conditions "determine" consciousness, and political conditions "play a part" in determining the economic conditions, and so forth. What cannot be forgiven Marx and Engels is their presumption in thinking that their sketch for further "scientific" investigation of how "man makes history" is, in fact, a complete science. Yet, this is what is implied in Engel's statement, "History has proceeded hitherto in the manner of a natural process and is essentially subject to the same laws of motion," or, on the more limited terrain of capitalism, Marx's comment, with its implicit comparison to Copernicus, that "just as the apparent motions of the heavenly bodies only become comprehensible to one who knows their real movements, which are not directly appreciable by our senses; so a scientific analysis of competition is only possible to one who has grasped the inner nature of capitalism."[97]

---

[96] Engels to J. Bloch, London, 21–22 September, 1890, *Selected Correspondence*, p. 498; and Engels to C. Schmidt, London, 27 October, 1890, *ibid.*, p. 507.
[97] Engels to J. Bloch, cited above, p. 499; and *Capital*, Vol. I, p. 330.

With their scientistic laws of motion, Marx and Engels came close to betraying the real insights of their version of the "new science." In fact, on the basis of his laws of motion, Marx works out a sort of "iron law of capitalism," comparable to Ricardo's iron law of wages. Thus, in this vein, he writes in the Preface of the first German edition of *Capital* (1867), "What we are concerned with primarily is, not the higher or the lower degree of development of the social antagonisms which arise out of the natural laws of capitalist production, but these laws in themselves, the tendencies which work out with an iron necessity towards an inevitable goal. A country in which industrial development is more advanced than in others, simply presents those others with a picture of their own future."[98] Here, Marx emphasizes the inevitable nature of history, which seems to follow logically from his laws of motion.

In his better moments, however, Marx has his doubts. Thus, writing in 1877 to a Russian periodical about the applications of his analysis of capitalism to Russian conditions, he states that "The chapter on primitive accumulation does not pretend to do more than trace the path by which, in Western Europe, the capitalist order of economy emerged from the womb of the feudal order of economy. It therefore *describes the historical movement* [italics added] which by divorcing the producers from their means of production converts them into wage workers (proletarians in the modern sense of the word) while it converts those who possess the means of production into capitalists." How will this apply to Russia? Well, says Marx, "once taken to the bosom of the capitalist regime, she will experience its pitiless laws like other profane peoples. That is all." Then, indignantly, he adds, "But that is too little for my critic. He feels he absolutely must metamorphose my historical sketch of the genesis of capitalism in Western Europe into an historico-philosophic theory of the general path

[98] *Capital*, Vol. II, p. 863.

every people is fated to tread, whatever the historical circumstances in which it finds itself." Comparing part of Roman
history with that of the United States, Marx comments,
"Events strikingly analogous but taking place in different historical surroundings led to totally different results. By studying each of these forms of evolution separately and then
comparing them one can easily find the clue to this phenomenon, but one will never arrive there by using as one's master
key a general historico-philosophical theory, the supreme
virtue of which consists in being super-historical."[99]

Here, we have a different Marx, a Marx with a larger vision.
To understand this Marx, we must come to grips with the
very problem with which he wrestled: the relation of the
rational to the empirical, of the true to the certain. As we have
seen time after time, this is the key problem of a possible
human science. Marx is in this bind; and we are there with
him.

Now, the problem facing Marx is well put by the critic and
scholar, George Lichtheim, when he says, "Thus processes
such as the development of feudalism out of primitive tribal-
ism, or the growth of bourgeois society within the feudal system, had to be related to changes inherent in the logic of the
anterior stage. Unless this could be done, the study of history,
for all the scholarly precision of the historians, was bound to
remain a merely empirical enterprise—hence pre-scientific." In
his "rational" mood Marx, seeking a logical development
which is formally necessary, and hence inevitable, could say,
"Of course it is much easier, from an analysis of the hazy
constructions of religion, to discover their earthly core; than,
conversely, to deduce from a study of the material conditions
of life at any particular time, the celestial forms that these may
assume. But the latter is the only materialistic method, and
therefore the only scientific one."[100] This extraordinary state-

[99] Marx to "Otechestvenniye Zapiski," cited above, pp. 378–379.
[100] For the first quotation, Lichtheim, *op. cit.*, p. 142. In this statement
we can see something like a formulation of the problem debated so

ment represents the extreme of Marx in this matter.

There is another cast to Marx's thought, however, equally important. In his description and analysis of the epochs of historical development, as we saw, he leaves it as a real question whether capitalism was inevitably bound, by a sort of abstract inner logic, to emerge from feudalism. Thus, feudalisms other than Western European might not supply the necessary and sufficient conditions for the rise of capitalism. For example, a Protestant ethic might be necessary (this, of course, was Max Weber's extrapolation of Marx); or, an example more acceptable to Marx, the discovery of the New World might be necessary. Thus, special, *historical* conditions are required. Viewed in this way, the necessary logic in Marx's philosophy of history is historical, and not formal. The latter would be, to use Marx's own term, "super-historical."

Marx's waverings arise, I believe, from one source. He constantly seems to underrate one element, or historical condition —human consciousness. Because he correctly perceives that human consciousness is in some way connected to, or determined by, or corresponds with material conditions, Marx makes the error of thinking he can treat it as largely a dependent force. Thus, if he can discover the "laws of motion" governing the material conditions, and assume that they operate independently from human will, he can establish his deductive science. Now, the extraordinary thing is that the whole aim of Marx's "science" is eventually to place the phenomena it describes *under man's conscious control.* As we have seen, this is the real intent of his critique. Yet, fundamentally, he treats all of history as if man's level of consciousness had remained sta-

---

earnestly by modern philosophers of history, like Carl Hempel, representing the covering law theory, and William Dray, representing the continuous series position. For details, see Carl G. Hempel, "The Function of General Laws in History," conveniently reprinted in *Theories of History*, Patrick Gardiner (ed.) (New York, 1959); and William Dray, *Laws and Explanation in History* (Oxford, 1957); and *Capital*, Vol. I, p. 393. This last quotation is part of the important footnote wherein Marx evokes the names of Darwin and Vico as his predecessors; see p. 261.

tionary. It is this, in fact, which vitiates especially his analysis of the most modern epoch, capitalism.

For example, a case could be made out that, given the level of consciousness of the Romans, there was no escape for them from the logic of their social arrangements. The latter, as Marx tries to show, led inexorably to a social decline. We can even go along with Marx in believing that, given the level of material development in antiquity, the level of consciousness about economics, sociology, and so forth could be no higher. Hence, the Romans were doomed. When we come to the present, however, we are in quite different historical conditions and circumstances; and these Marx tends to underrate. Thus, on one side, Marx underrates the very class consciousness that he has bestowed on the workers, which has helped allow them to form unions and to influence—or control in part—their wage rates. As Lichtheim remarks about Marx's assumption that the capitalists will try to intensify exploitation to affect the fall in the rate of profit (thus keeping real wages from rising even though productivity has improved): "There is nothing wrong with the logic of this argument, but it does not fit the observable facts under modern conditions, given the growth in organized labour's bargaining strength."[101]

In this last example, Marx has used abstract rather than historical logic. So, too, he ignores the possibility of men voluntarily changing the capitalistic system, in the light of better knowledge in the new human sciences (for example, economics and sociology). He has done this largely because he has chosen to ignore the rising level of consciousness. By doing so, he demonstrates a surprising and fundamental desertion of his historical approach. It is, however, the same surprising antihistorical bias of his spirit which we have seen in his thoughts about the postcapitalist epoch. What we found there was a utopia. In that utopia, of course, man secures at one stroke consciousness and control over the hitherto blind motions of

[101] Lichtheim, *op. cit.*, p. 188, fn. 1.

social phenomena. Engels gives us the most lyrical description of that happy event.

> The whole sphere of the conditions of life which environ man, and which have hitherto ruled man, now comes under the dominion and control of man, who for the first time becomes the real, conscious lord of nature because he has now become master of his own social organization. The laws of his own social action, hitherto standing face to face with man as laws of nature foreign to and dominating him, will now be used with full understanding, and so mastered by him. Man's own social organization, hitherto confronting him as a necessity imposed by nature and history, now becomes the result of his own free action. The extraneous objective forces that have hitherto governed history pass under the control of man himself. Only from that time will man himself, more and more consciously, make his own history—only from that time will the social causes set in movement by him have, in the main and in a constantly growing measure, the results intended by him. It is the ascent of man from the kingdom of necessity to the kingdom of freedom.[102]

To the nonbeliever, memories of earlier, nineteenth-century geological and biological debates are awakened. Such a complete change as Engels describes appears cataclysmic and nonhistorical. Further, as a historian, the nonbeliever might think that efforts at man's conscious control of his destiny have already been increasing. Thus, the American Revolution can be viewed as an instance in which a people formally set up a new institution, a constitutional convention, to contrive a government which would embody the people's sovereignty.[103] Marx himself recognized the French Revolution as announcing a new order of politics: the application of *reason* to human affairs. These, surely, were efforts, however short they fall of perfection, to "will" one's political destiny. And even in mid-nineteenth-century capitalist England, efforts to pass social

---

[102] *Basic Writings*, p. 109.
[103] For the geological-biological debates, see, for example, John L. Greene, *The Death of Adam* (Ames, Iowa, 1959). For the constitutional convention as a new political device, see R. R. Palmer, *The Age of the Democratic Revolution* (Princeton N.J., 1959), Vol. I.

legislation were made, based on statistical inquiries and parliamentary investigations into social conditions. Marx dutifully studied and used these; but because he underestimated the role of consciousness, he did not correctly see the direction in which they pointed.

The net result is that, while much of Marx's work on the past is useful and important, much of it is also perverted by polemical considerations into an abstract and nonhistorical logic. The Marxist future, as we have seen, is a complete leap out of history.[104]

15

It is impossible to talk of Marx's views on consciousness without bringing in the related topic of ideology. Marx's work here is fundamental. It represents a new way of looking at the world and at man, expressed in a vocabulary which has reshaped parts of our language. In effect, Marx's theory of ideology concludes the line of thought stretching to him from Descartes (and does so by fusing the empirical with the idealist epistemological position).

Descartes had declared that, with thought, man constructs the world.[105] Marx reverses this formulation—it is his real standing-on-the-head operation—and claims that the material world produces thought. Now, in itself this notion is not

[104] It must be pointed out that the Russian Revolution of 1917, whatever its successes, is empirical proof of the failure to leap out of history and to obtain at once the "kingdom of freedom" (i.e., conscious control of all objective forces). Of course, it could be and has been argued that this was the wrong revolution. But this argument, in turn, might be construed as a commentary on the predictive powers of Marx's "science."

[105] In a footnote to *Capital*, Vol. I, p. 414, Marx makes explicit his view of Descartes: "Descartes, like Francis Bacon, looked forward to an alteration in the form of production, and to the effective control of nature by man, as a result of a change in the ways of thinking . . . we are told that Descartes' method applied to political economy has begun to free that science from the ancient fables and superstitious notions about money, trade, etc."

original; Marx could have found it in any of his empirical predecessors, like Hobbes or Locke. It is what Marx does with the notion that is original.

First of all, he derives it immediately from Feuerbach, with all the critical overtones involved in the latter's writings. As Sidney Hook puts it nicely, "Instead of Descartes' 'Cogito ergo sum,' Feuerbach proclaimed a 'Sentio ergo sum.' Sensory experience was the criterion of existence, not logic or reason, no matter how divine."[106] Marx, however, does not leave sensory experience as mere sense experience. He transmutes it into a radically *social* perception or consciousness. This last emerges from the following logic.

According to Marx, man *knows* only by *acting* into nature: he *creates* his knowledgeable world. Thus, starting with the need to produce and reproduce life, men, by laboring, create social relations which accord with their material productivity. Men, also, Marx tells us, "produce *ideas, categories,* that is to say the abstract ideal expressions of these same social relations." In short, ideas are not given a priori, not even in a Kantian form; they are produced by men interacting with their environment. Marx formulates this in *The German Ideology* as follows: "Men are the producers of their conceptions, ideas, etc.—real, active men, as they are conditioned by a definite development of their productive forces and of the intercourse corresponding to these, up to its furthest forms. Consciousness can never be anything else than conscious existence, and the existence of men is their actual life process."[107]

Here, of course, Marx has recalled our attention to his stress on the conditions—conditions which are by their nature social —which surround man from the moment of his entrance into the world. These conditions are historical and transitory. To offer an example of my own, while the physiological apparatus of a primitive may be exactly the same as that of modern man,

---

[106] Hook, *op. cit.,* p. 225.
[107] Marx to P. V. Annenkov, cited above, p. 47; and *Basic Writings,* p. 247.

each will focus on very different things: what interests one, will escape the other's attention; what has no "meaning" for the first may be vital to the second.[108] Thus, every society will have its own way of looking at the world; and, on the larger scale, every epoch will have its characteristic consciousness rooted in its particular material conditions.

Marx calls the elements of such a consciousness the "illusion of the epoch." More at length, he expostulates that "Upon the different forms of property, upon the social conditions of existence, rises an entire superstructure of distinct and peculiarly formed sentiments, illusions, modes of thought and views of life." For this superstructure, Marx also reserves the term "ideology." Characteristically, he attaches it to classes, and thus transmutes it into class consciousness as well. "What else does the history of ideas prove," he asks dramatically, "than that intellectual production changes its character in proportion as material production is changed? The ruling ideas of each age have ever been the ideas of its ruling class."[109]

In essence, ideology is the mistaken, or, better still, the inverted perception of reality. In ideology, Marx informs us, "Men and their circumstances appear upside down, as in a *camera obscura* . . . this phenomenon arises just as much from their historical life process as the inversion of the retina does from their physical life process." As long as this inversion remains unrecognizable, men have an ideological outlook. Only by piercing the veil of illusion, what in some places Marx calls the phenomenal form, and penetrating to the inner reality can we go beyond ideology to science. Thus, science is the

[108] See, for example, Karl R. Popper, "Evolution and the Tree of Knowledge," Herbert Spencer Lecture, 30 October, 1961, at Oxford University. An interesting approach to the epistemological problem is Michael Polanyi, "Tacit Knowing: Its Bearing on Some Problems of Philosophy," *Reviews of Modern Physics*, 34, 4 (October, 1962).

[109] *Basic Writings*, p. 26. For the history of the term "ideology," see George Lichtheim, "The Concept of Ideology," *History and Theory*, IV, 2 (1965). Also, the relevant passages in Karl Mannheim, *Ideology and Utopia*, and the brief comment thereon in Charles Frankel, *The Case for Modern Man* (Boston, 1960), pp. 124-126.

discovery of the "actual substrate" underlying the phenomenal form; it is the reality behind the appearance.[110]

Marx, of course, believed that he had discovered the science of economic movements, as part of his discovery of the true instead of the apparent laws of motion of history. Moreover, he did not consider his critique as a part of philosophy, for philosophy in his eyes was merely a branch of ideology, soon to be eliminated. Thus, where Hegel had progressed from religion to philosophy, Marx would hold that he had taken the giant step from philosophy to human science.

Was Marx's "science" itself exempt from being an ideology? Did not it too spring from definite, transient historical circumstances? To this profound challenge, Marx turned the useful shield of definition. Ideologies are the unrecognized, unconscious, and therefore uncontrolled products of material conditions. In this state, they are alienated from men. Material conditions, however, as we have seen, necessarily evolve. At some point, and Marx saw this as about to occur in his own time, material conditions will fall under the control of men. Classes will be eliminated, and with them particular class consciousnesses and thus ideologies. Men will then be able *consciously* to achieve their own ends. This conscious knowledge and control is what Marx calls science.

Now, I have already suggested certain doubts about the scientific validity of Marx's thought; and these need not be repeated. What is important here is to discern the kernel of truth hidden in Marx's formulation of ideology. In order to do this, it must first be made clear that Marx did not dogmatically assert that a capitalist could only have capitalist ideas: Engels was the living refutation of such a simple-minded notion. Nor, in fact, did Marx put the emphasis in his theory of ideology on the explanation of the social origin of ideas; though, of course, only a certain range of ideas could arise in a given epoch. What he did stress was that ideas, once produced, owe their

---

[110] *Basic Writings*, p. 247; Engels to C. Schmidt, London, 27 October, 1890, *Selected Correspondence*, p. 505; and *Capital*, Vol. II, p. 591.

acceptance by large segments of society, especially by the ruling class, to their effectiveness in expressing "reality," i.e., class interests.

In sum, the fundamental consequence of Marx's concept of ideology is a new epistemological position. In his formulation, as we have seen, ideas are not innate in the Cartesian manner, or mere copies of sense impressions in the manner of Locke and Hume, or even "categorized" in the Kantian fashion; they are functional tools, produced by man in his effort to live. Moreover, they are produced and accepted under *historical* conditions; this is why history is central to Marx's vision. Hence, after Marx, ideas and ideologies must be treated in a naturalistic and historical rather than supernatural fashion, and are no longer to be considered timeless and unchanging, or to be held sacred and sacrosanct. This is the agonizing, Promethean penalty man must pay for his increased consciousness.

16

It is time to arrive at a summary statement about Marx's philosophy of history. I shall consider first some fundamental criticisms which may vitiate important parts of Marx's system, and then go on to a positive reckoning of his achievements.

The first criticism of Marx must be on the immediate terrain of his own work as an economist. The economic conditions, according to Marx, are basic to the development of society. Without a clear and sure understanding of the mechanism of economics (taking the word in its broadest sense) which drives society, we cannot grasp the *real* changes in history. Marx himself attempted to supply a science of economics, especially as it applied to the capitalist epoch. Obviously, if this scientific underpinning of his entire structure of history is faulty, a tremor is felt through the whole edifice. And this is the case. On numerous key points in his economics, Marx has been seriously and damagingly questioned. Some examples are the labor theory of value, the problem of surplus value, and the theory of technological unemployment. With all his accomplishments as an economic analyst, Marx, as Joseph Schumpeter points out, "was essentially period-bound as a theoretical technician."[111] This last is only natural; like any scientist constructing hypotheses and models concerning certain phenomena, Marx was bound to have much of his work falsified or superseded. Thus, it is only when such work is considered as itself fixed and final, and then made the basis, not of another model, but supposedly of the total reality of man's historical life that trouble arises. Marx's presumption, unfortunately, was to consider his economic theory in just these latter terms.

The next criticism takes its rise from Marx's work, but is not censorious of his particular efforts. As we have seen, Marx calls attention to man as a tool-maker, and stresses the importance of technological change in history. With brilliant flashes of insight, he supplies instances of the effect of a new tool on the relations of existing society. Alas, again Marx's own vision in this matter falters when he comes to his own time and to the immediate future before him. For example, he can see the mote in Ricardo's eye, as when he criticizes the latter's theory of rent—its assumption that the soil would deteriorate and become less fertile. "There is no doubt," Marx admits, "that as civilization progresses poorer and poorer kinds of land are brought under cultivation." But he adds, alluding to the modern application of chemistry to soils, "There is also no doubt that, as a result of the progress of science and industry, these poorer types of land are relatively good in comparison with the former good types." But having called Ricardo to task for ignoring possible scientific and technological change, Marx himself falls into the same fault. For example, he does not correctly see the possible effect of advancing technology on the standard of living of workers (a myopia less justly shared

[111] Schumpeter, *op. cit.*, p. 319.

today by Soviet Marxists visiting America, for example, and
denying the reality of the automobiles owned by "workers").
Nor could he effectively foresee that one consequence of technological change was to be a "managerial revolution," in
which ownership of the means of production, or lack of it,
becomes a more or less meaningless concept; worker ownership of stock, or even capitalist ownership, today has nothing
to do with control.[112] Nor did he see that technological
change was about to shatter his simple picture of a growing
polarization of classes—capitalist and manual workers—and,
combined with political factors, to introduce the great middle-
class mass (of, say, America) and, beyond that, the class of
technically trained nonmanual personnel. In this new world of
tools, and of men educated to use them in a new way, Marx's
conceptual schemes seem primitive and anachronistic. What,
for example, does "expropriation of the worker" mean in a
"capitalist" society where the worker owns stock, has social
security and unemployment benefits, and sends his son to
M.I.T. (probably on a scholarship supplied by General
Motors)?

Marx's great error, and it is my third and last fundamental
criticism of his system, one that I have touched on earlier, is
that he underestimates or else totally ignores some of the non-
economical forces making for historical change. These forces
are primarily of two sorts: ideas and psychological drives. I
shall not say much about the latter here; I have already
touched on Marx's treatment of personality as merely an economic category, and I shall leave the detailed discussion of
how psychological drives may affect historical changes for the
chapter on Freud. Suffice it to note now Marx's complete dismissal of the psychological elements in history, and to give as
only one instance the absence of any discussion about aggres-

---

[112] Marx to Engels, London, 7 January, 1851, *Selected Works*, p. 61;
and Marx to Engels, London, 26 November, 1869, *ibid.*, p. 272. On the
matter of ownership and control of industry, still one of the best books
is one of the first, Adolph Berle and Gardiner Means, *The Modern
Corporation and Private Property* (New York, 1933).

sive elements in man's behavior persisting into the communist epoch.

As for the role of ideas, the pertinent feature of Marx's work to note is that almost never are scientists or political leaders significantly mentioned. Occasionally, Marx will cite a scientist's idea, as analogy to his own work; but the data (with which, of course, he was familiar) of the history of the scientific revolution, the impact of a Copernicus, Kepler, Galileo, or Newton, simply do not exist for his history. Marx's repudiation of the "progress of the human mind" school is complete. In this aspect, Comte might just as well never have written the six volumes of his *Cours*. Thus, scientific ideas, which develop so strongly as an independent, internal, and logical response to problems of a particular discipline, are largely dismissed by Marx. While he exempts them from the category of ideology (though, of course, he correctly views them as influenced by the material conditions of society), in turn, Marx underestimates the effect that this rising level of semiautonomous scientific knowledge can have on historical development.[113]

Similarly, although Marx claims not to deny some causative power to social and political ideas in history, he considers only economic conditions as ultimate or fundamental causes of historical change. Thus, nowhere in his history is a phenomenon such as Mohammedanism mentioned in an important way. Yet, the empirical evidence certainly suggests that Mohammedanism originated in economic conditions which had not changed significantly for centuries, and that this new religious move-

---

[113] Marx, of course, gave lip service to the transforming power of natural science. Thus, as Wilhelm Liebknecht reports, "Soon we were talking about natural sciences and Marx scoffed at the victorious reaction in Europe who imagined that they had stifled the revolution and had no idea that natural science was preparing a new one. King Steam, who had revolutionized the world the century before, had lost his throne and was being superseded by a still greater revolutionary—the electric spark." (*Reminiscences of Marx and Engels*, p. 98). But natural science for Marx was largely an abstraction—he was not particularly concerned with studying how the electric spark had come into being—rather than the concrete product of *creative* individuals, operating in relative autonomy outside an ideological framework.

ment went on to form and shape a whole new culture out of which major centers of civilization arose.[114] Marx needs to reconcile his view that economic changes alone explain major ideological shifts with this sort of historical data; nowhere does he do so. Hence, we are forced to the general conclusion that Marx's economic interpretation of history tends to operate *in vacuo*, and to allow no countervailing intellectual or social forces, i.e., new relations devised by a new level of consciousness. In short, Marx has conveniently thrown out of his model of history a number of the most important variables.[115]

Nevertheless, with all these drawbacks—the shaky economic theory, the underestimation of continuing technological change, and the short-changing of noneconomic causal factors —Marx's philosophy of history still marks the transition from philosophy to social theory, though the latter, to use Hegel's image, has only half emerged from the Sphinx.[116] Marx, by way of his philosophy of history, has set up a historical sociology which, with all its faults, allows for heuristic development. The concern with the economic conditions of social development, while excessive and one-sided, can and does lead to much needed empirical studies. Marx himself showed the way, though in too dramatic and polemical a fashion. A comparison with Comte's sociology illustrates the realism and useful scientific nature of Marx's work.

More specifically in relation to the discipline of history itself, Marx's contributions can be summed up as follows. Though he never directly investigated the epistemological basis of historical knowledge, his whole theory suggests a defi-

---

[114] For a similar case, the Hebrew religion, see Henri Frankfort, *et al.*, *Before Philosophy* (Baltimore, 1951), especially chap. VIII.

[115] So, too, Marx throws aside the possibility of reforming the capitalist system by parliamentary legislation *over the long run*, while acknowledging various Factory Acts of his own period as temporary steps forward (See *Capital*, Vol. I, p. 284.) His pessimistic conclusion arises, I think, from his conviction that "welfare" legislative acts were only so many "fetters" on capitalism, to be broken rather than striven for increasingly. Cf. Mehring's comment, *op. cit.*, p. 101.

[116] For Hegel's image of the Sphinx, see pp. 164–165.

nite view on the matter. Clearly, Marx believes that true and certain historical knowledge is possible, and that he himself has been able to seize on historical reality. This he accomplishes through his application of *critique* to the mere appearances and illusions obscuring the foundations, the substructure, of knowledge. The critique, as we have already seen, starts with man as a producing animal, and traces his upward course. It emphasizes the transformative effect of struggle, envisioned as a dialectic struggle, and locates that struggle in a new social classification: economic class. Further, Marx is the first philosopher of history to place *revolution* (however qualified), as the active means of social change in the modern period, at the heart of his theory. Thus, according to Marx, the dialectic struggle, rooted in economic conditions and classes, ultimately takes the political form of revolution, violent or otherwise. All of these notions, today, have become matters of "historical reality" to be studied by the historian, the social scientist, and the historical sociologist.

Was Marx not only a critical historian, but also an historicist? The answer to this important question is mixed: in one sense he was, and in another he was not. Certainly, he believed very strongly in historical patterns, or epochs, in which all parts of the social structure relate to one another: the sort of "wind mill produces feudalism" pattern. Thus, he saw the task of the historian as one of analyzing the elements of a time-circumscribed pattern, in which all the parts were interrelated in a unique and necessary manner. This, however, the historian could only do when equipped with theoretical understanding of the real and fundamental way in which societies function and develop (in other words, with Comte's social statics and dynamics in a very different and new dress). Marx's critique sought to give the historian this correct theory. The result according to Marx, is a true historical science.

At this point, the nonhistoricist aspect of Marx appears even more strongly. Enlightened by his new science, Marx shows himself, for example, intolerant of the pattern of capitalist society, historically necessary though it might be. Like the *philosophes* in relation to the Middle Ages, he directs his wrath against a particular stage of human progress, in this case, his own period. He even falls into the snobbery of the aristocratic reactionaries of the nineteenth century, when he ridicules that part of industrial development which has transformed "a few vulgar and half-educated upstarts into 'eminent cotton spinners,' 'extensive sausage makers,' and 'influential blacking dealers.' "[117] But this is only the "carbuncle" Marx at work; in his better moments, he could analyse the entrepreneurs of modern industry in a cooler and more rational fashion, fitting them into the total context of capitalist society. When operating in this latter fashion, Marx takes the historicist insights and combines them with his own analytic apparatus.

Part of that analytic apparatus, as we have seen, applies to the forces making for *change* in a given pattern of society. Thus, Marx's really grand contribution to historical study is his effort to set up a *scientific* theory which will explain the *evolution* of man in society. This effort stems from Vico, with the latter's stress on man's creative power, goes beyond the inspired versions of Hegel and Comte, and anticipates Darwin's efforts for the biological world. Marx, by positing a capitalist society, of which he was the first discoverer and historian, alongside and after a feudal society, gave a new ordering to the realm of social phenomena. Moreover, in capitalism he perceived, correctly, as Schumpeter points out, "a form or method of economic change" which, by its nature, never is and "never can be stationary."[118] Marx tried to show, in detail, why capitalism pulses steadily toward fundamental change, and how it does so. He then applied his scheme to earlier epochs. Thus, history became for Marx the record of progress. His genius was to see that this progress was not only of the mind, of an increasing level of consciousness, but also of

[117] *Capital*, Vol. I, p. 435.
[118] Joseph Schumpeter, *Capitalism, Socialism, and Democracy*, 2nd ed. (New York, 1947), p. 82.

the material conditions with which mind interacted. The result was a sweeping new vision of the whole of man's past and future life.

This was the true prophetic aspect of Karl Marx. Often his vision faltered, and his gaze slid around unpleasant obstacles to his theories. Further, he may have misconstrued drastically the actual relations of mind and matter, of individual and society. But the credit is his for insisting on the absolute necessity of analyzing their interaction in naturalistic terms. As a result, we can see emerging from his philosophy of history, with the remnants of polemic still clinging fast to it, the shape of a theory which seeks to explain scientifically the real, evolutionary progress of human society. This is, for our purposes, the sublime part of Marx's attempt at a Promethean revolution.

IX

Spengler

Cried Alyosha. "I think every one should love life above everything in the world."

"Love life more than the meaning of it?"

"Certainly, love it, regardless of logic as you say, it must be regardless of logic, and it's only then one will understand the meaning of it."

DOSTOYEVSKY,
The Brothers Karamazov

1

ALMOST three quarters of a century after Marx's *Manifesto*, to be precise in 1918, the first volume of Oswald Spengler's *Decline of the West* appeared. Its impact on the reading public was extraordinary. Indeed, as every critic then and now has pointed out in astonishment, this ponderous tome of hundreds of pages of recondite philosophy of history had quickly sold out—36,000 copies is the figure given—by the time the second volume, equally large, appeared in 1922. Refusing to have the first volume reissued in its original form, Spengler revised it in outward appearance, though leaving unchanged the basic ideas. Appearing in 1923, this second version now stands in the definitive German edition as the accepted first volume: together the

first and second volumes have sold well over 100,000 copies in
Germany, and, by 1940, over 25,000 copies in the American
translation.[1]

The initial critical attention is just as impressive as the first
sales figures. Thus, an Argentine professor of sociology,
Ernesto Quesada, devoted his entire academic course in 1921
to a consideration of Spengler's work, and published his findings in a 616-page book in the same year. Treating Spengler as
a great sociologist, Quesada saw the *Decline* as bringing with it
"a fundamental change in our way of considering social phenomena and their everlasting evolution." In Germany, Spengler was dealt with more as a historian; and by 1922, Manfred
Schroeter, in his *Der Streit um Spengler*, could list some 400
critics who had commented on the first volume.[2]

While we may attribute part of the book's renown to its
appearance at the time of Germany's "decline" and defeat in
World War I, there exist firmer reasons for its continuing
importance. We can see these reasons more clearly now, when
the book has lost most of its allure for the contemporary public and achieved what one scholar has recently called "a kind
of highly topical oblivion."[3] For us, however, the fundamental
importance of Spengler's *Decline* is that it poses, even if errati-
cally and repetitiously, disturbing challenges in both the critical and speculative branches of philosophy of history.

Let us begin with the critical side. Here, Spengler ostensibly
rejects the entire tradition of the subject as we have so far
studied it. He not only attacks Descartes' dissecting and

[1] The American translation is by Charles Francis Atkinson, in two
volumes, the first published in 1926, and the second, in 1928. The pub-
lisher is Alfred A. Knopf (New York). References to *The Decline of the
West* will be to this edition. The details on sales are from Oswald
Spengler, *Today and Destiny*, translated by Charles Francis Atkinson,
arranged by Edwin Franden Dakin (New York, 1940), p. 361.

[2] Ernesto Quesada, *La Sociologia Relativista Spengleriana* (Buenos
Aires, 1921), p. 9. After *Der Streit un Spengler* (Munich, 1922), Schroeter
returned to his interest in Spengler, in *Metaphysik des Untergangs: Eine
kulturkritische Studie über Oswald Spengler* (Munich, 1949), which re-
produces much of the earlier book and adds a philosophical study.

[3] Erich Heller, "Oswald Spengler and the Predicament of the Historical
Imagination," in *The Disinherited Mind* (Cambridge, England, 1952),
p. 143.

analytic approach to knowledge, but he heaps scorn on every other approach—idealist, positivist, a priorist, and empiricist—as well. Marx, too, is dismissed contemptuously (although, as we shall see, there are actually many points in common between the two men). Instead, Spengler turns openly to three figures we have not dealt with: Nietzsche, Goethe, and Leibnitz. Behind them, Spengler also appeals covertly to an entire movement of German thought, embracing the neoidealist "revolt against Positivism" and involving especially the name of Wilhelm Dilthey. Though Spengler never openly mentions Dilthey, the latter surely must have colored his whole process of thinking.[4] On this "German" basis, as he puts it, Spengler claims to offer both a new epistemology and a new methodology of history: in short, a new logic of history.

Turning to the speculative front, Spengler takes arms against the advocates of the idea of progress. He denies a linear development in history, and instead reverts to a form of cyclical theory (which we last saw in Vico). In his new view of the way history unfolds, Spengler claims to have achieved a "Copernican Revolution," one which affords both a new perspective and a new periodization scheme. To support his claims, Spengler seems incidentally to have produced a uni-

[4] The phrase, "revolt against Positivism" is used by H. Stuart Hughes, *Consciousness and Society* (New York, 1958). This book gives an interesting account of the neoidealist movement. Hughes, however (on p. 376), denies the assertion of Pietro Rossi, in *Lo storicismo tedesco contemporaneo* (Turin, 1956), that, although Spengler never explicitly referred to Dilthey, he derived "the general statement of the problem" from him. On this matter, my own view is that statements of intellectual "derivation" are always dubious, unless either explicit acknowledgments or internal documentation can be supplied, but that certain similarities between Spengler and Dilthey's thought are undeniable. (One noteworthy difference, however, at least in degree, is that Dilthey's soul-types are ideal-types, presumably constructed a priori, whereas Spengler's soul-types are constructed from actual cultures of the past, i.e., historically.) To decide the matter for himself, however, the interested reader may consult the following works on Dilthey: H. A. Hodges, *The Philosophy of Wilhelm Dilthey* (London, 1952); Jean-François Suter, *Philosophie et Histoire chez Wilhelm Dilthey* (Basle, 1960); and Carlo Antoni, *From History to Sociology*, translated by Hayden V. White (Detroit, 1959), chap. I. My grounds for not dealing in this book with thinkers like Dilthey have already been stated in the Preface.

versal history, as well as a philosophy of history. For our modern Alexandrian age, the former has probably constituted a large part of his public appeal.

We must also notice one more element of Spengler's importance in this preliminary, and for the moment uncritical, account. It is that the *Decline* dramatically illustrates the claim of philosophy of history to have replaced traditional political philosophy, a claim which we first saw adumbrated in Condorcet's *Sketch*, and then made central in all of Marx's work. Spengler, in fact, originally intended his book to be a political tract. Moreover, it is tendentious throughout. This fact, however, while it makes the task of considering the *Decline* without partisan passion more difficult, must not be allowed to obscure the seriousness of Spengler's challenge in the field of philosophy of history, both critical and speculative.

2

There is a strange sort of "self-made" quality to Spengler's character and life, in spite of the fact that his education for a doctor's degree in the German universities was typical. He was born May 29, 1880, in Blankenburg in the Hartz Mountains, though his family soon moved to Halle. His father, descended from a line of mining technicians, was a postal official. The other item always mentioned is that his mother's sister had been a famous dancer, and some students of heredity (hardly well informed) have tended to see the combination of scientific and artistic interests in Spengler's life as springing from this background.

In any case, Spengler's family were sufficiently affluent to send him to a classical high school, and then to the universities of Munich, Berlin, and Halle (where he majored in mathematics and philosophy), and eventually to provide him with a small inheritance. Before that, however, he had received his doctoral degree in 1904, for his thesis on the pre-Socratic philosopher, Heraclitus. After passing his state examinations, he taught in a variety of high schools, ending up at Hamburg in 1910. In the next year, he resigned his post and, moving to Munich, took up a quiet existence as a scholar. Thanks to the small income left him by his mother, who had just died, occasionally supplemented by payments for reviews and articles, Spengler was now able to devote full time to his work on the *Decline*.

The idea for the *Decline*, according to Spengler, came to him in relation to the Second Moroccan Crisis. This incident, like a flare, lighted up the European landscape and foreshadowed the coming German-French conflict of 1914. Moreover, "It became evident," Spengler tells us, "that a political problem could not be comprehended by means of politics themselves and that, frequently, important factors at work in the depths could only be grasped through their artistic manifestations or even distantly seen in the form of scientific or purely philosophical ideas."[5] Thus, turning from his original intention of writing a book to be entitled "Conservative and Liberal" (although this did come to form the chapter on the State in the *Decline*), Spengler worked his materials into a philosophy of history. Finished in draft form by 1914, the book was ready for publication in 1917.[6]

By the time of the second volume, Spengler had also answered some of the critics of his first volume with a short article, "Pessimismus," and had written the first of a number of outright political tracts, "Preussentum und Sozialismus."[7]

[5] For a similar decision, in relation to World War II, see F. S. C. Northrup, *The Meeting of East and West* (New York, 1946).

[6] On the data relating to Spengler's life and work, August Albers, who was a clerk for Spengler's German publishers and who became his faithful disciple, has written an account, "Oswald Spengler," *Preussiche Jahrbücher*, CLXXXXII, 2. Heft (May, 1923). See, too, H. Stuart Hughes, *Oswald Spengler: A Critical Estimate* (New York, 1952), chap. I and *passim;* and the brief biographical note in *Today and Destiny*, cited above, which includes the interesting comments by Spengler's American publishers, the Alfred A. Knopfs, who saw him a number of times.

[7] The first named can be found in the collection, *Reden und Aufsätze* (Munich, 1937), and the second in *Politische Schriften* (Munich, 1932).

Other works of a combined philosophical-political nature, such as *Der Mensch und die Technik* (Munich, 1931) and *Jahre der Entscheidung* (Munich, 1933), were also produced by Spengler.[8] But the only book that really counted and that makes him an imposing figure is his first: *The Decline of the West.*

Brief as is this sketch of Spengler's life and work—there is very little more, as he was extremely reticent about revealing himself except in his great work—it allows us to project a few generalizations about him. The first thing to note is that he never held a university post, and, unknown until 1918, never had any real academic standing.[9] While we cannot be dogmatic about this matter, it seems likely that the fact cited above had real repercussions in both Spengler's style of writing and in his scorn for intellectuals and scholars.

Few academicians would have chanced, in a serious, scholarly work, the poetic and dramatic style used by Spengler. Nietzsche, who suffered for it, is one of his few predecessors here. Yet, the poetic intensity of Spengler's writing is perhaps the most important reason for his power over our imagination, if not over our reason. By its means, he lights up aspects of history whose features would otherwise remain in darkness. Substitute the word "pen," and we could say of Spengler what he luminously said of Michelangelo: that he found "a way with the chisel into a buried world." Though Spengler's style often becomes too much for us—turgid, strained, and repetitious—at its best, it is unforgettable. Such a passage, for example, is the one on Cecil Rhodes, where Spengler literally *creates* a greater than life-size figure for us.[10]

Spengler's disdain for intellectuals and scholars is something

[8] The first has been translated into English, by Charles Francis Atkinson, as *Man and Technics* (New York, 1932), and the second as *The Hour of Decision* (New York, 1934), Part I.

[9] See Hughes, *Oswald Spengler*, p. 98, for data on a few university offers made after 1918; and p. 118 for the only "scholarly" circle with which Spengler made contact.

[10] See *Decline*, Vol. I, p. 275, for a statement about Michelangelo; and Vol. I, pp. 37–38 for the passage on Cecil Rhodes.

we shall deal with again in terms of his general theory. Here I wish only to add that, glorifying the peasants in theory, in his own life he was also more at home with them, and with taxi-drivers and similar types, than with other thinkers like himself.[11] Did Spengler's exaggerated notion of his own originality come because he was largely self-taught in many of the areas with which he dealt? Because he deprecated the labored findings of the established scholars? Collingwood, for example, labeled him either "ignorant" or "reticent," and maliciously added that Spengler had not given him "a single genuinely new idea."[12] In any case, Spengler is constantly boasting of his originality in such phrases as "no one before has seen," or "it is a fact hitherto never appreciated," or "never before established," and this is a note that seems to grow increasingly loud and annoying by the second volume.[13]

More serious, however, is the possibility that what I have called Spengler's self-made or self-taught quality may well have affected his ability to think logically and clearly. Unexposed to the checks of other, and trained, minds, Spengler could indulge freely in vague and wooly speculations. Contradictions between his own actions and his theories did not disturb him: extolling technics as the only fit occupation for contemporary man, Spengler wrote lyric passages of philosophy; praising war and the wielding of the sword, Spengler, who was extremely near-sighted and who suffered from a heart condition, occupied himself from 1914 to 1918 with the *Decline;* and condemning the sterility of the modern family and the resultant population decline as a sign of decadence, Spengler remained unmarried and without children. These examples, of course, can be dismissed as *ad hominem* arguments; and, indeed, they do not in principle affect his theories.

Far more important is Spengler's sometimes extraordinary

[11] *Today and Destiny*, p. 360.
[12] R. G. Collingwood, "Oswald Spengler and the Theory of Historical Cycles," *Antiquity*, I, III (September, 1927), 313–314.
[13] For additional examples, see *Decline*, Vol. I, p. 400; and Vol. II, pp. 48, 90.

treatment of various philosophers, literary figures, and historical episodes, as well as his cavalier and convenient use of various "facts." Descartes, for example, is labeled a Jansenist; Spinoza, as "a Jew and therefore, spiritually, a member of the Magian Culture," is characterized as a descendant of "Talmudic 'more geometrico' methodology," while no mention is made in this connection of such geometric-minded non-Jews as Descartes and Hobbes; and so forth.[14] This sort of criticism of Spengler, however, cannot be correctly judged until both the grounds for his work and the general structure of his thought are more fully presented.

3

Spengler's political views do not concern us per se, but only as they relate to his philosophy of history.[15] Nevertheless, as the political is such an important part of Spengler's intention—we have already seen his initial framing of the *Decline* as a work on "Conservatism and Liberalism"—we had best deal with it right off, even before tackling the philosophy of history proper. Indeed, only by isolating and identifying the annoying political aspects of Spengler's work, and I confess my prejudices immediately, can we obtain a measure of objectivity for the rest.

The political affects Spengler's work in two ways: (1) it is an integral part of his philosophy of history, being part of any culture which he treats; and (2) it is an external element which anachronistically colors his approach to all the cultures which he studies. Let us look more closely at both these points.

In any culture, according to Spengler, the political elements

[14] *Ibid.*, Vol. I, pp. 66, 413.

[15] Hughes, *Oswald Spengler*, is concerned mainly with Spengler as a political phenomenon, and treats him more as a symptom than as a creator of political moods (see pp. 117, 164). André Fauconnet, *Oswald Spengler* (Paris, 1925), while devoting the first half of the book to Spengler as a philosopher, treats him as a political thinker and figure in the second half.

must be completely in tune with the general "spirit" of the whole organism. While we shall not understand the full meaning of this until we deal with the role of "culture" in Spengler's philosophy of history, we can perceive here that Spengler is merely restating the "holistic" position. For example, his vision of an integral connection between the dynastic principle of Louis XIV and the differential calculus, or the Greek polis and Euclidean geometry, is really comparable to Marx's view of the connection of the windmill and the feudal lord.[16] The spring or unifying element behind the two conceptions is different, in one case, spiritual (to be defined later), in the other, economic, but the basic principle is the same.

It follows from this view that the political element in a culture is neither accidental nor transmittible as a tool is to some other time or place. Within all political arrangements, however, there is one constant for Spengler: law and political rule are always "class" devices. In this surprising affirmation of Marx, Spengler asserts that "every historical world-picture contains a political-economic *tendency* dependent, not upon what this man or that thinks, but upon what is practically intended by the class which in fact commands the power and, with it, the legislation." While Spengler defines class somewhat differently from Marx—Spengler's class is more political than economic— he, too, insists on a class struggle taking place, even if only in constitutional guise. At one point, undoubtedly with Montesquieu in mind, Spengler makes the significant comment that "the spirit of laws is always a party spirit."[17]

The aim of all politics, internal and external, is survival. Man, as Spengler remarks in one of his works (*Man and Technics*), is a "beast of prey." In addition to such Darwin-like metaphors, Spengler also talks of the will of the strongest, and repeats with Hegel that "World-history is the world-court,"

[16] *Decline*, Vol. I, p. 7.
[17] *Ibid.*, Vol. II, pp. 64, 153. Of course the idea of politics as a class struggle had already been developed before Marx, by Vico, whose echo frequently seems to be heard in the pages of the *Decline*. Cf. Vol. II, p. 79, and see p. 365.

adding that "it has ever decided in favor of the stronger, fuller, and more self-assured life—decreed to it, namely, the right to exist, regardless of whether its right would hold before a tribunal of waking-consciousness."[18]

For Spengler, the internal and external arrangements of a political body are always related, but the external must dominate; that is, foreign policy takes precedence over domestic, and the class conflict of the latter must be subordinated to the national struggles of the former. Reversing Clausewitz's dictum, Spengler insists that policy is only war by other means. Spengler's approval of war as a natural and commendable act of creativity takes concrete form in his proud affirmation of the "uprising of 1914," which, he tells us, was "Prussian through and through" and "transformed souls in one moment." In the light of his declared view about politics as survival and the will of the strongest, Spengler's protests about the harshness of the Treaty of Versailles sound a bit incongruous; however, his exhortations to his people to prepare for another war looked forward to a reversal of that decision.[19]

Espousing external war, Spengler also embraces many of the cliché positions of early nineteenth-century conservatism. Glorifying both the nobility and the peasantry, he constantly denigrates the middle classes and the urban "mob." He contrasts virtuous "Blood" with filthy "Money." At one point in his rather naïve and mixed-up passages on economics, he characterizes trade and the middleman as "parasitism, completely unproductive and, therefore, land-alien." In a vague way, Spengler is even on the side of entail.[20]

[18] *Ibid.*, Vol. II, p. 507. By "waking-consciousness," Spengler means the "understanding" (*Verstand*).

[19] See *Hour of Decision*, p. xi; and *Decline*, Vol. II, pp. 363, 367, 422, 430. Spengler also gently insinuates that the "crash of 1918" was the work of the German monied class. See Vol. II, p. 410, fn. 1.

[20] While Spengler calls Edmund Burke a "true statesman" (*Hour of Decision*, p. 14), many of his ideas seem to reach beyond Burke to more reactionary figures, like Ludwig von der Marwitz. See *Decline*, Vol. II, pp. 478, 485.

Along with such social-economic views, Spengler has the usual assortment of conservative or reactionary political notions. He is opposed to parliamentarianism, and sees (alas, in 1918, perhaps correctly) elections degenerating into farces. As against political parties, which essentially, he feels, can only be bourgeois in nature, Spengler favors the struggle of factions, which he views as in some way "organic."[21] Freedom of the press and such-like "liberal" notions are only illusions, for they mean simply the freedom of Money to corrupt and control the people in the bourgeoisie's own narrow interest. While Spengler identifies all of the elements listed above, economic and political, as existing at a certain stage—the decline—in all cultures, it is obvious that on the eve of 1918 and the Weimar Republic they take on a rather special contemporary importance.

On the positive side, Spengler favors what he calls "Prussianism." This catchall term embraces not only Socialism, but Imperialism and Nationalism. By Socialism, Spengler does not mean Marx's theory "but Frederick William I's Prussian practice which long preceded Marx and will yet displace him—the socialism, inwardly akin to the system of Old Egypt, that comprehends and cares for permanent economic relations, trains the individual in his duty to the whole, and glorifies hard work as an affirmation of Time and Future." In Spengler's scheme of economics, work is not a commodity but a duty, and the individual seeks not his own selfish betterment but the service of the state. To effect this, the whole national productive force is to be brought under the state's control, while leaving a certain amount of scope for personal enterprise. As one commentator sums it up, "For a society conceived in these terms, corporatism is the logical form of government." This corporate state, however, from which political parties will be absent, is to be under the rule of a hereditary monarch,

[21] *Decline*, Vol. II, pp. 415, 448–449, 464.

like Frederick William I, and graced by a nobility which, to use Spengler's sporting term, is "in form."[22]

Now, it is this last element which (along with Race, to be discussed later) perhaps most distinguished Spengler's politics from the Nazi movement. While his stress on the nation, its aggressive foreign policy, and its "socialist" economy lent itself readily to an identification with National Socialism, the tone and meaning of Spengler's formulation was quite different. "The traditions of an old monarchy," he prophesied, "of an old aristocracy, of an old polite society, in so much as they are still healthy enough to keep clear of professional or professorial politics, in so far as they possess honor, abnegation, discipline, the genuine sense of a great mission (*race-quality*, that is, and training), sense of duty and sacrifice—can become a centre which holds together the being-stream of an entire people and enables it to outlast this time and make its landfall in the future." Alas, the charismatic upstart, Hitler, was neither polite nor possessed of a sense of honor, and Spengler was true enough to his ideal to hold himself aloof, and even to oppose, the Nazi movement which had enough in common with his own political beliefs to betray them effectively.[23]

Spengler believed that it was Germany's mission to try to make the "landfall" sketched above. But his historical sense told him that Western culture was in its decline, and that "Caesarism" was more likely than a traditional monarchy to succeed the present reign of Money. Nevertheless, he seems not to have recognized Hitler as one of the "great fact-men" who seize the role of Caesar. Rather, Spengler imagined the modern Caesar as a successor to the Cecil Rhodes type of leader.[24] In any case, whereas Burckhardt (with his *terribles*

[22] Hughes, *Oswald Spengler*, p. 109; and Fauconnet, *op. cit.*, p. 214. See, too, *Decline*, Vol. I, p. 138; and Vol. II, p. 330. It is interesting to note that Spengler greatly admired Mussolini.

[23] Cf. Hughes, *Oswald Spengler*, p. 112 and *passim*; and see *Decline*, Vol. II, p. 431.

[24] *Today and Destiny*, p. 363. Whatever the particular form of Caesarism, it meant for Spengler a return to "formlessness." See *Decline*, Vol. II, p. 431.

simplificateurs) and Nietzsche (with his commanders of the
herd who, pretending to follow, will lead with an iron will)
had merely foreseen the coming Caesarism, Spengler identified
and described his coming as a predetermined point on a fated
cyclical movement.[25]

In the *Decline*, the elements of what I have called Spengler's "conservatism" are omnipresent. And this brings us to the
second point with which I started: that the political is not only
an integral part of any culture which Spengler studies, but that
his own political convictions anachronistically color his studies
of all cultures. Only if we recognize this fact—one which,
admittedly, can only be tested as we go into his theory—can
we deal effectively with Spengler's philosophy of history,
making allowance for his and our political bias, and concentrating on his critical and speculative theories about history.
Spengler himself claimed that his treatment would "employ no
distorting modulus of personal ideals, set no personal origin of
co-ordinates, be influenced by none of the personal hopes and
fears and other inward impulses which count for so much in
practical life; and such a detachment will—to use the words of
Nietzsche . . . —enable one to view the whole fact of Man
from an immense distance, to regard the individual Cultures,
one's own included, as one regards the range of mountain
peaks along a horizon."[26] While it must be flatly stated that
Spengler fell far short of his own ideal, we ought to follow his
injunction in our own approach to him as one of the "mountain peaks" in the field of philosophy of history.

4

Spengler gave to his political-cum-philosophy of history work
the title "Der Untergang des Abendlandes." We are also told

[25] As we have seen above, however, Spengler momentarily wavered
(because of his enthusiasm for the "old monarchy") on the necessity of
Caesarism.
[26] *Decline*, Vol. I, pp. 93–94.

that he approved the use of "Decline of the West" as an English rendering of his title. Now, the word "Untergang" in German has an astronomical significance, as in the idea of the "declining" or "setting" of the sun. Thus, the thought arises that Spengler intended by his title to implant in his reader's imagination the idea, not of a decline of a society owing to naturalistic or historical reasons, but of a decline which is inevitable because it is "in our stars." Basically, I believe, Spengler was what I shall call an astrological historian. He is really talking about his own work when he says, "Astrology, in the form in which from Gothic to Baroque the Western soul knew it—was dominated by it even in denying it—was the attempt to master one's *whole* future life-course; the Faustian horoscope, of which the best-known example is perhaps that drawn out for Wallenstein by Kepler, *presupposes* a steady and purposeful direction in the existence that has yet to be accomplished."[27]

My suspicion that Spengler saw himself as the modern historical Kepler, drawing up the Faustian horoscope, is made greater by a number of rather occult references to the influence over our destiny exercised by the heavenly bodies. Thus, talking of certain critical points in history, Spengler comments that they are "yet another hint that the Cosmic flowings in the form of human lives upon the surface of a minor star are not self-contained and independent, but stand in deep harmony with the unending movedness of the universe."[28] Elsewhere, he talks of "the belief in his star which every born man of action possesses," and defines race, or the feeling for a common destiny, as *"something cosmic and psychic,* periodic in

[27] *Ibid.,* pp. 146–147. See *Today and Yesterday,* p. 357, for Spengler's approval of the English title.

[28] *Decline,* Vol. II, p. 392, fn. 1. See the rest of this significant footnote for Spengler's mystical approach. Kepler, as is well known, like Spengler, was interested in astrology and in the harmony of the cosmic flowings, and covered up much of his respectable scientific contribution with a great deal of mystical nonsense. For a very readable account of Kepler's work, see Arthur Koestler, *The Watershed: A Biography of Johannes Kepler* (Garden City, N.Y., 1960).

some obscure way, and in its inner nature partly conditioned by major astronomical relations."

Spengler's astrological view of history is, I believe, of the greatest importance in his work. It allows him to see a cyclical movement in history—an eternal recurrence—one which results from the astronomical theory of the revolution of the heavenly bodies. Further, it permits Spengler to claim powers of divination and prediction, whereby he can perceive human destiny. At the same time, it provides him with a periodization scheme which allows him to say at what point on the cycle our destiny stands at a given moment. Moreover, causation, for Spengler, resolves itself into cosmic destiny, and is therefore no longer a problem for the historian. In general, too, astronomic images, such as rise and fall, or dawn and decline, permit a historian like Spengler to embrace the notion that culture or society is an entity which moves *as a whole* in cyclic fashion. Thus, he need not entertain the disturbing idea that one part of the culture, for example, the political, may be progressing while another, possibly the social, may be suffering a reverse.[29]

Nevertheless, while in my judgment the "astrological" is the major motif in Spengler's philosophy of history, its note is rarely sounded aloud. It serves only as the great cosmic backdrop for Spengler's more microscopic drama of life. Thus, for the bulk of his work, Spengler uses other, "biological" images. Perhaps he realized that his astrological approach was too unacceptable, suggesting charlatanism, or that, once stated, it could not readily be applied in the fine detail of actual cultural history. In any case, the inspiration of Kepler gave way in practice to that of Goethe.

The prime question Spengler set for himself was: "Is there a logic of history?" His answer was "yes," but it is an *"organic logic."* This logic, Spengler tells us, is "an instinctive, dream-sure logic of all existence as opposed to the *logic of the inor-*

[29] Cf. Collingwood, *Antiquity,* Vol. I, p. 316.

ganic, the logic of understanding and of things understood—a logic of direction as against a logic of extension—and no systematist, no Aristotle or Kant, has known how to deal with it." What this new organic logic tells us, and Spengler overlooks the tautological aspect of his remark, is that there is a world-as-history in contrast to a world-as-nature. The world-as-history relates to becoming; the world-as-nature, to the system of all things become. According to Spengler, the first man before him to divine this distinction was the immortal Goethe. "That which Goethe called *Living Nature*," Spengler proclaims, "is exactly that which we are calling here world-history, world-as-history."[30]

Thus, following Goethe, Spengler makes a fundamental distinction between the historical and the natural worlds. As a result, for Spengler, the unity of the positive, scientific universe is broken.[31] Over the world-as-history lies what Spengler calls the "Destiny Idea," while the "Causality Principle" reigns over the world-as-nature. Again and again, Spengler stresses this basic dualism in the *Decline*, working it out in an involved and involuted fashion wherein each member of the pair reappears in a new garb. I list only some of the ingenious masquerades worn by the dualism: world-as-history versus world-as-nature; Destiny versus Causality (which are related as Time and Space); Form (*Gestalt*) versus Law (*Gesetz*); Physiognomic versus Systematic; Will versus Thought; Cosmic versus Microcosmic; periodity versus polarity; feel (*Fühlen*) versus feeling (*Empfinden*); Being (*Dasein*) versus waking-being (*Wachsein*); plant-like beings versus animal-beings; reason (*Vernunft*) versus understanding (*Verstand*); Race versus Language; Totem versus Taboo; Politics versus

---

[30] See *Decline*, Vol. I, pp. 3, 25, 117.

[31] We have already seen the beginning of this break in Hegel. By the late nineteenth century it had become a major position of German neoidealism. For details concerning the various contributions on the subject, by professional philosophers like Rickert, Windelband, and Dilthey, see, for example, R. G. Collingwood, *The Idea of History*, (Oxford, 1946), pp. 165–176.

Religion; Castle versus Cathedral; and Female versus Male.[32]
Spengler's brilliance, undoubtedly somewhat perverted here, is
demonstrated by the skill with which he spins out this seemingly endless dance of the two partners.

Erratic, despite its ingenuity, as Spengler's *development* of
the dualism may appear, the idea itself is a fundamental position in modern philosophy of history. Simply stated, it holds
that history is *not* subsumed under the generalizing sciences.
Nor are its methods the same as those of the natural sciences.
What the historian needs, according to Spengler, is an *eye*,
"The power of seeing and not that of calculating, depth and
not intellect." Speaking of Goethe, Spengler remarks: "Sympathy, observation, comparison, immediate and inward certainly, intellectual *flair*—these were the means whereby he was
enabled to approach the secrets of the phenomenal world in
motion. *Now these are the means of historical research*—precisely these and no others." *Par excellence*, Spengler informs
us, the method of history is "intuitive perception." Contemplation and vision (*Anschauen*) are the desired experiences, for,
as a becoming, history can only be experienced, lived through
(*erleben*), and not cognized in the form of mechanical laws.[33]

History, then, is the study of unique "becomings," which
can only be contemplated intuitively. This, let us note, is a
basic historicist position. At one point, Spengler tries to sum it
up with a quotation from Goethe, who, writing to his friend
Eckermann, remarks, "The Godhead is effective in the living
and not in the dead, in the becoming and the changing, not in
the become and the set-fast; and therefore, similarly, the reason (*Vernunft*) is concerned only to strive towards the divine
through the becoming and the living, and the understanding
(*Verstand*) only to make use of the become and the set-fast."

---

[32] For these various dualities, see *Decline*, Vol. I, pp. 97, 100, 308; and
Vol. II, pp. 4, 5, 12–13, 15–16, 117, 122, 144, 327.

[33] Cf. Burckhardt's statement that without *Anschauung* he could not
write his histories, as well as Dilthey's view that it is necessary to experience (*erleben*) history. See *Decline*, Vol. I. pp. 48–49, 95; and Vol.
II, pp. 25, 117.

Obviously, we have already encountered these words in our treatment of the *Decline*, and Spengler himself confessed about the quotation above, "This sentence comprises my entire philosophy."

Enjoined by Spengler to look at the world-as-history intuitively and with an organic logic, we discover that all "history is founded upon general biographic archetypes," organic beings, which, like everything organic, go through the phases of birth, youth, age, and death. More specifically, these organic beings are *cultures*. In Spengler's words, *"Cultures are organisms,* and world-history is their collective biography." Thus, Spengler clearly identifies for us the subject and object of history: instead of Hegel's "nation" or Marx's "class," it is "culture" which acts in history and which is also the object of our historical study.

Spengler's view of cultures as "biographic archetypes" or as organisms also allows him to add a refinement to his general historical method. Now, to intuition the historian can join a more scientific approach: comparative morphology. Again it is Goethe who supplies the hint with his distinction in biology between the term *homology*, signifying morphological or structural equivalence, and the term *analogy*, relating to functional equivalence. Thus, the lungs of terrestrial and the swim bladders of aquatic animals are homologous, while lungs and gills are analogous. Extended to history, this method allows us to go beyond shallow analogies and comparisons, such as that of Napoleon and Caesar, and to perceive, for example, that the homologous form to Napoleon is Alexander the Great: both stand in the same phase of a declining culture, while Caesar comes later. Hence, for Spengler, Napoleon and Alexander are "contemporaries," while Caesar's contemporary is yet to appear in the Western culture.

With his new morphological method, Spengler can run through all of past history, correctly estimating relationships, or so he claims, which were previously misconceived. Thus, for Spengler, the Classical Dionysiac movement is

homologous with the Renaissance and only analogous with the
Reformation. He also claims that he can fill in gaps, for example, from known elements in art to corresponding unknown
elements in the political forms, or, as in Chinese Culture, to
"predict" (by comparison with the Western Gothic phase)
the existence of a mystical period *even though* no data relating
to it has survived. Shocking and strained as some of Spengler's
morphological relationships appear at first sight, they at least
suggest a new approach to the ancient and frequently jejune
practice of superficial historical analogy.[34]

How did Spengler come upon these discoveries? By seeing
with the eyes of Goethe. "The deep, and scarcely appreciated,
idea of Goethe, which he discovered in his 'living nature' and
always made the basis of his morphological researches," Spengler tells us, "we shall here apply—in its most precise sense—to
all the formations of man's history." Thus, when studying
natural phenomena, Goethe lived into (*erfühlen*) instead of
dissecting them. As a result, Spengler informs us, referring to
the great poet's strange, interesting, and debatable scientific
achievements, "To the spiritual eye of Goethe the idea of the
prime plant was clearly visible in the form of every individual
plant that happened to come up, or even that could possibly
come up. In his investigation of the 'os intermaxillare' his
starting-point was the *prime phenomenon of the vertebrate
type;* and in other fields it was geological stratification, or the
leaf as the prime form of the plant-organism, or the metamor-
phosis of the plants as the prime form of all organic becoming."[35]

[34] While historical analogy is widely used by historians, there seems
to be no theoretical treatment of it. See the absence of any entry for the
subject in the *Bibliography of Works in the Philosophy of History, 1945–
1957,* issued by *History and Theory* (The Hague, 1961), Beiheft I. I
have sought to amend this situation in part with my introductory article
in the volume, *The Railroad and the Space Program: An Exploration in
Historical Analogy,* Bruce Mazlish (ed.) (Cambridge, Mass., 1965). For
some of Spengler's comments on the subject of analogy, see *Decline,*
Vol. I, pp. 111–113; and Vol. II, p. 285.

[35] *Decline,* Vol. I, p. 105. For an understanding of Goethe's scientific

I cannot discuss Goethe's scientific work here—his real contribution to the study of plant life and of anatomy, or his odd battle against Newton's theory of color—but only underline the fact that Spengler derived from him the notion of an intuitively perceived culture as the prime, organic historical phenomenon. Goethe's great enemy, in the eyes of Spengler, was Darwin. Thus, in spite of the fact that Spengler, sometimes unknowingly, fills his pages with Darwinistic images of struggle and survival, he has nothing but scorn for the English naturalist. It was Darwin, Spengler charges, who had sacrificed Goethe's Nature-Theory to the nineteenth-century cult of the useful and the material. As a result, "the organic logic of the facts of life was supplanted by a mechanics in physiological garb. Heredity, adaptation, natural selection, are utility-causes of purely mechanical connotation." The consequence for history is that "the historical *dispensations* were superseded by a naturalistic *movement* 'in space' . . . the word 'process' eliminated Destiny and unveiled the secret of becoming, and lo! there was no longer a tragic but only an exact mathematical structure of world-happening. And thereupon the 'exact' historian enunciated the proposition that in the history-picture we had before us a sequence of 'states' of mechanical type which were amenable to rational analysis like a physical experiment or a chemical reaction, and that therefore causes, means, methods and objects were capable of being grouped together as a comprehensible system on the visible surface. It all becomes astonishingly simple."[36] In sum along with Darwin, an indictment against Condorcet, Comte, Marx, and their ilk is strongly implied.

Abandoning, too, the idea of linear progress held by both the positivist historians and, supposedly, by Darwin, Spengler

---

contribution, see Rudolf Magnus' rather laudatory *Goethe as a Scientist*, translated by Heinz Norden (New York, 1961); and Erich Heller's more succinct and interesting "Goethe and the Idea of Scientific Truth," in *The Disinherited Mind*.

[36] *Decline*, Vol. I, p. 155, and cf. p. 370.

effects what he calls his "Copernican discovery." Instead of the Ptolemaic system of history, whereby modern Western man saw all world-happenings as circling around him and his development, Spengler substitutes a new perspective: the Copernican, wherein eight mighty cultures—Indian, Babylonian, Chinese, Egyptian, Arabic, Mexican, as well as the Classical and Western—flourish independently and go through their fated cycles of birth and death as separate worlds of self-contained values. As such, each must develop its own possibilities of self-expression.

One result of Spengler's new vision is the destruction of the old periodization scheme. What he calls the "jejune" subdivision of history into "Ancient, " "Medieval," and "Modern" is entirely shattered (though, as we shall see, a suspicious similarity appears to exist between it and Spengler's substitution). In its place are merely the separate cultures, passing through their organic life cycles. Another result, already foreshadowed in Spengler's recommended method of intuition, is the elimination of the possibility of "history-in-itself." There are only various *perspectives* on history, enjoyed by each culture. Moreover, historical consciousness itself differs for each culture; thus, to jump ahead a bit, according to Spengler the Greeks were ahistorical in comparison to Western man who views history as an infinite development.[37]

A new perspective and a new periodization scheme (or absence of one), these are the concomitants of Spengler's organic logic of history. To them Spengler adds a suggestion as to the language in which history is written and, therefore, how it is to be read. His task, Spengler tells us, is comparable to Galileo's, who perceived that the book of the world-as-nature was written in mathematical language. Spengler's great discovery is that historical phenomena are not merely events or objects

---

[37] *Ibid.*, Vol. II, pp. 26–29. Interestingly enough, Collingwood, who thought little of Spengler's philosophy of history in general, shared this particular conviction with him. I suggest, however, that this points up the shared attitude to *methodology*, as distinct from *content*, which bound Collingwood more closely to Spengler than he cared to admit.

(for the understanding) but *symbols*—expressions of the spiritual. Thus, facts are not important in themselves (history-in-itself?) but only because they form the symbol language of history. Interpreting this language with marvelous ingenuity and acuteness, Spengler presents us with a dazzling analysis of the symbolic meaning attaching to such diverse phenomena as the colors and brushstrokes used by artists of different cultures and different time periods; the clothes worn by different people; the different sorts of mathematics, drama, and funeral customs; the different ways of fighting wars and arranging political matters; and so on and on.

Obviously, what Spengler is seeking is the "spirit" of a culture or a period. This, for him, is the substance of history, for he has already disposed of the search for the "causes" of happenings in the world-as-history. Naturally, each spirit will be *sui generis* for each culture, and will pervade all aspects of the culture. Because it pervades and animates all aspects, every fact and happening in the culture serves, in turn, as we have seen, as a symbol of that culture and spirit.

5

Basic to every culture-spirit is a people's conception of time and space. These are the great categories which impose their forms on every perception.[38] But Spengler's vision is not Kantian. Time and space are *not* the same for everyone, eternal verities which thereby allow for universal truths. They are specific and different ways of seeing, enjoyed by each culture, and differentiating it from every other. Opposed to universal mankind, a common humanity, Spengler poses culture-man, unique and cut off from men of another culture. Thus, for classical man, time and space are bounded and nonextended—for example, a Euclidean geometry of magnitudes and a drama

[38] Almost as important, however, for Spengler seems to be a people's feeling for death.

of the "blind Causal of the moment" were all he could perceive—whereas, for Western man, time and space are unlimited and infinite, and his mathematics typically a differential
calculus of functions and his drama "an *inexorable* logic of
becoming." In short, time and space in Spengler are relative to
a given culture.[39]

Indeed, it is this apparently overwhelming "relativism" of
Spengler which most impressed many of his original readers.[40]
Spengler made no bones about his relativism. Concerning philosophy, he announced that "there are no eternal truths. Every
philosophy is the expression of its own and only its own time."
Similarly, "There is no timeless and solely-true way of art, but
only a history of art." Ethics, of course, are in the same situation.

Now, bold as Spengler thought his declarations, they were
really only the commonplace dictums of the day. Certainly,
Nietzsche had sounded forth the relativity of philosophy—
merely the "confession of the philosopher," as he called it—
and of ethics in no uncertain terms. And Spengler's views on
art were the small change of reaction to Winckelmann and
his ideal of timeless art drawn from his Greek studies, a
reaction in effect ever since the early nineteenth century,
joined now by Spengler with borrowings, often unacknowledged, from the debates of the German art historians of
his time, men like Riegl, Semper, Worringer, and others.
What Spengler added to the existing relativism, however,
was a persistence in demonstrating this relativity in *all*
fields, including, significantly, modern science, and, further,
a treatment of this relativism in terms of *culture as a whole*.

Spengler realized, indeed, that the most fundamental challenge to his relativism came from the field of mathematics.
Surely, here was a field in which knowledge was cumulative,
carrying over from one culture to another, *regardless* of their

---

[39] *Decline*, Vol. I, p. 130. Put another way, "Each Culture must necessarily possess its own destiny-idea."
[40] See, for example, Fauconnet, *op. cit.*, p. 5.

different conceptions of time, space, and destiny? No, says Spengler, mathematics is a *part* of philosophy, and we have already seen that every philosophy is merely the expression of its own time. "*There is no mathematic but only mathematics,*" Spengler announces. "What we call 'the history of mathematics'—implying merely the progressive actualizing of a single invariable ideal—is in fact, below the deceptive surface of history, a complex of self-contained and independent developments, an ever-repeated process of bringing to birth new form-worlds and appropriating, transforming and sloughing alien form-worlds, a purely organic story of blossoming, ripening, wilting and dying within the set period."[41] Thus, the Western appropriation of classical geometry is merely an outward possession of a thing learnt, and not an inward development of the Western soul.

Similarly, Spengler undercuts the claim of natural science to cumulative objectivity by attaching science to religion. Thus, against the prevailing rationalist view of a conflict of science and religion, Spengler views the two as related attempts to do away with fear by setting up laws of causality. "Always," he informs us, "science has grown up on a religion and under all the spiritual prepossessions of that religion, and always it signifies nothing more or less than an abstract melioration of these doctrines, considered as false because less abstract." Thus, for example, the Renaissance notion of God approximates the idea of pure endless space. Religion and its companion, science, therefore, are only intellectual form-worlds which are true for the particular culture in which they take shape, flourish, and then die.[42]

---

[41] *Decline*, Vol. I, pp. 56, 60–61.

[42] For these various views, see *Decline*, Vol. I, pp. 381, 395; and Vol. II, 13, 271. The classic work on the conflict of science and religion is A. D. White, *A History of the Warfare of Science with Theology in Christendom* (1896). For a somewhat different point of view, however, stressing the connection instead of the conflict of science and religion, see Alfred North Whitehead, *Science and the Modern World* (1925), chap. I. For a sort of indirect support of Spengler's idea of science as a relative "intellectual form-world," see Thomas S. Kuhn, *The Structure of Scientific Revolutions* (Chicago, 1962).

What are we to say of Spengler's seemingly total relativism? The first thing to remark is that he supports his position by an informed and perceptive knowledge of such matters as mathematics—which he had concentrated on in school—art, literature, and music. Of all the philosophers of history with whom we have dealt, Spengler is probably the most gifted in these areas (though undoubtedly surpassed by Condorcet and Comte as a pure mathematician). Thus, his pursuit of relativism in these subjects, even if ultimately we judge it incorrect, is a *tour de force*. We gain constantly from his brilliant *aperçus*.

The second thing to note is that Spengler's work joins, on one side, to the investigations undertaken by ethnologists, anthropologists, and psychologists concerning the different conceptions of time and space (which, of course, underlie all mathematics) held by primitive, mythical-minded peoples. On the other side, it relates to the speculations and researches of the sociologists of knowledge. Without going into details, I suggest the validity and value of a comparison of Spengler with, say, Mircea Eliade on myth, or Karl Mannheim on the epistemological basis of knowledge.[43]

Finally, we must study the connection of Spengler's relativism with skepticism, and the significance of this connection for Spengler's own work in philosophy of history. The only possible philosophy, Spengler tells us, for modern Western man is that which corresponds to Classical Skepticism. In a rather tricky passage, Spengler defines the difference between the two skepticisms. "The Classical skepticism is ahistoric, it doubts by denying outright. But that of the West . . . is obliged to be historical through and through. Its solutions are got by treating everything as relative, as a historical phenomenon, and its procedure is psychological. Whereas the Skeptic philosophy arose within Hellenism as the negation of philos-

---

[43] See, for example, Mircea Eliade, *Cosmos and History* (New York, 1959); and Karl Mannheim, *Ideology and Utopia* (London, 1936). Spengler's own application of the "sociology of knowledge" approach may be seen in his *Decline,* Vol, I, pp. 334, 379–380, 396; and Vol. II, p. 209.

ophy—declaring philosophy to be purposeless—we, on the contrary, regard the *history of philosophy* as, in the last resort, philosophy's gravest theme. This *is* 'skepsis,' in the true sense."[44] Thus, Spengler's skepticism concerns *absolute* knowing, it does not deny *relative*, i.e., historical, knowledge. From a given perspective we can gain knowledge which is correct, relative to that perspective, by definition. Hence, all knowledge is *historical*—situated in time and space—i.e., it is becoming.

The problem we are left with, however, is to reconcile Spengler's historical knowledge, even though relative in the sense above, with his earlier view that cultures are, in essence, unknowable one to another. One or two quotations from the *Decline* will set up the problem. "Truths are truths only in relation to a particular mankind." Thus, Spengler admits, "my own philosophy is able to express and reflect only the Western (as distinct from the Classical, Indian, or other) soul, and that soul *only* in its present civilized phase by which its conception of the world, its practical range and its sphere of effect are specified." Or, talking of the world of the Bible, he remarks "how alien to us all the inner life of Jesus is," and concludes that "Such sensations are unapproachably remote from men who live in and with a dynamical world-picture."

How, then, does Western man come to feel—for surely Spengler has already disdained mere understanding (*Verstand*) —the soul-forms of other cultures? Ah, says Spengler, we must learn to *see* with different eyes, "not from this or that 'stand-point,' but in a high, time-free perspective embracing whole millenniums of historical world-forms." We must duplicate Copernicus' act in the world-as-nature with a similar act in the world-as-history. By so doing, we emancipate ourselves from "the evident present in the name of infinity." Only if we can put "our Western feeling" out of action shall we be able to penetrate, for example, "into the essence of the world-image that underlay the Classical attitude."

[44] *Decline*, Vol. I, p. 45.

Fortunately, before Spengler's eyes "there seems to emerge, as a vision, a hitherto unimagined mode of superlative historical research that is truly Western . . . a morphology of becoming for *all* humanity . . . a duty of penetrating the world-feeling not only of our proper soul but of all souls whatsoever that have contained grand possibilities and have expressed them in the field of actuality as grand Cultures." This research "pre-supposes the eye of an artist, and of an artist who can feel the whole sensible and apprehensible environment dissolve into a deep infinity of mysterious relationships." This artist, it would seem, by his vision is able to rise above the relative knowledge which Spengler previously claimed was all that was permitted to mortal man. Spengler hails this artist's coming with the glad cry that "Now, at last, it is possible to take the decisive step of sketching an image of history that is independent of the accident of standpoint, of the period in which this or that observer lives—independent too of the personality of the observer himself, who as an interested member of his own Culture is tempted, by its religious, intellectual, political and social tendencies, to order the material of history according to a perspective that is limited as to both space and time."[45]

Then, having transcended space and time, Spengler adds that it is the historian's business not to praise or blame the "material" of history, i.e., the symbols of a culture, but solely to consider them morphologically. Admittedly, the reader is shaken after this declaration about historical impartiality by Spengler's vehement "I prefer one Roman aqueduct to all Roman temples and statues" and numerous other such apparently "partial" statements, but Spengler's casual defense is simply that items such as the temples and statues were not "in harmony with the tendency of the age."

According to Spengler, the reason we know what is the tendency of the age is because we are the first culture to have escaped our own perspective—in fact, this is *our* spiritual tendency—and therefore are able to view from on high the

[45] *Ibid.*, p. 93. See, too, p. 159.

necessary course of every culture. Hence, intimately tied to Spengler's transcendence of his own "relative history" is his unwavering conviction that the history of every culture is predetermined. Its destiny is inevitable, and indeed it is the triumph of *our* culture that we alone "can foresee the way that destiny has chosen for it."

Now, by determinism and inevitability, Spengler emphatically does not mean that history is under the necessity of causal laws. Causality, as we have already seen, can be applied only to the world-as-nature. For Spengler, "Real history is heavy with fate but free of laws." As such, we can *divine* the future but not reckon or calculate it. This divinable fate, however, does not take away our freedom; it is, instead, our necessary freedom. Obedience to the "laws" (in Spengler's terms, the destiny) of history is what makes us free. "We have not the freedom to reach to this or to that," Spengler tells us on the last page of the *Decline*, "but the freedom to do the necessary or to do nothing. And a task that history necessarily has set *will* be accomplished with the individual or against him."[46]

It is from this insight into destiny that Spengler claims to be able to judge what is "necessary" and therefore in harmony with the tendency of the age. "Judge," of course, is the wrong word, for Spengler would insist that he is merely describing and classifying morphological phenomena. Judgment, however, is what we ourselves shall have to pass on Spengler's views—I have already labeled his basic view of history, "astrological"—but for the moment we must reserve such judg-

---

[46] *Ibid.*, Vol. I, p. 118; and Vol. II, p. 507. Spengler does allow, in a rather strange way, for what he calls "accidents," or "incidents," or "Chance" in history. Thus, he remarks that "Chance decreed that the heavy attacks of the Huns should break themselves in vain upon the Chinese 'Limes'" with the result that the Huns turned westward (Vol. II, p. 41; see also Vol. I, p. 107, fn. 1; and Vol. II, pp. 44, 109 for other examples). These accidents, however, Spengler dismisses as mere surface ripples in a flowing tide. His comments that "it should have been Antony who won" (Vol. II, p. 191), or that Russia's "destiny should have been to live without a history for some generations," instead of being pulled by Peter the Great into a Western orbit (Vol. II, p. 193), are a little more difficult to make congruous with his position on inevitable destiny.

ment and pass it only when we have studied his total system. Thus, we turn now from Spengler's metaphysics, from his critical philosophy of history, to his speculations on the nature and development of actual, historical cultures. It is a shift in degree, for the critical and speculative in Spengler constantly overlap.

6

Spengler's effort to write cultural history is based on his initial concept of culture. Unfortunately, his conception of culture is not always marked by either consistency or clarity; and, therefore, we are forced to make more systematic than it actually is his avowedly intuitive and diffuse perception of his "prime phenomenon." Culture, he tells us, is an organism. As such, it goes through a fated cycle of birth, youth, age, and death; occasionally Spengler uses the alternate images of spring, summer, fall, and winter. While every culture, like every human being, has roughly the same duration—on the basis of his historical studies, Spengler fixes the figure at about 1000 years—it moves in a particular style and rhythm: Spengler talks of the *andante* of the classical and the *allegro con brio* of the Faustian spirit.[47]

Pushing "primitive Cultures" aside, as "neither an organism nor a sum of organisms," Spengler claims the existence of the eight Cultures mentioned earlier: Indian, Babylonian, Chinese, Egyptian, Arabic, and Mexican, in addition to Classical and Western.[48] In practice, Spengler deals mainly with the Classical, the Western, and the Arabian (although this is a poor

[47] *Decline*, Vol. I, p. 109. Does one hear an echo of Spengler in Hitler's claim to have founded a 1000-year Reich? Or is this simply the usual millennial dream in new guise?

[48] *Ibid.*, Vol. I, p. 18. Anthropologists might be expected to look askance at Spengler's dismissal of primitive "cultures." For a suprisingly favorable treatment of Spengler, however, see A. L. Kroeber and Clyde Kluckhohn, *Culture: A Critical Review of Concepts and Definitions* (New York, 1963), pp. 48-49.

third), and makes a number of references where convenient to all the others except the Mexican. At one point, however, he also introduces a confusing discussion of Mycenaean and Minoan "Cultures," dallies with them as "Inter-Cultures," and then a few pages later, further compounds our difficulties by dismissing the Minoan Culture as merely belonging to "the Egyptian provinces," acknowledging thereby that it is not an independent Culture.[49]

Spengler has told us that the defining characteristic of a Culture is that it embodies and actualizes "a single, singularly-constituted soul." Thus, he further complicates our problem when, in Volume II of the *Decline*, he suddenly informs us that "A single soul is the mark of every genuine order or class" (examples of classes are the nobility, the peasantry, the city masses, etc.) and that "Culture and class are interchangeable expressions." Since Spengler believes in "class conflict," as we have seen, it would appear that each sub-soul fights to make its version of the Cultural soul supreme. Or is the latter the dialectic product of the fight? Spengler does not clarify the matter for us.[50] Indeed, it would seem that here Spengler's politics have overshadowed his philosophy of history.

However defined, the next question is: How do these souls or cultures arise? At this point, Spengler becomes lyrical and informs us that "A Culture is born in the moment when a great soul awakens out of the proto-spirituality (*dem urseelenhaften Zustande*) of ever-childish humanity, and detaches itself, a form from the formless, a bounded and mortal thing from the boundless and enduring. It blooms on the soil of an exactly-definable landscape, to which plant-wise it remains bound. It dies when this soul has actualized the full sum of its possibilities in the shape of peoples, languages, dogmas, arts, states, sciences, and reverts into the proto-soul." One factor affecting the Culture itself is the landscape; Cultures are bound

[49] *Decline*, Vol. II, pp. 87, 99. Cf. p. 88.
[50] *Ibid.*, Vol. II, pp. 18, 332. For an explanation seemingly more tolerant of Spengler's inconsistency, cf. Hughes, *Oswald Spengler*, p. 107.

to a given soil, and "there is a mother-landscape behind all expression-forms."[51] It is not people, in Spengler's formulation, who create Cultures, but Cultures which create and shape people. As one example, Spengler claims that the Jews have been forged into a race by their Destiny.[52]

This brings us to Spengler's conception of the carriers of Culture: people and race. Actually, for Spengler the two are identical (differing only from population), for by "race" he does not mean a Darwinian unity of physical origin (and it is this which, of course, the Nazis embraced) but a group of people united in their acceptance of a particular Destiny. Thus, race involves a "cosmic and directional," not a material unity. Attacking the ideal of blood-purity and "the silly catch-words 'Aryan' and 'Semite' that have been borrowed from philology," Spengler also refused to define his race by language. These entities are quite distinct: "To Race belong the deepest meanings of the words 'time' and 'yearnings'; to language those of the words 'space' and 'fear.' " Interesting, and confused, as is Spengler's discussion of the nature of language, it suffices for our purposes to see that his definition of a race is not based on a common tongue. Race, for Spengler, is really a spiritual commitment by a people. A race, or people, "can change speech, name, race [in the sense of physical qualities], and land, but so long as their soul lasts, they can gather to themselves and transform human material of any and every provenance."[53]

Equipped with this insight, Spengler can now approach the classification of cultures in a new way. Thus, he declares that the erroneous "scholars' notions of people, language, and race" have been "the determining reason why the Arabian Culture has never yet been recognized as an organism." Misled by their notions, the scholars have reasoned that Persian is an Aryan

[51] *Decline*, Vol. I, p. 106; and Vol. II, p. 278. Cf. what I have said earlier about Spengler's "sociology of knowledge" approach.
[52] See *Decline*, Vol. II, pp. 127, 165.
[53] *Ibid.*, Vol. II, pp. 114, 165, 318.

language, that hence the "Persians" are an "Indogermanic people," and that therefore Persian history and religion are the
affair of "Iranian" philology. Brushing all this nonsense aside,
Spengler firmly places the so-called Persians and their history
under the Arabic Culture.

Impressed as we may be by Spengler's daring and original
development of his concept of Culture, however, we are still
without a satisfactory solution to the problem of how cultures
originate. Indeed, it is exactly this question as to the origin of
cultures that Toynbee saw Spengler as leaving unanswered,
and therefore requiring a new study of history. We can only
guess at what Spengler had in mind, from his acknowledged
discipleship to both Leibnitz and Goethe. Leibnitz's self-devel-
oping, completely isolated monads, and Goethe's "*Urphäno-
men*," both are there, apparently from nowhere. So with
Spengler's prime phenomenon. In the tenth century, Spengler
announces, "The Faustian soul suddenly awoke and manifested
itself in innumerable shapes." Its coming is explanation
enough; to explain how it originated would be to fall into the
mire of causal, world-as-nature explanation.

Spengler's Cultures not only arise out of nowhere; they
flourish, or so it seems, in independence and even isolation
from one another. Thus, people of one Culture cannot alter
their world-feeling, and when they borrow elements from another Culture it is only an outward item and never the inward
feeling attached to it which they borrow. Further, as we have
seen, except for Spengler-like individuals of the Western Culture, inward knowledge of other Cultures is impossible.

Spengler does qualify seriously, however, though without
acknowledging it, his view of cultures as isolated plants (thus,
implicitly, allowing his "organic" metaphor to break down).
First, he introduces his concept of "historical pseudomor-
phosis," which he defines as "those cases in which an older
alien Culture lies so massively over the land that a young Culture, born in this land, cannot get its breath and fails not only
to achieve pure and specific expression-forms, but even to de-

velop fully its own self-consciousness." Such is the case with
the Arabian Culture. And so, too, with a new Culture, the
Russian, which Spengler suddenly introduces.[54] Worse, at
one point, Spengler even broadens his historical pseudomor-
phoses to include, to some degree, almost all his Cultures.
"True," he admits, "all Cultures (the Egyptian, the Mexican,
and the Chinese excepted) have grown up under the tutelage
of some older Culture. Each of the form-worlds shows certain
alien traits." Further, in a number of places he slips into admitting such a development as "an ever-increasing admixture of
Eastern elements" (in the Classical Roman world) or, in reference to Magian monotheism, into saying that "A new soul had
come up, and it lived the old forms in a new mode," or even
into confessing that "It is not possible to draw a strict frontier
between the late Minoan and the young Mycenaean art."

Yet, on sum, Spengler's basic commitment to "organic"
metaphor forces him to bypass a topic such as cultural diffu-
sion, and to treat his Cultures as individual, discreet flowers in
a historical field. He is interested in the "soul" of a closed
Culture, not in the naturalistic, causality-tainted process of
cultural change. As with the question of a Culture's origin, so
with the question of how a Culture develops: the answer is the
pronouncement of the mystic word, "Destiny."

7

The actual Cultures on which Spengler concentrates, as we
have noted, are three: the Classical, Arabic, and Western. He
identifies their respective souls as Apollonian, Magian, and
Faustian.[55] The time periods occupied by these Cultures,

[54] *Ibid.*, Vol. II, pp. 189, 192. For Spengler on Russian culture, see Vol.
II, pp. 192–194 and *passim*.

[55] Nietzsche, in his *Birth of Tragedy*, divided the Greek soul into
Apollonian and Dionysian, with the latter bearing a good deal of
resemblance to what Spengler identifies as "Faustian" in the Western
soul. Of course, even before Nietzsche, there is Goethe's *Faust*.

though there is some overlap and Spengler is not very consistent, are roughly from about 1100 B.C. to the time of Aurelian in the third century A.D.; from either 1 A.D. or the time of Augustus to either 1000 or 1250 A.D.; and from about the tenth century to the present.[56]

Very briefly, the Classical soul, the Apollonian, "chose the sensuously-present individual body as the ideal type of the extended." More concretely, the Apollonian ideal is the self-sufficient and finished nude statue. In mathematics, the ideal is Euclidean geometry, concerned as it is with timeless magnitudes. So too, Classical man lacked all idea of an inner development and therefore of all history, inward and outward. His tragic dramas are characterized by the illogical, blind casual of the moment—*Oedipus Rex*. He willed to have no history, no duration, neither past nor future; and therefore he destroyed his body at death by burning, did without the clock, built his cities out of perishable timber, and took no thought concerning his political or economic welfare of the morrow. His deepest wish was to live in a timeless, closed space.[57]

Arabic Culture is complicated by its "Pseudomorphic" quality, and perhaps for this reason is the vaguest of Spengler's main Cultures. In any case, the Magian soul is distinguished by its feeling for cavernous space—think of the early Christian caves and of the Mohammedan mosques—and by its affinity for algebra, astrology, alchemy, mosaics, and arabesques. It shows itself in the sacraments and scriptures of the Persian, Jewish, Christian, "post-Classical," and Manichaean religions alike. Whereas Classical man concentrates on the pure Present, Magian man sees history as consisting of a beginning and an end to the world that is also the beginning and the end of man— consider the Judaic and Christian view of time. In this

[56] The charts at the back of Volume I of the American edition of the *Decline* place Spengler's inspirations in much too tight a straightjacket and thereby crush his spirit. They should be used merely as a guide to what he had in mind.
[57] See especially *Decline*, Vol. I, pp. 129ff., 183ff.

"Arabic" vision, according to Spengler, man is viewed as without will, and Spengler cites both the Arab word, Islam, meaning submission, and the work of St. Augustine.[58]

The prime symbol of Faustian man is pure and limitless space, and his conception of time is of a destiny which stretches out into infinity. His typical mathematics is the differential calculus. Tragic drama for the Western soul arises as the outcome of an entire, developing life—the inexorable logic of becoming—as exemplified in Shakespeare's *Lear* or in Goethe's *Wilhelm Meister*, a typical *Bildungsroman*. The autobiographical tendency of modern man is unique. Clocks and museums exist to preserve the past, and Faustian man's view of history is of an infinite time stretching away wherein he can exercise his *will*. Whereas Classical history is merely one of anecdotes and incidents, Western history, Spengler claims, is one of great connections and developments.

Clearly, even in these few examples of Spengler's articulation of his three major Cultures, we can discern a few guiding principles. Typically, Spengler first identifies what he considers to be the attitudes of the Culture to time and space. He then demonstrates these attitudes at work as they inform and pervade such diverse areas of the Culture as its mathematics, drama, history, funeral customs, architecture, politics, economics, and so forth. Indeed, by the time he has finished, Spengler has dealt with the totality of the Culture, applying to all its aspects the divining rods of space and time. Concurrently, he has been steadily comparing each of his Cultures with the others. While we shall reserve critical judgment a bit longer, here we can at least express admiration for the resourcefulness and the unbounded "Faustian" imagination with which Spengler has pursued his effort in comparative cultures.

[58] For the Arabic Culture, see especially *Decline*, Vol. II, chaps. VII, VIII, IX.

8

However Cultures may differ as to their feelings for time and space, they are all alike in that they go through the same phases, eventuating in civilization. For Spengler, civilization is the inevitable conclusion, the destiny of every Culture. It is the phase of the Culture in which the thing-become succeeds the thing-becoming, death follows life, and the petrifying world-city replaces mother-earth. In short, it is the last phase of a culture-form which is dying.[59]

The general characteristics of a civilization, according to Spengler, are briefly the following. Intellectually, it is marked by a fact philosophy as against metaphysical speculation and by a completely eclectic art and literature. Economically, it is dominated by money, and politically, by imperialism—that is, by energy directed outward under the control of a Caesar. The basic core of civilization, however, is the world-city— what Spengler calls "megalopolis"—and its attendant provinces. Within this world-city there is a new sort of nomad, a parasitical city dweller, rootless, traditionless, without a past. The city population is a mass, not a people or race. It is futureless. At the end, there is depopulation, the city crumbles, and the only thing left is the fellah type in the provinces. As it passes into a nonhistorical state, the decaying civilization turns to what Spengler calls a "second religiousness."[60]

While our present civilization is similar in its major features to the description just given, Spengler devotes a good many pages to indicating some of its specific lineaments. He sees modern civilization as really *English* in its nature, with the English economic imperialism conquering French culture in

[59] For earlier stages of the debate on culture versus civilization, see my remarks in the chapter on Kant, p. 109. Of general interest on this subject is Raymond Williams, *Culture and Society, 1780–1950* (New York, 1960).

[60] *Decline,* Vol. I, p. 424; and Vol. II, p. 310.

the Napoleonic Wars.[61] The new Caesars, Spengler's modern "heroes," are men like Cecil Rhodes and G. B. Shaw's Undershaft (the munitions manufacturer of *Major Barbara*)—"factmen of the grand style"—who, like Caesar himself, amass money only so that they can convert it into power. These figures are the true representatives of the Will-to-Power and of the Faustian ethic.

For Spengler, we are in a period of Alexandrian eclecticism.[62] Nothing original lies before us. Modern art is decadent, a "tedious game with dead forms." Even our science and mathematics are exhausted.[63] All our thinkers are, in any case, mere causality-men instead of destiny-men. Far better now, Spengler advises us, to build a bridge than to write a poem or paint a picture. And better still, of course, like Rhodes, to build an empire.

Clearly, it is our own time which most interests Spengler, and it seems obvious that his general view of civilization is highly colored by his specific judgment of the contemporary period. His politics begin to overshadow his philosophy of history. As he remarks, "Looked at in this way, the 'Decline of the West' comprises nothing less than the problem of Civilization." Our situation, since the nineteenth century, he tells us, is comparable to the epoch of Hellenism in the Classical Culture. Napoleonic imperialism is similar to that of Alexander's, and the World War is morphologically like the Punic Wars, when Rome fought Carthage under Hannibal. We, like the classical world, are in "The Period of the Contending States." Thus, instead of regarding the present era as a time of progress, Spengler views it as the mere ripening of Western culture to

[61] *Ibid.*, Vol. I, p. 150. Eduard Meyer, *Spenglers Untergang des Abendlandes* (Berlin, 1925), p. 5, has the genial notion that Spengler's "civilization" could as well be labeled "Americanisation."

[62] Compare some of Nietzsche's remarks (in various of his works) on our present Alexandrian period, or T. S. Eliot, in *The Waste Land*.

[63] It would be interesting to know whether Spengler would hold to this view at the present, in the light of recent developments in mathematics.

its limit, an inevitable destiny. This "Decline of the West,' Spengler tells us, is therefore one which we must stoically accept. Our Culture is finished.

9

Anyone who attempts a summary of Spengler's philosophy of history must constantly avoid two extremes. On the one hand, he must not, as so many of Spengler's early readers did, allow himself to be swept away by the poetic phrases and the apparently immense erudition to be found in the *Decline.* Closer reading shows Spengler's metaphysics, for example, to be largely a farrago of pretentious and contradictory nonsense and the erudition often spurious. On the other hand, the critic must not allow himself to be so annoyed by the metaphysics, the political motives, and the specific errors in data as to miss the real contributions to his subject made by Spengler.

Incongruous as it may appear at first glance, Spengler's task was the same as Voltaire's: to write cultural history. The method of execution and the leading ideas were, of course, vastly different, as was the specific interpretation given to the "spirit" which infused the various and varying cultures treated. Nevertheless, by stressing "cultures" as the unit of study, Spengler drew historians back to the path cleared by the *Essai sur les Moeurs et l'Esprit des Nations.* Spengler's Cultures, however, as we have seen, soar far above the actual culture of nations, for they have been hypostatized into self-sufficient entities. This is so, surely, because in part Spengler sought to rise above the narrow Western view, with its "nationalistic" history, and, at the same time, to go beyond what he considered the Enlightenment's naive structuring of history as a linear progress toward Western man.

Now, I have already hinted that Spengler's cultural history was strongly colored by his own national political desires. In fact, in the preface to the first edition of the *Decline* he places

his book "beside the military achievements of Germany," and
in the preface to the revised edition openly and proudly declares his philosophy of history "*a German philosophy*."[64]
Thus, it is mainly in theory, and only partly and spasmodically
in practice, that his book transcends the more limited perspectives of national history.[65]

With this qualification in mind, we must consider next the
contribution involved in Spengler's search for the "spirit" of
his Cultures. The search itself is something of a commonplace
(though as such it can be dangerous). Thus, we look for a
"spirit" of the Enlightenment period, or, in other forms, a
"climate of opinion," or a "Protestant Ethic." Closely related
is the study of national character.[66] In all this work, Spengler's
book holds a strange place: while it resolutely places "spirit"
above "materialism"—economic or otherwise—spirit is conceived as a fixed, biological matter rather than as a free, human
force. This is a most important point, to which we shall return
a bit later on.

In his conception of the spirit of a Culture, Spengler assigns
a central place to categories of time and space. Here, I believe,
is one of Spengler's most illuminating contributions. He is
aware that different peoples seem literally to *see* differently,

[64] It is worth noting that Spengler's phrase about placing his book
beside the German military achievements is omitted without explanation
from the English translation.

[65] In my view, one of the more successful parts of Spengler's "transcendence" is his concept of Magian Culture, not because in itself it is
wholly convincing, but because it frees us from the simple view of
Christianity as being, on one hand, a product largely of "Classical" times,
and, on the other hand, spiritually the same in the late Middle Ages as in
the third or fourth century. Further, by means of the Magian concept,
Spengler seeks to set up a non-Western-oriented treatment of the
Mediterranean-Middle East world. Other critics, however, even those
favorable to Spengler, like Eduard Meyer, consider it a vague and useless
construction.

[66] On the concept of national character, see such examples as David
Potter, *People of Plenty*, (Chicago, 1954); and Margaret Mead, *And
Keep Your Powder Dry* (New York, 1942). These works illustrate some
of the difficulties and rewards of working in this field. The "Protestant
Ethic" refers, of course, to Max Weber's pioneering effort in this
general area.

that perception is not a simple matter of the blank mind merely copying sensations or even of imposing fixed temporal and spacial forms on sensations.[67] With enormous insight—his real claim to being a seer—Spengler has then applied this awareness to deciphering the symbols of Classical, or Magian, or Western drama, architecture, music, and so forth, in terms of their *particular* time-space structure. While often one-sided in his interpretation, Spengler has cast a blazing light on that side of the Cultures which he sought to illuminate. It is only very recently that others have followed Spengler in this exciting approach, examining the changing nature of time in literature or in life.[68] Whoever works in this field must always be indebted to Spengler.

Praiseworthy as are Spengler's efforts in this matter, however, they bring in their train some serious defects. Once he has fixed on the time-space spirit of a Culture, Spengler sees only it and sees it everywhere. For example, convinced that Classical man is basically ahistorical, and wishes to live in a pure Present, Spengler can insist that Greek man built out of perishable materials in order that his cities might be without duration. So, too, according to Spengler, Classical man burned his dead, for he envisioned no duration beyond the present, bodily moment. Is it possible, one asks, that Spengler could have overlooked the marble Parthenon, which looms so large in our own stereotype of the Greek city, and the numerous tombs lining the Appian Way outside of Rome?

It is Collingwood who, himself prone to so many of Spengler's faults, puts his finger on the difficulty. Spengler's fallacy, Collingwood tells us, "lies in the attempt to characterize a culture by means of a single idea or tendency or feature, to deduce everything from this one central idea without recognizing that a single idea, asserted in this way, calls up its own

---

[67] An interesting book in this connection is E. H. Gombrich, *Art and Illusion* (New York, 1960), even though Gombrich is critical of Spengler's ideas.

[68] See, for example, Hans Meyerhoff, *Time in Literature* (Berkeley, 1955); and Georges Poulet, *Studies in Human Time* (New York, 1959).

opposite in order to have something to assert itself against, and henceforth proceeds, not by merely repeating itself, but by playing a game of statement and counter-statement with this opposite."[69] It is this fallacy, for example, which blinds Spengler to Nietzsche's brilliant insight into the tension between the Apollonian and Dionysian elements of the Greek culture.[70] The result is that, instead of the rich diversity and "Heraclitean" conflict of Classical life, Spengler gives us only a frozen image. Spengler's gaze, piercing as it is, is that of Medusa.

By emphasizing only one side of a subject, Spengler constantly indulged in the technique of the half-truth; and one is ominously reminded of Adolf Hitler and *Mein Kampf*. For example, one might concede that modern civilization harbors all the traits or tendencies Spengler ascribes to it. Must one thereby agree with Spengler's completely one-sided and therefore distorted presentation? Basically, his trouble is that he simply *asserts;* he never really argues or seeks to test his statements, which would involve attention to the "other side" of his truth. For instance, contrasting what he calls the Magian Consensus, which he characterizes as nonterritorial and geographically unlimited, with the Faustian ideas of fatherland, mother-tongue, ruling house, etc., Spengler concludes that Magian man becomes enthused at the word "international," whether it be coupled with socialism, pacifism, or capitalism, because in that word "is the essence of his landless and boundless Consensus."[71] Well and good! But what does one do about the cosmopolitan leanings of the enlightened *philosophes?* Was the somewhat antisemitic and anti-Christian Voltaire *not* a Faustian? Are all international-minded socialists, pacifists,

[69] *Antiquity*, Vol. I, p. 316. This article by Collingwood comprises one of the best critiques of Spengler. (There is a second article, "Cycles and Progress," *Antiquity* [December, 1927], which is nowhere near as good as this first.) What Collingwood shares with Spengler, however, is not only a view of the Greeks as ahistorical, but a belief in the intuitive method connected with a denial of lawlike, causal analysis in history.

[70] Cf. E. R. Dodds, *The Greeks and the Irrational* (Berkeley, 1951).

[71] *Decline*, Vol. II, p. 320.

and capitalists Magian and not Faustian-souled? Who, then, is left as a true Faustian? To raise these questions is to see immediately how flimsy is the tissue of Spengler's assertion.

The half-truth and the unsupported assertion are not Spengler's only faults. One can also list innumerable simple errors of fact, and an equally long list of arguable interpretations.[72] Even if we agree with Meyer and other critics favorable to Spengler, and I think their point well taken, that specific errors of data do not per se invalidate Spengler's general position, a problem still remains.[73] For if the data are used, not merely to illustrate his theses, but as the raw material from which he extracts and upon which he extrapolates his theses, then errors are grave indeed. And this, alas, is frequently the case. Thus, Spengler's idealization of the peasantry is based on their supposed closeness to the "abundant proliferation of primitive peoples," where wives are picked only for their childbearing and not their economic qualities.[74] On the other hand, civilized man is condemned for his sterile, childless marriages, i.e., depopulation. How inconvenient for Spengler (and here I am not attacking the valuation he places on a high birth rate) that anthropological studies show tribe after tribe indulging in marriage mainly as an economical arrangement, as well as having very low birth rates, while the high birth rate in "civilizations" like Japan and even Western Europe, the latter with its "romantic" marriages, has become a matter of serious concern.

If we turn once again from specific details to Spengler's general theory, we face additional doubts. Are cultures really organisms, whose life cycles are fixed like the life of some insect or fish, and to which we can legitimately attribute a

[72] How, for example, can Spengler say of Dostoevski, comparing him with Tolstoy, that the former "does not even know" what the Western form of a *problem* is (Vol. II, p. 195), when the whole of *Notes From the Underground* is devoted to *the* Western problem as Dostoevski understood it?

[73] Similarly, we could dismiss Spengler's numerous erroneous predictions as mere specific misreadings.

[74] *Decline*, Vol. II, p. 104.

spirit? Is this, to borrow a word from Spengler, even a helpful analogy? We have already noted earlier that Spengler's biological vision makes it impossible for him to explain cultural change other than as a fated, predictable development. Now, we must add another fundamental criticism of Spengler's cultural concept: while, as an abstraction, we can talk of the "spirit" of a culture, that "spirit" is only the reflection or abstraction of the psychological processes of real people, living or dead. Spengler's formulation, however, denies the idea of the historical process as a mental process, where the past is conserved in the present.[75] Moreover, it denies thereby that man can affect his future—this reflects Spengler's scorn for the thinker in general—and it also removes from man any burden of "guilt" or responsibility for his actions. Spengler preaches, instead, a very Prussian notion of obedience and acceptance.

By viewing cultures as fixed and limited organisms, Spengler may facilitate, of course, the study of comparative cultures. And his attention to homologous rather than to merely analogous relations is refreshing and suggestive. The price Spengler pays, however, is twofold: he completely ignores *historical* growth, and he neglects any aid which might be forthcoming from historical sociology. Thus, it is interesting to note that Spengler's main followers have been anthropologists rather than historians or sociologists. For example, Ruth Benedict has warmly and openly modeled her book, *Patterns of Culture*, on Spengler's insights. Her Zuñis, Kwakiutls, and Dobus are, to some extent, small, isolated, self-sufficient cultures, which can be looked at *as if* they were infused with one dominant spirit.[76] Historical change need not enter Benedict's picture, and, in fact, she neglects Spengler's pattern of organic change and, of course, his "decline" of culture into civilization.

[75] This is also Collingwood's criticism, in *The Idea of History*, pp. 181–182.

[76] It must be admitted, however, that even Benedict's application of Spengler's scheme to the limited terrain of these small cultures has been criticized as yielding a false unity.

It is this latter element, I suggest, which gives the hint as to Spengler's main deficiency in history. While he talks at great length about the general characteristics of "civilization," it is clear that he does not understand either modern civilization or modern history. Whatever insights he may have into Classical and Magian "culture and civilization," he has few into the real character of his own time. His comprehension of phenomena such as capitalism and industrialism (compare Marx's insights, for example), representational democracy, the socialist movement, and the rise of modern science and technology is simply flat. Concerned as he is about psychology and "spirit," Spengler never once mentions his contemporary, Sigmund Freud, nor reckons with his theories of mental life. Max Weber and Émile Durkheim might as well never have written on sociology, nor E. B. Tylor and Sir James Fraser on cultural anthropology. Is it unfair to expect Spengler to have read these men, or at least to be familiar with their ideas, thereby taking them into account?

It is Spengler's blindness to the important ideas and movements of his own time which marks the bankruptcy of his intuitive method. (It also suggests the inherent weaknesses of the entire nineteenth-century movement of historicism.) Priding himself on *Anschauung*, on the artist's vision, it is clear that Spengler did not *see* his own time. Extolling empathy for and sympathetic insight into the art forms of other "cultures," he had none for his own. It is from this myopia that the really fatal drawback to his proposed morphology of world-historical cultures emerges. He could not even envision the possibility of his vision being incorrect. Confusing the undoubted origin of all creative thought in some moment of intuition and insight with verification by that same intuitive insight, Spengler removed all possibility of the critical evaluation of his own insights. What is left, then, is poetry; and magnificent and wonderful as poetry can be, it is not history. Worse, when the poetry is absent or not dominant in Spengler's philosophy of history, all that remains is a rather shoddy and superficial political "inspiration."

X

Toynbee

Falling towers
Jerusalem Athens Alexandria
Vienna London
*Unreal**

T. S. ELIOT,
The Waste Land

1

IN THE summer of 1920, when Arnold Toynbee was already
mulling over his first attempt at *A Study of History*, Spengler's *Decline* was placed in his hands by chance in the person
of Professor Lewis Namier.[1] "As I read those pages," Toynbee tells us, "I wondered at first whether my whole inquiry
had been disposed of by Spengler before even the questions,
not to speak of the answers, had fully taken shape in my own
mind." Closer examination, however, revealed two important
differences between Toynbee and his German counterpart:
Toynbee was interested in the origins or geneses of civilizations, and he wished to approach this problem by the method
of English empiricism rather than by means of German a

---

* T. S. Eliot, "The Waste Land," *Collected Poems 1909–1962* (Har-
court, Brace & World).

[1] It is interesting to note that Namier, who guided Toynbee to the
larger view, devoted most of his energies to work on restricted topics
concerning institutions. See, for example, his *The Structure of Politics at
the Accession of George III.*

priori.[2] These, then, are Toynbee's own two claims to original fame.

The chance influence on Toynbee exercised by Namier manifested itself even before the Spengler volume. Thus, Toynbee recalls that in the Bosnian crisis of 1908–1909, Namier, then a fellow undergraduate at Balliol, and back from spending a vacation at his family home in Austria, brought with him an awareness of the interconnection of Central European events with seemingly isolated England. Such an awareness was unique in the peaceful, parochial atmosphere of the prewar days. The lesson Toynbee derived was that "The smallest intelligible fields of historical study were whole societies and not arbitrarily isolated fragments of them like the nation-states of the modern West or the city-states of the Graeco-Roman world."[3]

World War I itself, which caught Toynbee lecturing on Thucydides, a historian of the Graeco-Roman world, brought another sudden illumination. In Toynbee's words, "the experience that we were having in our world now had been experienced by Thucydides in his world already. . . . I, in my turn, had run into that historical crisis that had inspired him to write his work. Thucydides . . . had been over this ground before." Apparently convinced that 2000 years had brought nothing new to human life, and incidentally confirming Thucydides' view that his history was an "everlasting possession," Toynbee summed it up by saying, "He and his generation had been ahead of me and mine in the state of historical experience that we had respectively reached; in fact, his present had been my future." From this fact, Toynbee drew the conclusion that "Whatever chronology might say, Thucydides' world and my world had now proved to be philosophically contemporary." Moreover, Toynbee asked rhetorically, "if this were the true relation between the Graeco-Roman and the Western civilizations, might not the relation between all the civilizations

[2] Arnold Toynbee, *Civilization on Trial* (London, 1946), pp. 9–10.
[3] *Ibid.*, p. 9.

known to us turn out to be the same?"[4]

By the end of the 1914–1918 cataclysm, Toynbee was ready to start answering his question. The sketch which he made in 1920, grew by 1954 into a majestic 10-volume work which has achieved renown and sales comparable to that of Spengler's *Decline*.[5] In the course of two million words or so Toynbee pursued his search for the origins of civilization (which he had decided was the only intelligible unit of study), employing the empirical method, and guided by the conviction of the contemporaneousness and therefore comparability of all his civilizations. The result is, as all his critics agree, a mammoth edifice of history. It is also, in my own view, the pyramidal detritus of a profoundly outdated and diffused mind. (Of course, it must also be added that Toynbee appears to be a man of large and generous soul.) Toynbee is, par excellence, the Alexandrian historian of the very Alexandrian-like period of our modern world which he condemns so heartily.

2

Toynbee became a historian, as he placidly informs us, "because my mother was one before me."[6] The history which primarily engaged his attention was ancient history, and it was the classical world which served as his model. Indeed, as Toynbee tells us, his original intention in the *Study of History*

---

[4] *Ibid.*, pp. 7–8.

[5] The first three volumes of *A Study of History* appeared in 1933, the next three in 1939, and the remaining four in 1954. In 1946, D. C. Somervell made an abridgement of volumes I–VI, approved by the author; references to this useful summary of Toynbee's work will be cited as *Abridgement*. An abridgement of volumes VII–X has also been made, in 1957. With volume XII, subtitled "Reconsiderations," appearing in 1961, Toynbee has finally finished his masterpiece.

[6] This incredibly superficial "explanation" of his own origins as an historian, while touching, can hardly inspire confidence in Toynbee's forthcoming attempts to explain the origins of civilizations. One wonders, for example, why he followed his mother and not his father, whom he seems never to mention.

was merely to write a comparative history of the declines of Graeco-Roman and modern Western civilizations. Although he moved quickly from this "binocular view of history" to a vision which embraced all known civilizations, the original inspiration remained central.[7]

In terms of training and convictions, at least, Toynbee's grounding in ancient history should have been secure. At home, the classics along with the Bible were his constant companions. We are told that at his public school, Winchester, where Greek and Latin were the staples of education, he learned to express himself in Greek elegiac verse. On to Balliol College, Oxford, with a classical scholarship, Toynbee took his degree in this field, and then a Fellowship. After a nine-month tour in Greece, he returned to teach at the College. Then he married the daughter of Gilbert Murray, an outstanding classicist and a direct advisor on his *A Study of History*.

It is thus with great surprise that one sees Toynbee taken to task by other classicists for serious and fundamental omissions of facts and distorted interpretations. The evidence against him appears quite convincing, even to the amateur in the field. The explanation seems to be that Toynbee has submitted his admittedly enormous erudition to the narrow needs of his system, a strange outcome to his supposedly empirical method.[8]

In any case, a number of Toynbee's leading ideas are obviously derived from his love affair with ancient history. First in importance is his use of the Graeco-Roman experience as the model for the history of all other civilizations. Finding such marks as a time of troubles, a Universal State, and a Universal Church in the Hellenic world, Toynbee goes looking and finds

---

[7] *A Study of History*, Vol. X, p. 97.

[8] See W. Den Boer, "Toynbee and Classical History: Historiography and Myth," in *Toynbee and History, Critical Essays and Reviews*, M. F. Ashley Montagu (ed.) (Boston, 1956), pp. 222–223; also, David M. Robinson, "The Historical Validity of Toynbee's Approach to the Graeco-Roman World," in *The Intent of Toynbee's History*, Edward T. Gargan (ed.) (Chicago, 1961).

them too in such civilizations as the Syriac, Indic, and Sinic to name but a few. While most scholars have attacked this as a Procrustean bed on which to stretch and rack the facts of vastly different civilizations, at least one scholar has defended it, *as a method*, on the grounds that the measuring of "new cases against an old one, taken as a standard, is simply a version of what might be called the method of 'hypothesis.' "[9]

Next is the influence of Greek tragedy on Toynbee's scheme. In general, he seems to see civilizations as dying, not of external blows, but of self-destruction. As one commentator puts it, Toynbee's civilizations die, "as Greek tragic heroes die, out of blood guilt, pride, and blindness."[10] The alternative to such a death is also derived from Greek drama, and here Toynbee explicitly acknowledges his debt to Aeschylus' *Agamemnon,* with its *"pathei mathos"*—"learning through suffering." Through suffering, men and perhaps a whole society can be saved; their salvation comes because suffering permits them to go beyond the mundane realities of this world to a vision of God's nature and purpose.[11]

Lastly, beyond any specific element or influence, the classical materials are all-pervasive in Toynbee's mind. Classical myths inspire him, classical authors constantly supply him with apt quotations, and classical history gives him a ready armory of illustrations. In Toynbee's own view, his classical education, with its immersion in a completed, oecumenical civilization, which emphasized the things of the mind, was "a priceless boon."[12]

To this priceless boon of a classical education, Toynbee gradually added knowledge of all other civilizations. Since the 1780s, archaeologists had dug up no less than seven buried and

[9] William Dray, "Toynbee's Search for Historical Laws," *History and Theory,* I, 1 (1960), 34. Dray, however, also warns against the misuse of the Graeco-Roman model as a Procrustean bed.

[10] Charles Frankel, *The Case of Modern Man* (Boston, 1959), p. 176.

[11] *A Study of History,* Vol. X, p. 235. Cf. William H. McNeil, "Some Basic Assumptions of Toynbee's A Study of History," in *The Intent of Toynbee's History,* p. 37.

[12] *Civilization on Trial,* p. 4.

forgotten civilizations, and Toynbee set himself to read their reports. Travel in and reading about existing non-Western civilizations supplied additional materials to Toynbee's powerful memory. Like some modern-day Alexander conquering by the pen, Toynbee levied tribute for his writings on the Ottoman society in Turkey, the Minoan in Crete, the Far Eastern in Japan and China, the Hindu society in India, and so on and on. At the end, the binocular vision of history, ground to the Hellenic-Modern prescription, gave way to a kaleidioscopic vision of the historical universe.

Unbelievable as it may seem, during much of this historical activity, Toynbee also served as Director of Studies at Chatham House. As part of his work there, he edited and wrote large parts of the massive yearly volumes of *The Survey of International Affairs*, as well as producing separate works on problems in international relations. Thus, he was professionally involved in the study of the modern world and its politics as well as of the ancient civilizations and their cultures. One might well expect a rich brew from this mixture.

Finally, to the general sources of Toynbee's thought and inspiration must be added a few significant individual names. They are, usually, to be found mentioned in *A Study of History* itself. Most prominent is Henri Bergson, the French philosopher. Questioning nineteenth-century positivism and its postulates of assured, scientific progress, Bergson talked eloquently of such things as "creative evolution," *élan vital*, and of the distinction between mathematical and durational time. He stressed psychological and religious insight and intuition instead of analytical reason. Bergson's impact on the young Toynbee at Oxford was abrupt and enduring; it colored both Toynbee's thinking and even his writing henceforward.[13] So, too, Walter Bagehot's *Physics and Politics* is an obvious source of some of Toynbee's ideas on the "cake of custom" surrounding static societies, and the need for a challenge to evoke

[13] For a brief summary of Bergson's views, H. Stuart Hughes, *Consciousness and Society, passim,* is convenient.

a novel response. The Comte de Gobineau's *Essay on the Inequality of Human Races*, shorn of its racism, sets forth in preliminary form many of Toynbee's conceptions about civilizations. Further, like Spengler, Toynbee is constantly quoting Goethe and even Eduard Meyer. Indeed, the extensive footnotes to the *Study of History* give us all we need to know about Toynbee's intellectual biography. It is, of course, the particular synthesis which Toynbee constructs out of his eclectic materials which ultimately interests us.

3

Toynbee's system is today so well known and so easily available that little summary seems needed here.[14] Nevertheless, for the sake of having a common platform from which to launch our considerations of his work, the following very brief précis may be useful.

Toynbee begins by searching for an intelligible unit of historical study. In place of the average, present-day historian's concern with nations, Toynbee suggests we study "civilizations," the whole in which, for example, the national parts can alone be intelligibly explained. Starting with our existing Western Civilization, Toynbee finds it "affiliated" by certain traits to the Graeco-Roman or what he calls Hellenic Civilization. As Somervell's abridgement puts it succinctly, "The marks of this relationship are (a) a universal state (e.g., The Roman Empire), itself the outcome of a time of troubles, followed by (b) an interregnum, in which appear (c) a Church and (d) a Völkerwanderung of barbarians in an heroic age. The Church and the Völkerwanderung are the products, respectively, of the internal and external 'proletariats' of a dying civilization."[15]

---

[14] For example, the abridged version by D. C. Somervell, which carries an even more abridged outline at the end, is a handy way of reading Toynbee.

[15] *Abridgement*, p. 567.

The Hellenic Civilization is our "model" or "ideal type," and Toynbee uses it, though not slavishly, to identify and define all other civilizations. Employing it flexibly, we discover five living civilizations: our own Western, the Orthodox Christian, the Islamic, the Hindu, and the Far Eastern Society. In practice, Toynbee divides the Islamic into an Arabic and Iranic Civilization. Then follow the nonliving civilizations: Hellenic, Syriac, Indic, Sinic, Minoan, Sumeric, Hittite, Babylonic, Andean, Mexic, Yucatec, Mayan, and Egyptiac.[16] There are also two sets of "fossilized" relics of similar societies now extinct: one set includes, for example, Monophysite and Nestorian Christians, as well as Jews and Parsees, and the other set Mahayanian and Hinayanian Buddhists, as well as Jains.[17]

Some of Toynbee's civilizations are wholly unrelated to any other civilization: such are the Egyptiac and Andean. Others are unrelated to earlier civilizations, but are related to later ones; that is, without parents, but with children. Some are "affiliated" through universal churches, while others are related by inheritance of the organized religion of the dominant minority of the earlier civilization; and so forth.[18]

Next, Toynbee sets himself to defend the comparability of his 19 (or 21) civilizations. Distinguishing his civilizations, as

[16] Toynbee also debates whether or not we should divide the Orthodox Christian Civilization into Orthodox Byzantine and Orthodox Russian, and the Far Eastern into Chinese and Japanese-Korean in which case we would have 21 civilizations as a total.

[17] The major objection to Toynbee's "fossil" classification has centered about his description of the Jews as a "fossil." See for example, Maurice Samuel, *The Professor and the Fossil* (New York, 1956). While I am not competent to participate in the details of this argument, I can suggest that it is interesting to note Sigmund Freud's comparable use of the term "fossil" for his own people, in *Moses and Monotheism*, translated by Katherine Jones (New York, 1958). My own impression in this matter is that Toynbee's classification of the Jews as a "fossil" illustrates no particular bias or distortion on his part, but is simply part of the general confusion of his system. Nevertheless, while in principle he has a perfect right to set up any classification he finds useful, the heuristic value of such a classification, in practice, is another matter.

[18] *A Study of History* (New York, 1962), Vol. I, p. 120 ff. This is really the crucial volume for the study of Toynbee's methodological conceptions and leading ideas.

units, from primitive societies, he nevertheless implies that his task is similar to the anthropologist's. The concept of the "unity of civilization" (our old friend, the linear theory of progress?) is attacked, as is the theory that all civilization has been "diffused" from one center: Egypt. Toynbee's conclusion is that his civilizations are "philosophically contemporaneous" members of a single "species."

How do civilizations arise and what causes them to decline? This is the core of Toynbee's first six volumes, his major effort at a philosophy of history. The basic problem is to trace the breakthrough of a primitive society to a civilization. What causes the first groups to shatter the "cake of custom"? It is not Race, Toynbee tells us in an extended argument, nor is it an easy and comfortable Environment. Both of these incorrectly make psychical traits a fixed property of physical factors. The clue is offered to us by Mythology. The great myths—and Toynbee ransacks the Bible, Goethe's *Faust*, the Scandinavian *Voluspa*, Euripides' *Hippolytus*, and many others for examples of encounters between Gods and Demons—suggests that man creates civilizations as "a response to a challenge in a situation of special difficulty which rouses him to make a hitherto unprecedented effort."[19] For the first civilizations, the challenge has indeed been that of the material Environment: for example, progressive desiccation of grasslands, or tropical forests, or bleak plateaus. Thus, it is hard, not easy, conditions that produce the challenge to which an unpredictable response must be made. Of course, for later civilizations, the challenge can come from the human as well as the natural environment.

Among the stimuli Toynbee discusses are: hard countries, new ground, blows, pressures, and penalizations. His conclusion is that the challenge must be severe, but not cripplingly severe: in short, the Golden Mean. (I have not indicated the great range of examples Toynbee uses to illustrate his theses;

[19] *Abridgement*, p. 570.

these, of course, form the bulk of his book.) Once brought into existence, some civilizations become "arrested." Thus, the Ottoman and Spartan civilizations (we shall take up later the legitimacy of treating these as civilizations), vitiated by specialization and caste, no longer met their challenges with fresh responses. Others continue to grow.

Growth or progress in civilization, according to Toynbee, is not to be measured in terms of either political or military expansion or in improvement in technique. In fact, military expansion is a symptom of decline, and technology may well improve when "real civilization" is declining. "Real progress," Toynbee tells us, "is found to consist in a process defined as 'etherialization,' an overcoming of material obstacles which releases the energies of the society to make responses to challenges which henceforth are internal rather than external, spiritual rather than material."[20]

Toynbee's analysis of "etherialization," with his catchy phrases of "withdrawal and return," *mimesis*, creative minorities, and so forth, need not detain us here. Basically, we have already seen the main outlines of his explanation for the origins of civilization; and that, as we remember is the lacuna which he originally set himself to fill in Spengler's philosophy of history. For this latter reason, too, we need not pursue Toynbee in his schema for the breakdown of civilizations, other than to remark on such leading ideas and phrases as the nemesis of creativity; idolization of an ephemeral self (or institution, or technique); schism in the body social; internal and external proletariats; and the creative genius as a saviour. For all past civilizations the normal rhythm of breakdown has been $3\frac{1}{2}$ beats: rout-rally-rout-rally-rout-rally-rout.

At the end of Volume VI, Toynbee suggests that our own civilization is far advanced in a "Time of Troubles." Our first rout apparently was the sixteenth-century Wars of Religion, our second the French Revolutionary Wars, and our

---

[20] *Ibid.*, p. 576.

third the General War of 1914–1918 (it is not clear whether the 1939-1945 War is to be included as part of the earlier twentieth-century war, or not). We seem, therefore, to be on the verge of entering the universal state which, as in the Hellenic Civilization, heralds the decline and fall.

But Toynbee holds out a shred of hope. While our present situation appears sinister, there is no known law of historical determinism—though Toynbee has gone far to demonstrate that previous civilizations have performed as if there were such a law—which compels us to pursue the doomed path. Like Bunyan's "Christian," our present encounter may bring forth the correct response. In Toynbee's rather mystic communication at this point, it is suggested, implicitly, that we can rescue our civilization by increased "etherialization." Explicitly, he exhorts us that "we may and must pray that a reprieve which God has granted to our society once will not be refused if we ask for it again in a humble spirit and with a contrite heart."[21]

In the last four volumes, the swell of the religious note is increased, though with some change in key. While Toynbee does offer new details on such matters as his Universal States, Universal Churches, and Heroic Ages, his interest has openly shifted from religion as a possible seedbed of civilization to civilizations as the carriers of religion. Now, civilizations are merely "the handmaids of religion," providing "an opportunity for fully-fledged higher religions to come to birth."[22]

Toynbee's shift, however, is not only away from a concern with civilizations to an acknowledged preoccupation with religion, but from Christianity per se, as the sole vehicle of salvation, to a "higher religion." As Toynbee himself admits, "I was brought up to believe that Christianity was a unique revelation of the whole truth. I have now come to believe that all the historic religions and philosophies are partial revelations of the

---

[21] *Ibid.,* p. 554.
[22] *A Study of History,* Vol. VII, p. 445. Cf. Pieter Geyl, *Debates With Historians* (London, 1955), pp. 165–166.

truth in one or other of its aspects." Indeed, Buddhism and Hinduism, because they are nonexclusive, have a special lesson to teach about the mystery of Existence, and Toynbee confesses that "This Indian standpoint is the one from which the last four volumes of my book have been written."[23] It comes as no surprise, therefore, to those who have followed the drift of Toynbee's thought through the first six volumes to hear him declare himself fundamentally a religious thinker rather than a historian.

4

Toynbee's effort at a study of philosophy of history is so earnest, so much in a good cause, and so marked by an apparent air of judicious and open-minded scholarship that, as one reads it, one fights against the sickening realization that he is in the presence of the old "Emperor's clothes" story.[24] Yet, the ultimate judgment on Toynbee must be condemnation by historians for his poor understanding of history, and by philosophers for his weak logic and insipid metaphysics. Nor does the combination add up miraculously to good philosophy of history. In spite of noble passages, commendable insights, and exemplary industry, *A Study of History*, in my opinion, will

[23] *Toynbee and History*, p. 6–7. Indeed, Toynbee gives actual form to his new "syncretistic religion," by composing on the model of the Litany of the saints an invocation to "Christ Tammuz" and other "Christs," and to Mother Isis, Mother Cybele, and Mother Mary. See *A Study of History*, Vol. X, p. 143. The shades of Comte and his religion of humanity seem to be invoked by this litany.

[24] For those who have forgotten their Hans Christian Andersen, this is the story of two Western tailors employed to weave special clothing out of fine spun gold for the Chinese Emperor. Pocketing the gold for themselves, the tailors pretend to weave, claiming that only stupid people cannot see the exquisite gold threads of the garment they are weaving. Everyone, including the Emperor, afraid to appear stupid, pretends to see—and proceeds to admire—the cloth. At last the work is "completed," and when the Emperor, wearing the nonexistent robe, walks naked in front of his subjects, they, of course, fall down in admiration. Only when a little boy cries out—"Why, the Emperor is naked!"—does everyone admit the imposture.

be only a curiosity in 20 or 30 years.

Our task now, however, must be to seek what there is of value, even if it is only a negative value, in some of its leading ideas.[25] Let us begin with three key points in Toynbee's *Study*: (1) his plea for a new unit of historical study; (2) his desire for comparability or generalizations in history; and (3) his belief in the empirical method.

Toynbee begins by demonstrating the "Relativity of Historical Thought." Showing that modern historians "cannot abstract their thoughts and feelings from the influence of the environment in which they live," in this case an environment dominated by the Industrial System and by Nationality, Toynbee indicts his contemporaries for their parochial views. It is the same demand as Spengler's for a Copernican revolution in history. Toynbee's conclusion to this by-now truism is rather surprising: "So far, we have simply found that in the foreground of historical thought there is a shimmer of relativity, and it is not impossible that the ascertaining of this fact may prove to be the first step towards ascertaining the presence of some constant and absolute object of historical thought in the background. Our next step, therefore, is to take up the search for an intelligible field of historical study independent of the local and temporary standpoints and activities of historians upon which we have focused our attention hitherto."[26]

The quest for an "absolute" object of historical thought—and Toynbee wastes no more time discussing the logical relationship of this desire with his earlier demonstration of the relativity of historical thought—leads Toynbee to attack nationalistic histories as partial views, and to ridicule the history of "mankind" as an empty category. These strictures, of course, strike a pleasant note to modern sophisticated ears, and

[25] One difficulty here is that Toynbee's critics have already subjected both his data and his methodology to withering attack. It is hard, therefore, to say anything new on the subject; perhaps our special interests in philosophy of history will provide a few original insights.

[26] *A Study of History*, Vol. I, p. 16.

our initial approval of Toynbee's efforts is strengthened by his attack on those historians who choose a subject simply because of the availability of information in national archives or in chance collections. "Is Ptolemaic Egypt the most important and interesting phenomenon to study," Toynbee asks, "or does the historian choose it simply because Ptolemaic papyri are abundantly available?" The criticism is effective.[27]

So, too, we find ourselves nodding approvingly when Toynbee announces that we must first study wholes, not parts. It is only later that we wonder, as one commentator puts it, "how we can say anything at all about the whole until *after* we have looked at its parts?"[28]

Our difficulties really begin, however, when Toynbee informs us that the wholes to be studied are civilizations. The word that Toynbee uses interchangeably with civilization is "society." Thus, he talks at whim about Hellenic Civilization or Hellenic Society, ignoring the inconvenient fact that civilizations and societies are *not* necessarily the same things. Certainly, his own use of these terms in practice belies his equation of them in theory. In any case, in the whole of Volume I, the fundamental volume for Toynbee's methodology and theories, the word "civilization" is nowhere closely defined. In a vague way, it seems to mean a culture unified about a religion, as with Islamic Civilization. As for "Society," that is first defined for us in a footnote on page 45 of Volume I, quoting de Gobineau to the effect that "What I understand by society is a union, more or less perfect from the political point of view, but complete from the social point of view, of men living under the direction of similar ideas and with identical instincts." Toynbee's own definition comes in a later volume: "A society, we may say, is a product of the relations between individuals, and these relations of theirs arise from the coinci-

---

[27] Cf. Geoffrey Barraclough, *History in a Changing World* (Norman, Okla., 1956); and Christopher Dawson, *The Dynamics of World History* (London, 1957), for similar appeals for nonparochial views on history.

[28] Frankel, *op. cit.*, p. 189.

dence of their individual fields of action. This coincidence combines the individual fields into a common ground, and this common ground is what we call a society."[29]

Admittedly, words such as civilization, culture, and society are difficult to define. Nevertheless, Toynbee's claim to the establishment of a new, intelligible unit of study demands more precision than he affords us. Is it not obvious that Arabs and Africans who may share common elements of Islamic *civilization*, i.e., the religious culture and its attendant ideas and institutions, live in vastly different *societies*, defined according to Toynbee's "relations between individuals?" What understanding can we possibly secure if we confuse these two quite different, though possibly overlapping, *species*, to use Toynbee's term?

The utter vacuity of Toynbee's thought evidences itself in such examples as his treatment of the 'Osmanlis and the Spartans (studies which are, incidentally, in themselves fascinating) as arrested *civilizations*. Toynbee's *sang-froid* is staggering here, for he does not even bother to explain why Sparta, for instance, is a separate civilization or society instead of a part of the Hellenic whole. And, as Pieter Geyl, one of Toynbee's severest critics, points out, the attempt to illustrate the growth of civilizations from hard conditions by the examples of Holland and New England is false in its very essence, for neither of the two is itself a civilization.[30]

It is, probably, from this wholesale muddle that Toynbee's genial idea of the "fossil" societies arises. While Jewish "Civilization," for example, may have been still thriving in the Diaspora, Jewish "Society," in the sense of a territorially based "relations between individuals" was, before the state of Israel, only a poor shadow cast by the Ghetto group. So, too, per-

---

[29] *Abridgement*, p. 211. The quotation from de Gobineau is given by Toynbee in French, and the translation is my own.

[30] Toynbee's effort here is not only methodologically false; it also exhibits errors in fact. See Geyl, *op. cit.*, p. 99; and *Toynbee and History*, p. 301. Similar examples of compounded errors of theory and fact in Toynbee can be compiled endlessly.

haps, with the Parsees in India. Further, one wonders why Toynbee, on his own definitions, has not classified the Egyptiac Civilization as either a fossil or an arrested civilization? But this is to expect consistency from a scheme which has none.

Vitiated in its innermost parts from the very beginning, Toynbee's development of his ideas cannot be taken seriously. Nevertheless, on the sands we have just sifted through our fingers, he proceeds to erect his house of Tarot cards. Having "identified" his 19 (or 21) units, he declares them "philosophically contemporaneous" and therefore comparable. While we may once again applaud the desire for comparative history as a welcome relief from narrow, isolated monographs, we are left gasping by what Toynbee does with his resultant generalizations. Though, unlike Spengler, Toynbee, in perhaps their major difference, is interested in cause and effect relationships, his causes all too often turn out to be "laws" established by "analogies." Thus Toynbee claims to have established "empirically" a "law" that the geneses of civilizations require contributions from more races than one. He also sets up a "law" concerning challenge and response.[31] These "laws," discovered in some civilizations, are then applied, *by analogy*, to other civilizations.[32] Of course, Toynbee, in his usual judicious fashion, first warns his reader that "while Analogy is a vastly suggestive and significant pointer, we cannot afford to follow its indications blindly and mechanically."[33] Then, blandly, he proceeds by analogy to establish the cause of the decline and fall, for example, of the Sumeric Society: "According [i.e., according to the 'law' that societies succumb to internal troubles rather than to external invasions, which are

---

[31] *A Study of History*, Vol. I, p. 278; *Abridgement*, pp. 132, 323. See Dray, *op. cit.*, pp. 40–41, for a discussion of Toynbee's use of "laws."

[32] W. Den Boer's comment is apropos. Toynbee, he says, "evidentally is too deeply rooted in a tradition which opened the Bible at random in order to explain all the world's events, to abandon this method offhand." (*Toynbee and History*, p. 233.)

[33] *A Study of History*, Vol. I, p. 134.

mere consequences of the first]" he says, "we shall not identify the slayers of the Sumeric Civilization with the trans-
frontier barbarians who descended on 'the Kingdom of the
Four Quarters' in the eighteenth century B.C. We shall detect
the fatal strokes in events that had occurred some nine hun-
dred years earlier: the class war between Urukagina of Lagash
and the local priesthood and the militarism of Urukagina's
destroyer Lugalzaggisi; for those long-past catastrophes were
the authentic beginning of the Sumeric time of troubles." As
one stunned commentator remarks about a similar example,
"Surely . . . a cause must be proximate as well as adequate to its
effect. It would have been cold comfort for a Romanized
Briton about to be submerged by the barbarian hordes to be
told that he was paying for the sins of the Athenian mob
nearly 1,000 years earlier."[34] Are we too suspicious in believing that Toynbee is not really thinking of natural causes but of
Greek "fate" and Christian "sin," visited unto the remotest
generation? In any case, his generalizations, derived from his
comparison of philosophically contemporaneous societies, have
turned into strange causal demons.

Of course, if Toynbee's "laws" were really such, there
could be no objection to his employing them in all instances
where they apply. Indeed, we should applaud his scientific
acumen. It is because he fools himself about these laws and the
supposed empirical method by which he has established them
that Toynbee is a dangerous Pied Piper. As we recall, against
Spengler's a priori approach, Toynbee prides himself on his
empirical method. This method he describes as marshalling
"the relevant concrete facts of history." Or, at another place,
discussing the stimulus toward civilization, he implicitly defines it by saying, "Let us review the evidence in favour of this
proposition and then the evidence against it, and see what
inference emerges."[35]

Now, there are three comments necessary about Toynbee's

[34] *Abridgement*, p. 262; *Toynbee and History*, p. 107.
[35] *Abridgement*, pp. 88, 247.

so-called empirical method. The first is that he seems to mean
by empiricism a sort of naive Baconianism. Secure the hard
facts of history, and a law will emerge from them. There is no
hint in Toynbee of the interplay of the empirical and rational
approach, as suggested by earlier thinkers such as Vico and
Comte, or by practitioners of the modern scientific method.[36]

The second thing to note is that, on Toynbee's assumptions,
errors in the "concrete facts" would seriously impair the validity of his inferences. Since this is the area in which Toynbee
has been most constantly and severely attacked by reputable
historians, the blows to his work would seem irreparable except to those who wish to believe despite the evidence. Thus, a
student of Chinese history points out that modern scholarship
reverses Toynbee's picture of North China as a "hard" country, hence a stimulus to the growth of civilization, and South
China as a "soft" environment. Toynbee, it seems, drew his
data from a work based only on traditional and legendary
Chinese accounts. Another scholar, a geographer, cites innumerable examples of Toynbee's shallow and incorrect
knowledge of landscape and environmental conditions.[37] Indeed, in every area touched on by Toynbee, trusted scholars
have controverted him. Only a reading of them can show the
thin crust of his widespread erudition.

Lastly, however, it could be retorted that Toynbee's facts
are mere illustrations of his generalizations and "laws," and
that even if some of the illustrations are wrong, the theses are
not. In this case, of course, Toynbee would have to give up his
claim to inferential reasoning from the concrete facts. The
problem would then be: from whence has Toynbee derived
his "laws"? He has certainly not secured them from the social

[36] On the problem of historical "facts," see, for example, Carl L.
Becker, "What are Historical Facts?" in *The Philosophy of History in
Our Time*, Hans Meyerhoff (ed.) (Garden City, N.Y., 1959). (The other
articles in Meyerhoff's anthology should also be consulted.) E. H. Carr,
What is History (New York, 1962), devotes his first chapter to "The
Historian and his Facts."

[37] *Toynbee and History*, pp. 253–254, 298.

sciences; though, as he revealingly comments in an Annex to the first volume, "we" have never objected to historians "employing the sciences (i.e., Political Economy, Political Science, etc.) in a menial capacity as hewers of wood and drawers of water."[38] Nor has he obtained them from limited empirical studies by historians, such as those concerning, say, the rise of modern science or capitalism as factors in the general growth of Western civilization. Instead, as Toynbee candidly tells us, he has found his generalizations in Myth.

On Toynbee's account, all the findings of modern science and history have already been satisfactorily intuited in mythical thought. The problem, as he frequently points out, is merely "to re-translate the imagery of myths into the terminology of Science."[39] It is from the Bible and from Greek myths that Toynbee draws his "law" concerning challenge and response; modern geographical studies can only confirm in scientific terminology what we already know in the imagery of myth. And so with the law of the Golden Mean, Withdrawal and Return, New Wine in Old Bottles, the Nemesis of Creativity, and other such stories of the Gods. Ignoring all the critical analysis of myth, whether by anthropologists or Freudian psychologists, biblical scholars or ordinary historians, Toynbee eventually claims support for his ideas in Jung.

Toynbee's general argument has an air of plausibility for, as he reminds us, " 'History' grew out of Mythology." What he does not seem able to remember is that, in so doing, history became the *logos* which went beyond *mythos*. One might expect him to blush when he writes: "The biological and psychological analogies are perhaps least harmful and misleading when they are applied to primitive societies or to arrested civilizations, but they are manifestly unsuited to express the relation in which growing civilizations stand to their individual members. The inclination to introduce such analogies is merely an example of that myth-making or fictional infirmity

[38] *A Study of History*, Vol. I, p. 466.
[39] *Ibid.*, p. 299.

of historical minds."[40] But Toynbee has awareness only for
the mote in the other person's eye. His trust in his own vision
is total. We secure the full flavor of the historical feast Toynbee spreads before us when, commenting on the intrusion of
the Devil into the universe of God as being the model for
challenge and response, he says, "the event can best be described in these mythological images because they are not em-
barrassed by the contradiction that arises when the statement
is translated into logical terms."[41] Neither is Toynbee!

Closely connected, if not identical, with mythology as a
source of Toynbee's generalizations is religion. We have already seen how pervasive the religious inspiration is throughout the *Study*, and how Toynbee moved from Christianity as
the unique revelation to a belief in the emergence of a "higher
religion" at the end of his ten volumes. It is religion in this
rather syncretistic vision, where Toynbee is really equating
God with the *élan vital*, which gives Toynbee his supreme
generalization or "law" as to the direction of history: "The
goal of human endeavours: the mutation of Man into Superman."[42] Derived from religious myth, this goal can then be
used to measure, empirically Toynbee would say, the value of
each and every civilization; and such a measurement would be
absolute and not merely relative. In his comment, "My View
of History," Toynbee presents this thesis as if provisionally
and with sweet reasonableness: "While civilizations rise and
fall and, in falling, give rise to others, some purposeful enterprise, higher than theirs, may all the time be making headway,
and in a divine plan, the learning that comes through the
suffering caused by the failures of civilizations may be the
sovereign means of progress."[43] In *A Study of History*, how-

---

[40] *Abridgement*, p. 211.

[41] *A Study of History*, Vol. I, p. 278.

[42] *Ibid.*, pp. 194, 249, and cf. p. 159.

[43] *Civilization on Trial*, p. 15. This is remarkably like the conclusion
of Thomas Malthus: "I should be inclined . . . to consider the world and
this life as the mighty process of God, not for the trial, but for the
creation and formation of mind, a process neccessary to awaken inert,
chaotic matter into spirit, to sublimate the dust of the earth into soul, to

ever, God's purpose is presumed to be known.[44]

Toynbee's thinking about religion is rather extraordinary. Although he makes it his primary criterion both for defining and classifying his civilizations, he spends almost no time in analyzing the nature of religion. There is not even the shadow of an attempt at a sociology of religion. When talking of the Babylonian, the Minoan, or the Egyptiac Society, Toynbee is perfectly aware that "Here too, the relations between the Gods were simply a transposition of political facts into theological terms."[45] But this insight fails him when he comes to the "higher religions." He does not see that Christianity, Mohammedism, Hinduism, and so forth may also be a "transposition." Or that only Western Christian man may want to be a Superman, and that he, Toynbee, is egocentrically projecting this desire onto the rest of mankind as a goal.[46] Religion, the fundamental constituent of civilizations, seems to stand outside of Toynbee's empirical method.

5

In terms of his own claims, Toynbee must be ajudged to have failed.[47] It should be admitted, however, that his failure, especially in regard to the empirical method, is hardly unique among historians, but rather points in a glaring way to the

---

elicit an ethereal spark from the clod of clay." Humbler than Toynbee, however, Malthus also recommended that "we should reason from nature up to nature's God and not presume to reason from God to nature." (*Population: The First Essay* [Ann Arbor, 1959], pp. 122–124.)

[44] See, for example, *A Study of History*, Vol. I, p. 285.

[45] *Ibid.*, p. 118.

[46] Toynbee does not deign even to argue against Feuerbach and his ilk, and he ignores completely sociologists of religion like Max Weber. On a different tack, is there not a problem for Toynbee in the fact that the Black Race, i.e., Africans, have had fairly advanced, though perhaps not universal or monotheistic, religions without producing what he has classified as a civilization?

[47] For Toynbee's willingness to judge others in history, see *Abridgement*, pp. 262, 310, 547; and *A Study of History*, Vol. III, p. 470.

weakness and ambiguity of historical explanation in general. Thus, "Everyman the Historian" can usually find numerous "facts" which, carefully selected, illustrate his thesis.[48] Without any malicious desire to distort the evidence, he can overlook the data which would go contrary to his interpretation for the simple reason that there exist neither really adequate criteria concerning acceptable evidence nor "critical" experiments which can be performed.[49]

Where Toynbee, then, differs from other, more acceptable historians is in the enormity of his failure as contrasted with the extravagant claims for success which he has put forth. In place of the average historian's attempts at limited generalizations, based on careful though usually one-sided consideration of documentary evidence, Toynbee has offered sweeping, universal generalizations "derived" from sources more dubious than the usual. Myth has counted for more than historical evidence. The result is that there is nothing of heuristic value in Toynbee. He poses no historical problems for which further evidence may be sought. How shall we test, even by the admittedly loose methods prevailing in historical explanation today, his thesis of the Golden Mean or of Challenge and Response? Toynbee's "whole" of history is not amenable to correction or even extension of its parts. Worse, as a result of his misguided efforts, he has helped to discredit legitimate attempts at using generalizations and the generalizing sciences in writing history.[50]

Further, to this sort of null history, Toynbee has added a

[48] I am inspired to this phrase by Carl L. Becker, *Everyman His Own Historian* (New York, 1935).

[49] The difficulties in this matter, which jeopardize the work of such professional and highly regarded historians as Professors R. H. Tawney and H. R. Trevor-Roper as they argue about the role of the gentry in the Great Rebellion of 1640, is brilliantly illustrated by J. H. Hexter's analysis in "Storm Over the Gentry," *Reappraisals in History* (Evanston, 1961).

[50] For a more legitimate effort to deal with the problem of generalization in history, see *History and Theory*, III, 1 (1963), where the entire issue is devoted to "Symposium: Uses of Theory in the Study of History."

pretentious metaphysics: his claim to a philosophy of history. His illogicity and oversimplification do not shock the reader who runs, mainly because they are insulated in a sort of *Time Magazine* style: "The Tarsian Jewish apostle of Christianity *in partibus infedelium*," for example, is St. Paul. A few instances should suffice to indicate the kind of oversimplification in which Toynbee indulges.[51] "The geneses of all civilizations," he tells us, "could be described in a sentence written by a Western philosopher-statesman of our age one month after the close of the General War of 1914–18: 'There is no doubt that Mankind is once more on the move. The very foundations have been shaken and loosened, and things are again fluid. The tents have been struck, and the great caravan of Humanity is once more on the march.' "[52] After this illuminating description of the geneses of civilizations, we are bowled over by Toynbee's calm and judicious comment: "Can we yet say anything more about the transition from a static condition to a dynamic activity in which the genesis of every civilization consists?" Next, in his quest for a further answer, Toynbee asks why civilizations did not "begin to occur until less than 6000 years ago, when Man, after his ascent from Sub-Man, had been lying torpid on the level of Primitive Humanity for some 300,000 years?" Was man "torpid" during those 300,000 years when, for example, he learned the use of fire, progressively improved the making of flints and flakes until he turned them into nonutilitarian objects of reverence, employed the spear-thrower and the bow and arrow, made clothes of skins, turned caves into shelters, and then decorated their walls with

[51] It must be admitted that Toynbee's style has its good points, too. Some of his lines are brilliant, as when he describes the ruins of the Mayan Civilization: "The forest, like some sylvan boa-constrictor, has literally swallowed them up and is now devouring them at its leisure, prising the fine-hewn, close-laid stones apart with its writhing roots and tendrils." (*Abridgement*, p. 80.)

[52] *A Study of History*, Vol. I, p. 196. The Western philosopher-statesman is J. C. Smuts, one of Toynbee's favorite authors. Later, we shall see Toynbee quote Smuts a number of times as the spokesman for "Western Physical Science."

magnificent paintings? Can he be said to have awakened only 6000 years ago, when 10,000 years ago, living by hunting and gatherings, he took the utterly revolutionary step of domesticating plants and animals and founding fixed villages: the so-called Agricultural Revolution?[53] Is it that these are merely material changes, of no weight in Toynbee's metaphysical world, and therefore dismissed as well from this empirical world?

Has Toynbee read many utopian works to be be able to state: "To arrest a downward movement is the utmost to which most Utopias aspire, since Utopias seldom begin to be written in any society until after its members have lost the expectation of further progress"? How many other societies beside the Hellenic (if that) and the Western have produced the utopian genre of works? Did Bacon write his *New Atlantis*, Cabet his *Voyage en Icarie*, and Bellamy his *Looking Backward* to arrest a downward movement? Similarly, why does Toynbee imply that the expulsion of the American Tories by the victorious colonists at the end of the Revolutionary War is the result of the "total war" view introduced by nationalist democracies—true enough in itself—and ignore in this context similar treatment of nonmilitary population by nondemocratic "religious" states: the Spanish treatment of the Moors and Jews, the French persecution of the Huguenots, and so forth?

The line between oversimplification and illogical thought is thin, and Toynbee constantly crosses back and forth. On the illogical side I would put such an example as Toynbee informing us that "the nucleus of the Sinic character which stands for Yin seems to represent dark coiling clouds overshadowing the Sun, while the nucleus of the character which stands for Yang seems to represent the unclouded Sun-disk emitting its ray," and then two pages later remarking that of the various symbols

---

[53] Cf. Gordon Childe, *What Happened in History* (New York, 1946) or the issue of *Scientific American* (September, 1960) devoted to "The Human Species."

expressing the alternation between a static condition and a dynamic activity in the universe, "Yin and Yang are the most apt, because they convey the measure of the rhythm direct and not through some metaphor derived from psychology or mechanics or mathematics."[54] A similar instance is Toynbee's declaration that "so long as an act of will was postulated as the first cause in the background, it was in vain for theologians to lay down that predestination was irrevocable, since it was logically impossible to believe that an omnipotent power was incapable of revoking its own decrees"; Toynbee does not seem to see that the other view is also logically impossible, and that theologians have argued both positions with equally illogical conviction.[55]

There is no need to multiply instances. Moreover, in case they escape firsthand observation, innumerable examples are readily encountered in the articles of his numerous critics. What these examples add up to is the paucity of decent philosophy, as well as history, in Toynbee's philosophy of history. What he really offers us is a heroic though misguided attempt at universal history, covered over with a patchwork quilt of metaphysics, and pushed forward on the stage of the world as a well-dressed philosophy of history. As I have suggested before, we are in the presence of the Emperor's clothes.

6

Earlier, I stated that Toynbee is an "Alexandrian" historian. "Alexandrian" civilization itself can be characterized as a polyglot one: eclectic, syncretistic, borrowing its elements

---

[54] *A Study of History*, Vol. I, p. 210. Toynbee's ability to use analogies is awesome. "In the *Magnificat*," he tells us, "we shall hear Yin's song of joy at passing over into Yang." The verse in which Toynbee perceives this happening is: "My soul doth magnify the Lord, and my spirit hath rejoiced in God my Saviour; For he hath regarded the lowliness of his handmaiden." (*Ibid.*, p. 203.)

[55] *Ibid.*, p. 247.

from the four corners of the earth, and never synthesizing them into a single, harmonious culture. Interestingly enough, Toynbee himself characterizes a disintegrating civilization, which is dying of "schism in the Soul," by what he calls the sense of Promiscuity: vulgarity and barbarism in manners; vulgarity and barbarism in art; *Lingue Franche;* and syncretism in religion.[56]

Now, the great poem of our time describing and itself inspired by the Alexandrian quality of our age is T. S. Eliot's *The Waste Land*. Written in the shadow of World War I (1922), it surveys the desolate landscape of our culture, using as its measure the myth of the *Golden Bough* and the legend of the Holy Grail. Eliot's poem, too, has learned footnotes from a number of the literatures of the world, of all time periods. It employs bits and pieces from many languages: Greek, Latin, Italian, French, German, and even Sanskrit. Using these eclectic devices, Eliot informs us that our twentieth-century Western world is sterile, without faith, and on the point of dissolution. Our culture is "A heap of broken images," mere "withered stumps of time" from which the spirit has fled. Only a miracle in the shape of Eliot's syncretistic religion seems able to save us.

Even from this brief account, it is apparent that *A Study of History* is the attempt at a prose counterpart to *The Waste Land*. Toynbee, too, writes on the eve of the 1914 holocaust, in which he detected Western civilization burning itself up. He ranges over many civilizations and cultures, guided by the myths of the past. Sir James Frazer's *Golden Bough* is as precious to him as to Eliot. So, too, Toynbee brings the literatures of all the world under tribute to his eclectic enterprise, and interlards his pages constantly with quotations (almost always untranslated) from sources in Greek, Latin, German, French, and even Chinese and Hindustani. His message is the same as

[56] I have left out the last element, *Cuius regio eius religio,* as not pertinent; nor need I stress further the applicability of syncretism in religion to Toynbee's own case.

Eliot's: our Western civilization is disintegrating, lost without faith in a no-man's land. Only a miracle in the form of a "higher religion" can bring us salvation.

Alas, as we have already noted with Spengler, what is possible for great poetry is not acceptable in more earthbound history, or philosophy of history. As Toynbee himself acknowledges, the latter's wings are tied, or should be tied, to fact. While the historian can hope for the gift of poetic insight, and even for a poetic style, he cannot invoke in his favor the alluring dispensation of poetic license.[57] Yet, as we have seen this is exactly what Toynbee has done.

7

Toynbee's major fault is similar to Spengler's: he has neither understanding nor affection for the new elements of his own civilization. Extolling the need for civilizations to break the "cake of custom," Toynbee does not like the taste of the crumbs in his own mouth. He is, as I remarked earlier, a man of profoundly outdated mind and tastes. There is no place in his scheme for any of the new ideas, institutions, or achievements of the last 400 years of modern civilization. He is opposed to the modern national, democratic state. He intensely dislikes modern science and technology, and the industrial society that they have created. Modern art for Toynbee simply illustrates the decadence and degeneration of our civilization. Moreover, he refuses to recognize that the industrial and scientific revolutions have created what is now a *new* civilization. I believe that he is blind to this development for two reasons: (1) the industrial and scientific are not "religious" revolutions; and (2) at least outwardly, the same Christian religion con-

[57] Who cares that Keats, in his poem, "On First Looking into Chapman's Homer," mistakes Cortez for Balboa as the discoverer of the Pacific? It does not affect either the truth or beauty of the poem. In the case of a historian, such an error would cause us seriously to question his understanding of the events under consideration.

nects the middle ages and the modern period. Lastly, Toynbee denigrates the modern attempt at empirical social analysis and consequent piecemeal reform of social institutions in favor of a miraculous spiritual improvement, and exemplifies his dislike of the former by the very methodology of his *Study*.[58] In short, whatever is contemporary finds no resonance in his soul.

Toynbee's understanding of the creative achievements of modern science can be measured by the names he cites. His outstanding spokesman to express the "language of our modern Western Physical Science" (which, as we have seen, is for Toynbee simply a translation of mythical language) is—J. C. Smuts![59] Such developments as non-Euclidean geometry (Gauss, Bolyai, and Lobachevsky all worked in the middle of the nineteenth century, and Riemann's classic work was published in 1868), Planck's 1901 quantum theory, Einstein's relativity work from 1905 on, Heisenberg's 1927 indeterminacy principle, and the general drift of modern science to probability theories do not seem to have come within Toynbee's ken. Surely, while we need not expect an historian of civilizations to understand these and similar achievements in detail, we might hope for an awareness of them in his attitude toward modern science, and even for his admiration.

As for technical accomplishments, these for Toynbee "are all trivialities which do not touch the heart of what we mean by a civilization *in any respect* [italics added]." In words slightly reminiscent of Edmund Burke, Toynbee goes on to say that "A civilization does not consist in machine-sewing or rifle-shooting or tea- and coffee- and cocoa-drinking or tobacco-smoking. It does not even consist in reading and writing or in metallurgy. . . . To equate this kind of thing with 'Civilization' with a capital 'C' is an absurdity which would be

[58] Cf. Frankel, *op. cit.*, p. 189.
[59] *A Study of History*, Vol. I, p. 284. On p. 272, Toynbee talks of a "parable . . . taken up by the modern Western biologist." Again, his protagonist is J. C. Smuts.

inconceivable to a cultivated mind that was either Hindu or Hellenic or Western *of an earlier generation* [italics added]."[60] Ignoring Toynbee's strange sort of logic, which, by correctly denying that the items listed comprise the whole of a civilization, also denies that they are essential elements "in any respect," we can only agree with him in his placing himself, against the modern strawman he has set up, with an "earlier generation."

Similarly, Toynbee ignores almost all the recent work in the social sciences. For example, his understanding of men and their motives is not enlightened by the labors of Freud or his followers: his comprehension of societies by Tylor and Boas; his analysis of institutions by Durkheim and Max Weber; or his insight into social and economic phenomena by Marx (though he is undoubtedly influenced by him) and Keynes.[61] Toynbee needs none of their work to supply him with the hypotheses to be tested against his "empirical method": his sources are of another world.

To anyone who reads Toynbee carefully, it must be clear that he regards the last 400 years of Western civilization as a steady decline because during that period it has witnessed a decline of traditional religion. Blind to any other possible achievements of the modern world, he has ransacked the "withered stumps of time" to buttress his thesis that without religion, civilization decays. From the Reformation, with its split of the Universal Church, on through the scientific and industrial revolutions which have led the internal proletariat to increasing anticlericalism and "irreligion"—a development contrary to Toynbee's role for them—the path has been downward.[62]

---

[60] *Ibid.*, p. 429. Burke's similar statement can be found in his *Reflections on the French Revolution* (New York, 1955), p. 110.

[61] Toynbee's loose sort of "analysis" can be seen, for example, in his treatment of the "internal proletariat." Whatever the civilization, the internal proletariat are always the same; industrialism, for instance, according to Toynbee, has not changed them significantly.

[62] For the growth of proletarian irreligion, cf. E. J. Hobsbawm, *The Age of Revolution* (London, 1962), pp. 217 ff.

With all the powers of industriousness and insight Toynbee undeniably has, his private faith has caused him to be intolerant of any public path by which to reach "etherialization" other than the traditional religious one. The great advances of our civilization, for example, in Condorcet's "social art," that is, in social security and material prosperity, and in law, order, and humanitarianism (in spite of glaring lapses), these count for nothing. So, too, with the "etherialization," the rise to a higher level of consciousness, achieved by the creative acts of modern physics and biology and by the insights of modern psychology and social science. For Toynbee, man and his culture have remained basically static during 6000 years; indeed, Toynbee's treatment of civilizations as "philosophically contemporaneous" requires that he view them *sub specie aeternitatis*. The result, to sum up, is that Toynbee, like St. Augustine before him, has reverently placed his candle on the altar of the City of God; he has shed little light, however, on man's earthly pilgrimage through time.

XI

Freud

*"History . . . is a nightmare
from which I am trying to
awake."**

JAMES JOYCE,
Ulysses

1

IT MAY surprise some readers to see Freud described as the last
of the great classical philosophers of history. Yet, the description is an accurate one. The founder of psychoanalysis is in the
tradition of Comte and Hegel, and especially of Vico, whose
fulfillment he can well be considered. Like the latter, Freud
worked out a new science—in this case, psychoanalysis instead
of philology—which offered important clues for solving the
riddle of man's past.

In his initial work, of course, Freud concerned himself
mainly with the individual's past, and he studied his subject in
the office and the clinic rather than in the historical world.
Focusing on unconscious mental processes, hitherto neglected
or misunderstood, he discovered new methods and devised a
whole range of new theories to explore the unplumbed depths
of his patient's character. The result was a novel and startling
view of individual man.

* James Joyce, *Ulysses,* The Modern Library edition, (Random
House).

Then, boldly, Freud extrapolated his psychoanalytic findings to men in general and to the collective past. As part of this
effort, he envisioned a new genesis, or origin, of man as a
cultural animal, and then traced the path of humanity through
time. He concerned himself with such topics as the psychological roots of religion and morality, the direction of history,
and the means by which that direction is pursued. He analyzed
the actors in the historical drama, both the hero and the masses
who follow him, and attempted to work out a group psychology as earlier he had labored at an individual psychology.
Lastly, as he had analyzed individual neuroses in his clinical
experience, so he tried to analyze the neuroses of the group in
historical experience. The only cure for the latter (as for the
former), according to Freud, is consciousness of the hitherto
unconscious past. Thus, in his new version of an old subject,
philosophy of history becomes both a diagnosis and a therapy
for the ills of mankind.[1]

2

Freud, in his own life, embraced the adage "Physician, cure
Thyself," and managed his therapy by means of a second
adage, the Socratic "Know Thyself." Once possessed of his
self-analysis, he could work at the task of discovering an objective science of all mankind's psychological processes. Thus,
the inner elements in Freud's biography are more important
than usual, and would have to be understood, at least to some
extent, if one wished to comprehend the origins of psychoanalysis per se.[2] This sort of insight, however, we must forego
here, and restrict ourselves to some largely external details of

---

[1] In the anthology *Psychoanalysis and History* (Englewood Cliffs, N.J.,
1963), I tried to indicate some of the ways in which Freud's theories
have been applied by historians, as well as the implications of Freud's
work for speculative philosophy of history. See especially my introduction to that volume.

[2] Some of the essential works in this endeavor are *The Origins of Psychoanalysis: Letters, Drafts and Notes to Wilhelm Fliess, 1887–1902*,
Marie Bonaparte, Anna Freud, and Ernst Kris (eds.) (Garden City,

his life which serve as useful background to his work in philosophy of history.

Born in Freiberg, Moravia (now part of Czechoslovakia), in 1856, Freud moved at the age of four with his family to Vienna. Here, in the intellectual atmosphere of the Austrian capital, he spent most of his life. Only in his last year, because of the Nazis, did he leave Vienna for London, where he died in 1939.

The young Sigmund's family relationships were very complicated. His father Jakob, a surprisingly mild prototype for the Oedipal figure, had married for a second time, aged 40, when he was already the sire of two sons, as well as a grandson. Thus, Sigmund Freud, the firstborn of the second marriage, was at birth an uncle, while his own half-brothers were about the same age as his mother. There were numerous other familial complications in the young Freud's life—the death of a younger brother at 14 months, the rivalry of a year-old nephew—but I shall simply conclude this part of his biography by remarking, with Ernest Jones, that the paradoxes of his family circle were calculated to stimulate the future psychoanalyst's inquiring mind.[3]

In his *Autobiography*, which, like Vico's, was written for a collection of important lives, Freud remarks preemptorily: "My parents were Jews, and I have remained a Jew myself."[4] Freud's "Jewishness" is unquestionably important, though probably not for the reason advanced by one scholar, who seeks to establish and explain psychoanalysis as an expression of Jewish mysticism.[5] I would remark, rather, on two major effects on his work of Freud's being a Jew. The first is that he

---

N.Y., 1957); Freud's *The Interpretation of Dreams*, translated by James Strachey (London, 1954); his *Autobiography*, also translated by Strachey (New York, 1935); and Ernest Jones, *The Life and Works of Sigmund Freud*, 3 vols. (New York, 1953–1957).

[3] For details, see Jones, *op. cit.*, Vol. I, pp. 3 ff. It is interesting to compare Freud's unusual position in his family with that of Leonardo da Vinci, to whom Freud, of course, devoted a treatise.

[4] *Autobiography*, p. 9.

[5] See David Bakan, *Sigmund Freud and the Jewish Mystical Tradition* (New York, 1958).

felt keenly his disabilities in antisemitic Vienna. (For example, his path to academic advancement was temporarily blocked by his "race," as were other appointments.) As Freud put it, "When, in 1873, I first joined the University, I experienced some appreciable disappointments. Above all, I found that I was expected to feel myself inferior and an alien because I was a Jew. I refused absolutely to do the first of these things."[6] The important thing for our purposes is that Freud, while not feeling inferior, did feel himself "alien." The result was that "at an early age," as he tells us, "I was made familiar with the fate of being in the opposition and of being put under the ban of the 'compact majority.'" Thus, as an Ibsenite hero, Freud could stand stubbornly by his ideas, even when almost everyone (for he always needed at least one supporter, such as his friend, Fliess) was opposed to him.[7] And, as an "alien," he could view aspects of his culture in a way forbidden to those who belonged to it without reflection or question.

The second effect is that, although Freud rejected the Jewish religion (as he rejected all religion), and considered himself a Jew only by race, he was strongly immersed in parts of his people's cultural heritage. Thus, for example, he learned much about human nature, and its displacement and condensation of feeling, from the age-old accumulation of Jewish jokes and anecdotes.[8] More importantly, an early reader of the Old Testament, Freud never outgrew his curiosity about the genesis of the Jewish (and later the Christian) religion, nor his "romance" with the monumental figure of Moses.[9] These con-

[6] *Autobiography*, p. 11.

[7] Cf. Ibsen's play, *Enemy of the People*.

[8] See Freud's *Jokes and Their Relation to the Unconscious* (1905), with its frequent use of Jewish jokes as illustrative material. An interesting book, based on Freud's work, is Martin Grotjahn, *Beyond Laughter* (New York, 1957).

[9] More properly, this might be called "family romance," because Freud's identification of himself with Moses appears similar to the mechanism involved in the myth of the hero who has "two families." Cf. *Moses and Monotheism*, translated by Katherine Jones (New York, 1958), Part I, for Freud's own treatment of this myth.

cerns returned in later life, to haunt his pioneering explorations into psychoanalytic philosophy of history.

Much had to take place before that time, however. Dallying with the notion of studying law and engaging in social activities, the residue perhaps of his boyhood dreams of becoming a Minister of State, Freud decided instead at the time of leaving high school to study medicine. His decision was taken, in part, under the inspiration of hearing at a public lecture Goethe's essay on Nature. The other name Freud mentions at the time as strongly attracting him by his theories is Charles Darwin.[10]

Freud's choice of medicine as a career was equivocal. His real interests lay elsewhere, in "philosophical" speculation which, as a young man, he had ruthlessly to check. As he wrote his friend, Fliess, "I see that you are using the circuitous route of medicine to attain your first ideal, the physiological understanding of man, while I secretly nurse the hope of arriving by the same route at my own original objective, philosophy. For that was my original ambition, before I knew what I was intended to do in the world."[11] Undoubtedly, it was partly for this reason that Freud was negligent in pursuing his medical studies, spending over them three years longer than necessary.

Although entered into with a divided heart, Freud's medical work was of crucial importance to his creation of clinical psychoanalysis and to all that follows from that creation. It was not simply that, as Toynbee would put it, medical practice served as Freud's moratorium.[12] It was, rather, that psychoanalysis could only be created by a mind able to fuse together

---

[10] *Autobiography*, p. 10. In this connection, it is interesting to note that Goethe's influence on Freud was pervasive, supplying him with many of his quotations and perhaps some of his basic ideas. Cf. Philip Rieff, *Freud: The Mind of the Moralist* (Garden City, N.Y., 1961), *passim*. Goethe's influence on Freud should be compared with his similar influence on Oswald Spengler, though with vastly different results.

[11] Jones, *op. cit.*, Vol. I, p. 29; and *Origins of Psychoanalysis*, p. 143.

[12] See *A Study of History*, abridgement of Volumes I–VI, by D. C. Somervell (New York, 1947), pp. 217–230, for what Toynbee also calls "withdrawal-and-return."

the scientific approach to relatively controlled experimental data, i.e., Freud's patients, with speculative insights into such wide-ranging and diffuse subjects as philology, mythology, literature, and philosophy. In understanding dreams, for example, the "chimney sweepings" of the patient Anna O. and the insights of poets were of equal importance to Freud.[13] Thus, his genius lay in bringing forth a science that was partly based on medical therapy, out of and concerning man's humanistic strivings.

In fact, even before he turned to the development of psychoanalysis, there was an important body of pure physiological research to Freud's credit. He did work in the histological, pharmacological, and anatomical fields; wrote monographs on cerebral paralysis and on the aphasias; and barely missed being the discoverer of local anesthesia by cocaine. Of course, we cannot follow here his early work in neuropathology, or even his turning to a study of hypnosis, under the influence of Charcot and Bernheim, and then the gradual entrance into the dark woods of psychoanalytic investigation itself.[14] For our purposes, it is Freud's initial commitment to a particular scientific approach, which we can label physiological, that must concern us most.

I stress this point sharply. Freud's contribution to philosophy of history is, in one sense, the resumption of the ancient task of Hecataeus and his followers: the union of medical research and history.[15] As such, it cannot be fully understood without our grasping the medical aspect, the clinical basis of psychoanalysis, which underlies all of Freud's extrapolations to history. We cannot, for example, judge Freud's perception of the role of the Oedipus complex in man's early history without first weighing the evidence presented for its existence among

---

[13] For the case of Anna O., who coined the phrase "chimney-sweeping" to describe her "talking cure," and who was actually Breuer's patient, see *Studies in Hysteria* (with Josef Breuer) (1895).

[14] For some of the details, see Jones, *op. cit.*, Vol. I, p. 79.

[15] For the work of Hecataeus, see C. M. Bowra, *The Greek Experience* (London, 1957).

his patients. Nor can we come to a verdict about his notion of an "archaic heritage" without a similar trial.

Alas, the comprehension of clinical psychoanalysis requires at least a large chapter or book unto itself, tasks which we can hardly undertake here. Nevertheless, accepting this lacuna as temporarily unavoidable, we can at least seek out the lines of the scientific-medical theory to which Freud committed himself.[16]

The crux of his position derived from the physiological school of Helmholtz and DuBois-Reymond, mediated through the example of Freud's teacher, Brücke. In this school, physiology was conceived in the image of physics, with the latter's quantification and measureability of all phenomena as the ideal goal. Thus. ultimately, psychological phenomena were to be understood in terms of chemical and physical laws, and, for example, the theory of conservation of energy in physics was to be matched by a "law of constancy" in psychology. Hence, Freud worked out in great and tortuous detail what he called "the most fundamental attributes of the psychical mechanism (the law of constancy)," i.e., the tendency of the mental apparatus to maintain a constant tension, and he did so in such various forms as the "pleasure principle" and the "Nirvana principle."[17] He never abandoned his image of the psychical mechanism as an energy system, and constantly employed electrical metaphors as in the statement, "The expenditure of force on the part of the physician was evidently the measure of a *resistance* on the part of the patient." Indeed, at the end of his life, Freud still looked forward to the establishment of an acceptable connection between psychological and biochemical processes, and for the translation of his strange psychological terms into physiological and physical language.[18]

[16] For a useful summary of Freud's theories in clinical psychoanalysis, see Ives Hendrick, *Facts and Theories of Psychoanalysis* (New York, 1958).

[17] *Origins of Psychoanalysis*, p. 149; see especially the editor's note, p. 138.

[18] *Autobiography*, p. 53. One thinks of the comparable hopes of such

The breakthrough came when Freud, still in theory hoping for a physical explanation of psychic phenomena, accepted in practice the given data of his own and his patients' psychic life and sought for the *meaning* in it. Almost in spite of himself, and as if still afraid of his speculative impulses, Freud came to see that, at least initially, mental acts must not be treated as mere somatic processes but must be *interpreted* as meaningful. It is with a voice full of mocking self-admonition that Freud could finally point out, in his great book *The Interpretation of Dreams*, that "anything that might indicate that mental life is in any way independent of demonstrable organic changes or that its manifestations are in any way spontaneous alarms the modern psychiatrist, as though a recognition of such things would inevitably bring back the days of the Philosophy of Nature [i.e., Schelling] and of the metaphysical view of the nature of mind."[19]

It was probably his experiences with Charcot and French psychiatry that gave Freud the strength to break with the German physiological tradition, while retaining it as his own, distant ideal. Thus, in the introduction to his translation of Charcot, Freud remarked that "French clinical observation undoubtedly gains in independence in that it banishes the physiological point of view to second place."[20] With his new independence of the need to explain psychological processes solely in physiological terms, Freud could turn fully to interpreting the meaning of mental acts (while still positing a physical model behind them). In a remarkable burst of creative energy, he passed from mere hypnosis to true analysis, and thus to the meaning of such psychic phenomena as dreams, errors, jokes, and, of course, neurotic symptoms.

---

thinkers as Descartes and Locke. In their case, however the wish was for the establishment of a scientific morality.

[19] *The Interpretation of Dreams*, pp. 41, 96. It is interesting to compare the sales of Freud's epochal book—*The Interpretation of Dreams* sold 351 copies in the first six years after publication—with the sales of Spengler's *Decline* and Toynbee's *Study*.

[20] *Origins of Psychoanalysis*, p. 44.

His achievement is staggering. The science of psychoanalysis seems to have emerged full-blown like Minerva from Freud's Jove-like forehead.[21] Novel theories, concepts, and techniques, which I can only name here, abound in his work: the theory of the unconscious; the difference between manifest and latent content; the infantile root of neuroses and the sexuality of infancy; the similarity of dreams and neurotic symptoms and the link of the normal and the psychotic; the concepts of repression, censorship, wish-fulfillment; the Oedipus complex; the techniques of free association and symbol analysis; the definitions of id, ego, and super-ego; and many, many more.

3

Having once made his breakthrough, indeed, concurrent with and basic to it, Freud came to realize that the meaning of the mental acts revealed to him by his patients and by his self-analysis was intimately tied to the experiences of childhood. These, in turn, were indissolubly based on the relationship of the child to its social environment: at first and most important, the family, and then the society and culture at large. Gradually, Freud's interests turned increasingly to the latter involvement, and it is this aspect of his work which I shall treat under the heading, philosophy of history. Meaning, for Freud, had become meaning in a cultural context, and it is absurd to pre-

[21] Actually, Freud's predecessors are many, and it is largely our lack of knowledge which makes his achievement seem so spontaneous. As has been remarked about the "Dark Ages," the only thing dark about them was our knowledge of them. The fact that Freud had predecessors, of course, does not detract from the originality of his synthesis of previous work. In the first chapter of *The Interpretation of Dreams* Freud himself indicates his debt to many of his predecessors. On one aspect of previous work, see Lancelot Law Whyte, *The Unconscious Before Freud* (New York, 1960). On the question of how "scientific" psychoanalysis is, see the symposium, generally hostile (I believe misguidedly so) to Freud, *Psychoanalysis, Scientific Method, and Philosophy*, Sidney Hook (ed.) (New York, 1959).

tend, as some of his neo-Freudian critics have, that Freud ignored the social conditions of the mental acts which he sought to interpret in a scientific fashion.

Thus, after such major works in individual psychology as *The Interpretation of Dreams* (1900), *The Psychopathology of Everyday Life* (1901), *Jokes and Their Relation to the Unconscious* (1905), and *Three Essays on the Theory of Sexuality* (1905), Freud, while continuing constantly to write papers on his clinical findings, began to publish such works in group psychology as *Totem and Taboo* (1912–1913), *Group Psychology and the Analysis of the Ego* (1921), *The Future of an Illusion* (1927), *Civilization and Its Discontents* (1930), and *Moses and Monotheism* (1939), as well as important papers on such subjects as Leonardo da Vinci, War and Death, and Demoniacal Possession.

It is to the corpus of his work in group psychology that I shall direct my attention, while cautioning again that his work in individual psychology is the underpinning of all his theories in philosophy of history—the support on which he rests the major weight of his argument. At the base of this support itself is Freud's underlying commitment to nineteenth-century scientific method. With this caution, knowing how badly prepared we are, we may now attempt the descent into Freud's underground world of history.

4

At the very entrance to Freud's historical world, it is well to consider briefly the nature of his recital. The model for Freud's work in the area of culture is the "case history," but now macroscopic in its use. His approach to the origins of the group neurosis known as history is still clinical, and he writes up his reports as if he were dealing with an individual patient, only of larger dimensions. All of Freud's theories in philosophy of history are thus "grounded," to use an energy metaphor, in his observations of living subjects and in the method by which he writes up these findings.[22]

The case history itself, however, is a somewhat suspect scientific document. As Freud remarked about one of his earliest reported accounts, in the *Studies in Hysteria*, "I still find it a very strange thing that the case histories I describe read like short stories and lack, so to speak, the serious imprint of science." His opponents were equally quick to make this comment, as when Krafft-Ebing, chairman of the session of the Society of Psychiatry and Neurology in Vienna listening to the paper on "The Etiology of Hysteria" (1896), remarked dryly: "It sounds like a scientific fairy tale." For himself, Freud produced the consoling thought that "it is obviously the nature of the material itself that is responsible for this [the short story aspect] rather than my own choice."[23]

So, too, *Totem and Taboo* was labeled by one reviewer, an anthropologist, as a *Just So* story. While apropos in the sense that Freud was a great admirer of Kipling's tales, this remark once again seeks to dismiss Freud's work as largely a fairy tale.[24]

Now, in a strange way, these criticisms inadvertently point to the crucial feature of Freud's case histories; yet they miss the essential point. Freud's concern is with "fairy tales," but with their *analysis* and not with their mere *recital*. Clearly, this is not to say that Freud's analysis in a particular case is always correct; that remains for further discussion. It is to say that in external appearance his reports look suspiciously like short

[22] This way of proceeding points up Freud's differences with Jung; see further pp. 394-395. Cf. also to Toynbee's way of proceeding, pp. 359 and 369-370.

[23] *Origins of Psychoanalysis*, p. 13; and Jones, *op. cit.*, Vol. I, p. 263. Freud's case-history approach, with its union of medicine and history, helps illustrate our earlier comparison of him with Hecataeus.

[24] The story behind this is rather mixed up. As Jones tells it, Freud "quoted this joke from an English anthropologist, ascribing it to an American one, Kroeber (misprinted Kroeger), who had cited it; it actually came from R. R. Marett." (Jones, *op. cit.*, Vol. III, p. 323). See, too, Freud's *Group Psychology and the Analysis of the Ego*, translated by James Strachey (New York, 1960), p. 69.

stories or fairy tales, without thereby being such. Instead, these "short story" reports are intended to be sober, scientific case studies of cultural events.

There is another, similar ambiguity involved in Freud's use of what he called "scientific myths." On one level, these are merely hypotheses or useful fictions, heuristic devices to allow for a provisional ordering of the data. Thus, as he wrote to Albert Einstein, "Does not every science come in the end to a kind of mythology?" On another level, however, myths in their primitive form are perhaps the earliest means of scientific cognition of *actual events*, and to be taken seriously as such.[25] And on a third level, they merely represent psychic, but not historical, reality. Freud wavered among these definitions, and seemed unconscionably undisturbed about using them so loosely.

The difficulty is compounded, however, because Freud was not only *constructing* a scientific myth but presumably *analyzing* historical myths. We see the confusion illustrated in his comments in *Group Psychology and the Analysis of the Ego*. There, starting with the "scientific myth of the father of the primal horde," his own construction, he then passes immediately, as part of his hypothesis or scientific myth, to the historical development of the heroic myth. Thus, Freud supposes that after the murder of the father by the brothers grouped together, "some individual in the exigency of his longing, may have been moved to free himself from the group and take over the father's part. He who did this was the first epic poet; and the advance was achieved in his imagination. This poet disguised the truth with lies in accordance with his longing. He invented the heroic myth."[26] Methodologically, of course, Freud's *analysis* of the heroic myth must come first, and lead him next to the *construction* of his own scientific myth, which

[25] As Philip Rieff points out, Freud may have borrowed this use of myth from Frazer (Rieff, *op. cit.*, p. 224). The statement to Einstein occurs in "Why War?", *Collected Papers of Sigmund Freud*, 5 vols. (London, 1949–1950), Vol. V, p. 283.

[26] *Group Psychology*, pp. 86–87.

is then to be checked against further data of all sorts. As Freud presents his work, however, the reader is made to move the other way, and he does so with the awkward feeling that, in fact, it is the way Freud himself moved. Ambiguity, so close to Freud's heart, has here led close to incomprehensibility.

Now, however, it is time to enter into the details of Freud's historical account. We shall then see, in action, his employment of the case study and the scientific myth, and judge how useful and valid is his novel approach.

5

In a postscript, written when he was 79, to his *Autobiography*, Freud made the following revealing, although perhaps slightly misleading, statement:

My interest, after making a lifelong *détour* through the natural sciences, medicine and psychotherapy, returned to the cultural problems which had fascinated me long before, when I was a youth scarcely old enough for thinking. At the very climax of my psychoanalytic work, in 1912, I had already attempted in *Totem and Taboo* to make use of the newly discovered findings of analysis in order to investigate the origins of religion and morality. I now carried this work further in two later essays, *The Future of an Illusion* (1927), and *Civilization and Its Discontents* (1930). I perceived ever more clearly that the *events of human history*, the interactions between human nature, cultural development and the precipitates of primaeval experiences (the most prominent example of which is religion) *are no more than a reflection* of the dynamic conflicts between the ego, the id, and the super-ego, which psychoanalysis studies in the individual—are the very same processes repeated upon a wider stage [italics added].[27]

In pursuit of his cultural interests, besides the books mentioned, Freud completed at the very end of his life *Moses and Monotheism*.

Freud, himself, was especially taken with *Totem and Taboo*,

[27] *Autobiography*, pp. 148–149.

his initial production. As he wrote his friend, Ferenczi, "I am writing Totem at present with the feeling that it is my greatest, best, perhaps my last good work."[28] Comparing it to his first great work, *The Interpretation of Dreams*, Freud predicted for *Totem* the identical hostile reception accorded to the former. Obviously, then, he looked upon *Totem* as occupying the same fundamental position in respect to group psychology as his book on dreams had occupied in respect to individual psychology.

The key motif or, better, "scientific myth" for *Totem* came from Charles Darwin. "In 1912," Freud tells us, "I took up a conjecture of Darwin's to the effect that the primitive form of human society was that of a horde ruled over despotically by a powerful male. I attempted to show that the fortunes of this horde have left indestructible traces upon the history of human descent; and, especially, that the development of totemism, which comprises in itself the beginnings of religion, morality, and social organization, is concerned with the killing of the chief by violence and the transformation of the paternal horde into a community of brothers."[29] If we look at this passage closely, remembering too Freud's youthful enthusiasm for Darwin's theories, we can confidently put forward the suggestion that Freud, in *Totem*, saw himself as, first, completing Darwin's evolutionary account of the "descent" of the human species from its primal animal form, and, second, tracing the resulting "origin" of human society. We can see now that Freud was seeking to understand *in a scientific way* the genesis of man as a cultural animal, using the science of psychoanalysis as the lens by which to study his chosen species' evolution.

The immediate inspiration for Freud's work, however, seems to have been the investigations of his disciple Jung into the literature of mythology and comparative religions. Freud felt these efforts misguided (in any case he was on the verge of

---

[28] Quoted in Jones, *op. cit.,* Vol. II, p. 353.
[29] *Group Psychology,* p. 69.

a break with Jung) because they went from the interpretation of myths to explanation of clinical findings instead of the other way around.[30] Freud determined to see what could be done by applying the key of certain and sure psychoanalytical findings to the rusty lock of unknown prehistory and dimly known myth.

Dutifully, Freud read the general scholarly productions relating to his new field. He also read, with more enjoyment, the important contributions of anthropologists like Frazer (*Totemism and Exogamy*, 4 vols.) and comparative religionists like Robertson Smith (*Religion of the Semites*). Neither the dull nor the interesting books, however, fundamentally altered Freud's vision; he had derived that from Darwin and from his own work in psychoanalysis. Thus, he remarked to Ferenczi, "I am reading thick books without being really interested in them *since I already know the results; my instinct tells me that.* But they have to slither their way through all the material on the subject [italics added]."[31]

We have already had a brief synopsis of what Freud's instinct led him to. He himself repeated his "Just So" story a number of times, and gives an especially useful précis, which shows us how he used his borrowed material, in *Moses and Monotheism*. There he tells us that in *Totem* he made use of

... certain theoretical reflections of Charles Darwin, J. J. Atkinson, and especially Robertson Smith, and combined them with findings and suggestions from psychoanalytic practice. From Darwin I borrowed the hypothesis that men originally lived in small hordes; each of the hordes stood under the rule of an older male, who governed by brute force, appropriated all the females, and belaboured or killed all the young males, including his own sons. From Atkinson I received the suggestion that this patriarchal system came to an end through a rebellion of the sons, who united against the father, overpowered him, and together consumed his body. Following Robertson Smith's totem theory, I suggested that

[30] *Totem and Taboo*, translated by James Strachey (New York, 1962), p. ix. Cf. Jones, *op. cit.*, Vol. II, p. 351.
[31] Quoted in Jones, *op. cit.*, Vol. II, p. 352.

this horde, previously ruled by the father, was followed by a totemistic brother clan. In order to be able to live in peace with one another the victorious brothers renounced the women for whose sake they had killed the father, and agreed to practise exogamy. The power of the father was broken and the families were regulated by matriarchy. The ambivalence of the sons towards the father remained in force during the whole further development. Instead of the father a certain animal was declared the totem; it stood for their ancestor and protecting spirit, and no one was allowed to hurt or kill it. Once a year, however, the whole clan assembled for a feast at which the otherwise revered totem was torn to pieces and eaten. No one was permitted to abstain from this feast; it was the solemn repetition of the father-murder, in which social order, moral laws, and religion had had their beginnings.[32]

Did Freud really believe in the murder of the primal father as an actual event? First of all, when challenged, he retorted, "I am not an ethnologist, but a psychoanalyst. It was my good right to select from ethnological data what would serve me for my analytic work." Next, his thesis is watered down a bit by the admission that "the story is told in a very condensed way, as if what in reality took centuries to achieve, and during that long time was repeated innumerably, had happened only once."[33] The real qualification occurs at the end of *Totem* itself. Discussing the overvaluation of their psychic acts by primitives, Freud posits that "Accordingly the mere hostile *impulse* against the father, the mere existence of a wishful *phantasy* of killing and devouring him would have been enough to produce the moral reaction that created totemism and taboo. . . . No damage would thus be done to the causal chain stretching from the beginning to the present day, for psychical reality would be strong enough to bear the weight of these consequences." Having conceded this much, however, Freud then retreats to his original position: "Primitive men . . . are uninhibited," he concludes, "thought passes directly into action. With them it is rather the deed that is a substitute for

[32] *Moses and Monotheism*, pp. 167–168.
[33] *Ibid.*, pp. 169, 102.

the thought. And that is why, *without laying claim to any finality of judgment*, I think that in the case before us it may safely be assumed that 'in the beginning was the Deed.' [italics added]"[34]

What shall we say of Freud's great myth? First, I must note that my précis has ignored the detail with which Freud pursues the stages of "causal connection," stretching from the beginning to the present time; however, this lacuna is permissible because the question of the original "deed" is independent of the later development (which, in any case, I shall treat later on). Second, I must point out that Freud, at least in principle, is perfectly in the right, as long as he does not distort or suppress ethnological data, in wishing to employ the touchstone of psychoanalysis on the materials of anthropology. In that case, the judgment on the validity of his psychoanalytic findings must come from the clinic and not from the field and bush. Third, I must confess that my précis gives little ground for judging Freud's application of psychoanalysis to prehistory; I have not even touched on the wealth of illustrative and comparative materials (for example, the comparison of the compulsion involved in primitive taboos with the *délire de toucher* of individual psychotics, or the ambivalence centering around the totem worship with that animating everyday life), which is spread before us in *Totem*. The book must be read fully for these details.

Finally, I must further insist that alongside of Darwin's "conjecture," it is Freud's clinical concept of the Oedipus complex which constitutes the basic inspiration for his great scientific myth. Discovered in his self-analysis, confirmed in the dreams of his patients, and illustrated by Greek tragedy and the plays of Shakespeare, the Oedipal wish to eliminate the father and to possess the mother became the nucleus, not only of the neuroses, but of Freud's theories concerning history as well. Indeed, his first identification of the Oedipal wish pub-

[34] *Totem and Taboo*, pp. 159–161.

licly is in *The Interpretation of Dreams*, where he noted its
coherence with the myth that "Kronos devoured his children,
just as the wild boar devours the sow's litter; while Zeus
emasculated his father and made himself ruler in his place."[35]

Freud's problem, therefore, was to identify the role of the
Oedipus complex not only in present-day neuroses and dreams
but in the past, in the universal neurosis and nightmare, history.
He took as his fundamental assumption "The existence of a
collective mind, in which mental processes occur just as they
do in the mind of an individual."[36] He applied this view of the
basic unity of human nature to the materials supplied him by
Darwin, i.e., to man, *as an animal*, living in a primal horde, on
the edge of emergence into humanity. The result, as we have
seen, was an attempt, scientifically, to explain the role and
operation of man's psyche, his spirit, in the evolution of the
human species. Put in its simplest form, Freud was responding
to the age-old question, what separates man from other animals? His answer: the Oedipus complex.

The overwhelming result of Freud's solution to the riddle is
that sex is no longer a *natural* function, as in Darwin, but an
unnatural, psychological, and therefore *human* function. Man
is the first animal to be self-conscious about his sexual activity.
This *self-consciousness* takes the form of the Oedipus complex. It is what defines man as man, his essential attribute and
definitive break with the rest of the animal kingdom.

Now, whatever judgment we level on Freud's particular
formulation, one thing must not be lost sight of. He has placed
the psychological factor at the center of any attempt to explain man's history. He has taken Vico's external thunderclap
and tried to give it a scientific explanation as an internal
Oedipus complex, whose development he has then traced
through man's early stages. Further, he has replaced the rather

[35] See *Origins of Psychoanalysis*, pp. 30, 173 for the role of the Oedipus
complex in Freud's own life. For the allusion to the Kronos myth, see
The Interpretation of Dreams, pp. 256 ff.
[36] *Totem and Taboo*, p. 157.

shallow approach to the mind and its progress, taken, for example, by Condorcet and Comte, with a subtle and probing
approach to mental processes, now defined to embrace unconscious as well as conscious psychic states. In short, after Freud,
no history or philosophy of history worthy of its name can
afford to neglect the psychological, if not the psychoanalytic,
aspect.[37]

6

With this said, we can look at certain criticisms of his work.
One such criticism is to ask: why only the Oedipus complex as
animating the primal event? As one authority on Freud writes:
"His identification of the prototypical event with the primal
father murder excludes other possibilities that ought not to be
left unconsidered. The murder of the father is but one theme
in the myth literature extant; the fraticide motif occurs quite
as significantly as that of parricide." Thus, "the great murder
myth of the Old Testament is the killing of primal brother by
primal brother," the Cain and Abel story, while the myths
about Joseph and his brothers, Arthur and his knights, and
even the play about Hamlet and his father's *brother* point our
interest in the same direction.[38] Even though Freud would
probably respond by identifying sibling rivalry as a displacement of the more fundamental Oedipus complex, we are left
with some niggling doubts.

But chronologically, even before the Cain-Abel murder
myth in the Old Testament, there is the earlier, more genetic
myth of Paradise. Why did Freud not use this myth for his
prototypic event? Indeed, in *The Interpretation of Dreams*,
starting from a clinical observation concerning dreams of
being naked, that is, dreams of exhibiting, he pointedly re-

[37] This new requirement in history was actually prefigured in Freud's
own shift from a physiological to an "interpretative" scientific approach.
[38] Rieff, *op. cit.*, pp. 214–215.

marked: "When we look back at this unashamed period of childhood, it seems to us a Paradise; and Paradise itself is no more than a group phantasy of the childhood of the individual. That is why mankind were naked in Paradise and were without shame in one another's presence; till a moment arrived when shame and anxiety awoke, expulsion followed, and sexual life and the tasks of cultural activity began."[39] Here we have a psychic "event," incidentally closer to Vico's myth, which satisfies Freud's assumption of "a psyche of the mass in which psychic processes occur as in the psychic life of the individual," and which explains the beginning of cultural life. The same shame and guilt are involved as in the murder of the primal father, though in rather different form.

Why did Freud prefer the latter myth? Is it enough to answer that Freud *felt* the Oedipus complex as more fundamental in his own life? That his commitment to Darwin and the theory of the survival of the fittest led him irresistably to a theory of murderous conflict based on sex? That his clinical work, leading him to believe the Oedipus complex basic to all the neuroses, dictated its extrapolation to the mass psyche? I cannot answer the first two questions, they are merely hints; and the validity of the third question can only be judged in the light of present-day revisions of Freud's psychoanalytic theory —revisions which are beyond the scope of this work.[40]

Thus, accepting the sketchiness and question-raising aspect of my treatment of Freud's theory of the Oedipus complex, I must be content here not to pass final judgment on the actual details of his theory in *Totem and Taboo*, but simply to invoke admiration for his pioneering attempt at finding psychological meaning in the hidden "events" of the past. As Freud remarked about his own efforts, we glimpse "a hypothesis

---

[39] *The Interpretation of Dreams*, p. 245.
[40] An orthodox Freudian, of course, would insist, quite correctly, that all children, and certainly male children, must pass through an Oedipus complex as part of their development. See, too, the fascinating attempt by Alex Comfort, "Darwin and Freud," *Darwin and the Naked Lady* (New York, 1962), to root the Oedipus complex in biological evolution.

which may seem fantastic but which offers the advantage of establishing an unsuspected correlation between groups of phenomena that have hitherto been disconnected."[41]

7

If *Totem* appears fantastic, *Moses and Monotheism* has seemed to most scholars even more so.[42] The *Moses* book, however, is a natural development of the *Totem* hypothesis, continuing the story of man's cultural evolution from the totemic organization of society to the emergence of the monotheistic religions. Like *Totem*, it seeks to establish an "unexpected unity" and to do so by psychoanalytic hypotheses. A brilliant, exaggerated *tour de force*, filled with illuminations, it illustrates the speculative impulse, which Freud as a young man had "ruthlessly to check," springing too abruptly and detached from the empirical data. Yet, it is a serious and important book, to be read with deep interest.

The work is rooted in Freud's lifelong involvement with the legendary Moses. As Ernest Jones remarks, "There is every reason to suppose that the grand figure of Moses himself, from Freud's early Biblical studies to the last book he ever wrote, was one of tremendous significance to him. Did he represent the formidable Father-Image or did Freud identify with him? Apparently both, at different periods."[43] Thus, in 1912, the same year as he was writing *Totem and Taboo*, he began to compose an essay on the meaning of Michelangelo's Moses statue in Rome. Based on extended contemplation of the statue, for Freud had sat before it for hours, the essay "The Moses of Michelangelo" was finished in 1914. I shall single out only one point about this work. It is Freud's acute ability to *observe* details, such as that the tables in the statue were held

[41] *Totem and Taboo*, p. 141.

[42] See, for example, the critical reviews by A. L. Kroeber and Salo W. Baron, reprinted in *Psychoanalysis and History*.

[43] Jones, *op. cit.*, Vol. II, pp. 364–365.

upside down, and then to use these details in the construction of a psychoanalytic interpretation. Basing himself on this observation, Freud opposes the general view that the statue represented Moses as about to rise and chastise his disobedient followers dancing around the Golden Calf. Instead, he interprets the statue as showing Moses, suddenly aware that the sacred tables are about to fall to the ground, restraining himself with a mighty effort.

The same attention to the small detail and then the construction upon it of a psychological analysis is manifested in *Moses and Monotheism*. Written over various periods, finished under the shadow of the Nazis in 1939, broken and uneven in style, the book is nevertheless a true example of Freud's method. It starts with sharp attention to a small detail, Moses' name, and proceeds from that along its "fantastic" path.

The opening thesis of the book is that Moses was an Egyptian, not a Jew. Freud reaches this conclusion on two grounds: (1) a philological investigation of the name, Moses; and (2) an analysis of Moses' birth and exposure in terms of other "birth of the hero" myths. Freud next postulates that Moses was a follower of Amenhotep IV, the Egyptian Pharoah (c. 1375 B.C.) who changed his name to Ikhnaton and set up the worship of the one God, Aton. With the counterrevolution against Ikhnaton's monotheism by the priests of the old-style worship, Moses, according to Freud's account, seized on an unusual destiny. Rejected by his own people in Egypt, Moses "chose" the Jews (henceforth the "chosen" people of God), a barbarous, uncultured people, and, leading them out of bondage, shaped a "holy nation" out of them. Freud adds that Moses also introduced the Jews to the custom of circumcision, otherwise practised only by the Egyptians.

At this point, Freud pauses to hear the reproach "that I have built up this edifice of conjectures with too great a certainty, for which no adequate grounds are to be found in the material itself."[44] Reminding the reader that he has already himself

[44] *Moses and Monotheism*, p. 35.

stressed the hypothetical, the heuristic, character of his investigation, Freud plunges on to his second major thesis. Basing
himself on a "discovery" of the biblical scholar, Ernst Sellin,
Freud surmises that the Jews, chafing under the Mosaic laws,
murdered Moses, the father figure. This re-enactment of the
primal horde experience was as traumatic as the first experience. Forgotten and repressed through a long latency period,
the material was psychologically "remembered" by Moses' followers, the Levites, even after their merging with other Jewish
tribes, the Midianites. Without following Freud's involved account of the relations of the two segments of the Jewish race,
we come to his conclusion that, with the Israelitic prophets,
the original Mosaic religion was restored.

The unraveling of this history, Freud tells us, has been made
difficult because the texts have been transformed and distorted.
"The distortion of a text," however, he points out, "is not
unlike a murder." It leaves traces, and these we can decipher
with the magnifying glass of psychoanalysis.[45] Since the latter
tells us with certainty that "religious phenomena are to be
understood only on the model of the neurotic symptoms of
the individual, which are so familiar to us, as a return of long-
forgotten important happenings in the primeval history of the
human family," we know exactly what to look for in mankind's history. The murder of Moses, recapitulating the primal
crime, is the "long-forgotten important happening" which has
generated the obsessional neurosis that has taken form as the
Jewish religion. Totemism has been supplanted by monotheism.

It is not only the Jewish religion, however, which Freud's
inquiry seeks to comprehend. It is the Christian as well. According to Freud, it is against the background of a growing
and widespread feeling of guilt among the Jews and the inhabitants of the Mediterranean world that Paul, a Roman Jew
from Tarsus, must be understood. Paul correctly traced the
feeling of guilt back to the primal murder, which he labelled

[45] *Ibid.*, p. 52.

"original sin." A crime against God the Father, it could only be expiated through death. A son of God, Christ, made the necessary sacrifice, and took upon Himself the collective guilt.

The matter, however, according to Freud, is even more complicated than this. Freud says of Christianity, "Meant to propitiate the Father Deity, it ends by his being dethroned and set aside. The Mosaic religion had been a Father religion; Christ became a Son religion. The old God, the Father, took second place; Christ, the Son, stood in his stead, just as in those dark times every son had longed to do." Thus, though Freud does not say this overtly, the Christians managed the double feat of assuaging their guilt and yet retaining their desire to replace the Father. One evidence of this is Holy Communion, in which the believer incorporates the flesh and blood of the Redeemer, repeating thus the act of the old totem feast. The Christians also gave up the act of circumcision; and although Freud once again does not say this directly, he may well have been thinking that circumcision, as the symbolic act of castration, no longer held terrors for them.[46]

The final comparison Freud makes between the two religions is unexpected. "In certain respects," he tells us, "the new religion was a cultural regression. . . . the Christian religion did not keep to the lofty heights of spirituality to which the Jewish religion had soared. The former was no longer strictly monotheistic; it took over from the surrounding peoples numerous symbolical rites, re-established the great mother goddess, and found room for many deities of polytheism." Then, with a momentous "And yet," Freud continues, "Christianity marked a progress in the history of religion: that is to say, in regard to the return of the repressed. From now on, the Jewish religion was, so to speak, a fossil."[47] Shades of Toynbee!

As with *Totem*, only more so, the *Moses* thesis is hard either

---

[46] *Ibid.*, pp. 111, 116.
[47] See *Ibid.*, pp. 112–117.

to prove or to disprove. The events which it claims to explain are buried under the swirl of time, and there is little clear documentary evidence surviving. Some of Freud's subsidiary theories, such as the inheritance of acquired mental traits (a form of Lamarckian psychoanalysis, which we have not yet discussed), raise additional difficulties. Many of his "facts" are suspect: Moses' name may have been Egyptian, but the Jews, then as now, have frequently taken their names from the dominant culture in which they lived; the murder of Moses is dubious; and various of Freud's philological identifications are simply incorrect.[48] We can only conclude, therefore, that Freud's application of psychoanalytic insights to the traditional accounts of the origins of the Jewish and Christian religions results merely in a tenuous connection with what is, to begin with, unsatisfactory empirical data. The *Moses* book is indeed a very speculative work in the philosophy of history. What remains from Freud's work here is a chain of great "ifs," and a number of ingenious suggestions.

8

In *The Interpretation of Dreams*, Freud declares confidently that "we may expect that the analysis of dreams will lead us to a knowledge of man's archaic heritage, of what is psychically innate in him." Moving by way of the interpretation of adult patients' dreams to the childhood wishes animating them, Freud can perceive that "behind this childhood of the individual we are promised a picture of a phylogenetic childhood—*a picture of the development of the human race,* of which the individual's development is in fact an abbreviated recapitulation influenced by the chance circumstances of life [italics added]."[49] It is the effort to picture this development of the

[48] Cf. *Psychoanalysis and History*, p. 55.

[49] *The Interpretation of Dreams*, pp. 548–549. Actually, this passage was added in 1919, but it truly represents the early movement of Freud's mind from dreams to concern with the psychic phenomena of the group.

human race that led Freud to write such works as *Totem* and *Moses;* and it is why we are justified in regarding him as the last of the classical philosophers of history.

The connection between dreams and *Weltanschauungen*, or stages of thought, is sketched for us in the following statements. "Thought," Freud enunciates in *The Interpretation of Dreams*, "is after all nothing but a substitute for a hallucinatory wish. . . . Dreams, which fulfill their wishes along the short path of regression, have merely preserved for us in that respect a sample of the psychical apparatus' primary method of working. . . . What once dominated waking life, while the mind was still young and incompetent, seems now to have been banished into the night—just as the primitive weapons, the bows and arrows that have been abandoned by adult men, turn up once more in the nursery."[50] In *Totem*, Freud talks of another means of wish-fulfillment: projection. By projection, primitive man constructed his world system. "Under conditions whose nature has not yet been sufficiently established, internal perceptions of emotional and intellective processes can be projected outwards in the same way as sense perceptions; they are thus employed for building up the external world, though they should by rights remain part of the *internal* world." Thus, primitive men had developed "a picture of the external world which we, *with our intensified conscious perception*, have now to translate back into psychology [italics added]."[51]

In his "translation," Freud claims to have uncovered the following story. In "the evolution of human views of the universe . . . an animistic phase followed by a religious phase, and this in turn by a scientific one." Freud describes these phases: "At the animistic stage men ascribe omnipotence to themselves. At the religious stage they transfer it to the gods, but do not seriously abandon it themselves, for they reserve the power of influencing the gods in a variety of ways according to their

[50] *Ibid.*, p. 567.
[51] *Totem and Taboo*, p. 64. Cf. *The Future of an Illusion*, translated by W. D. Robson-Scott (Garden City, N.Y., no date), p. 25.

wishes. The scientific view of the universe no longer affords any room for human omnipotence."[52]

We can recognize quite clearly the ideas of Comte in this scheme. Although Freud does not mention the founder of positivism by name, the "successive stages of these three world systems" have a definite affinity to the schema expressed in the *Cours*. In fact, at one point Freud equates the animistic stage with the mythological. Also, he draws much of his material on animism from the anthropologist E. B. Tylor, who had come under the influence of the English Comtists; and, earlier, in *The Interpretation of Dreams*, he speaks of "the intellectual period which has now been left behind, when the human mind was dominated by philosophy and not by the exact natural sciences."[53] Therefore, while Freud may have temporarily shaken off, in his psychoanalytic work, the influence of positive science in the shape of Helmholtz and Brücke, he retained it in its full virulence in his philosophy of history.

What Freud's genius added to Comte was an analysis of the psychic development of the individual to match that of the race. "We are encouraged," Freud informs us, "to attempt a comparison between the phases in the development of men's view of the universe and the stages of an individual's libidinal development. The animistic phase would correspond to narcissism both chronologically and in its content; the religious phase would correspond to the stage of object-choice of which the characteristic is a child's attachment to his parents; while the scientific phase would have an exact counterpart in the stage at which an individual has reached maturity, has renounced the pleasure principle, adjusted himself to reality and turned to the external world for the object of his desires." Thus, ontogeny recapitulates phylogeny in this new, psychic *Bildungsroman*.[54]

[52] *Totem and Taboo*, p. 88.

[53] The *Interpretation of Dreams*, p. 63. For Tylor and the English Comtists, see Rieff, *op. cit.*, p. 209.

[54] *Totem and Taboo*, p. 90. Although Freud alternates in his view of the mind between metaphors of evolutionary growth and images of the mind as a series of layered ruins, as in the cities of antiquity (cf. *Civiliza-*

9

It is interesting to speculate briefly—scandalously so if our concern were with Freud's work as a whole—on the relationship between Freud's stages of libidinal development and his views on character types. Because his scheme changed on occasion, leading toward implied contradictions, this is a difficult topic. Nevertheless, he did clearly distinguish three stages in the libidinal development of the individual: the oral, the anal, and the genital. Each of these stages is connected with certain character traits: for example, Freud informs us, the early repression of the anal-sadistic stage results in traits of cleanliness and order; a fixation on early erotic sensation in the mouth produces generosity; and the continued interest in excrement gives rise to stubbornness.[55] In short, character results from the way in which we pass over, or become stuck in, these obstacle courses of our development.

From Freud's work of this sort other scholars have derived even more extensive and far-reaching conclusions. Thus, for example, Ernest Jones wrote an essay on "Anal-Erotic Character Traits," relating the traits of orderliness, parsimoniousness, and obstinacy to the same psychogenic factor, anal eroticism (in *Papers on Psycho-Analysis*), while social psychologists during World War II sought to analyze Japanese character

---

tion and Its Discontents, passim), his basic concept allows for the simultaneous existence of all the mental stages at once. Culture and the adaptation to reality, therefore, is a thin veneer covering the seething cauldron of the mind, and the most primitive behavior might erupt at any moment from the buried wishes of modern man. In this sense, Freud's evolutionary scheme differs from the biological, where earlier stages of development only manifest themselves in the embryo or as useless appendages; thus, man's gills do not reappear in mature life.

[55] For details, see Freud's *General Introduction to Psychoanalysis* (first delivered as lectures in 1915–17; I cite the translation by Joan Riviere |New York, 1953|), and "Character and Anal Eroticism," *Collected Papers*, (1907), Vol. II, pp. 45–50. An interesting synthesis of work in this area is Joseph J. Michaels, "Character Structure and Character Disorders," Chapter 19 of *American Handbook of Psychiatry* (New York, 1959).

structure in terms of toilet-training habits. More recently, Luther has been analysed in these terms by a number of writers, and some have gone so far as to identify Freud's anal-erotic character type with the entrepreneurs of capitalism.[56]

10

The main attention in *Totem* and *Moses* was to past stages of man's development. In *Future of an Illusion* and *Civilization and Its Discontents*, Freud speculated on the direction in which history might move. In a sense, he was studying the transition from the religious to the scientific stage of man's existence.

Freud's views on religion, as on all other subjects, fluctuate. "There are no grounds," he says, "for fearing that psycho-analysis . . . will be tempted to trace the origin of anything so complicated as religion to a single source." Yet, in effect, this is what Freud does. As he himself incautiously admits at one point, psychoanalysis "leads us to a result that reduces religion to the status of a neurosis of mankind and explains its grandiose powers in the same way as we should a neurotic obsession in our individual patients."[57]

First, as we have seen, Freud bases religion on the memory of the primal murder, and makes it take its rise from the original totemic observances and the taboos connected therewith. Now, in this second formulation, he treats religion as an illusion, defined as a belief which has wish-fulfillment as a prominent factor in its motivation, while disregarding its relations to reality.[58]

[56] See Erik H. Erikson, *Young Man Luther* (New York, 1958); Norman O. Brown, *Life Against Death* (New York, 1959), especially Part V; and Walter A. Weisskopf, *The Psychology of Economics* (Chicago, 1955).

[57] *Totem and Taboo*, p. 100; and *Moses and Monotheism*, p. 68.

[58] *The Future of an Illusion*, p. 54. For example, according to Freud, Aristotle's belief that vermin are evolved out of dung is an error, while Columbus' belief that he had discovered a new sea-route to India is an illusion.

The line between illusion and what can be called delusion—
an idea inaccessible to the arguments of reality—is thin, and
Freud sometimes wobbles across it. Thus, in *The Future of an
Illusion* he points out that "in the delusion we emphasize as
essential the conflict with reality; the illusion need not be necessarily false, that is to say, unrealizable or incompatible with
reality."[59] For example, depending on one's personal attitude,
the belief in the coming of a Messiah who will inaugurate a
golden age may be adjudged an illusion or a delusion. Initially,
Freud seems generally to have thought of religion as an illusion, as in the Feuerbachian tradition. By the time of *Civilization and Its Discontents* he has become more severe. Remarking that the paranoiac substitutes a wish-fulfillment for some
aspect of the world which is unbearable to him and carries this
delusion through into reality, Freud comments that "when a
large number of people make this attempt together and try to
obtain assurances of happiness and protection from suffering
by a delusional transformation of reality, it acquires special
significance. The religions of humanity, too, must be classified
as mass-delusions of this kind."[60]

Memory trace, obsessional act, illusion, or delusion: Freud
views religion as a childish attempt by man to deal with reality
(to propitiate God, the father figure). It is time he tells us, to
put away childish things, to grow up, and to face reality,
individually and as a species. Religion, he declares, is "the obsessional neurosis of humanity. It, like the child's, originated in
the Oedipus complex, the relation to the father. According to
this conception one might prophesy that the abandoning of
religion must take place with the *fateful inexorability of a
process of growth* [italics added], and that we are just now
in the middle of this phase of development."[61]

While admitting that adhesion to the universal neurosis may

[59] *Ibid.*, p. 53.
[60] *Civilization and Its Discontents*, translated by Joan Riviere (Chicago,
no date), p. 36. Cf. Jones, *op. cit.*, Vol. II, p. 339, for similarities and differences between religious and obessional acts.
[61] *The Future of an Illusion*, pp. 77–78.

protect the true believer from acquiring personal neuroses, Freud bases his dismissal of religion on three facts: (1) it is an undignified abasement of man's spirit: "At such cost—by the forcible imposition of mental infantilism and inducing a mass-delusion—religion succeeds in saving many people from individual nueroses;" (2) it obscures the "purely human origin of all cultural laws" and by shrouding the latter in "pretensions to sanctity" hampers the effort rationally to change and improve them; and (3) it is not really an effective assuagement of guilt: "If it (religion) had succeeded in making happy the greater part of mankind, in consoling them, in reconciling them to life, and in making them into supporters of civilization, then no one would dream of striving to alter existing conditions. But instead of this what do we see? We see that an appallingly large number of men are discontented with civilization and unhappy in it." There is only one solution. Religion must be supplanted by science, and mankind must move on to maturity. "The time has probably come," Freud announces, "to replace the consequences of repression by the results of rational mental effort, as in the analytic treatment of neurotics."[62]

11

Alas, however, man's problem is more complicated than it seems from Freud's optimistic espousal, at least initially, of universal psychoanalysis. Freud, himself, indicates the dimensions of the problem. In its briefest form, his argument is as follows. Civilization is necessarily based on coercion and instinctual renunciation; indeed, we can regard "instinctual repression as a measure of the level of civilization that has been reached." Thus, the taboo is basic to the origins of society, for the sexual desires banned by the taboo are sublimated in work;

---

[62] Jones, *op. cit.*, Vol. III, p. 359; and *The Future of an Illusion*, pp. 74, 66, 79.

this is Freud's explanation of the economic aspect of civilization.[63]

Next, the same primal murder which led to the institution of totem and taboo triggers the evolution of culture by its arousal of guilt feelings which are internalized in the individual in the form of the super-ego.[64] The feelings of the sons who were leagued against the father were—and are—ambivalent, i.e., made up of coexisting opposed feelings, particularly love and hate. Having loved as well as hated the father, they feel guilty about his murder. In almost Kantian fashion, Freud extrapolates from this initial ambivalence to the successive stages of growth of human society: love leads to the formation of families, binding them together, while its counterpart of hate is turned outward toward other families; then, love again leads to larger family groupings, communities, versus other communities; and so forth.

Summing up, Freud declares that "Since culture obeys an inner erotic impulse which bids it bind mankind into a closely knit mass, it can achieve this aim only by means of its vigilance in fomenting an ever-increasing sense of guilt. That which began in relation to the father ends in relation to the community. If civilization is an inevitable course of development from the group of the family to the group of humanity as a whole, then an intensification of the sense of guilt—resulting from the innate conflict of ambivalence, from the eternal struggle between the love and death trends—will be inextricably bound up with it, until perhaps the sense of guilt may swell to a magnitude that individuals can hardly support."[65]

In the face of this gloomy picture, Freud remains stoical. Though man may seek happiness, he reminds us, human happiness is not the purpose of the universe. Life is an eternal balance of the pleasure-pain principle—the law of constancy—

---

[63] *Totem and Taboo*, p. 97. Cf. *Civilization and Its Discontents*, p. 68, for Freud's comments on Eros and Ananke (Necessity) as the parents of human culture.

[64] *Civilization and Its Discontents*, p. 105.

[65] *Ibid.*, p. 122.

and the destiny of the individual is not perfectibility. Nor is the direction of history leading man to utopia. Instead, man's cultural existence, his history, is an eternal dialectical struggle between the forces of love and hate in which there can be no total victory, or surrender.

There can, however, be progress. "The voice of the intellect" grows louder, and "in the long run nothing can withstand reason and experience."[66] Religious illusion will give way to scientific analysis, and man can consciously and rationally change his sexual mores so as at least to make endurable the burden of guilt. Freud even looked forward, for psychoanalytic reasons, to the elimination of war.[67] Finally, the creation of the science of psychoanalysis is itself proof of man's growing rationalism.

Yet, progress for Freud is only a relative term; what he is really concerned with is the Darwinian theory of evolution extrapolated to the development of man as a cultural-historical animal. Resolutely, Freud declares that "the meaning of the evolution of culture is no longer a riddle to us. It must present to us the struggle between Eros and Death, between the instincts of life and the instincts of destruction, as it works itself out in the human species. This struggle is what all life essentially consists of and so the evolution of civilization may be simply described as the struggle of the human species for existence."[68] Starting with the riddle of the Sphinx—really Oedipus' curiosity as to the meaning of birth—Freud has courageously ended with the riddle of death.

---

[66] *The Future of an Illusion*, pp. 97–98.

[67] See Freud's "Thoughts for the Times on War and Death," *The Complete Psychological Works of Sigmund Freud, Standard Edition*, James Strachey and others (eds.) (London, 1953–), XIV; and Jones, *op. cit.*, Vol. III, p. 346.

[68] *Civilization and Its Discontents*, p. 103.

12

History is diagnosed as a neurosis. The prognosis is for continued dialectical tension. But who are the subjects, the patients so to speak, of history? Freud's answer is the classic one, given ever since the emergence of Greek tragedy: the hero and the crowd. There is little or no place in Freud's imagination for intermediate actors, for example, elites or classes, and he wastes no time in dealing with them. Instead, he concentrates on the leader and the led, on the individual and the opposition.

In his emphasis on the psychological factor, Freud stakes out an implicitly anti-Marxist position. "How impossible it is to deny the personal influence of individual great men on the history of the world," he declares, "what profanation of the grandiose multiformity of human life we commit if we recognize as sole motives those springing from material needs."[69] No one can deny the power of religious ideas, he points out, and, as we have seen, these spring largely from psychic rather than material causes.

Indeed, the "religious" hero is Freud's prototypic great man, and his power is rooted in the primal murder. The hero, in fact, is defined as "a man who stands up manfully against his father and in the end victoriously overcomes him."[70] Having overcome the father—authority—the rebel hero then replaces him, and rules in his turn.

The crowd, or masses, whom the hero rules, follow him, just as before they followed the earlier "father" because, by definition, "the great majority of people have a strong need for authority, which they can admire, to which they can submit, and which dominates and sometimes even ill-treats them." Uncreative, mere putty in the hands of the great man, the masses

---

[69] *Moses and Monotheism*, p. 65.

[70] *Ibid.*, p. 9. Psychologically, then, are we all heroes if we overcome the Oedipus complex and grow up to be mature adults? Alas, Freud does not say this.

are "chosen" by him and shaped into his creature; as Freud puts it in one of his more extravagant moods, "it was one man, the man Moses, who created the Jews."[71]

Freud pursues the symbiotic relationship of the leader and the led further. The source of the leader's strength is that he, like the father of the primal horde, is "free." Commenting that the will of the leader of the primal horde needed no reinforcement from others, Freud adds that "Consistency leads us to assume that his ego had few libidinal ties; he loved no one but himself, or other people only in so far as they served his needs. To objects his ego gave away no more than was barely necessary." Freud's conclusion is most interesting: "He, at the very beginning of the history of mankind, was the 'superman' whom Nietzsche only expected from the future."[72]

The masses, on the other hand, are linked to one another and to the leader by libidinal ties. Rejecting a stress on material self-interest, Freud, as we have seen, views history as a progressive series of ever-widening human circles, connected by love. As for the leader-led relationship, Freud reminds us of the ambivalent feelings held by the sons toward the primal father. "It is the longing for the father that lives in each of us from his childhood days, for the same father whom the hero of legend boasts of having overcome. . . . He (the father-leader) must be admired, he may be trusted, but one cannot help also being afraid of him."[73] Thus, love and hate are inseparably mixed in the psyche of the masses.

Freud's leader, the great man, is obviously derived, although by a good deal of extrapolation, from clinical evidence concerning the Oedipus complex. Whence comes Freud's derogatory view of the masses? The answer is, in part, from the spirit of his times. The mob, which manifested itself so dramatically at the time of the French Revolution, still haunted the

---

[71] *Moses and Monotheism*, p. 136.

[72] *Group Psychology*, p. 71. Cf. the story of Lenin's objection to the playing of Beethoven's "Appassionata" sonata in his presence because it made him want to stroke the heads of young children tenderly instead of rigorously forcing through a revolution.

[73] *Ibid.*, pp. 31, 43; and *Moses and Monotheism*, p. 140.

European mind in the late nineteenth and early twentieth century. Glorified by Marx as the proletarian masses, these same agglomerations were looked upon with other eyes by conservatives. To such students of the phenomenon, like Gustave Le Bon, who powerfully influenced Freud, they were "le canaille," or scum. Thus, when in Paris as a young man, Freud's imagination went back to the revolutionary mob. "The town and the people are uncanny," he wrote, "They seem to be of another species from us. I believe they are all possessed of a thousand demons. . . . I hear them screaming 'A la lanterne' or 'A bas dieser und jener.' They are the people of psychical epidemics, of historical mass convulsions."[74] Was Freud also, perhaps, instinctively foreseeing the "mass convulsions" against the Jews by the Nazi mobs?

The second source of Freud's depreciation of the masses is, I believe, his own need to be in the opposition. The group, Freud contended, has never thirsted after truth; it demands illusions. It is like the subject of a hypnotist, without a will or mind of its own, slavishly following suggestions. It is one with the primitive mind, and opposes the movement to the scientific stage of thought. While Freud was aware that a momentary crowd was different from a continuing group (for example, under the latter heading, he discussed the Church and the Army) he generally talked as if almost exactly the same psychic processes were active in both; thus *all* groups are made up merely of worshippers and followers of illusions. In opposition to such groups, Freud set individuals like himself, unafraid to seek and to make known new truths and thus to destroy old illusions.[75]

[74] Cf. Rieff, *op. cit.*, pp. 250ff; and see Jones, *op. cit.*, Vol. I, p. 184.
[75] Cf. Thomas Mann's short story, "Mario the Magician" (conveniently found in the collection, *Death in Venice*), and see Jones, *op. cit.*, Vol. I, pp. 190–191, for a significant description of the differences between an individual and the "mob." Did Freud, in his imagination identifying himself with Moses, expect the same fate as the founder of the Jewish people? Or, as Bakan, *op. cit.*, p. 164, suggests, was it Freud, rather than the Jews, who fantasied the murder of Moses?

13

Yet, with all his disparagement of the "horde animal," Freud reserves a most important task for the masses. They are the bearers of tradition. True, the tradition was started by the leader. As Freud says, "The super-ego of any given epoch of civilization originates in the same way as that of an individual; it is based on the impression left behind them by great leading personalities, men of outstanding force of mind, or men in whom some one human tendency has developed in unusual strength and purity."[76] But without the masses to carry them on, the cultural ideals set forth by the leader would wither and disappear. Even as early as 1883, Freud had glimpsed this double truth for himself. During a performance of *Carmen* the thought came to him that "the mob give vent to their impulses, and we deprive ourselves. We do so in order to maintain our integrity. We economize with our health, our capacity for enjoyment, our forces: we save up for something, not knowing ourselves for what . . . there is a psychology of the common man which is somewhat different from ours. Such people also have more feeling of community than we do: it is only they who are alive to the way in which one life is the continuation of the next, whereas for each of us the world vanishes with his death."[77]

In this connection, the question of how the mass of common men transmit the tradition, what Freud sometimes calls mankind's "archaic heritage," arises. Freud's answer, an uncompromising affirmation of the Lamarckian theory of the inheritance of acquired characteristics, has shocked all his subsequent critics.[78] According to Freud, tradition consists not only of

[76] *Civilization and Its Discontents*, p. 136.

[77] Jones, *op. cit.*, Vol. I, pp. 190–191.

[78] It is interesting to note that Freud apparently saw no problem in accepting both Darwin and Lamarck; of course, his way was made easier in this respect because of the large chunks of Lamarckian doctrine in Darwin. As for Lamarckism, in general its influence on nineteenth-century thinkers (for example, Nietzsche was also a Lamarckian) is one of the great neglected topics of intellectual history.

what is directly communicated, for example, by education, but of memory traces of what our forefathers experienced. "When I speak of an old tradition still alive in a people," Freud announces, "of the formation of a national character, it is such an inherited tradition, and not one carried on by word of mouth, that I have in mind." Nodding to "the present attitude of biological science, which rejects the idea of acquired qualities being transmitted to descendants," Freud placidly continues with his own conviction. "I admit, in all modesty, that in spite of this I cannot picture biological development proceeding without taking this factor into account."[79]

Freud's "proof" derives from two factors: (1) the "remnants of memory evoked by analytic work, which call for a derivation from phylogenesis," and (2) "a tradition based on oral communication could not produce the obsessive character which appertains to religious phenomena." His conclusion is that "If things are different, then we are unable to advance one step further on our way, either in psychoanalysis or in mass psychology. It is bold, but inevitable."[80]

In the face of this drastic, and perhaps arrogant, statement, what are we to say? I suggest two reflections. The first concerns the Lamarckian hypothesis itself. While most reputable scientific thought today dismisses it, there is a growing body of opinion which holds that evolution is more complicated than Darwin's theory of natural selection allows for, and that there may be something worth pursuing in the Lamarckian approach. Only expert knowledge can prevail here; for the moment, our one caution must be against condemning the Lamarckian thesis out-of-hand. In any case, in Freud's formulation written to his friend, Abraham, the thesis runs as follows: "Our intention is to base Lamarck's ideas completely on our own theories and to show that his concept of 'need,' which creates and modifies organs, is nothing else than the power unconscious ideas have over the body of which we see the

[79] *Moses and Monotheism*, pp. 127–128.
[80] *Ibid.*, pp. 128–130.

remains in hysteria—in short, the 'omnipotence of thoughts.' Fitness would then be really explained psychoanalytically; it would be the completion of psychoanalysis. Two great principles of change (of progress) would emerge: one through adaptation of one's own body, the later one through alteration of the outer world (autoplastic and heteroplastic)." Jones' comment on this is revealing. "In other words, Freud equated Lamarck's 'need' on an animal's part with Schopenhauer's will to power, the psychoanalytical omnipotence of thought."[81]

The second reflection is that Freud, violating his usual precept, has explained far too many effects with one simple cause. While, as Jones points out, a strong emotional experience can be incorporated in the individual's personality in such a fashion as to alter it permanently, why assume that this will *biologically* affect the offspring of that person? Can we not more easily account for tradition by the hypothesis, foreshadowed by Freud himself, that the great man, forged in the fires of a strong emotional experience, sets up ideals and institutions which then shape a whole people? Even in the small model of society, the family, a father's *example* is frequently enough to mold a child; there is no need to evoke the magic genes as explanation. Freud himself, from the hard flint of his psychoanalytic theories, struck out the early sparks of a theory of Identification, as well as mentioning *en passant* that ideas and ideologies—as he puts it, "an abstraction" or "a common tendency, a wish in which a number of people can have a share"—can take the place of the leader. And it is these suggestions, rather than his Lamarckian hypothesis, which have been heuristic and have inspired further work.[82]

[81] Jones, *op. cit.*, Vol. III, pp. 312–313. Cf. K. R. Popper's provocative statements in "Evolution and the Tree of Knowledge," Herbert Spencer Lecture, 30 October, 1961, Oxford University, or Erwin Schrödinger's views on simulated Lamarckism in *Mind and Matter* (Cambridge, England, 1958).

[82] Jones, *op. cit.*, Vol. III, p. 313; *Group Psychology*, pp. 40, 46–53. Erikson, *Young Man Luther*, illustrates the sort of imaginative development of these ideas which can take place. Comfort, *op. cit.*, p. 31, offers an interesting theory based on biological evolution as an alternative to Freud's explanation of castration fears in terms of racial memory.

14

I should like to conclude this discussion of Freud's views on the actors in history by re-emphasizing that his drama of the Hero and the Crowd, while carrying with it the poetic truth of catharsis, is too simple and dualistic a picture of historical reality. Freud's Moses and his Jewish followers are figures in a great Passion Play, not in history as it "actually happened" with all its complications. Initially, then, Freud would seem to have failed in persuading us to believe in his new actors in history.

Yet, from the ashes of this failure, new figures and subjects in history have arisen, which do bring conviction, and which cause us to look at the *dramatis personae* of the human past with fresh insight. Put very simply, the new actor, or subject, in history is Freudian man. Though very slowly, the conviction is gaining upon us that the figures who strut and fret for a moment about the stage of history are, like us, the figures revealed in clinical analysis. If, to this new unity of mankind, we are able to add a study of the changing conditions and circumstances of culture—rather than of genes—as they shape the constants of individual desires, we are on our way to an original and more meaningful understanding of the human beings who create, and are created by, history.

15

Implicit, if not explicit, in Freud's theories is his view that history itself, like psychoanalysis, is an attempt at a conscious scientific understanding of man. Thus, in *Totem*, he drops the interesting hint that the absence of historical consciousness is a sign of deep suppression. "The dread of uttering a dead person's name," Freud suggests, "extends, indeed, to an avoidance of the mention of anything in which the dead man played a part; and an important consequence of this process of suppression is that these peoples possess no tradition and no historical memory, so that any research into their early history is faced by the greatest difficulties." So, too, in *Moses* Freud remarks about Jewish "repression" concerning the Mosaic events, "A long time was to elapse, however, before historians came to develop an ideal of objective truth. At first they shaped their accounts according to their needs and tendencies of the moment, with an easy conscience, as if they had not yet understood what falsification signified."[83]

With this in mind, Freud applies to historical myths, the "day-dreams" of collective man, the same naturalistic approach as he does to the interpretation of dreams. He denies the supernatural origin of both dreams and myths, and seeks to pierce, by analysis, the screens behind which the real historical meaning lurks.[84] To do this, he uses the same psychoanalytic insights and theories which he stumbled upon in his clinical work. Indeed, he specifically compares his realization that the stories of childhood seduction told him by his patients are fantasies with the similar discovery that early so-called historical accounts are mere myth productions. "It will be seen then," Freud comments, "that my mistake was of the same kind as would be made by someone who believed that the legendary story of the early kings of Rome (as told by Livy) was historical truth instead of what it is in fact—a reaction against the memory of times and circumstances that were insignificant and occasionally, perhaps, inglorious."[85] Armed with his new analogical insight, Freud further realizes, for example, that the recorded episodes of so-called demonic possession in the Middle Ages correspond exactly to the details of spontaneous hysteria which he has observed in his patients. He also remarks that the later transformation of the previously ambivalent devil figure into a purely evil demon is connected

[83] *Totem and Taboo*, pp. 55–56; and *Moses and Monotheism*, p. 85.
[84] See *The Interpretation of Dreams*, p. 4; and *Totem and Taboo*, p. 97.
[85] *Autobiography*, p. 66.

with the increased repression associated with the Reformation and with the wave of guilt and fear brought in its train by the syphilitic infection then raging through Europe.[86]

Moreover, Freud recognizes that the distortion of historical reality embodied in myths is not merely a thing of the past. The tendency to suppress unpleasant memories is still with us. Thus, remarking on the French reaction to defeat in 1870, Freud says, "The 'grande nation' cannot face the idea that it can be defeated in war. *Ergo*, it was *not* defeated; the victory does not count. It provides an example of mass paranoia and invents the delusion of betrayal." Well could he have repeated this observation, but about Germany, in 1918. So, too, his comment in *Moses* about biblical sources could be applied to more contemporary sources: "If we find reasons for recognizing the distortions produced by them [repressed feelings], then we shall be able to bring to light more of the true course of events."[87]

Freud's own major contribution to historical method, in the attempt to bring to light the true course of events, is probably his injunction to observe details, even the most insignificant. He himself sets the example. In his clinical work, he practices a new version of Vico's total acceptance of the given, and insists on the *relevancy* and *meaning* of every statement and every piece of data. There are no accidents for Freud, no unconnected or undetermined bits of phenomena. Maintaining that no occurrence was so small or insignificant as to fail to come within the causal sequence of things, he announces in good positivist fashion that "Anyone thus breaking away from the determination of natural phenomena at any single point, has thrown over the whole scientific outlook on the world (*Weltanschauung*)."[88]

Stretched to its utmost, and applied to history, Freud's view

---

[86] *Origins of Psychoanalysis*, pp. 190–192; and Jones, *op. cit.*, Vol. III, p. 353.

[87] *Origins of Psychoanalysis*, p. 115; and *Moses and Monotheism*, p. 50.

[88] Cf. p. 45 of this book; and *General Introduction to Psychoanalysis*, p. 32.

opens up the startling prospect of a history in which, properly speaking, there are no unintended consequences. Man's wishes, unconscious as well as conscious, make up the motor force of history. What we call "accidents" are merely the hitherto unexplained expressions of his universal neurosis, awaiting a new psychoanalytic, that is, historical, interpretation.

Of course, my extrapolation of Freud's theories in such a manner is highly speculative. More germane to historical practice is Freud's own insistence that, like dreams, history, the expression of the psychic needs of men brought into conjunction with external conditions, can be interpreted. As a human product, it has meaning. By paying attention to the small details, by refusing to ignore inconvenient and unpleasant facts, we can slowly come to understand the human purpose which runs through the events of the past. For the moment, we stand only on the shores of the vast ocean of human time, trying to perceive its depth and extent through the small looking glass of individual psychoanalytic method.[89]

16

It is too early to attempt a final assessment of Freud's work in history, and of its impact on historical study. Only a few tentative statements can be made. The first is that Freud concerned himself almost wholly with the distant past. In love with antiquity, enamored of ruins, and collector of Egyptian figurines, Freud admitted that "my predilection for the prehistoric in all its human forms remains the same." His apparent accentuation of the past was confirmed for him in his daily experience with patients. As he remarked in *The Interpretation of Dreams*, "Dreams and neuroses seem to have preserved more mental antiquities than we could have imagined possible." On this basis, Freud concluded, "psycho-analysis may

[89] Cf. Donald B. Meyer's review of Erikson's *Young Man Luther*, in *History and Theory*, I, III (1961), 291–297.

claim a high place among the sciences which are concerned with the reconstruction of the earliest and most obscure periods of the beginnings of the human race."[90]

Like Orpheus, an earlier visitor to the underworld of man's desires, Freud could not refrain from gazing backwards. As a result, his vision ran the danger of becoming frozen to the past. There he saw a first cause, the primal event, which not only gave rise to social groupings and to morality but *determined* all subsequent events. It is a rigid scheme, in which man's nature is fixed for all time. Looked at in this way, Freud's philosophy of history is unhistorical; it denies the possibility of fundamental or important change in man or society. "As it was in the past, so shall it be in the future" could well be Freud's chant.[91]

This aspect of Freud, however, brings in its train a significant commitment, and leads to our second observation. Unlike Enlightenment thinkers, with whom he shared the belief in a fixed human nature, Freud did not see the past as a burden which could merely be thrown off or escaped from. There is no utopia, to take the place of Paradise at the other side of time, in Freud's scheme. The past is an incubus which must always be lived with and understood.[92]

It is this latter commitment which, paradoxically, turns Freud's relatively static view of histroy into a vision of progress of sorts. Man can, and does, rise to a higher level of consciousness about himself. In this new version of Hegel's increased self-consciousness, Freud forces us to become aware that thought operates on an *un*conscious as well as conscious level. He does not glorify irrationalism, but rather shows us that there is reason in what seems like unreason. Our history is not determined for us by an external "cunning of Reason," but

---

[90] *Origins of Psychoanalysis*, p. 278; and *The Interpretation of Dreams*, p. 549.

[91] Cf. Philip Rieff, "The Meaning of History and Religion in Freud's Thought," *The Journal of Religion*, XXXI, 2 (April, 1951), 114–131.

[92] Some neo-Freudians, like Brown, *op. cit.*, and Herbert Marcuse, *Eros and Civilization* (Boston, 1955), take a different view.

by our own "rational" unconscious desires. Thus, by means of Freud's brilliant insights, history is turned into the story of our gradual development, or evolution, toward scientific consciousness—and thus control—of ourselves and our environment, social and physical.

As we can see from the above, Freud's theories are almost always paradoxical and ambiguous, and often contradictory. Many of the specific explanations of various historical events or data which he advances are too pat, too devious, and too tenuous. Yet, at the end, we come away from reading him with the feeling that we have been given a revelation, a glimpse, of things previously sacred and veiled from our eyes. This, I believe, is the ultimate impact on us of Freud's *speculative* philosophy of history.

17

Lastly, however, there is a side other than the speculative to Freud's work which we must consider. This is the method, rather than the specific vision of history, which he bequeathed to his followers. That method is, of course, the psychoanalytic method: a naturalistic and scientific way of approaching the study of man and mankind (for example, unlike Toynbee, who uses unexamined myths as a key to real history, Freud examines and analyses the myths themselves in order to understand their role *in* history). Though Freud concentrates, as we have seen, mainly on prehistory, the method he uses is equally applicable to examining man's more recent past.[93]

In its simplest form, Freud's method embodies the following fundamental elements: close attention to *details*, and then, on the basis on these *observed details*, the setting forth of *hypotheses*. I have already discussed Freud's emphasis on acceptance of and attention to the "given." Not content, however, merely

[93] In this connection, I have already mentioned *Psychoanalysis and History* as offering some examples.

to record and classify the "facts," Freud insists on the need for theories. Hypotheses, he tells us, are always justified if they "bring coherence and understanding into more and more new regions." They are tools, or fictions, to facilitate the handling of material. When no longer useful, they may be discarded for others. "We must always be prepared," Freud warns, "to drop our conceptual scaffolding if we feel that we are in a position to replace it by something that approximates more closely to the unknown reality."[94]

The absolutely essential element in Freud's method, however, is *analysis*. He strenuously opposes the easy leap involved in intuitive synthesis, the method so facilely used, for example, by Spengler and Toynbee, and he scorns the holistic approach. Though acknowledging the peculiar gift involved in the "direct understanding" of materials, Freud comments that "the existence of such a gift cannot be counted upon generally, its effectiveness is exempt from all criticism and consequently its findings have no claim to credibility." Instead, returning to Descartes' analysis into parts as the method of achieving certainty, but without the Frenchman's rage for complete deductive rationality, Freud states his credo: "For my part I have never been concerned with any comprehensive synthesis, but always with certainty alone. This deserves that everything else be sacrificed to it."[95]

In sum, having elaborated a speculative philosophy of history in the grand, classical manner, Freud also left behind him a major contribution to the critical side of philosophy of history. He demanded of the historian a hard, earnest attention to detail, although in terms always of relevance and meaning. The lens by which to look at the detail is the psychoanalytic method. The result, at its best, is the sort of certainty involved

---

[94] *Group Psychology*, p. 69; and *The Interpretation of Dreams*, p. 612. Cf. *General Introduction to Psychoanalysis*, p. 306. Clearly, on the basis of his own remarks, Freud would have welcomed a scientific approach to his own work.

[95] *The Interpretation of Dreams*, p. 350; and Jones, *op. cit.*, Vol. II, p. 418.

in the modern scientific method itself: tentative, heuristic, and creative.[96] Only in this way, Freud seems to suggest, shall we come to know the reality and meaning of the historical world: a human reality with a human meaning.

[96] For a view of modern science in these terms, see Thomas S. Kuhn, *The Structure of Scientific Revolutions* (Chicago, 1962).

XII

Conclusion

AFTER the richness of the great theories with which we have been dealing, an attempt to summarize or to draw conclusions must be something of a poor enterprise. This is so because it is not the particular opinions, findings, or even hypotheses of our speculative thinkers which must absorb our major interest, but rather the analyses and reasonings by which they arrived at them. It is, in short, not the momentary rightness or wrongness of a theory which contributes most to scientific knowledge, but the heuristic elements of the process of thought underlying the theory itself. And this last emerges only from a detailed, critical analysis of the thinker's entire contribution.

Thus, the summaries now offered are like Condorcet's "hypothetical history." Or, to use another image, the track we are here cutting through the tangled and complicated theories of the great speculators on history serves merely to carry the traffic of a few oversimplified ideas; it gives little indication of the extensive country which lies so abundantly about. With this caution, however, we shall try to map some of the paths of thought that have been crisscrossing and running through the various speculative theories that we have been considering. Taken in the large, these can be identified under four major headings: (1) the epistemological question: how do we know. Intimately connected with this is the problem of the relationship of empiricism and rationalism; (2) the problem of methodology; (3) the problem of periodizing and schematizing the data of the past: and (4) what, for want of a better phrase, I shall call the condition of the modern historical consciousness. In fact, of course, these four subjects are interconnected.

1

The first path we enter upon is a brambly one. Indeed, stated in the abstract, many of the statements concerning the epistemological problem and the rational-empirical relationship may simply bore us, unless we are professional philosophers. In themselves, such statements are generally mere prolegomenas to the large speculative theories which follow upon them. Moreover, some of the views on epistemology are often promulgated separately from or confusedly mixed with notions about rationalism and empiricism as *procedural methods*. It is only the importance of the subject, therefore, which must sustain our spirits as we stumble through what will often seem like a wasteland.

It was Descartes who strikingly posed the rational-empirical dilemma at the beginning of the modern period. He sharply dissected and bisected the mind from the body, and yet gave the mind a way of knowing a world made up of extended bodies. Advising us to distrust the senses, to doubt all our received notions, he endowed the mind with the power to construct, *ab initio*, the self, God, and the world created by God along the paths thought out by the self. For Descartes the ideal path by which mind thought rationally was geometry. This, then, became the path by which the universe had also been thought out and constructed. And, because geometry and consequently the universe were constructions of the mind, conclusions based on them were true and certain. Thus, there was little place in Descartes' universe of thought for the, as he saw it, unrationalized, unconstructed, and hence untrue and uncertain empirical data we call historical.

Descartes' challenge invoked two major responses. The first

brought mind down to earth, and sought to root its ideas in sense impressions. On this view, thought comes after experience; it does not construct the latter. The second response was to spread the dominion of mind over the historical as well as physical world, and, somehow, to link thought with empirical data that, at least at first blush, *seemed* to exist independently of mind. Let us take the empirical path first.

It was the empirical-minded philosophers, like Hobbes, Locke, and Hume, who first rescued history on a significant theoretical level from Descartes' withering doubt. They did it by taking Descartes' division of mind and body, and transmuting it into a division between relations of ideas and matters of fact (to use Hume's terminology). In effect, this was a division between mathematics, where the relations were a priori, that is, matters of definition, and physics, where the relations were based on experience. As Locke phrased it, "Knowledge of bodies is to be improved only by experience." The extraordinary conclusion that flowed from this was that physics was a matter only of *probable* knowledge, and thus of "judgment and opinion, not knowledge and certainty." Nevertheless, "experimental philosophy" supplied the only reliable path by which man might proceed. It was the only form of knowledge which humanity, limited in its capacities, could obtain to meet the exigencies of actual life.

History was of the same nature as physics. It, too, was based on experience, and was a matter of the highest probability, rather than of certainty. Nevertheless, vindicated in its claim to be a respectable though uncertain form of knowledge by its sheltering relationship to Newtonian physics, history still faced the excruciating question: how does one determine the most probable knowledge? Thus, by the eighteenth century the problem had shifted for the empiricist thinkers from "Is history an acceptable form of knowledge?" to "How does one secure acceptable knowledge in this legitimate, though only probable, area?"

Voltaire gave an answer that essentially went back to Carte-

sian attitudes, but with a heavy infusion of Lockean empiricism. Subject the authorities of the past to the razor's edge of
reason and experience, he advised. Then we shall see how little
in their stories can be accounted as probable. In fact, we shall
discover that history's main lesson is that we need to discard
the incubus of the past. Reason, or, in other words, eighteenth-
century enlightened thought, and not tradition legitimates
man's ideas and institutions. Thus, implicitly, what Voltaire
did was to break the cause and effect relationship between the
past (i.e., history) and the present, and, like Locke, to offer
humanity a *tabula rasa*. Voltaire's particular version of history,
cultural history, allowed him to implement this view without
too much difficulty.

In essence, Voltaire had bypassed the problem of relating
the rational to the empirical approach. Condorcet confronted
it boldly. The crux of experiential knowledge was cause and
effect relationships. The latter were based on repeated sense
impressions. When these were sufficient in number, one had
highly probable, if not deterministic, knowledge. Easily found
in physics, could such knowledge also be discovered in history? Yes, Condorcet answered, for all events leading from the
past to the present are linked by an "uninterrupted chain." By
observing the chain of events, the historian could "reveal the
order of this change and the influence that each moment exerts
upon the subsequent moment." Moreover, Condorcet under-
took, by inductive reasoning, to derive useful truths, i.e., scientific generalizations, from the empirically established regularities.

Was Condorcet being naïve? Did he not recognize, as Hume
did, that the probability factor of a "law" is heightened only
by constant, repeated experiences of a like phenomenon: e.g., a
ball rolling down an inclined plane, traveling a given distance
in a given space of time? Where were such repeated experiences in history? And how were they to be observed? Yet, the
very extent of Condorcet's naïveté (if such it be judged) in
this matter seems, paradoxically, to have been the required

starting point for his work on the "social art." In this last, he came to grips with the problem of probability as a *mathematical* question, rather than, as in Locke or Voltaire, as a "credibility" question (where the evidence is weighed primarily on the scales of "reason," even though that "reason" is assumed to be based on experience). By so transposing the definition of probability, Condorcet edged toward a science of human behavior, on the basis of which man might control future political and economic decisions.

The application of the "social art" to the past, however, was tenuous. Indeed, Condorcet's bold endeavor to decipher the past by a simple cause-and-effect empiricism seems to have exhausted the potentialities of that way of approaching history, and exposed its deficiencies. Withal, the seeds of another sort of approach existed in Condorcet, for he had the fruitful notion of conceiving man's development over time in terms of stages of mental and technological—scientific advances. Hence, while Condorcet based his own view of the "progress of the human mind" on a misleading mechanical cause and effect relationship, others could take his inspiration and implement it by an appeal to dialectical processes. To do this, however, required a different conception of the relationship of rationalism to empiricism, of theory to fact.

It was Vico who, for our purposes, first made the breakthrough. Philosophers like Locke and Hume had vindicated history from the empirical side. Vico now did it from the rational side. He took Descartes' notion, that we understand only what we construct by the mind's activity, and applied it to history. Man makes his history, Vico announced, and therefore he understands it.[1] This is for Vico a truth beyond question: "That the world of civil society has certainly been made by men, and that its principles are therefore to be found

[1] By this momentous decision, Vico again severed historical knowledge from physical knowledge, and placed the former with the truths of mathematics. This by-product of his particular vindication of history reappears, though in different form, of course, in the neo-Kantian division of the *Geisteswissenschaften* from the natural sciences.

within the modifications of our own human mind."

Vico did not attempt to give a systematic exposition of his epistemological position. He made little effort, aside from the verum=factum formula, to struggle abstractly with the question of how we know. Nevertheless, in practice Vico did go on to wrestle in Herculean fashion with the problem of how we relate rational ideas to empirical data. The terms he used must be clearly understood: he called the rational the "true," and the empirical the "certain." Thus, he broke up into two parts Descartes' compound of "true and certain" as the correct marks of knowledge. The rational, Vico claimed, was the province of the philosopher, the empirical, that of the "philologians." As I have sought to translate Vico's thought, the first supplies us with theories, or hypotheses, and the second with the actual phenomena to be explained; or, to use other modern terminology, the former gives us an "ideal type" or model, and the latter the unrationalized, though not irrational, empirical reality of "what happened."

Vico's effort at theory falls into areas that today we label as, for example, anthropology, psychology, sociology, and theory of economic development. In his work, however, hypotheses about, say, myth or class struggles are diffused and confused with all sorts of other hypotheses. Thus, it remained for other thinkers to take what he called "philosophy" and to resolve it into separate, more rigorous disciplines of the cultural sciences. To cite a few examples (without necessarily claiming Vico as the actual inspiration), Adam Smith and his followers, starting from moral philosophy, broke off the particular field of economics; Comte developed a specific science of sociology; and Tylor and other anthropologists dealt with myth and primitive thought in terms of a specialized new study.[2] But it was Vico who first glimpsed their amorphous shapes and recognized

[2] This is the same sort of development which occurred in the natural sciences. Starting from "natural philosophy," disciplines such as physics and chemistry gradually emerged as autonomous fields of study (indeed, fully, only in the nineteenth century).

that only from such a series of mental outposts could the territory of reality—the terrain of actual "human choice"—be truly and certainly surveyed.

Immanuel Kant supplied Vico's epistemological deficiencies and gave a reasoned basis for the belief in the constructing mind. Opposing the empirical view that all knowledge comes from sense impressions, which bombard a more or less passive mind, Kant postulated a mind that "creates" its knowledge in terms of certain given forms and patterns, in a tight interrelationship with the phenomenal data. Extrapolating this view to history, Kant saw man as legitimately able to impose a teleological or "As-if" pattern on the otherwise apparent chaos of past events. We need not repeat here the discussion as to the difficulties with Kant's theories (see pp. 121–125); suffice it to say that his work gave confidence and support to those who wished to picture man as an active and constructing being, who in some way *makes* his own world rather than merely *copying* an already existing one.

The flaw in Kant's work, however, seemed to be his denigration of the very same "creative knowledge" which at first he had appeared to extol. Describing this knowledge as merely phenomenal, Kant talked of another sort of knowledge, noumenal, which lies beyond our grasp. And this, Kant admonished us, is the only "real" reality.

Hegel's genius was to seek to overcome this dualism. He attempted to reintroduce the ancient Heraclitean notion that we can know rationally the reality of the universe because that reality is itself rational. Thus, according to Hegel, the dialectic of the mind recapitulates the dialectic of the world. Fraught with complications and difficulties as is his scheme, it had the effect of once again bolstering the courage of those who believed that man makes his own history and therefore can come to know it. Moreover, Hegel himself supplied a brilliant and complex exposition of how the rational and the empirical must be reconciled in practice. Further, probably his major achievement was to implement his insight by translating the intuitions

of religion into philosophical statements, bearing within them
the seeds of social science hypotheses.

Certain ideas in Hegel coalesced for the early Marx about
the conception that man not only made his history, but was
"alienated" from what he had made. According to Marx, the
way to acquire true and certain knowledge of what man had
made and makes, and to bring it once again under his conscious
control, is critique. Marx was not particularly interested in
abstract epistemology; he seems to have borrowed loosely
from both Hegel and Comte. What he was interested in was a
correct understanding (and hence reconstructing) of social
institutions. To achieve this, he gradually metamorphosed
philosophical critique, heavily indebted here to Hegel and
Feuerbach's religious critique, into social science, specifically
economics. In large part, of course, his economics is imbedded
in a major effort at historical sociology, and here the connection with Comtean positivism, in spite of Marx's disclaimer,
looms significantly.

With Marx, the philosophical trail we have been pursuing
can conveniently be brought to an end. At this point, the
traditional epistemological question no longer serves as an important and meaningful part of the systems of the great speculators on philosophy of history who remain to be considered
(aside from Comte). In general, they have little to say on the
matter that is original. Thus, Toynbee may claim to be empirical, and Spengler to be a prioristic and intuitive; but neither
says anything new or philosophically sophisticated about the
problem. Instead, for them epistemology has turned into sociology of knowledge, and it is our social situation, our culture,
rather than our physiological apparatus which is presumed to
shape our perception of the universe. In short, it is ideology or
sociology of knowledge which interests our contemporary
speculative philosophers of history, and they are content to
leave other facets of the epistemological question to the abstract philosopher and to the experimental psychologist.

As for the rational-empirical relationship per se, that has

become a matter of scientific methodology. Even before Marx, Comte had tried to establish the characteristics of acceptable positive science. Claiming that only the historical development of a science can inform us as to the method necessary to deal with the specific material which composes its subject matter, Comte believed that the unity of the sciences resides solely in that each science seeks the following: to establish regularities of behavior amongst its observed phenomena, to state that regularity in the form of a general hypothesis, and to verify that hypothesis in terms of the empirical data.

After Comte, Freud, too, embraced the view that we must erect within each science what he called "conceptual scaffolding" and thereby reach out to "unknown reality." Throughout his work in psychoanalysis, he claimed to be proceeding scientifically: relating observed data by means of hypotheses, checking the latter against further evidence, and then using the tentatively confirmed hypotheses as tools with which to continue probing the unknown.

In sum, however, in modern speculative philosophy of history the general philosophical questions about epistemology and the connection of rationalism and empiricism are either treated superficially (as in Toynbee and Spengler), or have given way to the attempt, operationally, to relate theories to data concerning man's development as a cultural animal (as in Marx and Freud). With all the errors, confusions, and hesitations attendant on the latter attempt, it can still be considered a step in the direction of scientific knowledge. As we have seen, however, such a step could be taken only after the earlier metaphysical vindication of history as a legitimate form of human understanding.

2

In its halting journey toward the precise cultural sciences, philosophy of history took sustenance from the vital waters of religious thought. Many of the larger, metaphysical assumptions of our speculators, as I shall shortly emphasize, came from traditional theological notions. Yet, in the final analysis, the historical largely displaced the religious view of the world for modern intellectual man. The so-called "warfare of science with theology in Christendom" had its counterpart in the historical as well as the natural sciences.[3] Generally overlooked or played down, one could assert that the historical-theological battle was perhaps even more fundamental—because Judaism and Christianity claimed to be historical religious—than the scientific—theological battle. In fact, once history could vindicate itself as a legitimate form of knowledge its corrosive power could easily be turned against a religion claiming authority from a more or less mythical past.

The secularization of sacred history took place primarily under the generalship of Voltaire and other *philosophes* like him. Like Galileo shortly before them, they brought heavenly matters down to earth, and showed that they were like substances. Religious tradition could no longer hold itself at a distance, sheltered behind the clouds of revelation, but now found itself looked at searchingly by the resolving power of historical critique. After Voltaire and other enlightened thinkers had put their eye to the historical lens, religious tradition seemed to have dissolved into a mass of superstitious vapors.

The trouble with their work was that it tended to dismiss religion entirely as a historical phenomenon, instead of trying to understand its role in man's cultural evolution. Content to discern an eternal, natural religion, the *philosophes* stopped looking at religion historically. They treated it in the same way as they had treated myth. Thus, it remained for more idealistic speculators like Vico and Hegel to redeem religion as a serious subject for historical inquiry.

Vico, especially, from a committed point of view reintro-

[3] See, for example, A. D. White, *A History of the Warfare of Science with Theology in Christendom* (1896).

duced religion as a normal part of a unified history. For him, indeed, there could be no society—or history—without religion. As for Hegel, his extrapolation of Vico's view was to insist that in the present the role of religion was being taken over by philosophy. Viewing religion as a changing, historical entity (as against the *philosophes*' fixed interpretation), Hegel envisioned its last stage as an evolution into his reasoned metaphysics. According to the German thinker, the "birth-time" of this great spiritual revolution was his own epoch.[4]

Hegel's contemporary, Comte, however, had a slightly different view of what was happening during this epoch. According to Comte, religion was being replaced, not by philosophy (which had only been a way station during the sixteenth to the eighteenth centuries), but by science. The latter, like religion before it, offered what negative and critical philosophy could not: organic, cohesive, certain knowledge. Unlike religion, however, certainty in science was not a matter of faith and intuition but of positive methodology, which sought observed regularities of behavior rather than first causes. This sort of certain knowledge, Comte believed, could be obtained about social as well as natural behavior.

The upshot of Comte's work was an attempted redefinition

---

[4] Actually, it was Vico himself who prepared the way for this Hegelian transcendence of religion. By treating all religions other than the Judaic-Christian as a matter of psychological projections, the author of the *New Science* unintentionally naturalized religious beliefs. Where he stopped at the scriptures, Hegel could go on to these as well. The trail Hegel blazed was resolutely trodden by the neo-Hegelians, and by such potent thinkers as Feuerbach, Marx, and Freud. For them, whether economic or psychological in its roots, religion was a matter, not of extraterrestial revelation, but of very earthy projection. From this development, views such as the following could emerge. One, for example, by Hegel, that man, instead of being created in the image of god, had created god in his own image; it was only a short step from this to the assertion that therefore man was god, or potentially so. A second, for example, as advanced by Comte and Freud, that the religious way of thinking was only a stage in man's evolution toward scientific maturity; on this interpretation, humanity had progressed first to philosophy—Hegel's insight—and now was advancing to the scientific stage itself. At this point, religion, a childish memory, could simply be put away in the closet of man's past.

of the warfare of science and religion. The real battle, he indicated, was between science and philosophy, i.e., metaphysics. Religion and science, Comte claimed, actually embodied similar *Weltanschauungen*, with the latter only a more up-to-date version of the former. (It is interesting to note that Oswald Spengler came to hold this same view, even though, unlike Comte, he favored intuition over positive science. For Spengler, both religion and science attempt to set up laws of causality; see p. 330.

It was Karl Marx who re-established the original battle lines. Aligning Hegel's philosophical critique and Comte's positive science, he turned both batteries on the enemy, religion. As a result, religion, for Marx, existed merely as an ideology. From this point on, it was easy for Sigmund Freud—anti-Marxist as he was—to extend the notion so that religion became, not only an ideology, but a neurotic illusion. As such, naturally, it could give us no knowledge of the real world. Further, it followed that religion was itself a way of viewing the world which needed to be "cured" by scientific insight.

In our own time, the only one of our speculative philosophers of history who has sought to redeem the religious conception of history, has been Arnold Toynbee.[5] For him, the meaning of history lies in its progress toward a more etherialized religion, not toward various forms of science. Unrooted, however, in any analysis which bequeaths to modern man a cultural science at the same time as a philosopher of history—as Comte did with sociology, Marx with a theory of economic development, and Freud with psychoanalysis—Toynbee's work will probably have little lasting impact.[6] Exhortatory rather than heuristic, I suspect that its sounds will tend to fade away without much echo.

[5] Perhaps Comte's "turn" to religion in the *Système*, after his earlier, more secular work in the *Cours*, places him alongside Toynbee, whose religious commitment grows stronger in the later volumes of *A Study of History*.

[6] Clearly, Toynbee would have betrayed his vision if he had produced a cultural science.

3

Obviously, the naturalistic or scientific embrace of religion by some of our philosophers of history seems to have been even more deadly than the mere disdain of the *philosophes*. On the other hand, religious conceptions also left their mark on historical explanation. One of the strongest surviving elements of religion in much of nineteenth-century philosophy of history and social science was the concept of Providence. Translated into more secular vocabulary, as the "invisible hand" of Adam Smith, the "cunning of Reason" of Hegel, or the "historical materialism" of Marx, Providence became a sort of naturalistic Maxwell's "demon," regulating and controlling the behavior of human molecules. Later, indeed, this secularized concept of Providence could be reworked in an attempt at a more descriptive "law," for example, of the marketplace, or in the shape of game strategy, or of large-scale theories of social change à la Max Weber. From its very beginning in Vico, however, the Providential belief gave metaphysical assurance to those who sought for regularities of behavior underlying otherwise apparently chaotic and chance events.

The notion of theodicy also played a major role in various attempts at philosophy of history. As in Vico and Hegel, the acceptance of *all* of God's works, even the apparently evil ones, led to an "acquiescence in actuality." In its furthest development, on one side this helped lead to historicism. On the other, it led to the close observation of certain phenomena, previously dismissed on moral grounds; for example, of such phenomena as the acquisitive economic system and, eventually with Freud, of various unconscious human desires. Closely connected with views on Providence, the concept of theodicy ultimately fostered an attention to detail, an attention absolutely basic to empirical social science.

The idea of progress may well be another metaphysical assumption inherited from religion. For example, as one writer has suggested, the idea of progress may be merely a secularization of the eschatological pattern of Christianity. Another writer has talked about the "heavenly city of the 18th century." And various scholars have sketched the influence on later historical thinking of Judaic-Christian conceptions of time.[7] In any case ,whatever their particular nature and origin, shreds of religious notions have often clung to the vision of secular salvation known as the idea of progress.

In sum, by means of these various concepts—Providence, theodicy, and eschatology, as well as others, such as that of the existence at the beginning of a paradisal stage of existence, or of the origin of society in a sexual act—religious thought has left a tremendous legacy to the philosophies of history which have arisen in its wake. These, in turn, have carried some of the concepts mentioned into various nascent cultural sciences.

4

In the shift from a predominantly religious view of the world to a largely historical one, that is, a logical and scientific one, the philosophers of history whom we have been considering employed a bewildering variety of methods by which to reach historical knowledge. Therefore, any effort to order and classify their approaches is bound to end in an artificial unity, one which distorts the actual untidy and sometimes erratic nature of the creative process. Nevertheless, for expository purposes, I shall try to construct a Procrustean bed of sorts.

The basic dichotomy seems, at an initial glance, to be between those who favor what may be called an intuitive approach and those who favor a more analytic method. Thus, on the first side might be placed such figures as Kant, Hegel, and

[7] See Karl Löwith, *Meaning in History* (Chicago, 1949); Carl L. Becker, *The Heavenly City of the Eighteenth-Century Philosophers* (New Haven, 1932); and Mircea Eliade, *Cosmos and History* (New York, 1959).

Spengler. On the other side, Condorcet, Comte, Marx, and Freud. Vico might appear on both sides, and Toynbee would probably be pleased to be assigned to the analytic side. The intuitionists emphasize such words as *Anschauung*, empathy, sympathy, artistic contemplation, and vision. The analysts talk more about hypotheses, observation, experimentation, mathematics, and logic.

Fundamentally, however, the intuitive-analytic division is misleading on two counts. The first is that this division masks the more important split on the question of *verification*. For example, some of the analysts would admit that their hypotheses are *derived* from *intuitive* insight into observed phenomena: Vico (for the moment considered as an analyst) and Freud undoubtedly would, although Condorcet and Comte would probably demur. (In general, those who take a strict empiricist position on the epistemological question tend to prefer some form of inductivist phrasing.) The key question, then, is not "how do we obtain our hypotheses," but "how do we verify them." Those who, like Spengler, answer "intuition" are diametrically opposed to those who, like Marx and Freud, respond "logic and evidence."[8] This, to my mind, is the really radical split.

The second reason why the intuitive-analytic dichotomy misleads is that it averts our eyes from the more important division concerning what I shall here call the sympathetic "acquiescence in the given" (actually, a form or part of historicism). With significant lapses, the following can be considered historicist, in the sense defined: Vico, Kant, Hegel, Comte, Marx, Spengler (here my reservations would be the greatest), and Freud. Closely connected to the "acquiescence in the given" is the awareness of "cultural wholes." The two views combined add up to a willingness to study *all* of social

---

[8] I bypass here the difficult question of how we establish "logic and evidence" as acceptable criteria for explanation; that is a question of scientific methodology, as well as of philosophical speculation. See, however, Ernest Nagel, *The Structure of Science* (New York, 1961).

phenomena in an interrelated manner. (This, of course, is an ideal; in practice only greater or lesser parts are and can be studied.)

Thus, the real division works out to those who do and those who do not believe in the intuitive or imaginative creation of hypotheses; in the to-and-fro movement of these hypotheses in relation to the "acquiescence in the given"; and in the verification of these hypotheses by logic and evidence rather than by intuition. Taken together, these elements add up to what I have tried to identify as the heuristic method of history and the cultural sciences. In a rough and ready fashion, I would place Vico, Comte, Marx, and Freud under this last rubric.

5

Two other divisions of some interest and importance can be set up. One involves the problem of causality and the other the problem of the dialectic. On the first problem, there are those who embrace causality and those who reject it as a serious concern in historical speculation. Of the latter sort there is, for example, Spengler, who substitutes Destiny for causality. Of the former sort, Condorcet (typical here of many of the enlightened thinkers), Comte, Marx, Toynbee, and Freud can be cited. Among the latter, the noteworthy split is between those who embrace a rigid determinism and insist on complete causal predictability, and those who hesitate at or oppose such a decisive commitment. Thus, Condorcet, Comte, Marx, and, to a lesser extent, Toynbee, tend to a completely determined and predictable causal chain. Freud and, surprisingly enough, Voltaire had reservations. For example, as Freud remarked, "from a knowledge of the premises we could not have foretold the nature of the result. . . . We never know beforehand which of the determining factors will prove the weaker or the stronger. Hence it is always possible by analysis to recognize the causation with certainty, whereas a prediction of it by synthesis is impossible." Voltaire's more laconic phrasing we have already seen: "Every being has a father, but every being does not always have children."

Among proponents of causality, the classic view is that of a mechanical, Hume-like one-to-one cause and effect relationship. More subtle and complicated is the dialectical conception. On this latter view, development takes place in a sort of stepwise fashion. Instead of linear causation, we have a process in which, for example, a thesis gives rise to its opposite, and the resulting conflict produces a new synthesis. Thus, the "cause" of this last is not a simple, single thing, but the *struggle* of at least two elements. In an explicit, conscious fashion, the dialectical method itself was espoused only by Kant, Hegel, and Marx; but even among them, it had differing characteristics, and was put to somewhat different uses. As for the implicit use of dialectic, we find that in the work of Vico, Comte, and Freud, accompanied by varying degrees of consciousness about the method itself.

Closely related to dialectic, though there is no necessary connection, is the general notion of struggle. A few examples will illustrate the range of possibilities in this area. Thus, *philosophes* like Voltaire and Condorcet saw history as informing us of and being informed by the struggle between truth and error, reason and superstition, light (i.e., enlightenment) and darkness. Marx, on the other hand, perceived the struggle of economic classes, while Freud had antinomies of love and hate, Eros and Thanatos, "the instincts of life and the instincts of destruction." Kant talked of man's "unsocial sociability," Condorcet of the conflict of the "interests of each with the interests of all," and Toynbee of "challenge and response."

To sum up, whatever the particular result, all of our philosophers of history have taken a stance on the various problems we have just discussed. Most of these problems, such as the problem of causality, form part of critical philosophy of history. In addition, however, many of our figures have also concerned themselves either with the question of dialectical development or with the less complex question of struggle. Starting, perhaps, as a critical inquiry, this rapidly passes over into the speculative philosophy of history. Thus, as I have stressed before, the critical and the speculative for our thinkers are closely related, forming part of one continuous inquiry.

6

In considering the origin and development of man as a historical being, almost every one of our speculative philosophers of history has worked out a beginning point and then a schema concerning stages in history. Seen in the large, these schemas are also attempts at a new periodication.

Let us take the question of origin first. On this matter, our speculators again offer us a number of diverse suggestions. Vico, for example, envisioned as the beginning of human society a thunderclap scaring man into caves, and thus into monogamous sex relations. Condorcet, convinced that the beginning of society was impossible to discern in the dim past, restricted himself to the first observed society, which lived by hunting and fishing. Hegel, while talking vaguely of Reason (as bearing within itself potentially all that is to follow), actually started his historical survey with the rise of self-consciousness in the East, i.e., the Oriental world. Marx, on the other hand, started with the family and its division of labor as the first social relationship (with the first society larger than the family apparently being a nebulous "primitive community"). To conclude the list, Spengler had his cultures apparently spring autonomously from nowhere; Toynbee's civilizations arose from primitive societies in a "challenge and response" situation; and Freud began the evolution of cultural man with the killing of the father by the primal horde.

From these diverse starting points, our speculators then proceeded to carry the development of man as a cultural animal through various stages. In Vico's case, history is composed of cycles, spiraling upward, with each cycle comprising three ages: Gods, heroes, and men. Condorcet opted for a linear progress of a hypothetical human race, which passed to Enlightenment through ten stages. Comte announced his law of the three stages, where he envisioned a shift from the theological to the metaphysical, and then to the positive stage.

Hegel has a dialectical progression through the Oriental, Greek, Roman, and German Worlds. In Marx's version of history, there are four epochs, the Asiatic, ancient, feudal, and the modern bourgeois (with a prehistoric epoch of primitive communism), each marking a certain stage of intertwined tool-making and relations of production. Spengler's vision of independent, autonomous cultures, of course, eliminates the possibility of stages in mankind's development; however, within his cultures he does provide for a fated cycle of birth, youth, age, and death, with the coming of the latter equated with civilization. So, too, at first glance, Toynbee's scheme of 21 "contemporary" civilizations, each merely going through a seemingly predestined series of events—a time of troubles, Universal State, and Universal Church—according to a fixed "three and a half beat rout-rally rhythm" appears also to preclude the notion of humanity as a whole progressing by stages; however, his concept of "etherialization" may provide an element which allows for progress, and so for some form of stages of progress. With Freud, we have more or less a return to Comte's three stages, except that now the individual's psychic development recapitulates that of the species.

A number of those who believe in stages, though by no means all, also embrace what I call "holism." That is, they see each stage as a cultural whole, in which the political, economic, religious, and social arrangements, the legal institutions, the arts and sciences are all inextricably interrelated. In some cases, all the parts of the culture are viewed as animated by one spirit or *Zeitgeist;* in others, one part of the culture—for example, the economic—determines and conditions the others; in yet other cases, the unity perceived is a mere descriptive unity, abstracted from the data rather than animating or conditioning it. Among the "holists" of various sorts, I would name Vico, Hegel, Comte, and Marx. Spengler ought also to find a prominent place in this list, even though he did not believe in stages; his cultural wholes are isolated, autonomous entities, but none the less "holistic."

7

It should be clear now how many variations can be found in the means by which a philosophy of history can be constructed. A seemingly infinite number of combinations of views on such topics as epistemology, the rational-empirical relationship, the role of religion and of religious conceptions, scientific methodology, the use of intuition and of analysis, the question of verification, the concepts of causality, dialectic, and struggle, and the problem of origins and stages of cultural development appears to exist. To this list, we could add other possibilities, such as a decision on the primacy of passions or reason as the dominant force in history, or a choice as to a hero, or elites, or the masses as the central protagonist of the historical drama.

It should be equally clear that what counts is the particular, coherent articulation given to these elements in a specific philosophy of history. We understand any one part of the total structure of the thought of a Marx or a Freud only in terms of the other parts. A fair treatment of any of our speculative thinkers requires us, at least temporarily, to view the world in terms of the model, or paradigm, which he has constructed for us. Our question should be, not whether this is a correct picture of reality, isomorphic at all points, but whether the paradigm illuminates aspects of historical reality for us, giving us greater understanding of and operational power over parts of the phenomena.

8

We need not, however, and should not rest content with this
initial sympathetic approach to the whole of a system of
thought. Legitimately, I believe, we can usefully demand of
our philosophers of history, not a final answer on the abstract
question of, say, the nature of epistemology or causality, but a
hint about the further development of possible, precise
branches of the cultural sciences. In this sort of "putting to the
rack" of our speculative thinkers, however, we should bear in
mind the admonitions so well expressed by P. B. Medawar:

> 1. *There is no such thing as a Scientific Mind.* Scientists are a
> very heterogeneous group of people doing different things in
> very different ways. Among scientists there are collectors, classi-
> fiers, and compulsive tidiers up; many are by temperament
> detectives, many are explorers, some are artists, others artisans.
> There are poet-scientists and philosopher-scientists and a few
> mystics. What sort of mind or temperament can all these people
> be supposed to have in common? . . .
> 2. *There is no such thing as the Scientific Method*—as the
> scientific method, that is the point: there is no one art or coherent
> system of rules for the conduct of scientific inquiry which stands
> to its subject matter as logical syntax stands to any particular ex-
> ample of reasoning by deduction. Mill's Four Methods, for example,
> are best thought of as household hints. "An art of discovery is not
> possible," wrote a former Master of Trinity, "we can give no rules
> for the pursuit of truth which shall be universally and peremp-
> torily applicable."[9]

With this salutary flexibility in mind, I shall make the following, tentative claims for some of our speculative philosophers of history. As I see it, the contributions to the cultural
sciences are that: Vico's inspirations concerning philology and
hence primitive and ancient myth direct us to anthropology
and psychology; Voltaire's work meanders toward cultural

[9] P. B. Medawar, "Imagination and Hypothesis," *The Times Literary
Supplement*, 25 October, 1963, 849.

history; Condorcet's "social art" anticipates a nonhistorical sociology, as well as elements of statistical analysis and game theory; Hegel's form of cultural history serves as a bridge from religious to philosophical conceptions of man and the universe, and provides a metaphysical basis for emerging social theory; Comte, continuing a thought we encountered in Kant, firmly places social phenomena under invariable law and thus makes it subject to scientific study in the specific form of sociology; Marx, further developing Comte's historical sociology, sets up his theory of economic development—the obverse of the traditional "decline and fall" theories—as well as pointing out, by his analysis of ideology, the dimensions of a new sociology of knowledge. Spengler, by his insights into ways of viewing time and space, contributes both to anthropology and to sociology of knowledge; and Freud, starting from his clinical work in psychoanalysis, indicates to us lines of inquiry radiating out to fields such as social psychology, political science, and history itself.

This is an impressive list of achievements to come out of the alembric of philosophy of history. As it has worked out, many of our speculators, often in a futile search for a total knowledge, have produced elements of scientific knowledge which can serve in more limited inquiries. Others of our speculative thinkers never aimed at anything more than limited inquiries to begin with. As Medawar has indicated, however, it is from just such heterogeneous people and aims that the strange discoveries we call scientific take their rise.

9

Aside from its fructifying contributions to various of the cultural sciences, what else can be said of philosophy of history? What is its position today? I discern three answers.

The first is that philosophy of history finds itself situated in an "Alexandrian" culture. André Malraux points out that ours is probably the first culture which can collect together, simultaneously and in one location, so to speak, the artifacts, arts, and archeological evidences of all past and primitive cultures. As he reminds us, by our museums, a relatively new invention, and by our "museums without walls," i.e., photographic reproduction, we achieve this novel eclectic feat.[10] The same phenomenon obtains in history. For the first time, man seems to possess the full range of his past (though there are undoubtedly important gaps); every day seems to bring new discoveries, such as the deciphering of linear B. Man, therefore, is in the era of universal history, effectively and not just as an ideal.[11]

It is this situation that I call "Alexandrian," and that stimulates men like Spengler and Toynbee to attempt large-scale philosophies of history in the form of comparative civilization studies.[12] It would be ridiculous to pretend that Spengler and Toynbee have not had predecessors: Hegel and Comte both wrote up their philosophy of history, in part, in this way. What is different is the more truly universal quality of Spengler and Toynbee; while frequently faltering, they stumble on nevertheless to a non-European centric point of view. This is their proudly proclaimed "Copernican Revolution."[13]

I have already stated my reservations about the work of both Spengler and Toynbee. Here, I would only add that their grandiose efforts ought to inspire and not to deter others from doing more limited and rigorous work in the field of compara-

[10] See André Malraux, *The Voices of Silence*, translated by Stuart Gilbert (Garden City, N.Y., 1953).

[11] Cf. Raymond Aron, *The Dawn of Universal History* (New York, 1963).

[12] On a lesser scale, other scholars seek to provide comprehensive narrative accounts, with very modest pretensions, if any, at being speculative philosophers of history. See, for example, the interesting book by Herbert Muller, *The Uses of the Past* (New York, 1952), and William H. McNeill, *The Rise of the West* (Chicago, 1963).

[13] For example, because it is based on a wealth of materials simply not available to Hegel and Comte (for instance, recent anthropological and archaeological findings), Toynbee's *A Study of History* is, more than their works, truly Alexandrian and non-European in orientation.

tive studies, whether anthropological or historical.[14] When these more restricted studies reach a certain range and complexity of materials, efforts will once again be made to perceive large-scale regularities of behavior coursing through the development of man and society in time. Whether we call this philosophy of history or by some other name will not matter. Better grounded in empirical data, more demanding as to verification of more sophisticated hypotheses, these inquiries will be headed (though with a more accurate compass) in the same direction as are the pioneering efforts at philosophy of history of the speculators whom we have been observing and analyzing.

My second statement about philosophy of history today relates to its critical aspect. As I see it, the useful and promising area in critical philosophy of history pertains to linguistic analysis: the careful, critical analysis of terms and concepts used in historical explanation. There is a difficulty here, however. On one side, the injunction thrown out by thinkers like Locke, Hume, and Condorcet, concerning the need to resolve the ambiguity of words, has been caught up by our contemporary logical analysts. On the other side, the concern manifested by Vico about philology and the meaning of words, and more recently by Marx and Freud, has not found much of an echo among either philosophers or historians.

The trouble is that the working out of the logical implications of language by philosophers really does not even come close to the heart of the historian's concerns. Historical terms and concepts have *meaning* only within historical life per se. Language itself is historical, and is merely a *means* by which we seek to get at reality itself. As Vico and Joyce both knew, language is the prism by which we *perceive* the world. We do not start from Descartes' nonhistorical, abstractly thinking self, nor from Locke and Hume's blank tablet, bombarded by sense impressions to which we then attach words. Our language is not an Archimedean point, standing outside our

[14] For example, see the contributions to the periodicals, *Comparative Studies in Society and History*, and *Annales*.

own world of historical experience.

I do not want to belabor this thesis as an abstract philosophical issue. Nor do I wish to deny the very real contribution of analytic philosophers in calling our renewed attention to language and in cutting away masses of useless verbiage. Rather, I would like merely to suggest that the real problem in this area concerns the actual technical vocabulary and concepts used by historians. Further, I would claim that the primary responsibility for the critical look at their own linguistic tools is theirs.[15]

Simply as an example, let me quote one present-day historian on the matter. "History," as J. H. Hexter tells us, "has been poorest in its vocabulary of *general terms for dealing with limited areas during limited periods of time.* The determination of what general terms are useful is a matter not for amateurs but for experts." Then, momentarily taking his instances from a period not his own, Hexter continues, "In the civilizations of the ancient New East during the second millennium B.C. are the terms 'mythopoeic thought,' 'priest-king,' and 'temple-city' useful; are 'warlordship' and 'priestlordship,' 'pasture' and 'sown,' 'maritime' and 'riverine' convenient antitheses? If so, where and for how long? If these terms are of no use, what terms are? Only scholars who are on a standing of intimacy with the detailed historical data concerning the Near East from 2000 to 1000 B.C. can give adequately informed answers to such questions." As Hexter concludes, "What we may hope for is piecemeal advances as historian after historian re-examines the place and time with which he is mainly concerned, and seeks to contrive, for telling about what went on in that bounded place and time, a vocabulary of conceptions better suited to bring out its character than the fairly shopworn one now in use. Perhaps this bit-by-bit process of rethinking the very language of historical writing has already gotten under way."[16]

---

[15] As examples of what I have in mind, I would cite the work of Marc Bloch on feudalism, and of J. H. Hexter on early modern history.

[16] Hexter, *Reappraisals in History* (Evanston, 1961), p. 202; cf. the review of this book by J. G. A. Pocock, *History and Theory*, III, 2 (1963).

Now, in this sort of linguistic analysis in history, the abstract question, for example, of generalization is resolved by the very use of general terms, *insofar* as they apply to the historical data itself. Such general terms—warlordship, middle class, or feudal—are also concepts. They embody a theoretical analysis of the social institutions which they are used to describe. Feudalism, for example, is not a concept handed to historians by sociologists; nor, to take another example, is market economy one proffered by economists; both concepts are devised by historians from historical experience itself. And that is their *meaning*.

Hitherto, historians, adept in handling archival materials, have often been shamelessly unconscious and uncritical in their use of terms, concepts, and theories. They have not seen their work sufficiently as a *problem*, in which the reconciliation of theory and fact, of Vico's true and the certain, of the rational and the empirical has the central place. In short, they have not made the clear commitment to a scientific inquiry. Insofar as philosophy of history persists in the future, one part of it, which I have now been discussing under the heading, "linguistic analysis," will occupy itself with this decisive undertaking. As already stated, only the historians themselves, not the philosophers, can undertake this task; and they must tackle it as an operational concern, in terms of the language of history itself.

My third reflection on the position of contemporary philosophy of history involves some thought about the nature of "historical consciousness." Here I share the view that the major contribution of the speculative philosophers of history, aside from their thrust toward specific cultural sciences, has been in deepening our sense of historical self-consciousness and self-awareness. (Moreover, of course, it is the state or level of historical consciousness which is the background for the required efforts in linguistic historical analysis.) As a consequence of this growth in self-consciousness, we possess the potentiality for increased control over social phenomena.

Let us review briefly some of the highlights in this process.

It was Vico's genius to perceive the dim shadows of man's "bestial" past, and then to go beyond this awareness to the intuition that man is only really free to make his history when he becomes rationally self-conscious enough to control his brute passions. At this point, as we can see (and Vico probably did not), by such action man potentially frees himself from the blind, unintended consequences of mere nature. The first step in this direction, however, even before man seeks to control future consequences—the most difficult enterprise—is knowledge of how the past has unrolled. Belated consciousness of the past is thus the necessary prelude to present consciousness. This, at least, is how I extrapolate Vico's primary message. (The other major contribution Vico makes to our self-awareness is his theory concerning man's projection of his psychic desires upon the gods and forces of the universe.)

From a very different viewpoint—empiricism—a thinker like Condorcet pursued the growth of consciousness itself. Starting with Locke's view that the sense experiences of the child lead to the adult's reason, Condorcet extended this to the human race as a whole, and traced a continuous "progress of the human mind." Throughout, his emphasis is on the increasing rationality of man, and hence his scientific control over his actions.

Hegel, too, stressed the growing empire of reason, but his Reason had depths and subtleties (as well as vagaries) lacking in the *philosophes'* conception. Indeed, it is Hegel who most consciously intuited the centrality of growing self-consciousness for history. The meaning of history for him is essentially the increasing awareness by man of his position in time. Hegel calls this the realization in actuality by Reason of what is already in it potentially. But if we remove this mystical husk, we discover the kernel of Hegel's meaning: man is a cultural animal, shaped by his culture, and his culture is laid up for him by a historical process. At the core of this culture are religion and its modern surrogate, philosophy. It is the ideas embodied in these ways of viewing the world which determine our being and that of society. These ideas, we are now told, derive from Reason unfolding itself, an unfolding which has occurred, of course, in a dialectic fashion. At the end, Hegel's conclusion is similar to Vico's. By becoming conscious of these changes—and the level of this consciousness defines what we are and where we are in time—we may (Hegel hedged here) take into our own hands, and thus shape, the "laws of the land."

With Comte, consciousness turns into positive science. There is no place for psychological or, essentially, historical awareness in the *Cours;* there is only historically informed sociological awareness: a science of society. This, however, according to Comte, is a major step forward to greater control over man's actions. (Naturally, in the hands of other speculators, sociology might also be used as a background to self-knowledge.)

Marx, as we know, took Hegel's emphasis on consciousness and flipped it over on its back. Led on by Feuerbach, Marx declared that ideas do not shape the culture, but the culture shapes the ideas. To use Marxist terminology, the material conditions of production, which form the core of our culture, determine our consciousness. Marx's real contribution here is to call our attention to the technological and economic factors which affect our self-awareness. Like Condorcet and Comte before him, however, his "sociology of knowledge" tends to remain largely on the level of consciousness. Though he does provide for "false consciousness," Marx does not view this as a matter of the unconscious, but merely as a mistake as to so-called real interests. Rooting consciousness in "classes," Marx allows for the mistaken or false awareness by a class of its true position. When, however, this false consciousness is remedied, correct class consciousness (proletariat now; bourgeois earlier) becomes a revolutionary instrument. Thus, consciousness changes the world.[17]

[17] I have already discussed the logical difficulties of reconciling this view with Marx's theory of economic determinism. See pp. 252 and 292–294.

Marx's other contribution on this issue circles about his concepts of projection, alienation, and critique. Like Vico and Feuerbach, Marx saw man projecting his psychic desires into the superterrestial realm, where they discharge themselves without changing relations on earth. Making his own creations into external powers—religious and economic—man alienates them from himself. Only by critique, Marx insisted, can man dispel his self-created illusions and take back into his control the "Frankensteins" he has created. In this part of his thought, emphasized in his early works, Marx viewed critique as a matter of increasing self-consciousness, bestowing power on man.

In our own day, growing self-consciousness and its connection with scientific knowledge, physical and social, as discussed above, has been rejected by Toynbee. He values only religious consciousness, what he calls "etherialization." The latter, of course, has been called "projection" by many of his fellow speculators, and the conflict of views is clear.

One of the strongest contemporary voices emphasizing the role of projections is, of course, that of Freud. There is no need to repeat here the details of his analysis (see pp. 409–411). Freud's major contribution to our subject, of course, was his resolute concentration on the unconscious. Extending the range of the Socratic injunction, "Know thyself," to another, Dantesque level of understanding, Freud, for the first time, offered man a scientific method of comprehending the reason in his unreason. With the scalpel of psychoanalysis, Freud attempted to peel away the layers of man's past—personal and as a member of a species—and to show him how he had come to be. With all its mistakes and ego-wounding qualities (that is, to our *amour propre*), psychoanalytic history presents man with the possibility of a most radical historical consciousness.

Now, if I am right in believing that the speculative philosophers of history, taken together, have deepened and extended our personal and collective historical self-awareness, two consequences seem to me to emerge from this conclusion. The first is simple. It is that this historical consciousness itself serves as the major metaphysical backdrop for efforts in the particular cultural sciences (as well as for attempts at linguistic analysis of the sort I have advocated). As Isaiah Berlin has so well pointed out,

> . . . the categories in terms of which alone we conceive such basic notions as man, society, history, development, growth, barbarism, civilization, and the like . . . are destroyed or transformed by those changes in the total outlook of a man or a milieu or a culture which it is the hardest (and the most important) test of the histories of ideas (and, in the end, of history as such) to be able to explain. What is here involved is a deeply ingrained, widespread, long–lived *Weltanschauung*—the unquestioning (and not necessarily valid) assumption of one particular objective order of events or facts. Sometimes it is a vertical order—succession in time. . . . At other times we conceive of the order as "horizontal"; that is, it underlies the perception of the interconnections between different aspects of the same stage of culture.[18]

What Berlin calls *Weltanschauung*, I am here calling "historical consciousness."

The second consequence of a deepened historical consciousness, along with the new cultural sciences, is a new vision of ourselves. For example, we have come increasingly to see that what we thought to be unique attributes of man—reason, language, and so forth—are not restricted to him, but are shared in varying degrees by other animals, and even by machines. What is unique to man is his history. This he shares with no other animal. As we have contended, *homo sapiens* has been for most of his existence a part of *natural history;* only gradually has he emerged from this state to a true *historical*, i.e., self-conscious level of existence.

History, then, as we have defined it, as opposed to natural

---

[18] See the entire statement by Berlin in *History and Theory*, I, 1 (1960), 5–6. Cf. J. H. Talmon's comments in *Encounter*, 120 (September, 1963), 14–16. From a different viewpoint entirely, H. Scott Gordon, "Ideas of Economic Justice," *Daedalus* (Summer, 1953), previously mentioned, illustrates what I mean by metaphysical assumptions in back of particular cultural sciences.

history, is a gift which man has not always had. Indeed, it is an awareness which not all members of the human species have reached at the same time, and which even today some groups are just acquiring. Once possessed of historical self-consciousness, however, man sees, on one level, that he has had a "personal history"—he is aware of himself as an *individual* development in time. On another level, he perceives that he has had a *collective* history. It is the problem of integrating the two levels—of understanding how the society's history influences the individual, and how the individual's history shapes the society—that still stands as a challenge.

To my mind, Marx and Freud, elaborating on the hints and suggestions put forth by numerous of our other speculative philosophers of history, have pointed out some of the fundamental lines of inquiry in the taking up of this challenge. Thus, Marx has tried to show that the passage of man from natural history (Darwin's domain) to history must be studied in terms of technology and economics. Next, Freud has placed at the center of this transition the concept of psychological change, brought about under the influence of sexuality. Taking sex out of Darwin's reproductive-survival schema, Freud has studied its shift from a natural to a human activity, that is, to a self-conscious act. Thereby, he has made it the fulcrum of man's historical actions.[19]

Somewhere in the middle of these insights (suitably modified), into an economic-social development and a psychological development, a major breakthrough to increased historical understanding may be in the offing. If, as I assume, the major causal factor in history can be designated as "what man thinks," or, in other words, his self-consciousness as to his culture, then this thinking or self-consciousness plays the central role in "what happens," and in the way it happens. That is, wars, depressions, and so forth occur *in the way they do* because men, possessed of a certain level of self-awareness or

---

[19] In back of Marx and Freud, as we have seen, Vico, for example, had had similar premonitions.

knowledge, allow certain problems presented by nature and other men to be solved in that particular way.[20]

Unfortunately, at this moment we know very little precisely about what causes historical man to think and act as he does. Sociology of knowledge is at an early stage. Marx's determination of thought by material conditions is a very crude piece of theory. And Freudian psychoanalytic theories are as yet too limited in their application, not reaching to a satsfactory social psychology; they leave out too many of the surrounding aspects of the historical process. Thus, we still lack adequate theories concerning the reciprocity and interaction between what conditions or determines man's perceptions, thoughts, and desires and what these latter, in turn, condition or determine in the world we call historical.[21]

Our speculative philosophers of history, however, have tried, even if with halting steps, to lead us to increased historical self-consciousness; then to translate this notion into the more empirical question of the social-psychological nature of consciousness; and then to help refine this into the particular inquiries of anthropology, sociology, economics, and psychology. As a result, it may be that we now hold in our hands the threads which can ultimately guide us more confidently through the labyrinth of history, even though we shall never be able to fly free from the maze itself.

[20] See my comments on this, pp. 293 and 422–423. Of course, one must hastily add that the solution of one set of problems leads directly to other problems. This, however, is simply the human condition.

[21] Much of this answer, naturally, will come from disciplines such as physiological psychology and psycholinguistics. For the broader social, historical, and cultural aspects of man's consciousness, however, we must look elsewhere.

Selected Bibliography

The bibliography which follows is really an extended note to aid the reader interested in pursuing further a figure or subject that has aroused his interest. It is intended mainly to supplement the items mentioned in the footnotes to the individual chapters, though in a number of cases a citation found there is repeated.

GENERAL

A journal devoted exclusively to philosophy of history, both of the critical and the speculative sort, is *History and Theory*, 1960–. Its Beiheft 1 (1961) was devoted to a *Bibliography of Works in the Philosophy of History*, 1945–1957, and this was supplemented by a Beiheft 3 (1964) bringing the *Bibliography* up to 1961. Probably the best general introductory work on the subject, vastly stronger on the critical than the speculative side, however, is W. H. Walsh, *An Introduction to the Philosophy of History* (London, 1951). To supplement it, there is *Theories of History*, Patrick Gardiner (ed.) (New York, 1959). This book is a very useful anthology of both speculative and critical works in the philosophy of history. It has helpful introductions, as well as an extensive bibliography (which obviates the need to reproduce many of the items here); the bibliography, however, is not a critical one. A classic in the field is R. G. Collingwood, *The Idea of History* (Oxford, 1946). Of continuing interest are the pioneering works of Robert Flint, *History of the Philosophy of History* (Edinburgh, 1893) and *The Philosophy of History in France and Germany* (New York, 1874), which have offered standard coverages of speculative philosophy of history for many years. The more recent study by Karl Löwith, *Meaning in History* (Chicago, 1949), while written from a definite religious point of view, offers a brilliant though often too brief treatment of many of the figures covered in the present book. Frank E. Manuel,

Shapes of Philosophical History (Stanford, 1965) is a general treatment, covering the subject from the ancients to the present in broad strokes. German writers, as might be expected, have contributed numerous works on the general subject. Among them, a German counterpart to Gardiner's *Theories of History*, is Kurt Rossmann, *Deutsche Geschichtsphilosophie von Lessing bis Jaspers* (Bremen, 1959). Georg Mehlis, *Lehrbuch der Geschichtsphilosophie* (Berlin, 1915), Part II, pp. 343-512, is worth consulting, though it is really only an extended listing of figures in the history of philosophy of history. Ernst Bernheim, *Lehrbuch der historischen Methode* (Leipzig, 1908), pp. 685-735, is, of course, a standard work; the pertinent pages are indicated. A modern entry in the field is Fritz Wagner, *Geschichtswissenschaft* (Freiburg, 1951). From the Italian, there is Benedetto Croce, *The Theory and History of Historiography* (originally published in 1915), now available in English. I. S. Kon, *Die Geschichtsphilosophie des 20. Jahrhunderts: Kritischer Abriss*, 2 vols., translated from the Russian by W. Hoepp (Berlin, 1964) is a major new survey of the various schools of philosophy of history in the twentieth century, and offers Kon's own view, as a Marxist, of the problems in the field. Specifically on the critical side, a good start can be made with the following works: Maurice Mandelbaum, *The Problem of Historical Knowledge* (New York, 1938); Patrick Gardiner, *The Nature of Historical Explanation* (Oxford, 1952); and William Dray, *Laws and Explanation in History* (Oxford, 1957). A fine anthology is *The Philosophy of History in Our Time*, Hans Meyerhoff (ed.) (Garden City, N.Y., 1959).

VICO

The starting point for the English-speaking student of Vico is the translation by Thomas Goddard Bergin and Max Harold Fisch of the *New Science* (Ithaca, N.Y., 1948) and of the *Autobiography* (Ithaca, N.Y., 1944), as well as the very valuable introduction to the latter by Fisch. In addition to the standard *Opere*, F. Nicolini (ed.) (Milano, 1953), there is a French translation of the *New Science*, *Principes d'une science nouvelle* (Paris, 1953), which offers a valuable commentary and essay by Nicolini. See, also, F. Nicolini, "Jean Baptiste Vico dans l'histoire de la pensèe," *Cahiers d'Histoire Mondiale*, VII, 2 (1963). Two of the most brilliant treatments of Vico are Isaiah Berlin, "The Philosophical Ideas of Giambattista Vico," in *Arts and Ideas in Eighteenth-Century Italy:* Lectures given at the Italian Institute, 1957–1958 (Rome, 1960); and Giorgio de Santillana, "Vico and Descartes," *Osiris,* 9 (1950). Benedetto Croce, *The Philosophy of Giambattista Vico,* translated by R. G. Collingwood (London, 1913) did much to bring Vico to the attention of modern readers. Earlier, there was Robert Flint, *Vico* (Edinburgh and London, 1884). It appears to be the first major work on Vico in English. As one of a series on great philosophers, it tends to stress the metaphysical aspects of Vico, and to trace the development of his thought as presented in his earlier works. It suffers from accepting Vico's *Autobiography* literally, and, partly as a consequence of this, of underestimating his involvement with the Epicureans and their philosophy. On the other hand, while a bit dry and pedantic for modern tastes, it offers thoughtful, judicious statements on Vico by a man who was versed in the Italian commentaries on his subject, in general philosophy, and in the history of the philosophy of history: a background in depth against which he could judge the *New Science.* A similar sort of book, though more recent, is H. P. Adams, *The Life and Writings of Giambattista Vico* (London, 1935). Although a little dry and oversummarized, this book supplies an excellent précis of the entire life and work of Vico. As Adams admits, his aims are biography and historical criticism, rather than philosophical criticism; nevertheless, he does contend that Vico was post-Cartesian, owing to Descartes the commencement and core of his philosophy. The preface offers a useful bibliography. From a Marxist point of view, a stimulating treatment is the article by M. Lifshitz, "Giambattista Vico," translated from the Russian by Henry F. Mins, Jr., *Philosophy and Phenomenological Research,* VIII, 3 (March, 1948). I also found of interest Alfonsina Albini Grimaldi, *The Universal Humanity of Giambattista Vico* (New York, 1958); and Arthur Henry Child, "Making and Knowing in Hobbes, Vico, and Dewey," University of California Publications in Philosophy, Vol. 16, No. 13 (Berkeley, 1953). Useful, but somewhat tedious, is C. E. Vaughan, *Studies in the History of Political Philosophy Before and After Rousseau,* 2 vols. (Manchester, 1939), Vol. I, which has a chapter summarizing Vico's thought. See, too, his article, "Giambattista Vico: An Eighteenth Century Pioneer," Bulletin of the John Rylands Library, 6 (1921–1922), 266–288. Aloysius Robert Caponigri, *Time and Idea: The Theory of History in Giambattista Vico* (London, 1953) is disappointing. It is knowledgeable, but uneven in composition and judgment. There is also Thomas Whittaker, "Vico's new Science of

Humanity," *Mind*, 35 (1926), reprinted in *Reason and Other Essays* (Cambridge, 1934), 133–189; and, on a specialized subject, M. H. Fisch, "Vico on Roman Law," in *Essays in Political Theory Presented to George H. Sabine*, M. R. Konvitz and A. E. Murphy (eds.) (Ithaca, N.Y., 1948). Also, Eric Auerbach, "Vico and Aesthetic Historism," in *Scenes from the Drama of European Literature* (New York, 1954).

For those who can read Italian, some significant works are: Fausto Nicolini, *Commento Storico alla Seconda Scienza Nuova*, 2 vols. (Rome, 1949); Franco Amerio, *Introduzione allo Studio di G. B. Vico* (Turin, 1947), written from a Catholic viewpoint; Nicola Badaloni, *Introduzione a G. B. Vico* (Milan, 1961), written from a Marxist viewpoint; *Il Pensiero di Giambattista Vico*, una antologia dagli scritti, a cura di Paulo Rossi (Turin, 1959); and A. Corsano, *Giambattista Vico* (Bari, 1956).

THE ENLIGHTENMENT

R. V. Sampson, *Progress in the Age of Reason* (London, 1956); and Charles Frankel, *The Faith in Reason: The Idea of Progress in the French Enlightenment* (New York, 1948), along with the standard work by J. S. Bury, *The Idea of Progress* (London, 1920), are good introductions to one aspect of the Enlightenment view of philosophy of history.

VOLTAIRE

J. B. Black, *The Art of History;* a study of four great historians of the eighteenth century (London, 1926) is a standard work, treating Hume, Robertson, and Gibbon, along with Voltaire. A useful volume is J. H. Brumfitt, *Voltaire, historian* (New York, 1958). A book which looks at a specific example of Voltaire's antecedents is Haydn Trevor Mason, *Pierre Bayle and Voltaire* (London, 1963). It is an interesting effort to deal with the problem of ascertaining how, in fact, and in what way, Bayle influenced Voltaire. The author concludes that "Voltaire's critical attitude owes more to Bayle than to any other outside influence." Mason adds the interesting comment that "Voltaire wants to see history as a moral philosopher, but he is obliged by Bayle to look upon it as a scientist; this may partially account for his own confused attitudes on the subject" (p. 133). Concentrating on the consequences of Voltaire's historical work, there is Charles Rihs, *Voltaire; recherches sur les origines du matérialisme historique* (Genève, 1962). This is an interesting study which treats Voltaire as the classic representative of "l'idealisme historique" and considers him as the transitional historian between the theological conception of history and historical materialism. Reflecting the revived Italian interest in historical work of the Enlightenment is Furio Diaz, *Voltaire storico* (Torino, 1958).

CONDORCET

On Condorcet, in addition to the works cited in the footnotes to the chapter on him, there is a good treatment in Frank E. Manuel, *The Prophets of Paris* (Cambridge, Mass., 1962), chap. II; Manuel also offers a useful bibliography. There is also Sir James Frazer, *Condorcet on the Progress of the Human Mind* (Oxford, 1933).

KANT

Probably the best short treatment is Emil L. Fackenheim, "Kant's Concept of History," *Kant-Studien*, Band 48, Heft 3 (1956–1957). There are also a few interesting pages in Walsh's *Introduction to Philosophy of History*, cited above. See, too, Theodore Litt, *Kant und Herder* (Leipzig, 1930).

HEGEL

The literature on Hegel is enormous. In addition to works cited in the footnotes to the chapter, the following are noteworthy. The studies by Jean Hyppolite, *Introduction à la philosophie de l'histoire de Hegel* (Paris, 1948) and *Études sur Marx et Hegel* (Paris, 1955), show an alive and informed mind; the latter work includes a most interesting study, "La signification de la Révolution française dans la 'Phénoménologie' de Hegel." A pioneering treatment is Wilhelm Dilthey's *Die Jugendgeschichte Hegels*, Vol. IV of his *Gesammelte Schriften*), (Leipzig, 1921, first published in 1906). So, too, is Benedetto Croce, *What Is Living and What Is Dead in the Philosophy of Hegel*, translated by D. Ainslie (London, 1915). Other important works are Sidney Hook, *From Hegel to Marx* (New York, 1935); Karl Löwith, *Von Hegel zu Nietzsche* (Zurich, 1940), recently translated into English; Richard Kroner, *Von Kant zu Hegel*, 2 vols. (Tubingen, 1921–1924); Theodore Haering, *Hegel: Sein Wollen und Werk*, 2 vols. (Leipzig, 1929–1938); and G. R. G. Mure, *An Introduction to Hegel* (London, 1940). On Hegel's more specifically political thought, see *Hegel's Political Writings*, translated by T. M. Knox, with an introductory essay by Z. A. Pelczynsky (Oxford, 1964); and M. B. Foster, *The Political Philosophies of Plato and Hegel* (Oxford, 1935). There are also chapters on Hegel in George H. Sabine, *History of Political Theory* (New York, 1937); and C. A. Vaughan, *Studies in the History of Political Philosophy Before and After Rousseau*, Vol. II.

COMTE

Frank E. Manuel, in *The Prophets of Paris*, previously cited, has an interesting chapter on Comte, as well as a useful bibliography. For overall treatments of Comte, in addition to those mentioned in the footnotes of the chapter, see Edward Caird, *The Social Philosophy and Religion of Auguste Comte*, 2nd ed. (Glasgow, 1893); and L. Lévy-Bruhl, *La philosophie d'Auguste Comte* (Paris, 1900, with an English translation in 1903). Henri Gouhier, "La philosophie de l'histoire d'A. Comte," *Journal of World History*, II (1955) is a succinct though rather arid coverage. For Comte as a sociologist, see Georges Gurvitch, *Les fondateurs de la sociologie contemporaines: Comte, Marx et Spencer* (Paris, 1958). On Comte and the history of science, there is George Sarton, "Auguste Comte, Historian of Science," *Osiris*, X (1952); and Paul Tannery, "Comte et l'histoire des sciences," *Revue générale des sciences*, XVI (1905). Other special topics are dealt with in John Greene, "Biology and Social Theory in the Nineteenth Century: A. Comte and H. Spencer," in *Critical Problems in the History of Science*, Marshall Clagett (ed.) (Madison, Wis., 1959); and Thomas Whittaker, *Comte and Mill* (London, 1908).

MARX

If Hegel presents an embarrassment of riches, we are in an even worse situation with Marx. However, to add to the items listed in the footnotes of the chapter, the following might be listed: M. M. Bober, *Karl Marx's Interpretation of History*, 2nd ed. revised (Cambridge, Mass., 1950); widely regarded as authoritative, I found this summary and criticism of Marx by an economist, while solid and useful, also rather dull and unenlightening. More illuminating is Sidney Hook, *Towards the Understanding of Karl Marx* (London, 1935), which should be read in conjunction with his brilliant work, previously cited, *From Hegel to Marx*. Benedetto Croce moves on from Hegel to Marx in his *Historical Materialism and the Economics of Karl Marx*, translated by C. M. Meredith (New York, 1914). Maximilien Rubel, *Karl Marx: Essai de biographie intellectuelle* (Paris, 1957) traces especially the influence of French thought upon Marx. Worthy of renewed mention (it is already cited in the footnotes) as an outstanding critique of Marxism as a philosophical system is H. B. Acton, *The Illusion of the Epoch* (London, 1955). H. P. Adams, *Karl Marx in his Earlier Writings* (London, 1940) offers a useful summary of some of the initial efforts of Marx. On the now popular subject of alienation, an additional item, is Karl Löwith, "Man's Self-Alienation in the Early Writings of Marx," *Social Research*, II, 2 (Summer, 1954). On the equally popular subject of the development of underdeveloped nations, see Bert F. Hoselitz, "Karl Marx on Secular and Social Development: A Study in the Sociology of Nineteenth Century Social Science," *Comparative Studies in Society and History*, VI, 2 (January, 1964), 142–163. On Marxist morality, see Eugene Kamenka, *The Ethical Foundations of Marxism* (New York, 1962). Werner Blumenberg, *Karl Marx* (Hamburg, 1962) is a most interesting and up-to-date biography, with excellent illustrations and a useful bibliography.

SPENGLER

The most available and useful treatment in English has already been mentioned in the footnotes. It is H. Stuart Hughes, *Oswald Spengler* (New York, 1952). In Pietro Rossi, *Lo storicismo tedesco contemporaneo* (Turin, 1956), Part V is devoted to Spengler. There is also L. Febvre, "De Spengler à Toynbee: Quelques philosophies opportunistes de l'histoire," *Revue metaphysique et de morale* (1936); and Theodor W. Adorno, "Spengler nach dem Untergang: Zu Oswald Spenglers 70. Geburtstag," *Der Monat* (May, 1950).

TOYNBEE

Toynbee and History: Critical Essays and Reviews, M. F. Ashley Montagu (ed.) (Boston, 1956), already mentioned in the chapter footnotes, is indispensable reading. The entire issue of the magazine, *Diogenes*, 13 (Spring, 1956) is devoted to a consideration of Toynbee. *A Bibliography of Works on Arnold Toynbee, 1946–1960* forms part of the issue of *History and Theory*, IV, 2 (1965).

FREUD

For a critical treatment, see Philip Rieff, *Freud: The Mind of the Moralist* (New York, 1959), especially chap. VI, "The Authority of the Past"; also Rieff's articles, "The Authority of the Past—Sickness and Society in Freud's Thought," *Social Research* (Winter, 1954), and "History, Psychoanalysis and the Social Sciences," *Ethics* (January, 1953). Herbert Marcuse, *Eros and Civilization: A Philosophical Inquiry into Freud* (Boston, 1955); and Norman O. Brown, *Life Against Death: The Psychoanalytic Meaning of History* (Middletown, Conn., 1959) are attempts to go beyond Freud. Lionel Trilling, *Freud and the Crisis of Our Culture* (Boston, 1955) remains more within the orthodox Freudian framework. Hans Meyerhoff, "On Psychoanalysis and History," *Psychoanalysis and the Psychoanalytic Review*, 49, 2 (Summer, 1962), puts the emphasis on the historical nature of the psychoanalytic method. A most suggestive essay is Alex Comfort, "Darwin and Freud," in his *Darwin and the Naked Lady* (New York, 1962).

I refrain from listing here the numerous contributions now appearing which relate to the application of psychoanalytic methods to history per se rather than to philosophy of history; outstanding in this regard, however, are the various works by Erik H. Erikson. A number of important articles, on both Freud's philosophy of history and the application of psychoanalysis to history, are reprinted in my volume, *Psychoanalysis and History* (Englewood Cliffs, N.J., 1963), which also contains a selected bibliography. For further items, see the latter.

Indexes

INDEX OF NAMES

INDEX OF SUBJECTS

477